UNITED NATIONS ECONOMIC COMMISSION FOR EUROPE

NON-OBSERVED ECONOMY

IN NATIONAL ACCOUNTS

Survey of Country Practices

UNITED NATIONS
New York and Geneva, 2008

Note

The designations employed and the presentation of the material in this publication do not imply the expression of any opinion whatsoever on the part of the Secretariat of the United Nations, concerning the legal status of any country, territory, city or area, or of its authorities, or concerning the delimitation of its frontiers or boundaries.

Acknowledgements

The survey of national practices in estimating the non-observed economic activities in national accounts was carried out under the general supervision of Lidia Bratanova. Tiina Luige was in charge of processing and analyzing the results of the survey with assistance from Gauri Khanna, Vania Etropolska and Tihomira Dimova. Bénédicte Boudol formatted and prepared the results of the survey for print. Yves Clopt prepared the design and layout of the publication.

UNITED NATIONS PUBLICATION
Sales No. E.08.II.E.8
ISBN 978-92-1-116987-4 ISSN 0069-8458

Preface

The complete coverage of economic production is important in order to ensure good quality national accounts and exhaustive estimates of Gross Domestic Product (GDP). A lot of attention is paid to the possibility of missing economic activities, which often suggests that the GDP figures published by national statistical offices exclude large parts of the economy. Achieving exhaustiveness requires a lot of work since it is difficult to account for certain types of productive activities that cannot be observed and measured directly by the official statisticians when the national accounts and GDP are compiled. The groups of activities that are often *non-observed,* in the sense of not being directly observed and measured, are those that are *underground, illegal, informal or undertaken by households for their final use.* Furthermore, some activities may be missed because of *deficiencies in the basic data collection systems.* These five groups of activities comprise the non-observed economy (NOE).

Despite the difficulties, the goal of most national statistical systems is to ensure, as far as possible, that the *non-observed activities* are appropriately measured and included in the GDP estimates. This publication presents an inventory of the current practices of forty three countries, UNECE member countries as well as some countries outside the region, in measuring non-observed economic activities to ensure the exhaustiveness of their national accounts. The material was collected through a survey undertaken by the UNECE Statistical Division during 2005-2006. It is a continuation of a similar survey carried out in 2001-2002 where twenty nine countries participated. The countries' contributions are synthesized, organized and edited by the UNECE secretariat in order to allow for some cross-country comparisons of the methods used to estimate the size and importance of the different types of non-observed activities. The publication includes numerical examples and estimates provided by the member countries.

The publication refers to the work of OECD and Eurostat in defining the non-observed economy and developing the appropriate framework for producing exhaustive estimates of GDP. In 2002, the OECD released its *Handbook for Measurement of the Non-observed Economy*, which is considered as a basis for the work in this area. The term *non-observed economy* is also used by the European Union in connection with its programme to guarantee the exhaustiveness of the GDP. The Eurostat Tabular Framework used in this programme has allowed to harmonise the approach to NOE measurement in many countries.

The publication demonstrates the substantial efforts that the statistical offices of an increasing number of countries are undertaking to ensure the exhaustiveness of the GDP and to capture all economic activities that fall into the production boundary of the United Nations System of National Accounts 1993 (SNA93).

CONTENTS

INTRODUCTION

1. Background

In 2005-2006, the UNECE secretariat carried out a survey of national practices in estimating the non-observed economic activities (NOE) in national accounts.

Previous surveys had been conducted in 1991 and 2001/2002. The first 1991 survey covered nine countries and was presented as a collection of articles featuring the contributions from each country. The observations were published in 1993 as an *Inventory of National Practices in Estimating Hidden and Informal Activities for National Accounts.*

A second survey was conducted in 2001-2002 to which 29 countries responded. The purpose of the survey was to obtain an overview of the methods used in UNECE member countries. In this survey, for the first time, an attempt was made to compare and analyse country practices and trends, and to standardize the contributions in terms of terminology and presentation.

The joint UNECE/Eurostat/OECD Meeting on National Accounts in April 2004 asked the UNECE secretariat to carry out a new survey on NOE, thereby updating the Inventory and increasing its coverage.

The third survey was carried out in 2005-2006 and many more countries replied to the survey, UNECE member countries as well as non-members (e.g. OECD countries outside the region). As in 2001-2002, in this latest round participating countries were asked to provide estimates of the size of the non-observed economy in the GDP and to elaborate on the methods used to arrive at these estimates.

Forty five countries responded to the survey. Japan and New Zealand do not estimate the NOE. The 43 countries that provided information about their methods of estimating the NOE are: Albania, Armenia, Australia, Austria, Azerbaijan, Belarus, Belgium, Brazil, Bulgaria, Canada, Croatia, Czech Republic, Estonia, Finland, Georgia, Germany, Hungary, Ireland, Italy, Kazakhstan, Kyrgyzstan, Latvia, Lithuania, the Netherlands, Norway, Mexico, Moldova, Mongolia, Montenegro, Poland, Romania, Russian Federation, Serbia, Spain, Sweden, The former Yugoslav Republic of Macedonia, Tajikistan, Turkey, Turkmenistan, Ukraine, United Kingdom, United States and Uzbekistan.

The purpose of this latest survey is threefold. First, it presents an inventory of current practices to estimate the non-observed economy in different countries at different stages of economic development. Second, it provides a platform for comparison of the different approaches used as well as an insight into the associated difficulties when putting into practice the different methods. Finally, it serves as a useful reference for countries in their efforts to put forward a comprehensive estimate of GDP that takes into account both observed and non-observed economic activities.

2. Conceptual background

Main definitions

The **Non-observed Economy** refers to all productive activities that may not be captured in the basic data sources used for national accounts compilation. The following activities are included: underground, informal (including those undertaken by households for their own final use), illegal, and other activities omitted due to deficiencies in the basic data collection programme. The term 'non-observed economy' encompasses all of these activities and the related statistical estimation problems.

The following definitions of the main terms employed in the publication are based on the 1993 SNA.

Underground production: production activities that are legal but deliberately concealed from public authorities in order to avoid paying tax (e.g. VAT or income tax) or social security contributions; meeting statutory standards; or complying with official procedures and regulations such as the completion of administrative forms or statistical questionnaires. As well as "underground", which is the term most commonly employed, some countries also employ the terms "concealed activities", "hidden economy" or "black economy" to denote this type of activity.

Informal activities: legal production activities which are characterized by a low level of organization, with little or no division between labour and capital as a factor of production. The informal sector typically functions on a system of unofficial relationships and does not rely on official agreements. It is broadly characterised as consisting of units engaged in small-scale production of goods and services with the primary objective of generating employment and incomes for persons concerned. The definition of the informal sector corresponds with that of household unincorporated enterprises.

Illegal activities: productive activities which are forbidden by law or which become illegal when carried out by unauthorised persons. The following types of illegal activities are considered in the inventory: production/import/sale of drugs; prostitution; sale of stolen goods and smuggling of goods.

The updated version of the System of National Accounts, SNA 93 Rev.1 will include a special chapter dealing with informal economy and a more elaborated treatment of illegal activities. As these texts were not yet available at the time of analysing the results of the survey, the publication is based on SNA 93.

3. Eurostat tabular frameworks

Eurostat has carried out two rounds of Pilot Projects on Exhaustiveness (PPE) to address the differences in concepts, definitions, and methods employed in accounting for non-observed activities in national accounts in the EU Candidate Countries. The first one was conducted in 1998/99. A tabular framework that relates the NOE areas with statistical problems encountered by national accountants was designed by Eurostat to facilitate comparison across countries and to improve exhaustiveness. Eight types of non-exhaustiveness (T1-T8) were identified (see Annex).

A second Pilot Project was conducted in 2002/03. The classification was modified to clarify the boundaries between the different types. Seven types of non-exhaustiveness were identified (N1-N7). These are described in section 3.1. below.

The main aim of the two frameworks was not to provide a definitive classification of types of NOE but to ensure that the NOE is measured systematically, all potential NOE areas are covered and no activities are double counted. When countries use the same framework, comparison of NOE can be made at a more detailed level. It is also easier to ensure the exhaustiveness of methods and to exchange experience in their implementation. The frameworks have been used mainly in the EU candidate countries (where the PPEs were carried out) but also in some other countries, such as Albania, Bosnia and Herzegovina, Austria, Azerbaijan, Croatia, Kyrgyzstan, Montenegro, Serbia, Turkmenistan and Ukraine.

The UNECE survey makes use of the types of non-observed economy identified in the Eurostat tabular framework. Several countries used the T1-T8 framework in their responses, whereas others switched to the more recent N1-N7 classification. For countries in the survey that used the T1-T8 framework or did not classify their activities, the UNECE Secretariat made an attempt to classify the non-observed activities according to the N1-N7 classification, as reflected in Table 1. The allocation of activities to different types of non-exhaustiveness for these countries is thus subject to interpretation.

3.1. The N1-N7 framework

The N1-N7 framework was used within the second wave of the Eurostat Pilot Projects on Exhaustiveness. Seven types of non-exhaustiveness were identified (N1-N7)[1] instead of the eight types in the previously used T1-T8 framework.

The main difference between the two classifications is that while the T1-T8 framework relates the non-exhaustiveness types to the NOE problem areas, the N1-N7 framework is based on subdividing the producers according to their potential for non-exhaustiveness.

The seven types under this new framework can be broadly classified into the four categories of: not registered, not surveyed, misreporting and other deficiencies. The definitions associated with each category, such as legal person and producer, are also clearer in the N1-N7 framework. Enterprises are referred to as producers to ensure that all possible types of enterprises are involved, including non-market household enterprises. A more detailed description of the types is given in Box 1.

The N1-N7 classification is more appropriate to be used within the production (output) approach. As the output approach is the most widely employed by countries for GDP estimates, the N1-N7 types are considered a good basis for systematic and comprehensive assessment of the exhaustiveness of national accounts. The N1-N7 framework can be applied also to the expenditure approach as long as the basic data are obtained from producer surveys. When other data sources are used, it is sometimes recommended to record these exhaustiveness adjustments under N7 - other statistical deficiencies. The income approach is to a great extent based on the same data sources as the output approach and therefore the types N1-N7 can be used.

---

[1] Eurostat, 2005, *Eurostat's Tabular Approach to Exhaustiveness: Guidelines.*

The main aim of the breakdown into non-exhaustiveness types is to ensure complete, unduplicated coverage in order to produce accurate GDP estimates. The breakdown is not a goal in itself. Therefore, it is not of critical importance whether specific exhaustiveness elements are allocated to one particular N-type or another, as long as they are covered somewhere in the framework.

Box 1. Eurostat's tabular approach: types of non-exhaustiveness

Not registered
N1 - Producer deliberately not registering - underground
Producer deliberately does not register to avoid tax and social security obligations. Most often this refers to small producers with turnovers that exceed threshold levels above which they should register. Producers that do not register because they are engaged in illegal activities fall under type N2. **Type N1 does not include all underground activities, some of which are associated with type N6.**

N2 - Producers deliberately not registering - illegal
Producer deliberately does not register as a legal entity or as an entrepreneur because it is involved in illegal activities. Type N2 excludes illegal activities by registered legal entities or entrepreneurs that report (or misreport) their activities under legal activity codes.

N3 - Producers not required to register
Producer is not required to register because it has no market output. Typically these are non-market household producers that engage in production of goods for own consumption, for own fixed capital formation, and construction of and repairs to dwellings. Or, producer has some market output but it is below the level at which the producer is obliged to register as an entrepreneur.

Not surveyed
N4 - Legal persons not surveyed
Legal persons not surveyed due to several reasons such as: the business register is out of date or updating procedures are inadequate; the classification data (activity, size or geographic codes) are incorrect; the legal person is excluded from the survey frame because its size is below a certain threshold etc. This leads to (systematic) exclusion of the legal person from surveys when in principle they should be included.

N5 - Registered entrepreneurs not surveyed
Registered entrepreneurs may not be surveyed due to a variety of reasons: the statistical office does not conduct a survey of registered entrepreneurs; the registered entrepreneur is not in the list of registered entrepreneurs available to the statistical office, or if available, is systematically excluded from it; the registered entrepreneur is not in the survey frame because the classification data (activity code, size code, geographic code) are incorrect.

Misreporting
N6 - Producers deliberately misreporting
Gross output is under-reported and/or intermediate consumption is overstated, in order to evade income tax, value added tax (VAT), other taxes, or social security contributions. Misreporting often involves maintenance of two sets of books, payments of envelope salaries which are recorded as intermediate consumption; payments in cash without receipts, and VAT fraud.

Other
N7 - Other statistical deficiencies
Type N7 is subdivided into N7a - data that are incomplete, not collected or not directly collectable, and N7b - data that are incorrectly handled, processed or compiled by statisticians. The following areas should be investigated: handling of non-response; production for own final use by market producers; tips; wages and salaries in kind; and secondary activities.

4. The 2005-2006 survey

4.1 Overview

Forty five countries responded to the survey. Japan and New Zealand do not estimate the NOE. The 43 countries that provided information about their methods of estimating the NOE are:

- **European Union (EU) Members (18)**
  EU - 15: Austria, Belgium, Finland, Germany, Ireland, Italy, the Netherlands, Spain, Sweden and United Kingdom;
  EU - new members: Bulgaria, Czech Republic, Estonia, Hungary, Latvia, Lithuania, Poland and Romania.

- **OECD countries – non-EU (5)**
  Australia, Canada, Mexico, Norway and United States.

- **EU Candidate Countries (3)**
  Croatia, The former Yugoslav Republic of Macedonia and Turkey.

- **Countries from the Commonwealth of Independent States (12)**
  Armenia, Azerbaijan, Belarus, Georgia, Kazakhstan, Kyrgyzstan, Moldova, Russian Federation, Tajikistan, Turkmenistan, Ukraine and Uzbekistan

- **Other countries (5)**
  Albania, Brazil, Mongolia, Montenegro and Serbia

The survey is based on the concepts, definitions and terminology as recommended in the OECD *Handbook on Measuring the Non-observed Economy (2002)* and the Eurostat Projects on Exhaustiveness of National Accounts. The Handbook defines NOE as all productive activities that may not be captured in the basic data sources used for national accounts compilation. Illegal activities, deficiencies in data collection, informal activities that are not registered or recorded, and misreporting of production are examples of reasons associated with measurement difficulties.

Broadly, the survey is divided into several sections, each of which serves as an indicator of current practices adopted. These sections are broadly classified as: definitions and concepts used; data sources and estimation methods, and implications and effects on Gross Domestic Product (GDP) estimates.

In processing the countries' contributions, use was made, to the extent possible of the recommendations of the OECD *Handbook on Measuring the Non-observed Economy* and the Tabular Approach to Exhaustiveness (TAE) developed by Eurostat. In the Survey, an attempt was also made to standardise the presentation and the terminology in line with the recommendations of the OECD Handbook.

4.2 Main data sources and estimation methods

Countries used a variety of data sources for the estimation of non-observed activities. Several sources are quite common amongst countries, such as agricultural census, business statistics, household surveys, demographic data/population census, Labour Force Survey/labour statistics, taxation and fiscal data, police records, social security records and foreign trade statistics. Some sources are used only in one or a few countries, particularly the surveys to capture a specific activity (e.g. smuggling of tobacco). Other sources like Labour Force Survey and employment data, structural business surveys, household budget/expenditure surveys, and taxation data are widely used by countries.

The estimation techniques adopted spanned the three main approaches: production approach, expenditure approach and income approach. Often countries produce two estimates of non-observed activities by employing two of the three approaches, mostly the production method followed by the expenditure approach.

Countries use a wide variety of methods to estimate the GDP stemming from the non-observed economic activities. The following methods can be mentioned: the labour input method, commodity flow method, balancing input-output and supply-and-use tables, other reconciliation methods (e.g. comparison of theoretical VAT and actual VAT, theoretical income tax and actual income tax), comparison with norms, use of fiscal data and special surveys.

Of the above mentioned methods, a special mention should be made of the labour input method which is increasingly being used to measure value added and compensation of employees. The method was pioneered by Istat, the Statistical Office of Italy. Labour supply and demand data are compared to estimate inconsistencies in recorded labour. Data on labour supply are obtained from the population census and Labour Force Survey while labour demand is obtained from business statistics. A surplus of labour supply from household surveys over labour demand from enterprise surveys is an indication of non-observed production. It provides a lower bound as some labour input may be missing from both sources. Estimates of output and value added per unit of labour input are calculated and then applied to the data on labour input to account for output by unregistered and hidden labour.

In addition, some countries use the "expert method" usually in conjunction with one of the approaches described above. This method relies on the estimates of experts to assess the share of NOE in different activities using available data sources. However, this method is highly subjective.

5. Analysis

5.1 Impact on GDP

The size of the adjustments for the non-observed economy varies widely by groups of countries as indicated in Table 1. It should be noted that some country results may have been revised after the UNECE survey data was collected. The share of NOE in GDP in the CIS countries ranges from 10.7% (Belarus) to 31.6% (Moldova), whereas in the new EU member countries it is between 4.6% (Czech Republic, expenditure approach) and 18.9% (Lithuania). Amongst the OECD countries (both EU and non-EU), the adjustments for NOE estimates range from 0.8% (United States) to 14.8% (Italy) of GDP, though most of the countries lie in the less than 5% range.

In general, adjustments made using the expenditure approach are lower than those made using the production and income approach indicating a better coverage of activities in the data sources used to capture production. For example, in the Czech Republic the contribution of NOE to GDP using the income method was 6.6% whereas it was 4.6% with the expenditure method; in

Latvia the production method produced an estimate of 13.6% whereas a figure of 8.3% was reached using the expenditure method.

5.2 Observations of different types of non-observed activities

Table 1 provides information on the different types of non-observed activities estimated by countries. Ten of the 43 countries followed the N1-N7 classification. These are: Bulgaria, Croatia, Czech Republic, Estonia, Hungary, Latvia, Lithuania, Montenegro, Poland and Serbia. For the remainder, the classification into different types of non-exhaustiveness in Table 1 has been made by the UNECE Secretariat and should be treated as indicative. However, during the time when the survey results were analysed and the publication prepared, several more countries have started to use the N1-N7 framework.

Most of the countries made adjustments for misreporting (N6 – 35 countries), units deliberately not registered (N1 – 34 countries) and producers not required to register (N3 – 32 countries) (Figure 1).

Figure 1. Coverage of Non-Exhaustiveness Types

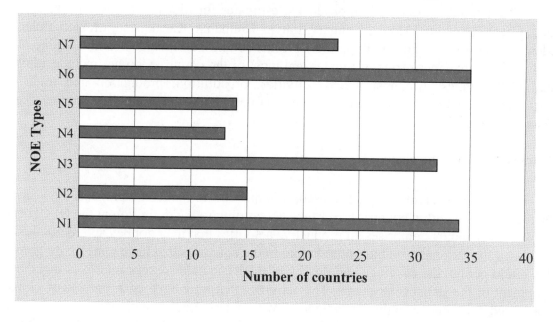

All the CIS countries (Table 1), made adjustments for producers who are not registered, either deliberately (N1) or not required to register (N3). For the new EU member countries, producers deliberately not registering (N1) were also common in addition to misreporting (N6) and other deficiencies (N7). Almost all of the new EU members and several of the CIS countries made also estimates for illegal production though these are often not published officially. In OECD countries, misreporting (N6), other statistical deficiencies (N7) and producers not required to register (N3) dominated the adjustments made.

Reports from all countries indicate that the volume of adjustments for non-observed activities is biggest due to misreporting of producers followed by producers deliberately not registering (underground). Within these two sets of activities the most common sectors identified are:

- construction – informal clandestine production in construction, own account construction;
- agriculture (including forestry, fishing and hunting) - own account production for sale and for final use, hidden employment, unrecorded output from agricultural plots;
- trade - informal household activities, wholesale and retail trade;
- health care and education - payment for services;
- transport - movement of goods and passengers; and
- housing - income from renting rooms and dwellings and imputed rent.

5.3 Illegal activities

Illegal activities deserve special mention due to the difficulties surrounding their estimation. Given the nature of activities (i.e. those that are forbidden by law), the problems of too few data sources and unreliable data lead to practical difficulties in their measurement. Commonly used data sources which help to quantify illegal activities are police records, crime statistics, information from health centres (drug consumption), and expert estimates. Few countries regularly produce estimates for illegal activities.

Fifteen countries reported on producing estimates for illegal activities. These are: Bulgaria, Croatia, Czech Republic, Estonia, Hungary, Latvia, Lithuania, Kazakhstan, Mexico, Poland, Serbia, Sweden, the Former Yugoslav Republic of Macedonia, Turkmenistan and Ukraine. In several countries, these are experimental estimates and most of the countries do not include adjustments in official GDP figures. Amongst illegal activities, prostitution, production and trade in drugs, production and sale of counterfeit goods, sale of stolen goods and smuggling are the areas that are commonly estimated.

6. Conclusions from the survey

Due to the different approaches used, it is difficult to make comparisons between countries and sometimes also within countries over time. According to the definition in the OECD Handbook, non-observed economy comprises all productive activities that may not be captured in the basic data sources used for national accounts compilation. In the countries that have gone or are going through the transition period, the coverage and quality of the basic data sources improves together with the development of the statistical systems. The activities that may have been previously considered as non-observed will increasingly be estimated within the regular national accounts compilation process. Therefore, the increase or reduction in the share of NOE in GDP may be either an indication of the changes in the economic activities, or due to the improvement of the statistical sources and methods, or both.

Many OECD and EU member countries have methods in place to ensure a maximum coverage of the national accounts. However, special studies to ensure exhaustiveness are often carried out once over a long time period. The approach is often different from the one used by Eurostat in the new EU member countries, and the data are not directly comparable. On the other hand, several countries are only recently starting to pay more attention to systematically measuring the non-observed economy. In some cases, its measurement can also be considered as politically sensitive and countries are careful in labelling as non-observed economy the activities captured under the framework of exhaustiveness of national accounts.

In general, three major groups of countries can be identified in respect to their approach towards measuring the non-observed economy (the countries are mentioned as examples, some countries may be placed in several groups):

- the countries rigorously following the Eurostat Tabular Framework (mainly the new EU members and Candidate Countries, but also several CIS countries, like Kyrgyzstan, Turkmenistan and Ukraine);
- the countries that have a thorough and systematic approach to ensuring exhaustiveness of National Accounts but do not (regularly) measure the NOE as such (e.g., Australia, Canada, Finland, Germany, Ireland, Netherlands, Norway, United Kingdom, United States);
- the remaining countries have different approaches:
    - using its own framework and methods: Italy (Italy is a pioneer in measuring NOE and a lot of the methods and approaches used in other countries are based on the so-called Italian approach);
    - focusing on measuring the non-observed activities in specific branches (often via special surveys) but not using a comprehensive framework; the measurement is often not linked to ensuring exhaustiveness of national accounts (e.g., Armenia, Georgia, Mexico, Mongolia, Tajikistan, Turkey);
    - focusing on informal sector and informal labour, mainly using the labour input method (e.g. Albania, Brazil, Moldova).

Because of the above mentioned reasons, it is difficult to identify clear trends in NOE dynamics across countries. Although some countries recorded an increase in the size of NOE in GDP estimates, by and large a declining trend can be observed.

In recent years, the countries are increasingly paying attention to ensuring the exhaustiveness of national accounts and improving data collection and estimation methods to be as exhaustive as possible in their GDP estimates.

Table 1. Adjustments for NOE activities[1]

Countries	Year	Size (%)	N1	N2	N3	N4	N5	N6	N7
New EU Members									
Bulgaria	2001	**10.2**	•	•	•	•	•	•	•
Czech Republic	2000	**4.6(E), 6.6(I), 9.3(O)**	•	•	•	•	•	•	•
Estonia	2002	**9.6**	•	•				•	•
Hungary	2000	**11.9**	•	•	•			•	•
Latvia	2000	**13.6(O), 8.28 (E)**	•	•				•	•
Lithuania	2002	**18.9**	•	•				•	•
Poland	2002	**15.7(O), 7.8 (E)**	•	•	•			•	•
Romania	2002	**17.7**	•		•			•	
OECD-EU Members									
Austria	2001	**7.9**	•		•	•	•	•	•
Belgium	2002	**3.0-4.0**	•		•			•	•
Finland		Not stated	•		•			•	
Germany		Not stated	-	-	-	-	-	-	-
Ireland	1998	**4.0**			•	•		•	•
Italy	2003	**14.8(L), 16.7 (U)**	•		•	•	•	•	
Netherlands	1995	**1.0**						•	•
Spain	2000	**11.2**	•			•		•	•
Sweden	2000	**1.3**		•				•	•
United Kingdom		Not stated	•		•		•	•	•
OECD Non-EU Members									
Australia	2000-01	**1.3**			•			•	•
Canada		Not stated	•	•	•			•	•
Mexico	2003	**12.1**	-	•	•	-	-	-	-
Norway	1995	**2.4 (O), 1(E)**			•	•	•	•	•
USA	1997	**0.8**						•	
EU Candidate countries									
Croatia	2002	**10.1**	•	•	•	•	•	•	•
FYR Macedonia	2003	**16.3**	•		•			•	
Turkey	2004	**1.66**	•		•			•	
CIS									
Armenia	2003	**28.9**	•		•			•	
Azerbaijan	2003	**20.7**	•		•	•	•		•
Belarus	2003	**10.7**	•		•				
Georgia	2004	**28.3**	•		•			•	
Kazakhstan	2003	**21.6**	•	•	•			•	
Kyrgyzstan	2003	**17.0**	•		•			•	
Moldova	2001	**31.6**	•		•			•	
Russian Federation	2003	**24.3**	•		•	•	•	•	•
Tajikistan	Not stated	**25.0**	•		•	•	•		
Turkmenistan	2005	**18.1**	•	•	•			•	•
Ukraine	2003	**17.2**	•	•	•	•	•	•	•
Uzbekistan	Not stated	**29.0-30.0**	•		•		•		
Other									
Albania	2003	**30.8**	•					•	
Brazil	2003	**12.79**	-	-	-	-	-	-	-
Mongolia [2]	Not stated	**13.0 or 30.0**	•		•				
Montenegro	2002	**8.8**	•		•			•	•
Serbia	2003	**14.56**	•	•		•	•	•	•

Notes:

O - according to output approach

E - according to expenditure approach

I - according to income approach

L - Lower bound estimate

U - Upper bound estimate

"-" – it is not possible to establish which types of the NOE are covered based on the country's contribution to the survey

[1] For some countries, the classification into different types of non-exhaustiveness has been made by the UNECE secretariat and should be treated as indicative. For more information, the reader should refer to the country description in this publication.

[2] Mongolia: two estimates: 13% and 30% were produced based on two different studies.

ALBANIA

1. General overview

In January 2003, Albania produced and released data for the non-observed economy for the first time. The data covered the period 1996-2003 and were produced by the Institute of Statistics in Albania (INSTAT) with technical assistance from the IMF.

The production and expenditure approach are used for estimation of GDP and the figures are based on concepts defined in the United Nations System of National Accounts 1993 (SNA 93). Comparing the two methods, the estimates based on the production approach are considered more reliable, given the quality and quantity of data available. The estimates of value added and output are split into the estimates for the observed and non-observed activities.

2. Sources and estimation methods

To ensure exhaustiveness of GDP estimates, expert estimates are used to measure economic underground activities based on existing data sources, covering the period 1996-2003. The method is based on experts' assessments of the share of NOE in each branch of economic activity. This share is then used for grossing up data on output, intermediate costs and value added for each branch.

The approach based on expert opinions suffers from a high degree of subjectivity. Therefore, INSTAT plans to move to a new methodology with the help of two technical assistance projects: one funded by the EU Commission (through the CARDS programme) and another one by the IMF.

One of these projects is a partnership between INSTAT and the National Statistical Institute of Italy (ISTAT), which started in 2004. The project aims at improving estimation of the non-observed economy in Albania, by developing and testing a methodology based on the labour input method (the so-called Italian approach). The results will then be compared with those obtained via the production approach.

At the core of the labour input method are three important steps:

- Obtaining estimates of labour input by integrating different sources of information representing the supply and demand for labour;
- Obtaining estimates of output and value added per unit of labour input for the same industry and size breakdown from a regular or special purpose enterprise survey;
- Multiplying the labour input estimates by the unit ratios for industry and size classes to calculate output and value added.

In each economic activity, the labour input estimates by size of enterprise provide the weighting factors by which to gross up enterprise survey based estimates of output and value added to totals. This procedure can be expected to give a more exhaustive coverage of production if the household survey data give more complete coverage of labour input to GDP than do the enterprise survey data. There are two reasons to suppose that this is likely:

- Household surveys pick up labour inputs that are not included in the enterprise survey, for example because these enterprises are too small to be registered, or because they are too small to be included in the survey;
- Individuals may report their labour input to households survey whereas enterprises may conceal those same inputs in order to avoid taxes or complying with administrative regulations.

2.1 Sources of data for the supply of labour

The Population and Housing Census of 2001 and the Living Standard Measurement Survey (LSMS) have since 2002 represented the main sources of information on the labour market in Albania. The first survey gives (almost) a complete enumeration of population and employment in the country. The second one is a sample survey of 3 660 households, covering all districts of the country. The main aim of this multipurpose survey is to measure the living standards of households. It also allows to measure employment in the informal sector and define some categories of under-employment. The following labour data can be obtained from these sources:

- Permanent, temporary, seasonal and occasional jobs;
- Employment details for employees, employers, own account workers, family workers;
- Employed persons with a secondary job;
- Employed persons by hours worked (less than 12, 13-24 hours, 25-35 hours, 36-39 hours, 40 or more hours);
- Part-time and full-time employees.

The data are broken down by the economic activity according to NACE two digit classification.

2.2 Sources of data for the demand of labour

The sources of information on labour supply are the establishment survey and the Structural Business Survey (SBS) conducted yearly since 1997. Data from SBS are useful to identify the number of jobs (registered jobs, main and secondary) by size of enterprise. The following data on employment are gathered from this survey:

- Employed persons at the end of the year;
- Self-employed at the end of the year (distinguished between propriety and family workers);
- Employees at the end of the year;
- Average number of employees, self-employed and total employment at the end of the year.

The number of unregistered workers is obtained by integrating the different sources of labour input from the supply and demand side. The total amount of value added for production by unregistered workers is obtained by applying the per capita value added by industry obtained as an average of small, medium and large enterprises, to the labour input figures.

3. The non-observed economy

The NOE estimation represents one of the highest priorities of improving the work on National Accounts, since the procedure used until 2003 in Albania was subjective and was based on coefficients that have been static during the period 1996-2003. In order to overcome this major drawback, the labour input method was used, adapted to the Albanian situation.

A preliminary estimate of labour productivity, broken down by branch and size class, has been calculated. This estimate allows to distinguish between the productivity of observed activities and that of the non-observed activities. The productivity of the non-observed activities is considered equal to the productivity of the less efficient enterprise.

Labour input can be measured using total employment and total hours worked. Consequently labour productivity can be obtained based on the aggregates of output, generally turnover or value added (GDP).

Productivity measures based on VA per employee were calculated by the National Accounts Department, for branches and for size classes. Two different measures of labour input have been used: the number of people employed in observed enterprises (according to SBS and balance sheets) and the number of people employed in enterprises underlying NA. In such cases imputed values calculated with the currently used procedure were incorporated in input and output measures. These results were compared with Italy and the following conclusions were drawn:

- In Albania, the VA per employee in small enterprises is bigger than in medium-size and big enterprises which is different from Italy;
- Such a comparison allows to take into account the role of smaller enterprises.

A methodology to reconcile national accounts aggregates with the total labour input as estimated by LSMS has been developed. The approach makes use of the basic data collected from different sources and can be summarized as follows:

1. The starting point is to determine (by branch and size class) the number of enterprises included in NA and those 'observed'; this is achieved by calculating the difference between (a) all observed enterprises (SBS + balance sheets) and (b) a number of enterprises derived from the Business Register; the difference provides an estimation of the hidden enterprises;

2. The second step consists of grossing up the labour input referring both to the non-observed (hidden) enterprises and to the hidden input of labour in the observed enterprises; this aggregate is calculated (by branch) as the difference (ΔI) between the number of posts declared by enterprises and an estimated amount of hidden labour (employed both by hidden and legal enterprises); it must be noted that the data from the LSMS survey was assumed to be exhaustive;

3. It is necessary to distinguish VA_{Obs} (observed VA), which refers to the observed enterprises and VA_{Corr} (corrected VA), which refers to the enterprises underlying National Accounts:

$$VA_{Corr} = VA_{Obs} + VA_{missing\ enterprises}$$

4. It is now possible to calculate (by branch) the Total Value Added (TOT VA):

$$TOTVA = VA_{Corr} \times \frac{Number\ of\ Entreprises\ underlying\ NA}{Number\ of\ Observed\ Enterprises} + \frac{VA_{SizeClass}}{Observed\ Labour\ Input} \times \Delta I\ [1]$$

where: $\dfrac{VA_{SizeClass}}{Observed\ Labour\ Input}$ indicates the productivity of the less efficient enterprises.

This procedure allows to obtain an estimate of VA including the underground economy. The procedure can be summarized as follows:

a) The NA target population expressed in terms of number of enterprises provides the starting point. This amount is obtained by deducting the number of "currently non-active" enterprises from the number of enterprises recorded in the Business Register. Only the enterprises recorded as closed in the survey of enterprises are considered "Non-active". It is important to stress that by using this methodology the number of enterprises underlying the NA estimates is larger than the number of enterprises considered in the Structural Business Statistics (SBS, defined as Observed Enterprises-E_{Obs}). This difference provides an estimate of the hidden enterprises.

b) As a first step, the input of labour declared by enterprises is grossed up. This procedure is consistent with grossing up the economic aggregates (output and intermediate cost) and multiplying, by branch and size class, the average number of employed people by the number of enterprises underlying the Structural Business Statistics (E_{Obs}). Thus, the "observed input of labour in the observed enterprises" (OL_{ObsE}) is obtained.

c) Then the average value of point (b) is grossed up to the number of enterprises considered as non-active by SBS and active in National Accounts ($E_{Non-active}$). In this way the "Non-observed input of labour in the non-observed enterprises" ($NOL_{Non-obsE}$) is obtained.

d) In the third step a comparison is made by branch of economic activity between the number of posts obtained in Living Standard Measurement Survey (LSMS) - $Labour_{LSMS}$ - with the total of posts obtained in points (b) and (c) ($OL_{ObsE} + NOL_{Non-obsE}$). The results of the comparison reveal that $Labour_{LSMS} > (OL_{ObsE} + NOL_{Non-obsE})$.

It is assumed that the difference ΔI is captured by:

$$\Delta I = Labour_{LSMS} - (OL_{ObsE} + NOL_{Non-obsE})$$

and is a further estimate of hidden labour (employed both by hidden and legal enterprises).

The procedure described in points (a) – (d) allows an identification of the National Accounts target population both in terms of number of enterprises and in terms of employed persons. Therefore, it is possible to estimate the corresponding value added (as well as output and intermediate costs), for each component of the observed and non-observed economy.

Let i=1,2,25, be the index for the branches and j=small, medium, large, the index for the dimensional class. It is possible to calculate the total value added (TOTVA) using the following formula:

$$TOTVA_i = \sum_j \frac{VA_{Corrj}}{E_{Obsj}} \times (E_{Obsj} + E_{Non-obsj}) + \frac{\sum_i VA_{Corri}}{\sum_i OL_{ObsEi}} \times \Delta I \quad [2]$$

where VA_{Corr} is the value added declared in the SBS survey and indicates the size class characterized by the minimum value added per capita. Equation [2] is reformulation of equation [1]. Equation [2] allows to estimate the NOE component using a different per capita value for the observed and for the non-observed components of the economy.

4. Implications and effects on national accounts and GDP estimates

Due to the lack of statistical information sources and experience, the expert method was used to calculate the non-observed economy during the period 1996-2003. However, this method suffered from a high degree of subjectivity and the percentages applied for estimation of NOE in each industry were fixed, despite the important changes that occurred in the Albanian economy during this period.

Therefore, it was considered necessary to develop new methods in accordance with the OECD *Handbook on Measuring the Non-observed Economy* (2002). The labour input method was considered to be the most suitable method for a good estimation of NOE in Albania. It is intended to serve as a conceptual framework for GDP exhaustiveness estimation in relation to the non-observed economy.

Based on the latest estimates for the period 2001-2003, the share of non-observed economy in the value added at basic prices (without FISIM) is presented in Table 1:

Table1. Value added produced by the non-observed economy
(per cent)

Branches	2001	2002	2003
Agriculture, hunting and forestry	11.4	11.3	11.0
Industry	7.7	10.1	12.8
Construction	67.7	73.2	77.0
Trade, hotels and restaurants	60.0	56.1	51.5
Services	15.5	15.5	17.5
Value added at basic prices (without FISIM)	**30.4**	**30.5**	**30.8**

ARMENIA

1. Sources

Valuable sources for estimating the non-observed economy are the data from sample surveys. Since 2001, the National Statistical Service of the Republic of Armenia has been conducting a labour force survey in coordination with the integrated household survey. In addition, within the TACIS Programme, a special labour force survey was conducted in 2004 in 2539 households. The survey showed that 22.7 per cent of the total persons employed were working without a formal labour contract. Hidden employment is more widespread among self-employed. According to the survey data, 78 per cent of employers and self-employed persons were carrying out unregistered activities, with 15.3 per cent of them describing their occupation as temporary, 32.3 per cent as continuous and 52.4 per cent as seasonal or occasional.

In 2002, a survey was conducted among institutions providing health services and selling pharmaceuticals to households, and among households consuming these products and services. According to the household survey, the volume of consumed health services was 6.65 times higher than the volume of health services provided by institutions and individual entrepreneurs. The volume of purchases of pharmaceuticals by households was ten times the volume of purchases reported by retail trade enterprises and private entrepreneurs.

In 2002, a sample survey of the financial results of registered non-commercial enterprises was also conducted. During the survey, 49.7 per cent of the enterprises were operational, 29.8 per cent were not active and 20.5 per cent could not be found.

2. Estimation methods

To produce estimates of non-observed economy, use is mainly made of data from regular statistical reports on the number of employed persons and the number of persons engaged in the production process. These two sets of data are used to determine the total number of persons employed and to calculate labour productivity and value added by economic branches.

However, using only the concept of 'employed person' is not sufficient. In order to reflect the complexity of the labour market, it is necessary to take into account concurrent jobs, work in unregistered units and part-time work. In addition, the temporarily unemployed are also included in the number of employed persons.

To calculate the number of persons actually engaged in production, official statistical data sources are supplemented with data from Labour Force Surveys (in particular, to determine the number of persons on enforced leave, holding several jobs or employed part-time). An average coefficient is calculated from these two sources, and the total number of persons on enforced leave, holding several jobs or employed part-time is determined by applying the coefficient to official data. These data are then allocated by branches of the economy according to the pattern established from the Labour Force Survey data.

The number of persons actually engaged in production is used as the basis for calculating labour productivity for the various branches. Value added for the "non-recorded" part of the economy is then determined on the basis of this labour productivity and the total number of persons employed.

Because of the nature of <u>agricultural production,</u> the non-recorded output from this branch is determined based on the results of annual checks of the reliability of data on numbers of livestock and crop areas. These data serve to correct for the underestimation of livestock output and crop yields. Overall, the hidden part of agriculture constitutes about 23 per cent of its value added.

For the <u>health sector,</u> the hidden activities are calculated on the basis of the health sample survey by comparing the results of household expenditures on health and the output of health institutions and private entrepreneurs providing health services to the population. Adjustments for total value added in this sector amounted to 58.2 per cent, against 30 per cent in 2001, i.e. the hidden activities revealed on the basis of this survey increased the adjustment for value added in health by 72 per cent (16 billion drams, in 2003: 1 USD= 579 drams).

The adjustment for value added in public enterprises, made on the basis of the 2002 sample survey data, made up 58.9 per cent, against adjustments of about 1 per cent made in the previous years.

2.1 Estimating value added produced by the registered unemployed persons with a gainful occupation

In order to estimate the number of economically active people, the number of workers officially recorded as unemployed but engaged in some kind of paid activity is estimated. According to the Armenian Employment Service, in 2003 the number of registered unemployed persons was 124 000, or 10.1 per cent of the economically active population. According to the data from the Labour Force Survey carried out in 2004, the level of unemployment was 31.2 per cent, which is three times higher than the officially registered figure. However, it appeared that 4.2 per cent of unemployed persons had a gainful occupation as an employer or self-employed.

Data on labour productivity and the number of persons officially registered as unemployed (but occupied as employers or self-employed), derived from surveys for the respective sectors, are used to calculate the gross value added attributable to this category of workers.

2.2 Estimating informal activities of households

Methods of determining the scope of the informal activities of population differ across economic branches depending on the available information. Household budget surveys, other sample surveys and tax data are used to estimate value added of the household sector.

For <u>industry,</u> estimates of output and value added are based on household budget surveys. Adjustments are made for production of wine for sale, sewing of clothes, repairs of furniture, electric appliances and recreation items, production of bread and confectionery, production of handicrafts and other similar work, and services relating to industrial activities.

For industry as a whole, value added created by the household sector amounted to 5.0 per cent of the total value added in industry, a 13.2 per cent share of the overall NOE adjustment in industry.

In <u>construction</u>, informal activities are estimated based on data from individual housing construction surveys. According to these surveys, the hidden share of individual housing construction by households constituted 22.1 per cent of the total NOE adjustment for construction, or 9.1 per cent of the total VA for construction.

Informal activities of households in <u>agriculture</u> are calculated on the basis of checks on the numbers of livestock and areas sown by crops. Adjustment for value added of households amounted to 13.4 per cent in agriculture, or 57.8 per cent of the total NOE adjustment for agriculture.

In <u>trade</u>, informal activities are estimated based on data from the household surveys. Adjustment for value added in individual entrepreneurship constituted 11.2 per cent of trade, or 17.2 per cent of the NOE adjustment for trade.

In <u>transport</u>, informal activities relating to transport of goods and passengers are calculated from data obtained through sample surveys of cargo and passenger transportation, as well as data on passenger transportation services in the city of Yerevan. The total volume of informal activities of households amounted to 21.0 per cent of VA in transport, or 76.5 per cent of the NOE adjustment for the sector.

In the <u>housing</u> sector, informal activities were estimated from household survey data as well as from the ratio of private and state-owned dwellings. Total adjustment constituted 25.6 per cent of VA of the sector, of which income from renting individual dwellings amounted to 10.6 per cent, or 41.4 per cent of the total NOE adjustment for this branch.

In <u>healthcare</u>, payments for services are calculated from data obtained through the household survey. The adjustment for the informal activities amounted to 8.0 per cent, or 15.3 per cent of the NOE adjustment for healthcare.

For <u>education</u>, the estimates of the informal sector were produced on the basis of a sample survey of students enrolled in the higher educational institutions to calculate the number of persons studying privately and total payments made to private tutors. The adjustment for the informal activities in education constituted 8.6 per cent, or 61.6 per cent of the NOE adjustment for the education sector.

In 2003, the adjustment for value added in informal economic activities amounted to 33.4 per cent (36 per cent in 1997) of the household sector, or 8.3 per cent of the GDP of Armenia.

3. Implications and effects on national accounts and GDP estimates

For the first time, estimation of the non-observed economy in GDP in Armenia was made in 1994. The hidden economy at this time amounted to more than 50 billion drams or 27 per cent of total GDP. In 2003, the non-observed economy amounted to 470.2 billion drams, or 28.9 per cent of total GDP.

The share of the informal activities of households in NOE was 28.6 per cent in 2003 against 26.5 per cent in 1997 (the share of the households sector in GDP amounting to 24.3 per cent and 21.3 per cent correspondingly).

The adjustments for the non-observed economy in 2003, as recorded in GDP, by economic branch, are given in Table 1 below:

Table 1. Adjustment for non-observed economy - 2003

	Total	of which (share in NOE adjustments for the branch) (per cent)		
	Share of NOE by branch (per cent)	Hidden employment (in registered and not registered enterprises)	Unemployed (as employers or self-employed)	Informal activities of households
Agriculture	23.2	40.8	1.4	57.8
Industry	37.6	83.8	3.0	13.2
Construction	41.0	65.4	12.5	22.1
Transport and communication	16.5	14.2	9.3	76.5
Trade	55.0	46.6	36.2	17.2
Other branches	12.3	59.7	2.4	37.9
Total GDP at market prices	**28.9**	**57.6**	**13.8**	**28.6**

Continuous work on improving the information base, statistical reporting and methods of statistical observation is carried out alongside the estimation of the non-observed economy. Great attention is paid to the development of administrative and statistical registers. In 1999 an annually updated business register of enterprises and entrepreneurs was created in the system of statistics. The registers are the main mechanism of improving the information base, enabling to expand the coverage of data used to calculate the main indicators of the system of national accounts.

AUSTRALIA

1. Concepts and definitions

The concepts and definitions used in the Australian System of National Accounts (ASNA) generally conform to the standards set out in SNA93. Some minor variations have been adopted to allow for Australian data supply conditions or user requirements.

Australian Bureau of Statistics (ABS) surveys are designed to ensure that survey results are consistent with national accounts concepts and definitions. Where administrative data are used, special care is taken to ensure the correct application of standards and the identification of possible gaps and overlaps. Where source data are known to differ from national accounting definitions and concepts, appropriate adjustment is made to align the data.

To ensure that GDP is as exhaustive as possible within the production boundary defined in the SNA, the various components of the non-observed economy are estimated along the lines indicated in the OECD publication *Measuring the Non-Observed Economy: A Handbook* (2002).

2. Sources and estimation methods

ABS puts considerable effort into producing exhaustive estimates of GDP and its components, including methods for assessing and remedying deficiencies in the basic data collection program.

A large number of collections are undertaken that feed directly into the national accounts compilation process. These collections range from periodic large economic and household surveys to annual or quarterly surveys of industry to provide current economic indicators. Additionally, a range of non-ABS data such as taxation and administrative data are used.

The quality of ABS statistics is underwritten by the application of good statistical methods during all stages of a collection, including the design stages. Substantial effort is put into developing statistical standards, including concepts, data item definitions, classifications and question modules. Standard rules are adopted for frame maintenance, field collection and estimation, and generalised processing facilities are available to support the use of these rules. ABS also has a Methodology Division that is responsible for ensuring that sound and defensible methods are applied to all collections and compilations.

Sample design and estimation systems are developed in accordance with internationally accepted standards. Accuracy is assessed in terms of both sampling and non-sampling error. Each source data area is also required to confront its data with other ABS data and with external information to ensure statistical coherence, as far as is possible, between the various data series that are input to the national accounts.

An important element in ensuring the quality of the national accounts is editing and data confrontation. The most important data confrontation exercise is the compilation of the annual supply-and-use tables which form the benchmarks for the quarterly and annual estimates of GDP and its components. ABS calculates all three measures of GDP, which are balanced in the supply-and-use tables to ensure comprehensive and consistent GDP estimates.

The application of supply-and-use tables provides the framework for checking the consistency of flows of goods and services obtained from different data sources. The supply-and-use framework is also used to calculate much of the economic data contained in the accounts and for detecting any weaknesses in the outputs. Any data deficiencies and inconsistencies that are identified through the data confrontation and balancing procedures are regularly fed back to data suppliers.

In summary, the compilation systems and methods used by ABS to compile the national accounts are designed to ensure that, as far as possible, all relevant transactions are captured and included in the GDP estimates. The basic data collection program is continually reviewed so as to reduce the amount of production that is non-observed. In common with the national accounts of most countries, illegal activities are not explicitly included but the accounts are designed to include items, which, while legal in themselves, are not reported to the taxation authorities. Illegal production can to some limited extent, feed into the overall measure of GDP where it is 'laundered' as legitimate activity.

3. The non-observed economy

Explicit allowances for the legal underground component of non-observed activity are currently included in estimates of GDP for Australia.

As already indicated, no specific allowances are made for illegal production, such as the production and distribution of narcotics, as it is difficult to measure such activity with sufficient reliability. It is recognised, however, that such illegal activity could be a significant component of Australia's total non-observed production.

As informal production is relatively unimportant in Australia, no attempt is made to distinguish between the formal and informal sectors in the sub-sectoring of the household sector.

With regard to production of households for own final use, the provision of owner-occupied dwelling services by households are a significant component of Australia's household final consumption expenditure. The provision of these services is included in the ASNA. Other 'own account' activities, such as the cultivation of crops and livestock for own final use and the undertaking of own-account construction, are of less significance for Australia than they are for many other countries. Nevertheless, Australia makes adjustments to its national accounts to take account of these sorts of activities in accordance with the relevant SNA93 guidelines. For example, an adjustment of around 2% is made to the value of gross mixed income to allow for the backyard production of fruit, vegetables, meat, fish, eggs, beer and wine by households for their own use.

3.1 Who is engaged in underground activity?

Underground activity tends to occur in areas where there is a low level of regulation and a high proportion of cash transactions. Thus it tends to be concentrated in small businesses engaged in activities such as construction, accommodation, cafes and restaurants, personal and other services and retail trade. In Australia, small businesses with few or no employees are the most likely to engage in the non-declaration of sales income. Areas such as catering, personal care, most repair services and domestic services, are examples of areas where small businesses are a significant source of supply. In particular, repair and maintenance work undertaken for households is often paid for in cash directly, so the scope for under-reporting the value of this type of work may be significant.

Underground activity does not exist or is less significant in highly regulated industries, the public sector, and industries where large businesses predominate, such as utilities, health, education, communications and finance. There are a number of reasons for this. In the case of publicly listed companies, ownership and management are usually separate, and management reports to independent boards. Management is usually rewarded for strong sales and profit performance and generally would not benefit from understating sales or overstating expenses. Large businesses are subject to independent auditing to detect fraud. These characteristics are also true of government owned corporations. In addition, large companies stand to lose business if discovered engaging in fraudulent activities. It is recognised, however, that misreporting of income by large businesses could occur to some extent.

Householders may also participate in the underground economy on their own account. Such activities, commonly referred to as 'moonlighting', generally involve individuals who are employees in the observed economy but who, outside of official working hours, participate in the underground economy. They do so by offering goods and services directly to consumers for 'cash in hand' and then not reporting this activity. The householder is in effect operating as a small unincorporated business. Alternatively, employees may undertake additional unrecorded paid work for an employer for 'cash in hand'. In this case, the unrecorded additional income would be classified as employee income.

Individuals who are thought to undertake this type of activity are normally people with trade or vocational skills, such as car mechanics and those involved in building-related trades, or workers who undertake cleaning and other types of labour intensive unskilled work after hours. Some professional employees, such as schoolteachers and architects, could also be involved. Individuals not in the formal workforce such as students and those who are unemployed may also operate in the underground economy.

3.2 Estimates of underground activity

Estimates of the underground economy in Australia have ranged between 1.3% and 15% of GDP. The lower estimates have been derived by ABS using tax audit information and statistical analysis. The higher estimates are normally based on monetary models, such as the currency demand model, which estimate the amount of underground activity by examining the amount of unexplained cash circulating in the economy. ABS does not support the use of monetary models for measuring the underground economy and considers that the higher estimates lack credibility.

For ABS, measurement of the underground economy is of prime interest. The focus is not on those transactions that may escape detection by the tax authorities. Unreported, undeclared or untaxed transactions are not synonymous with unmeasured transactions in the national accounts. Income that is not declared to the taxation authorities may still be recorded in ABS estimates of GDP depending on the measurement methods used. In estimating GDP, ABS makes use of many data sources, including taxation data, administrative data, household survey data and business survey data, some of which are expected to be relatively unaffected by underground activity.

For some key areas where the underground economy is expected to be particularly significant, the methods used also include a number of checks and balances through the supply-and-use estimation system.

3.3 Source of adjustments

The current method for adjusting the understatement of business income evolved from initial estimates of revenue foregone through understatement of business income in tax returns (on the assumption that businesses which understate income to taxation authorities similarly understate business activity in ABS business surveys). Since then, the factors underlying the adjustments have been reviewed periodically taking into account factors such as the estimated effect of specific measures undertaken by the Australian Tax Office (ATO) to reduce tax evasion. In the second half of 1999, ABS, in conjunction with the ATO, analysed the results of the ATO tax audits over a five year period to see if the results could be used to better quantify the size of any potential understatement. As a result of this study, ABS implemented a small upward revision to its previous income adjustment factors for both incorporated and unincorporated enterprises.

3.4 Adjustments made to GDP estimates for underground activity

In the compilation of GDP, ABS makes explicit upward adjustments for underground transactions that go unreported in the source data. The adjustments rely on indicative information from aggregated income tax audit information, anecdotal evidence and the data confrontation process inherent in the supply-and-use methodology used to compile the national accounts. The combination of these methods, together with a detailed "upper bounds" analysis, gives ABS confidence that there are no substantial amounts of production missing from GDP as a whole, although it is recognised that the quality of some components could be more significantly affected.

The adjustments are applied consistently to the income, expenditure, gross output and intermediate use for incorporation into the supply-use framework. Overall estimates of gross output, intermediate and final use together with factor incomes are balanced within that framework, so implicitly some of the underground economy adjustments would be altered in that process.

The income adjustments used are weighted net income averages derived from the results of the tax-based audits. They also take into account some earlier ABS analysis and assumptions (based on taxation data) about the ratio of small incorporated businesses to large businesses for each industry.

The explicit adjustments applied to the income side of the GDP account add about 1.3% to the level of GDP.

The adjustments applied to the income measure of GDP are also applied directly to the production-based estimate of GDP as they are directly related supply-side measures using more or less the same annual data sources. Based on the patterns indicated in historical aggregate tax audit data, around 63% of the income adjustment factor is added to output and 37% is deducted from intermediate consumption (with some variation between industries) to account for understatement of sales and overstatement of expenses by businesses.

To balance the income adjustments, a small 0.4% adjustment is made to the Household Final Consumption Expenditure (HFCE) estimate in the Use table. Generally, the data used to compile the expenditure measure are considered far less susceptible to understatement.

The adjustment is made at the industry level with two thirds of the adjustment being allocated to two industries, *Retail trade* and *Accommodation, Cafes and Restaurants.*

No adjustments are currently made to Gross Fixed Capital Formation (GFCF). This is because the data sources and methods used are not thought to be susceptible to any significant unreported transactions. Any required adjustments are left to fall out implicitly from the balancing process.

The adjustment factors used for each component are not varied from year to year, because new information only becomes available very infrequently. For this reason, the adjustments do not generally impact on GDP growth rates.

4. The income measure of GDP

4.1 Gross mixed income (GMI)

The GMI estimate is considered the most likely GDP income component to be understated due to underground activity. This is because small business income accounts for a very high proportion of the GMI estimate.

ABS currently adjusts its GMI estimates to allow for understated income (due to 'skimming') and the associated under or overstatement of costs. The adjustment to GMI is based on aggregated tax audit data and ABS assumptions. Due to a lack of data, no allowances are made for:
- employed persons who undertake paid work for themselves outside of official working hours unknown to the tax authorities;
- persons officially recorded as not in the workforce or in receipt of unemployment benefits who are actually working for themselves for undeclared cash payments.

While no adjustments are made for these activities, recent analysis indicates that they are unlikely to significantly affect the overall estimate for underground activity. Additionally, as the national accounts are a balanced system, some of this unrecorded activity may be corrected for in the compilation process due to the confrontation of data for the supply-and-use of products in the economy. For instance, if expenditure data identify outlays not recorded on the income and production side, the latter components of GDP are likely to be adjusted upwards in the national accounts compilation process, thus limiting the impact of the unrecorded income on GDP.

4.2 Gross operating surplus (GOS)

An upward adjustment is made to the GOS of small private non-financial corporations, based again on aggregated tax audits and ABS assumptions.

No adjustments are made to the GOS estimate for private financial corporations as these businesses are normally very large and highly regulated. Additionally, public sector non-financial corporations and the general government sector would not be involved in underground activity so no adjustments are required.

In relation to the GOS item, 'dwellings owned by persons', because of the methodology adopted, there is virtually no scope for this item to be understated due to missing underground transactions. The Census of Population and Housing provides the total number of owner-occupied and rented dwellings, and information about rents paid for rented dwellings. Being Census based, the stock of dwellings will not be understated nor is there any reason for persons who rent dwellings to understate the rent they pay.

4.3 Compensation of employees (CoE)

No adjustments are made to the estimates of CoE due to a lack of sufficient information. In businesses where cash receipts predominate, employees can be paid in cash. This is only an issue for the national accounts to the extent that the expense goes unrecorded by the business as it is the business expense rather than the income recorded by the employee that is used as the source data for CoE. Anecdotal evidence suggests that some unrecorded payments are made to casual staff and in other situations overtime and bonuses may be paid 'off the books'. Substantial components of CoE are, however, unlikely to be affected by the underground economy. These components are:

- the 10% of CoE that relates to employers' social contributions (superannuation and workers' compensation);
- the 25% of total wages and salaries paid to public sector employees;
- the approximately 50% of private sector employees who are employed by medium and large businesses (i.e., those with 20 or more employees) who in turn account for 70% of private sector wages and salaries.

For the remaining employees, although there are financial incentives for both employers and employees to enter arrangements for wages to be paid 'off the books', there are several factors which act to limit its extent, such as:

- it requires the complicity of two parties, the employer and the employee, which is inherently more risky than understating one's own income;
- businesses which employ labour totally off the books could expose themselves to substantial workers' compensation costs;
- employees such as casuals whose earnings are under the personal income tax threshold have nothing to gain by being paid in cash as they could expect a tax refund.

While it is acknowledged that some CoE will remain unrecorded in the national accounts, the above factors will limit the extent. It is also the case that an understatement of CoE expenses by businesses acts to dampen the likely understatement of GOS/GMI. So at the GDP level it is partially offsetting.

4.4 Taxes, subsidies

Due to a lack of information, no adjustments are made for missing taxes on products. Taxes such as the Goods and Services Tax (GST) are fully recorded in government accounts, but businesses could fail to pass on to government the full amount collected. In the case of skimming of receipts by businesses, GST on the amounts skimmed will have been collected but not passed on to government, and for 'under the table' transactions, a GST-free price may be struck. In principle, the adjustments made to GOS and GMI for unrecorded activity include these amounts so GDP itself is not missing the amounts that would normally have been paid to government. Subsidies, being governments payments, are unaffected by underground activity.

4.5 Imports

Imports would only be marginally affected by underground activity through either undeclared transactions or the undervaluation of declared transactions.

4.6 Income and production adjustment methods

4.6.1 Gross Mixed Income

ABS applies an overall adjustment of around 19% to unincorporated non-farm net business income, which translates into an adjustment to total GMI of around 10%. Different adjustments are applied to individual industries based on tax estimates, the assessed proportion of cash transactions and other factors. An adjustment factor is not applied to the agriculture industry (other than to forestry, fishing and hunting) as gross output is sourced from information other than business surveys. The market value of agricultural production is derived by collecting quantity data from agricultural establishments and marketing organisations and then multiplying by prices supplied by marketing boards, brokers, wholesalers, marketing reports and auctioneers. However, if sales are made to organisations other than those mentioned, it is possible that some underestimation could occur.

4.6.2 Gross Operating Surplus

For private non-financial corporations, company income is currently adjusted upward by around 7%. Again, different adjustments are applied at the individual industry level. The adjustments take account of expected differences in misreporting between small and large businesses. For large businesses an understatement of company income of 4% is assumed, while for small businesses a 19% adjustment is applied. In total, this translates into an overall adjustment to private non-financial GOS of around 3%.

In summary, the following direct adjustments are made to initial income estimate to account for underground activity:
- gross mixed income - 10.1%;
- gross operating surplus for private financial corporations - 3.2%;
- an overall adjustment to the level of GDP of around 1.3%.

The explicit adjustments applied in 2000-01 to the income side of the GDP account are shown in Table 1.

To estimate output and intermediate use adjustments by industry, the GMI/GOS adjustments are split into estimates for understated income (gross sales of goods and services) and overstated expenses. The former component provides the upward adjustment to output and the overstated expenses component provides the negative adjustment required for intermediate use.

Table 1. Gross Domestic Product Account, Income Estimates
2000-2001

	Estimate prior to adjustment	Explicit adjustment for missing underground transactions	Published estimate	Adjustment to initial estimate
	(Millions US dollars)	(Millions US dollars)	(Millions US dollars)	(Percentage)
Compensation of employees	321 731	...	321 731	...
Gross operating surplus				
Non-financial corporations				
Private	96 766	3 205	99 971	3.3
Public	18 912	...	18 912	...
Total	115 678	3 205	118 883	2.8
Financial corporations	18 110	...	18 110	...
General government	13 018	...	13 018	...
Dwellings owned by persons	55 771	...	55 771	...
Total gross operating surplus	202 577	3 205	205 782	1.6
Gross mixed income	54 202	5 277	59 479	9.7
Total factor income	578 510	8 482	586 992	1.5
Taxes less subsidies on production and imports	82 315	...	82 315	...
Gross domestic product	**660 825**	**8 482**	**669 07**	**1.3**

Source: Australian System of National Accounts 2001–2002 (cat no 5204.0) and unpublished estimates.

5. The expenditure measure of GDP

Consistent with adjustments made on the supply side, 0.4% adjustment is made to the household final consumption expenditure (HFCE) estimates. The rationale for making this adjustment is a belief that if businesses understate their income they are also likely to understate retail turnover and other sales revenue in the source data used to compile HFCE. No such adjustments are required for components of HFCE that are based on household surveys. The payment of unrecorded tips in for example, restaurants and the like have also been taken into account in estimating the likely understatement of HFCE. However, in the Australian context, such payments are unlikely to be a significant component of underground activity.

No adjustments are made to GFCF. ABS believes that its methodology for estimating residential construction and alterations and additions is reasonably reliable in spite of underground activity. 'Work done' data are sourced as far as possible from prime contractors and the data aligns quite well with local government approvals value data. Alterations and additions make use of Household Expenditure Survey (HES) data, which rely on what the purchaser paid rather than what the business received.

There could be some scope for underground activity in relation to non-residential construction, however, as for residential construction, the methodological approach adopted most probably accounts for this.

Regarding machinery and equipment, businesses are known to overstate their expenses by treating the purchase of capital goods as a current expense to get an immediate write-off. However, in the compilation of the national accounts benchmarks using the supply-and-use approach, more reliance tends to be placed on the supply of capital equipment than the expenditure data. It is, therefore, assumed that this item is unlikely to be the subject of any significant understatement.

The approach taken to derive the underground economy adjustments on the expenditure side was to use the industry output adjustments at the most detailed level as the starting point and to map these to the use side in a supply-use matrix. A substantial proportion of the industry output adjustments mapped to intermediate consumption or to areas of the account such as gross fixed capital formation where it is considered no adjustment is required because of the reasons given above. An adjustment was made where the mapping was to household final consumption expenditure. In this way the integrity of the adjustments on the supply-and-use side of the national accounts is maintained.

6. Possible upper bounds of underground activity missing from GDP

ABS has reviewed its adjustment for the underground economy in the estimation of GDP. In particular, it investigated the possible upper bounds of error around the adjustment. A paper containing the results of the review was released in March 2004, titled 'The Underground Economy and Australia's GDP'.

In undertaking the review, ABS systematically analysed each component of the income and expenditure measures of GDP and made judgements as to the maximum feasible level of understatement. Subjective judgments were applied at the most detailed level possible for each component. While such judgements are obviously subject to a large margin of error, when totalled they can provide a reasonable indication of what is plausible in terms of an upper bound on missing GDP.

The following key assumptions were made in order to make judgments about upper bounds for underground transactions:
- they are in cash;
- general government and government business undertakings are not involved;
- imputed transactions, including the value of owner-occupied housing services are not involved, by definition;
- large and medium businesses (defined as those with 20 or more employees) are unlikely to be involved in 'skimming' or overstating expenses to any significant extent;
- large and medium businesses are unlikely to understate compensation of employees' expenses;
- small businesses understating income are the major contributors to the underground economy.

6. 1 Upper bound income estimate

Based on these assumptions and a detailed analysis of GDP components, it was estimated that at least 65% of the goods and services included in the income-based GDP estimate are either not subject to underground economy transactions or subject only to a very minor extent. In particular, underground activity is unlikely to be occurring in the general government sector, public corporations, highly regulated industries and those industries where very large businesses predominate. It is possible therefore to rule out large part of forestry, mining, manufacturing, non-residential construction, transportation, communications, electricity, gas and water, finance and insurance, government administration, health and education. The remainder of GDP, which includes the production of small businesses and individuals, is potentially affected to a more significant extent.

Upper bounds were deliberately chosen to stretch what could be considered a plausible level of understated transactions. In undertaking the analysis, attention was paid to the fact that upper bounds for the GMI/GOS and CoE components of the income measure of GDP cannot be chosen independently of each other due to the inverse relationship between them (labour costs are a deduction item in the derivation of GMI and GOS). This had significant implications for the assessment of what is a plausible level of adjustment to each aggregate and to GDP itself. If an understatement adjustment were made to CoE it might have to be accompanied by a reduction in the adjustments to GMI and GOS to cover those circumstances where businesses truthfully account for their sales but understate their wage costs. However, in situations where businesses also understate their sales, a positive adjustment to both GMI/GOS and CoE would be valid and intuitively one would expect this to be the case for cash-based industries. However, even in this situation the more CoE is understated the less understated GMI and GOS will become, all else remaining equal.

Table 2 summarises judgments on what could be considered very generous 'upper bound' estimates for underground transactions in the context of the income measure of GDP. The estimates shown in Table 2 are built up from the upper bounds assigned at the detailed industry level. It should be emphasised that these are not to be considered ABS estimates of missing GDP. It simply represents the results of a sensitivity analysis using a range of various assumptions.

At first sight the upper bound for understatement of compensation of employees (2%) may appear low. However, the upper bound on compensation of employees paid by small private businesses is substantial and for industries such as construction, accommodation, cafes and restaurants and personal and other services it was assumed for the purposes of the study to be as high as 20%. As the source of data for compensation of employees is the employer and not the employee, the motivation for understatement by the employer is either not present or far weaker because compensation of employee type expenses are normally tax deductible.

The upper bound estimate for understatement of gross mixed income (37%) was set very high to take account of both the predominance of small businesses contributing to the gross mixed income estimate and also the potential for tradespersons, professionals and others to 'moonlight' on their own account. Again, even more generous allowances for the potential understatement of income have been made for the most likely affected industries.

An alternative approach to determining a possible upper bound for non-disclosed income is through the analysis of detailed population statistics. This approach is useful since a high level of accuracy can be attached to population counts. In undertaking the study, it was presumed that all underground activity involves participation by persons who are either employed or unemployed, or not officially in the labour force, such as full-time students. Again, assumptions were made about the possible extent of individual involvement in underground activity depending on labour force status and occupation. Using very generous assumptions about the proportion of people involved and average hours worked in the underground economy, the study produced upper bound results consistent with those shown in Table 2.

**Table 2. Upper bound estimates of underground activity missing from GDP
2000-2001**

	Estimate prior to adjustment for potentially missing underground transactions	Upper bound estimate of potentially missing underground transactions	Upper bound estimate of potentially missing underground transactions
	(Million US dollars)	(Million US dollars)	(Percentage of estimate prior to adjustment)
Compensation of employees	321 731	6 382	2.0
Gross operating surplus			
Non financial corporations			
• Private	96 766	5 356	5.5
• Public	18 912	…	…
• Total	115 678	5 356	4.6
Financial corporations	18 110	…	…
General government	13 018	…	…
Dwellings owned by persons	55 771	…	…
Total gross operating surplus	202 577	5 356	2.6
Gross mixed income	54 202	20 256	37.4
Total factor income	578 510	31 994	5.5
Taxes less subsidies on production and imports	82 315	…	…
Gross domestic product	**660 825**	**31 994**	**4.8**

Considering that the upper bounds for understatement used in the analysis were deliberately chosen to stretch the limits of plausibility for the detailed components of GDP, it strongly indicates that the largest possible upward adjustment required for income for the underground economy would be in the order of 5%. More probably it would be considerably less than this. Given the adjustments already made for underground transactions in the national accounts compilation, it is considered highly unlikely that the level of GDP could be understated by more than about 2% on account of missed underground transactions. Overall, ABS remains comfortable with its current adjustments as set out in Table 1.

6.2 Upper bound expenditure estimate

The expenditure approach to estimating GDP is, in principle, independent of the income and production methods as it is estimated from the demand side. In practice, however, it does utilise some common data sources and ultimately it is balanced with the other two approaches in the supply-and-use framework. As part of the review, a judgment was also made as to the possible significance of underground activity for each expenditure item.

The areas of expenditure considered most likely to be affected by underground activity are:
• residential construction and alteration and additions;
• household final consumption expenditure on goods and services.

The remaining expenditure items are unlikely to be affected to any extent. In particular, it is assumed that public sector transactions are not affected. Data for the public sector comes from administrative sources and expenditure of public funds is subject to strict financial and audit controls. Exports and imports would only be marginally affected by underground activity through either undeclared transactions or the undervaluation of declared transactions.

Expenditure on intangible fixed assets, e.g. computer software and mineral exploration, and ownership transfer costs are also unlikely to be affected to any significant degree (the former because they are depreciable costs to the business and the latter because transactions are unlikely to be in cash). In relation to expenditure on machinery and equipment, the national accounts use supply-side data (i.e. domestic production and imports of machinery and equipment) in conjunction with expenditure data, thereby providing a crosscheck to some degree. Also as machinery and equipment is a depreciable item for taxation purposes and because transactions are unlikely to be in cash, the degree of under reporting is likely to be limited, although businesses may write off some purchases as a business expense.

6.2.1 Residential construction and alterations and additions

The example most often mentioned in relation to the underground economy in Australia is that of building tradesmen doing work 'off the record'. ABS believes, however, that the estimates of investment in residential construction are reasonably reliable in spite of underground activity because of:

- the requirement for local government building permits for new buildings and significant alterations and additions;
- the targeting in surveys of prime contractors rather than sub-contractors;
- the involvement of financial institutions in making progress payments;
- the use of household survey data rather than data from businesses to periodically benchmark alterations and additions;
- the estimates not being based on the income declared by builders to income tax authorities.

The value of work done on new residential buildings is collected in ABS Building Activity Survey (BACS) quarterly. The population list from which jobs are selected for inclusion in the survey comprises all approved building jobs which were notified to ABS up to, but not including, the last month of the reference quarter. Statistics on the value of building work approved are derived by aggregating the estimated value of building work when completed as reported on building approval documents provided to local councils or other building approval authorities.

While it is difficult to build a dwelling without a building permit, values reported on building permits could be subject to understatement. While ABS generally accepts values provided by approving bodies, every effort is made to ensure data are provided on a consistent basis. Given the potential loss of revenue, councils are unlikely to issue a building permit for a house with a value that is unreasonably low. The price of new homes on the market is also well advertised and is a good gauge of their cost of construction. There may, however, be instances where data reported do not reflect the building completion value. For most project homes the reported value is the contract price, which may include the cost of landscaping as well as site preparation. In other cases, where a builder is contracted to construct a dwelling based on the owner's plans, the value may only be the builder's costs.

When compiling the national accounts, allowances are also added for net expenditure on new dwellings not included in the survey (e.g. dwellings on rural properties not requiring local government permits and architects' and professional fees).

Notwithstanding the use of a range of checks and balances, it is recognised that there could still be some understatement at the margin. For the purposes of the upper bounds analysis, an arbitrary (but generous) 10% understatement to value of building work done was allowed.

For alterations and additions to existing dwellings, the value of the work undertaken is estimated using data from the periodic Household Expenditure Survey (HES) in combination with information provided periodically from an external source on the home improvement market.

ABS has no evidence that the household-based HES collection significantly understates expenditure on alterations and additions. The following factors would act to minimise the level of understatement:

- there is nothing illegal about paying cash or agreeing on a competitive (low) price;
- the survey is confidential;
- the homeowner is not asked for details of the contractor or whether the correct taxes were paid on the transaction.

Nevertheless, some expenditure may remain unreported. In particular, individual respondents who are deriving income from the underground economy may have an incentive to also understate their expenditure in HES to have consistency between their recorded income and recorded expenditure. To allow for this, an arbitrary figure of 15% was allowed for the possible underestimation of alterations and additions. It was estimated that this amount combined with the 10% allowance for missing transactions in new construction would add around 0.6% to the overall level of GDP.

6.2.2 Household final consumption expenditure

Sales of goods and services to households are the other major area where underground transactions are known to take place. Personal expenditure on goods and services accounts for around 60% of Australia's GDP.

In Australia, household final consumption expenditure (HFCE) is calculated quarterly and annually using a wide variety of sources including business and household surveys as well as administrative data. The use of retail industry and other service industry surveys data are examples of the counterparty approach to estimation in the national accounts—the receipts of businesses selling to households are taken as the estimate of expenditure by households. If the receipts of businesses are subject to skimming or are completely unrecorded ('under the table' transactions), then the counterpart household expenditure estimates would be understated where these sources are used.

Many goods and services, however, are unlikely to be subject to significant skimming of receipts or cash settlements. Examples include the purchase of new motor vehicles, motor fuel, heating fuel, electricity, gas and water, medical and hospital care, telephone, postage, transport provided by public authorities, lotteries, banking and insurance. The operating expenses of non-profit organisations, which are included in personal expenditure, are not affected either, as non-profit organisations are not subject to income tax. Additionally, some expenditure items in the national accounts do not reflect actual monetary transactions. The most significant example is imputed rents for owner-occupied dwellings, which is calculated by multiplying average rents for privately rented dwellings by the number of owner-occupied dwellings.

Taking all these factors into account, expenditure on goods and services which are not subject to underground activity to any significant degree total around 50% of HFCE. For the 50% of personal expenditure items that could be subject to underground activity, it is unlikely that sales by large businesses would go unreported to any significant extent. According to ABS publication, *Small Business Statistics in Australia*, (2001)(cat. no. 1321.0), large and medium businesses (those with 20 or more employees) are the source of supply for around 73% of the goods and services sold to households.

Small businesses with few or no employees are the most likely to engage in the non-declaration of sales, particularly those engaged in the provision of services where it is easier to omit a proportion of their receipts. However, even here the scope for understatement of receipts has some limits, as businesses reporting their income to the ATO are likely to be detected by the taxation authorities if they hide too much income in relation to their operating costs or in comparison to other similar businesses.

Areas such as restaurants and take-away food, personal care, most repair services and miscellaneous goods and services, such as domestic services, are examples of areas where small businesses are a significant source of supply of consumer goods and services to households. Repair and maintenance work undertaken for households is often paid for in cash directly to the owner of the business so there is ample scope for under-reporting the value of this type of work. In contrast, purchases of goods such as food, clothing and furnishings are predominantly made from larger retail chains although purchases from small businesses are still significant in value.

Bearing in mind these restrictions on the extent of underground activity within HFCE, upper bounds were postulated. Factors that were taken into account included:
- the areas of expenditure unlikely to be affected by underground activity, as detailed above;
- the relative significance of government enterprises as sources of supply;
- the relative significance of large businesses as sources of supply;
- the relative significance of very small employing or sole trader businesses as a source of supply;
- the degree of government regulation;
- the likelihood of the various data sources used to compile HFCE estimates to pick up underground transactions, e.g. Household Expenditure Survey based estimates are thought to be less likely to understate or exclude the value of underground transactions than are estimates based on business survey data;
- the methodology used to derive the estimates.

Based on these assumptions, it was estimated that the upper bound for underground transactions relating to expenditure on goods and services excluded from the national accounts could at most amount to around 5.6% of personal spending or 3.4% of GDP. Given the large proportion of expenditure considered to be unaffected by underground activity (at least 50%) and the significance of large businesses in most industries, these percentages could be considered as very generous upper bounds.

The following examples illustrate the type of reasoning behind the choice of the upper bound estimates made. In the case of food, a 10% upper bound was used. ABS retail industry estimates indicate that around 70% of purchases are made from large businesses, so the 10% estimate implies a 33% understatement on average on the part of small businesses. For hotels, cafes and restaurant services provided to households, a total understatement of around 19% was used. In this case the proportion of these services provided by small businesses account for around 40% of the total. This means that the implied average understatement by small businesses would be 43%.

Given that only a proportion of small businesses within each industry are likely to be engaged in underground activity to any significant extent, the implied understatements would be even greater for those businesses actually engaged in underground activity.

Some corroborating evidence was obtained by comparing the results of the Household Expenditure Survey (HES) with the estimates provided in the national accounts. As previously mentioned, the HES is entirely independent of business reporting to either ATO or ABS, although there may be some tendency for people who derive income from the underground economy to also under-report their household expenditure in the HES. Comparative analysis of 1998–99 HES results with the national accounts household final consumption expenditure estimates for that year indicate that the HES estimates, when adjusted for known scope and definitional differences, are in fact around 11% lower than the corresponding national accounts figure. Much of this difference is attributed to some areas of well known understatement in household expenditure surveys—alcohol, tobacco and gambling. After correcting for this, the HES estimate is still around 6% less than the national accounts HFCE estimate and hence there is not a strong suggestion from that source that HFCE is understated.

In summary, the expenditure analysis indicated an extreme upper bound of 4% for underground activity using the expenditure-based GDP measure, made up of a maximum possible understatement of 0.6% from GFCF and 3.4% from HFCE. This is 3.8% higher than the current adjustment to the expenditure estimate of 0.2% of GDP. However, given the large part of expenditure that is not susceptible to underground activity and the generous assumptions used to determine an upper bound, the actual extent of understatement is thought to be considerably less than the upper bound of 4.0%.

7. Estimates derived from monetary models of the economy

Monetary modelling techniques have been used in Australia to derive estimates of the underground economy. Using these techniques, estimates as high as 15% of GDP have been derived by independent researchers for Australia. ABS and academic researchers have examined these models and concluded that they have serious flaws and cannot be taken seriously. Analysis was also undertaken to determine the possible implications for the detailed components of GDP if estimates of this magnitude were to be valid. The analysis concluded that the size of the adjustments required to accommodate under-reporting on this scale are highly unlikely to be assessed as plausible. Additionally, such levels of understatement would indicate implausibly high levels of household expenditure, in relation to after tax household income, on the limited range of goods that can be purchased 'under the counter'.

This conclusion is consistent with the international guidelines which consider such macro-economic modelling methods to be unreliable (OECD 2002, page 190).

8. Summary

In the compilation of GDP, ABS makes a 1.3% adjustment for underground transactions that go unreported in the source data. No allowances are made for illegal transactions, as these are explicitly excluded in ASNA from the production boundary that defines the scope of GDP (although it is recognised that they are included within the SNA production boundary). The adjustment relies on indicative information from aggregate income tax audit information, anecdotal evidence and checks and balances inherent in the national accounting methodology itself.

Within each of the three approaches to measuring GDP, areas where there is little or no scope for underground activities account for a substantial proportion of the total. Where understatement does occur it tends to be concentrated in particular areas, which could impact on the reliability of some components of GDP.

For the income measure, under-reporting would be mostly confined to the understatement of income by unincorporated small businesses, small corporations, and CoE paid by small businesses. There is no evidence to suggest that large corporate organisations are involved to any significant degree in underground activity. As most unincorporated businesses are small businesses, the GMI estimate would be the most affected. GMI, however, only accounts for around 8% of the unadjusted income measure of GDP; hence any understatement due either to missing income or missing businesses would have to be many times the current estimate to generate the outcomes that suggest GDP is significantly understated.

From a production perspective, there is again limited scope for many industries to be engaged in underground activities. Industries unlikely to be affected conservatively account for at least 65% of overall activity. Even for the remaining industries that are prone to underground activity (construction, accommodation, cafes and restaurants, personal and other services and retail trade), large businesses are unlikely to be involved to a significant degree and the scope for small businesses to be involved would be limited to some extent by the possibility of detection by the taxation authorities.

On the expenditure side, government expenditure and a large component of household final consumption expenditure are not susceptible to underground activity. Most private business investment expenditure is also unlikely to be susceptible. Underground activities are expected to be concentrated in some forms of household final consumption expenditure and in alterations and additions to dwellings. In the latter case, use is made of household expenditure surveys to benchmark the estimate. Activities where there is scope for some understatement amount to only a third of total transactions and very large adjustments would be required to these components to generate the outcomes that suggest GDP is significantly understated.

While the recent review of the underground economy using upper-bound analysis included some estimations for additional areas of economic activity that could be subject to understatement, such as moonlighting activity and wages and salaries, it was decided not to make any additional adjustments to those currently used. This decision was based largely on the highly subjective nature of the estimates, given the lack of objective data sources. Analysis indicates that the missing amounts are unlikely to have a significant impact on the total level of the adjustment to GDP. Overall, ABS considers that the 1.3% adjustment made for the underground economy in deriving GDP is an adequate adjustment for Australia.

AUSTRIA

1. Sources and estimation methods

Adjustments for the non-observed economy (NOE) in Austrian national accounts can be grouped as follows:

- Adjustment for non-response in statistical surveys (carried out in business statistics);
- Adjustment for under-recording in statistical surveys (mainly small units);
- Adjustment for misreporting by units responding to statistical questionnaires (under-reporting of output, over-reporting of intermediate consumption);
- Adjustment for producers intentionally evading registration (e.g. clandestine production);
- Adjustment for producers not obliged to register (e.g. private households);
- Other adjustments (e.g. tips).

The methods applied in the particular adjustment procedures are described below. Moreover, an attempt is made to allocate the methods and their results to the types of NOE (T1 to T8) according to Annex 4.1 of the OECD *Handbook on Measuring the Non-observed Economy*, although a one-to-one allocation is not always feasible. The results refer to the year 2001, since this is the year for which the most recent supply-and-use tables are available at the time of preparing the response to this survey. Thus, these data are fully balanced.

2. Handling of non-response

Adjustments for non-response are carried out along with the evaluation and processing of statistical surveys for both unit non-response and item non-response, i.e. before the data enter the national accounts. Hence, no additional adjustments are necessary in the process of compiling the national accounts aggregates.

2.1 Unit non-response

Unit non-response may occur for two main reasons. On the one hand, there are units which refuse to return the questionnaire. On the other hand there are units which were economically active in the reference period of the statistical survey, but which cannot be reached due to either a change of address, having closed down, or insolvency. Substitutions based on other (e.g. administrative) sources are made, if the missing unit is a large one or if it belongs to an industry with only a few units. Otherwise, imputations are made on the basis of the average of the particular activity and size class. The average rate for unit non-response in structural business statistics for 2001 was about 7.4%.

2.2 Item non-response

Item non-response means that a unit does return the questionnaire but does not fill in the full range of items asked. In this case, the missing item is imputed, based on the average of the particular activity and size class.

3. Adjustment for under-recording (VAT test)

3.1 Concept and original data

The VAT test provides the first indication of the exhaustiveness of the annual structural business statistics (SBS). This is a method to determine whether all survey units, which should theoretically be recorded, actually have been. It is easy for this not to happen, particularly with small companies and establishments, and for this reason special attention is given to survey units with low turnover.

The VAT test compares turnover according to SBS with the taxable turnover in accordance with the VAT statistics broken down by industry (NACE Rev.1 two-digit codes) and size classes (turnover strata).

3.2 Comparison by turnover strata

Since companies with large turnovers are well known, it is most frequently in the lower strata that statistical under-recording of output is suspected. The VAT test therefore compares the taxable turnover according to the VAT statistics with turnover according to the SBS for each turnover stratum, beginning with the lowest.

If the turnover of a NACE Rev.1 division according to the VAT statistics is larger than recorded in the SBS, it is assumed that it is under-recorded by the amount separating the two values. This method is continued in higher turnover strata until the difference between turnover in accordance with VAT statistics and SBS is reversed. The following turnover strata are used:

- stratum1: up to 0.363 million EUR
- stratum2: from 0.363 million EUR to 0.727 million EUR
- stratum3: from 0.727 million EUR to 3.634 million EUR
- stratum4: from 3.634 million EUR to 7.267 million EUR

Under-recording in the strata with turnovers of over EUR 7.237 million is not only rare but stands out in national accounts. It is corrected by individual research carried out by Statistics Austria. For those activities not covered by the annual SBS, the ratios of under-recording obtained from applying the VAT test on the 1995 non-agricultural business census are extrapolated (NACE Rev.1 M, N, O).

3.3 Assignment of hidden output, intermediate consumption, value added and employment

On the basis of the hidden turnover values calculated as described above for each NACE Rev.1 two-digit code and turnover stratum, all the other survey characteristics (intermediate consumption, inventory, formation of fixed capital, wages and salaries, workforce etc.) were computed for the relevant branches and strata according to the SBS.

4. Adjustment of intermediate consumption

A special additional survey was conducted in which the reporting companies were asked for further breakdowns of overall earnings and cost components (voluntary additional survey). On the basis of this (extrapolated) additional information, certain survey variables were corrected in order to adjust them to national accounts concepts. In particular, a series of figures were identified in the item 'Other operating expenditure', which do not count as intermediate consumption for the purposes of national accounts. Examples of such operating expenditure are tax-related charges (compulsory contributions to the chamber of commerce, compulsory contributions to the trade and industry pension insurance institute, fees and similar dues), transfers (such as membership contributions), fees for executives and differences in exchange rates. Adjustments to remedy these errors reduced intermediate consumption and increased value added by the same amount.

Misreporting in this case is not based on the intention to conceal income, but because respondents report the residual in their business balance sheets under this particular item in the questionnaire. Hence, this adjustment can be regarded as a conceptual transition from business accounting to national accounts. The correction factors arising from the adjustment were then applied to the data of subsequent years.

Adjustments are also necessary because the responding units report gross insurance premiums as intermediate consumption. Based on annual insurance statistics, the gross premiums are therefore replaced by the insurance service charge.

5. Revenues off the books (ROB)

Undeclared income from hidden economic activities of registered and/or surveyed small companies in particular was estimated on the basis of the data of the 1995 non-agricultural business census survey. The business census in 1995 covered NACE Rev.1 sections C to K and M to O. The addition of such ROB constitutes a major quantitative adjustment to the basic statistics for national accounts for the purposes of ensuring the exhaustiveness of GDP and GNI calculations. The ratios derived from the data set of the census survey were also applied for the subsequent years.

5.1 Theoretical approach of the study

The point of departure for identifying hidden income is the assumption that a self-employed person would like to earn the same income per working unit as he pays a dependent employee, i.e. his income targets are determined by the earnings of dependent employees in his immediate economic environment. If he were to earn less, he would, as a *'homo economicus'*, change his employment status. In cases where the data collected in the basic statistics indicate that self-employed persons have a lower income, there is a good reason for assuming that at least the difference between their and dependent employees' income is compensated for by earnings which are not declared to the tax authorities and to official statistics. The boundary between deliberately concealed activity and under-recording in basic statistics is, as experience shows, fluid, but it is not immediately relevant to the target of the most comprehensive recording possible of GDP and GNI.

A key additional assumption for such a comparison of income is a reference income for the self-employed which can be compared with wages and salaries. As in the previous studies, operating surplus (net of interests) was used as a reference income, which is derived from the data collected in the business census as indicated in Box 1.

Per capita income is determined from the data on employees from the business census. Information from the 1995 microcensus on average working hours of the self-employed and blue-collar and white-collar workers by industry was used to convert the result to income per working time unit.

Box 1.

> Gross value added
> − compensation of employees
> − consumption of fixed capital
> − taxes on production and imports
> + subsidies
> − interests
> ────────────────────
> = **reference income**

5.2 Extent of the study

The previous studies showed that, particularly in companies in the lower turnover size classes, the reference income for the self-employed was lower than the income of dependent employees. This observation supports the assumption that the difference is made up for by undeclared income, since it is easier for smaller units to carry out economic activities off the books. For this reason, the two lower size classes, with turnovers up to EUR 0.363 million and up to EUR 0.727 million, were studied. Corporations such as limited companies and stock corporations were excluded, as well as cooperatives.

To use the wide range of items asked from institutional units (enterprises) on the one hand and simultaneously allocate the ROB estimates by industry on the other hand, the study concentrated on those institutional units which equal one local kind-of-activity unit (establishment). These particular units cover about 99 per cent of all kind-of-activity units in the described turnover strata. Nevertheless, the ratios of ROB derived from the study were also applied to the remaining local kind of activities in the respective industry and turnover stratum.

Activities were broken down at NACE Rev.1 group level (three-digit codes). NACE Rev.1 section J (Financial intermediation), which does not lend itself to ROB, was excluded. Separate estimates were made for renting out of private rooms, which is not surveyed in the business census.

5.3 Methodological details

Since it could be assumed that the self-employed would not compare their income with those of their less qualified labour force (such as unskilled labour, cleaning personnel, etc.), there seems to be no point in simply using average income of dependent employees by branch and turnover size class as a reference value.

In addition to the information from the business census (blue-collar and white-collar workers by sex, wages and salaries) and the micro censuses (working hours of the self-employed, and of blue-collar and white-collar workers by sex), data on the varying income levels of men and women (blue-collar and white-collar workers by NACE Rev.1 sections) were taken from the statistics of the *Hauptverband der Sozialversicherungsträger* (*HV,* Main Association of Austrian Social Security Institutions), in order to determine the income of blue-collar and white-collar workers by sex, adjusted for working hours. The highest income – in most cases of male white-collar workers – was used for the purposes of comparison.

In addition, the concealed operating surpluses per capita, determined in the two lowest size classes, were also imputed for establishments in the higher turnover size classes if the company in question took the legal form of a sole ownership. For these companies the incentive to increase income with undeclared business is certainly no less than in small companies. Moreover, the legal form of a sole ownership makes this easier.

Freelance workers, who were included in the business census for the first time in 1995 (except for freelance artists), are a special case. The approach described revealed very few instances of hidden income in this group. However, the conclusion to be drawn from this is not that there is no ROB amongst freelance professionals but that the right method has not been selected for detecting it. In a study of the *Institut für Wirtschaftsforschung* (WIFO - Institute for Economic Research), specially calculated rates for 1988 were imputed, which were increased by the change in the consumer price index as an indicator for the increase in prices in the total economy within the period 1988 to 1995. This approach was supported inter alia by the fact that in the exceptional cases mentioned above in which hidden operating surpluses were detected by means of the income comparison, the results were higher than those for 1988 by a similar amount. The number of freelance artists was taken from the income tax statistics.

5.4 From hidden operating surplus to hidden output

The next step was to find out how much additional output is required in order to obtain the additional value added, defined by the additional estimates of hidden operating surpluses. Equating additional operating surplus with additional value added implies that ROB does not give rise to any other components of value added in the form of wage and salary payments. Since this represents expenditure for the owner of a company, he has no interest in concealing it. Any concealed payments to employees from hidden operating surpluses represent a zero sum gain within the additional estimated value added and do not increase this more.

Additional undeclared intermediate consumption is, however, a distinct probability. The first step is to distinguish between fixed intermediate consumption (such as rents) and intermediate consumption, which is difficult to obtain undeclared (such as energy), and variable intermediate consumption (such as material input). Whilst the first two are almost certainly included in declared intermediate consumption, and hence statistically observed, even if used for activities in the hidden economy, this is not the case for the third. An owner of a company, who is engaged in undeclared activities, is well advised in some branches (manufacturing, repairs and hotel and catering business) not to enter some purchases of intermediate products in the books in order not to arouse the suspicions of the tax authority by an obvious mismatch between material input and output, whereas the direct ratio of fixed costs to output is more difficult to reconstruct.

A decision had to be made by each branch to determine whether and to what extent concealed intermediate consumption is used to generate concealed operating surpluses. In this way, it was possible to extrapolate imputed output. In the remaining cases, the operating surplus or value added was equated with output (for example in trade).

5.5 Additions for tax evasion

Depending on the type of hidden production and taking into account the customs known to pertain in certain branches, a distinction was made between tax evasion with and without mutual agreement. The former is the case when the purchaser of a product or service pays the tax assuming that the producer will also do so (for example in the hotel and catering and taxi businesses). If the company owner does not, these taxes are an additional source of income for him and should therefore be added to hidden value added. In the case of tax evasion with the agreement of both parties, the purchaser does not pay the taxes because he knows that this forms part of undeclared activity or has suggested it himself.

5.6 Time series

The results obtained from the study for the year 1995 were also applied to the subsequent years.

6. Renting out of private rooms

Tourism is an unusually large industry in Austria, of which a significant proportion is outside institutional tourism. Additional calculations have always been made in Austrian national accounts for the renting out of private rooms, with a distinction being made between overnight stays on farms and on other premises. The basis for these estimates is tourism statistics (arrivals, overnight stays) and the consumer price statistics, which record overnight stay prices in private rooms every month.

It has to be assumed that the recorded overnight stays in private rooms do not give the entire picture. First of all, only 1500 of the 2500 municipalities are reporting overnight stays with no records kept in the other municipalities. It must also be assumed that there is under-recording in the reporting municipalities too, especially in the case of short holidays. Tourism statistics experts take the view that the overnight stays recorded under "other types of accommodation" (approximately 12% of the overnight stays in private rooms) belong to this category. An addition of 66% is therefore made in national accounts. Intermediate consumption is assumed to be 22% of the price for an overnight stay (15% for breakfast and 7% for other costs).

The additional estimates for value added arise from the additions to output less sales tax apportioned to value added at the net output/gross output ratio. Furthermore, estimates were made for VAT fraud without mutual agreement.

6.1 Provision of personnel

Based on information by insiders of this branch (NACE Rev.1 group 74.5) adjustments were made for two reasons. On the one hand, it is considered that a significant number of jobs is not registered in order to evade taxes and compulsory social contributions, on the other hand, under-recording is quite likely due to the particular nature of this branch (rather high fluctuation of employees and 'atypical' employment[2]).

7. Tips

7.1 Tips in hotels and restaurants

The income statistics of the *Hauptverband der Sozialversicherungsträger* (HV, Main Association of the Austrian Social Security Institutions) give average wages and salaries for the

---

[2] e.g. income below specific thresholds and/or limited conditions of social security, work on call

hotels and restaurants industry (NACE Rev.1 section H), which are significantly lower than in other branches. They are also well below the income of employees in trade, which is definitely a comparable group.

Since the data of the HV are adjusted in terms of days of insurance cover, seasonal effects can be ruled out. An adjustment for working time was also made using the results of the microcensus. Assuming that the income expectations in both branches are similar, the most obvious explanation is that employees in the hotels and restaurants industry make up their income to at least the level of employees in trade by means of tips. If the working conditions are taken into account (night work in hotels and restaurants), this assumption hardly seems to overstate the case.

An addition of approximately 30% to allow for tips was therefore added to the wages and salaries in the hotels and restaurants industries recorded in the 1995 non-agricultural business census.

7.2 Tips in hairdressing

In class O 93.02 (hairdressers, beauticians and chiropodists), an addition of 10% on the basis of the household budget survey was made to turnover and value added data, explicitly for tips and other non-recorded components of value added.

7.3 Tips in the taxi industry

There are no detailed income data for the taxi industry. Since this is also a classical tip industry, it is assumed that employees boost their income by the same ratio as estimated for employees in hotels and restaurants.

8. Hidden activities

8.1 Construction

Own-account construction of dwellings (construction of owner-occupied houses) is very common in Austria and a corresponding addition is made in the national accounts. For this purpose, the labour input by the owner, relatives, neighbours, casual helpers and clandestine workers for activities, which represent formation of fixed capital (newly constructed buildings, improvements and refurbishing of existing houses), is valued and added to output or value added in the construction industry. The same applies for own-account construction of agricultural buildings, which is not included in the output and value added of agriculture and forestry but construction.

Own-account construction of non-agricultural dwellings

This item comprises two separately estimated components, namely a) private persons' own-account construction of dwellings, and b) own-account maintenance and improvement of dwellings.

a) Private[3] persons' own-account construction of one and two-family houses

This is estimated on the basis of two sources, namely the annual housing construction

---

[3] Physical persons, not legal persons.

statistics and a study on casual work carried out at the beginning of the eighties by the *Forschungsgesellschaft für Wohnen, Bauen und Planen* (FGW – research company on housing, building and planning). The FGW study took a close look at construction work and construction costs in building one- and two-family houses and revealed that, on average, own-account construction accounted for about 23% and services of casual workers and clandestine workers accounted for about 4% of total construction costs in Austria. The own-account proportion is approximately 36% (31% own-account, 5% casual work) of the official construction costs recorded in the housing construction statistics. This rate is applied to the average construction costs of one and two-family houses built by persons in order to determine the value of own-account output.

b) Own-account improvements and maintenance of dwellings

In the investment account, capital spending on new construction and major repairs (dwelling improvements and refurbishing of existing dwellings, etc.) is estimated separately. Capital spending on improvements of dwellings in particular is strongly supported by cheap credit. However, subsidies can only be taken advantage of if approved companies carry out the work. The proportion of own-account work is thus lower than in the case of new buildings. Hence, a proportion of 30% was assumed.

Own-account construction of agricultural dwellings and buildings

The *Land- und Forstwirtschaftliche Buchführungsgesellschaft* (LGB – agriculture and forestry bookkeeping company) carries out sample surveys each year to determine expenditure on housing and other buildings and the value of corresponding own-account activities. Additions are then made in national accounts.

8.2 Motor vehicle repair

Under-recording in this branch is approximately 11% of output. This additional estimate is made by comparing the results of the consumer account (which does not distinguish between official and informal components due to its functional approach), with supply data from the input-output account. In the consumer account, a technical link is assumed to exist between the number of kilometers covered and the expenditure on repairs. As a result of this comparison, the 11% addition is then transferred to the national accounts. Under-recording of output in this industry is equal to under-recording of value added, since it may be assumed that the material used (such as spare parts) is already included in private consumption.

8.3 Employees in private households

NACE Rev.1 group 95 (private households with employees) was originally recorded on the basis of wage and workforce data from the *Hauptverband der Sozialversicherungsträger* (HV, Main Association of the Austrian Social Security Institutions). However, since the household budget survey recorded much higher values, new calculations were carried out for NACE Rev.1 group 95. The data for final consumption expenditure of households from household budget surveys were used together with the number of employees in this branch (according to the HV), updated for individual years and adjusted in accordance with the contractual wage index for cleaning.

9. Results

The adjustments for NOE in Austrian national accounts amount to about EUR 15.7 billion and 7.9% of GDP (without adjustments). The figures and their allocation to types of NOE are shown in Table 1.

Table 1. Allocation of adjustments to types of NOE

T1:	T2:	T3:	T4:	T5:	T6:	T7:	T8:	TOTAL
Statistically non-observed: non-response	Statistically non-observed: out of date registers	Statistically non-observed: units not registered or not surveyed	Non-observed for economic reasons: under-reporting of turnover/income	Non-observed for economic reasons: units intentionally not registered	Informal sector (not registered, under-reporting)	Illegal activities	Other types of GDP under-coverage	
adjustments for non-response in structural business statistics	VAT-test		Revenues off the books, adjustment of intermediate consumption, non-observed provision of personnel	Repair of motor vehicles, home helps / Own account production and clandestine work in private construction of dwellings			Tips	
Adjustments in millions of EUR for the year 2001								
4 062			8 325	2 464			873	**15 723**
% of GDP (without adjustments)								
2.0			4.2	1.2			0.4	**7.9**

AZERBAIJAN

1. Concepts and definitions

The concepts defined in SNA93 and in the OECD *Handbook on Measuring the Non-observed Economy* are followed to ensure exhaustiveness in the NA. In the computations of GDP, upward adjustments for the following areas of non-observed economy are included:
- underground production;
- informal sector;
- production by households for own final use;
- misreporting of data;
- production not recorded for statistical reasons.

The adjustments for illegal production are not included in GDP.

The analytical framework used for classifying the non-observed economy is as follows:
- Illegal activities:
    - Unregistered (illegal);
- Informal activities:
    - Unregistered (not required to register);
    - Data not reported;
- Activities concealed for economic reasons:
    - Unregistered (intentionally);
    - Misreporting;
- Activities not observed for statistical reasons:
    - Non-response;
    - Incomplete coverage of respondents;
    - Out of date registers.

A classification of the non-observed activities according to reasons for non-exhaustiveness was introduced in 2005. This work was based on Eurostat's exhaustiveness projects carried out in the EU Candidate Countries.

2. Sources and estimation methods

The main sources used for estimating the non-observed economy are the special sample surveys in the industries with a high share of informal activities. For example, a survey of informal trade based on direct observation and questioning of sellers has been conducted for many years giving reliable results. In agriculture, the calculation of informal production is based on a special survey of farmers' households. Data from administrative sources and expert estimates are also used.

Due to the shortage of directly observed information from regular reports and through special surveys, balancing input-output tables is an important method for estimating the non-observed economy. However, these tables have so far been compiled only once. Another instrument is a supply-and-use table. The compilation of supply-and-use tables in Azerbaijan on a regular basis began in 2004 and has helped to reveal a number of cases where there was a lack of correspondence and balance. In some cases, balancing of supply-and-use for selected products is also made, including in volume terms. However, the balancing models have one principal shortcoming. They allow making adjustments for one of the indicators being balanced, assuming that the other one is reliable. In practice, it can happen that both indicators are not reliable and the effectiveness of the balancing model is decreased. Therefore, the balancing method should be combined with other methods based on additional information.

Since 2001, pilot surveys of different aspects of the labour market in Azerbaijan (informal employment, underemployment, etc) have been conducted. Starting from 2005, the information base for estimating the non-observed economy is expanded considerably. From the second quarter of 2005, employment surveys of about 12 000 households are conducted on a regular basis. Additional data on informal employment will also be obtained from the survey of child labour (SIMPOC)[4] carried out with the support of ILO.

3. Implications and effects on national accounts and GDP estimates

All adjustments for the non-observed economy have implications on GDP estimates.

GDP is computed by three methods (production, income and expenditure method). Adjustments for informal and hidden economic activities are made for GDP calculated by all three methods. In the calculation of GDP by the production method, adjustments are made for industrial production, construction, transport, trade, and consumer services.

In calculating GDP by the income method, adjustments are made mainly for mixed income. This indicator is calculated as the difference between the gross value added and wages and taxes on production.

In calculating GDP by the expenditure method, the main adjustments are made to households' expenditure for final consumption. The value is calculated on the basis of trade data. Small adjustments are made to fixed capital formation, mainly in construction of private dwellings.

The adjustments by economic branches are made mainly in the branch departments of the statistical office and are taken into account in the compilation of national accounts. The national accounts experts have the right to question the estimates produced by the branch departments and revise them if they do not correspond to the macroeconomic findings.

The non-observed economic activities are absent in the oil sector (oil extraction, transportation and processing). The share is also not high, in construction, despite the wide-scale construction work in the country. This can be explained by the high cost of drilling, and construction and mounting works connected with oil extraction, which is carried out with the aid of foreign investment.

With the greater level of extraction and export of oil, the share of the oil sector in the country is increasing, which leads to a decrease in the share of other industries and consequently the share of the non-observed economy in GDP. But this process does not imply a decrease in the size of the non-observed economy in the country.

---

[4] Statistical Information and Monitoring Programme on Child Labour

In 2003 the adjustments for the non-observed economy amounted to 20.7 per cent of the total value of GDP (see Table 1 and Table 2).

Table 1. NOE effects on GDP estimates

	2002			2003		
	Adjustments for NOE in GDP	**Share of NOE adjustments in value added by industries**	**Share of NOE in GDP**	**Adjustments for NOE in GDP**	**Share of NOE adjustments in value added by industries**	**Share of NOE in GDP**
	billion manats	per cent	per cent	billion manats	per cent	per cent
Industry	2 050.4	18.1	6.8	2 555.1	19.2	7.2
Agriculture, hunting and forestry	1 334.9	32.0	4.4	1 561.2	35.6	4.4
Fishing	51.5	92.1	0.2	60.1	100.0	0.2
Construction	156.1	5.9	0.5	797.7	19.9	2.2
Wholesale and retail trade, repair of motor vehicles, motorcycles and personal and household goods	889.2	39.2	2.9	1 156.4	45.6	3.2
Hotels and restaurants	5.6	4.7		16.9	10.2	
Transport and storage	720.0	30.4	2.4	598.6	21.3	1.7
Communication	0.6	0.1		6.8	0.9	
Financial intermediation						
Real estate, renting and business activities	93.2	13.5	0.3	91.9	8.6	0.3
Public administration and defense: social security	4.2	0.4	0.0	32.6	2.5	0.1
Education	205.1	16.5	0.7	168.0	14.3	0.5
Health and social work	147.9	36.1	0.5	167.3	29.9	0.5
Other community, social and personal service activities	169.0	20.9	0.6	177.9	30.0	0.5
FISIM						
Taxes on products and imports						
Subsidies on products						
Gross domestic product			19.2			20.7

Table 2. Estimation of total NOE output by type of activity - 2003
(billion manats)

NACE Section	T1	T2	T3	T4	T5	T6	T7	T8	Total
Total:	1 524.3		2 415.0		1 892.4	1 244.3		4 622.2	11 698.2
A								2 081.6	2 081.6
B					94.6				94.6
C			1 640.8					6.9	1 647.7
D					1 797.8	825.1			2 622.9
E								2.2	2.2
F	1 524.3					330.8			1 855.1
G			616.8					925.1	1 541.9
H								24.5	24.5
I								916.5	916.5
K								122.9	122.9
L						88.4			88.4
M			63.0					147.0	210.0
N			94.4					141.5	235.9
O								254.0	254.0

BELARUS

1. Introduction

The estimation of the non-observed (hidden and informal) economic activities in the compilation of macroeconomic indicators has been extremely topical in Belarus since the 1990s. The NOE has been growing considerably in the course of the implementation of economic reforms and transition to a market economy. This is due to the expansion of the private sector as a result of privatization and the emergence of new enterprises. Imperfections of accounting the activities in the new sectors of the economy and the need to maintain the living standards of the population have also contributed to growth of the non-observed economy.

2. Sources and methods of estimation

The non-observed (hidden and informal) economy comprises all economic activities that are hidden from statistical observation. Accounting for the non-observed economy is carried out in three stages:
- when estimating the output of goods and services of the economy by branch;
- at the stage of reconciliation (balancing) the main national accounts indicators;
- when compiling input-output tables.

When estimating the output of goods and services by branch, estimates of hidden and informal economic activities are made using the following methods:
- the commodity-flow method (on the basis of input-output tables and balances for the following selected goods and services: cement, petrol, alcohol, public catering, transport and communication services);
- combined methods of estimating indicators (alternative calculations of value added);
- indirect methods requiring comparison of data from various sources (comprehensive surveys, sample surveys of households and administrative data sources);
- methods of comparative analysis based on the estimates of the ratio between inputs and outputs in various groups of enterprises.

The sample surveys of households are the main source of information on the informal sector of the economy. The surveys provide data on income and expenditure of households for a wide range of goods and services. The sample consists of 6 000 households, or 0.2 per cent of the total number of households in the country. In order to have a representative sample for the country, separate samples were designed for both urban and rural population. In agriculture the output of individual household plots is estimated on the basis of the data of individual household plots surveys (household books). In transport, since 2003, regular surveys have been conducted on the number of passengers transported by individual entrepreneurs' buses.

Services rendered by entrepreneurs are estimated from data on the number of licenses issued to private individuals to perform certain kind of services such as road transport, medical treatment, concert tours, etc. The reason for using this method is that individual entrepreneurs provide a large proportion of these services and collecting objective information from them directly remains problematic.

The GDP estimates from the production and expenditure side are reconciled at the stage of balancing of the main SNA indicators. Household final consumption expenditure is adjusted for households' consumption of services rendered by private entrepreneurs. The Ministry of Statistics and Analysis also compiles annual input-output tables. These tables provide a basis for reconciliation and balancing of the statistical data on flows of goods and services obtained from different sources. The compilation of input-output tables reveals deficiencies in the accounting for the supply and use of goods and services with further adjustments to the indicators.

3. Implications and effects on national accounts and GDP estimates

The share of the non-observed economic activities in the GDP of Belarus was estimated to be 11.1 per cent in 2002. For 2003 it was 10.7 per cent, of which agriculture accounted for 4.6 per cent, trade and public catering - 3.4 per cent, housing construction - 1.3 per cent, industry 0.4 per cent, transport 0.2 per cent, and other services 0.3 per cent.

BELGIUM

1. Introduction

In Belgium, the switch from the ESA 79 to the ESA 95 provided an opportunity to make fundamental changes to the layout of the national accounts [5]. The revision concerns both the choice of statistical source material and the method of calculation. The method of estimating the underground economy has also been totally revised.

2. Concepts

The production boundary, as defined in the SNA 93 and the ESA 95, describes the range of productive activities that should be accounted for in the measurement of gross domestic product (GDP), and is therefore the boundary relevant to considerations of exhaustiveness. The details specified in SNA93 (§ 6.18) and ESA 1995 (§ 3.08) are the reference for the compilation of the Belgian national accounts.

The conceptual framework for producing an exhaustive measurement of output in the national accounts uses the concept of the underground economy [6].

The underground economy consists of the black economy and the illegal economy. The black economy consists of clandestine enterprises and unreported activities. At present, no estimates of the illegal economy are carried out in Belgium.

The illegal economy comprises activities which fall within the production boundary of the national accounts, but which are not permitted by law.

Clandestine enterprises are the non-registered production units. Non-registered means: "non-recording in statistical files of economically active units "[7]. These enterprises do not meet the legal requirements concerning payment of social security contributions etc.

The adjustment made for the purpose of estimating exhaustive value added for clandestine operations is called the adjustment for hidden labour.

---

[5]   The compilation of the national accounts is the responsibility of the National Accounts Institute (NAI). The NAI does not have any staff of its own, but coordinates the work done by the three associated institutions: a) the National Statistical Institute (NSI), which takes charge of collecting the basic data, except for the foreign trade data; b) the Federal Planning Bureau (FPB) which is in charge of compiling the input-output tables and the budget forecasts; c) the National Bank of Belgium (NBB) which is in charge of compiling the annual real and financial national accounts, the quarterly accounts, the regional accounts, the foreign trade statistics (including the collection of basic data) and, jointly with the FPB, the detailed accounts of public authorities.

[6]   The concepts applied by supranational bodies (UNECE, Eurostat) are described in: Willard J.-C., The Underground Economy in National Accounts, *Guide-Book to Statistics on the Hidden Economy,* UNECE, 1992, pp. 79-103. Currently it is not the practice of Belgium to apply all the proposed concepts.

[7]   Decision of the Commission of the European Communities of 24.07.1998 on the treatment for national accounts purposes of VAT fraud.

Unreported activities are the activities not declared by enterprises whose production and value added should be included via the calculations based on the registers of production units.

The adjustment made for the purpose of estimating exhaustive value added is called the adjustment for tax evasion.

The adjustment for tax evasion consists partly of an adjustment for under-declared taxable income and partly of an adjustment for VAT fraud.

There are two different types of VAT fraud:
- fraud with the complicity of the buyer, i.e. the seller and the buyer agree not to invoice the VAT. The VAT which was payable by law is therefore not the subject of a transaction, and the amount of the fraud therefore does not form part of GDP.
- fraud without complicity i.e. the buyer pays the VAT but the seller does not pay it over to the authorities. This amount is the subject of a transaction between seller and buyer.

The adjustment for VAT fraud therefore concerns VAT fraud without complicity. In practice, this type of fraud occurs in branches which sell to households as consumers. The VAT is not tax-deductible for households, so the tax authority does not receive any application for repayment of VAT which might allow tracing the seller. The amount of the VAT fraud without complicity is treated as part of the turnover in the Belgian national accounts.

3. Sources and estimation methods

An exhaustive figure for GDP is obtained by taking the results of surveys and extrapolating them as accurately as possible for the population on the basis of registers, applying the definitions of the ESA 95 as closely as possible, and including the underground economy in the methods of calculation[8].

The calculation of GDP is based on an exhaustive register of production units. The conceptual differences between the data from administrative sources and the ESA95 definitions are calculated in detail. An estimate of the black economy is also made at detailed level. No adjustment is made as yet for illegal activities. A consistent calculation of GDP according to the output, expenditure and income approach is obtained by integrating the supply-and-use table (SUT).

3.1 Principal data sources

Repertory of production units

The estimate of GDP is based on the *business register* compiled by the National Statistical Institute (NSI). This database contains all economic agents active in Belgium[9]. The basic

---

[8]   "In general, we can say that the criteria for completeness are: the existence of an accurately determined reference universe of production units, the possibility of determining whether units are missing, the possibility of making adjustments for missing units and the existence of general systematic adjustments for evasion and undeclared labour." GNP Committee, CPNB/166 (Eurostat), Report to the Council and The European Parliament on the application of the Council Directive on the determination of GNP at market prices, 1995, §2.4.

[9]   Enterprises which are not registered for VAT are not considered legal persons and do not employ staff are currently missing. The intention is to include these producers in the register in the near future.

information for compiling the register is supplied by a number of government agencies (VAT, Department of Social Security [DSS], National Register) which maintain partial records of units for their own purposes (namely enterprises registered for VAT, businesses employing staff and legal entities).

On the basis of this register, the NBB constructs a *repertory* each year, containing for all enterprises (companies, self-employed persons, NPIs) identification numbers and characteristics relevant for the national accounts. By using the combination of the following characteristics, it is possible to calculate in a detailed and standardised manner the administrative aggregates (e.g. turnover, purchases, wages) from which the ESA95 variables will be calculated at a later stage, and to select the most appropriate basic source:

- NACE code (determines the branch to which the unit belongs);
- category (determines which basic source[10] is used to estimate the activity of the unit);
- institutional sector code (determines the institutional sector in which the unit is included).

The aggregation of variables available in the different source files is always based on the characteristics (NACE code, sector code) entered in the repertory. This method ensures that the results obtained via different sources are mutually comparable. The basic aggregates at national level are always calculated per branch and per institutional sector.

Principal basic sources [11]

The method of calculation makes maximum use of administrative data. The principal administrative sources are the annual accounts filed by non-financial companies, the VAT returns of VAT-registered enterprises, and the returns from the Department of Social Security (DSS) and the Department of Social Security for Provincial and Local Public Services (DSSPLPS) submitted by employers.

In Belgium, virtually all limited liability companies have to publish their accounts in accordance with a standardised format laid down by law, at the Central Balance Sheet Office of the National Bank of Belgium. The annual accounts file is therefore the preferred source for estimating the ESA95 aggregates for the production and primary generation of income account for non-financial companies.

Large companies[12] have to file accounts using the full format; SMEs are allowed to use the short format. These reporting formats are in fact data extracts from the internal accounts of the enterprises, where large companies have to supply more information than SMEs.

---

[10] The categories used in the case of non-financial enterprises help to determine the selection of the preferred basic source for calculating the administrative aggregates.

[11] The description of the source material and the method of calculating value added is confined to those sectors for which adjustments for the underground economy are relevant, namely non-financial corporations (S11) and households (S14).

[12] An enterprise is regarded as large for the purpose of company law if: a) the average size of its workforce on an annual basis exceeds 100, or b) it exceeds more than one of the following thresholds: b1) annual average workforce: 50, b2) annual turnover (excluding VAT): EUR 6.25 million, b3) balance sheet total: EUR 3.12 million. An enterprise with separate legal personality which does not fulfill these criteria comes under the SMEs (small and medium-sized enterprises).

All enterprises with a turnover of more than 0.5 million Euros must adhere to the 'Minimum Standardised Accounting System'. This accounting plan (introduced by the Royal Decree of 1983) puts into practice the legislation on book-keeping and annual accounts of enterprises, dating from 1975. The accounting laws specify the content of the various headings in the balance sheet and profit and loss account (revenue and expenses). In this way, the accounting plan specified for book-keeping purposes can be translated into the breakdown of transactions according to the ESA95.

The VAT returns are used to deduce the turnover (proxy for P1), current purchases of goods and services (proxy for P2) and purchases of investment goods (proxy for P51). The information on turnover and current purchases is used in most branches to estimate the value added of units registered for VAT included in the household (S14) sector, and to produce an additional estimate for the activities of companies for which no (usable) annual accounts are available.

The activity of most non-financial enterprises (supply of goods and services) comes under the VAT rules. Only a small number of activities are exempt from VAT (legal services, medical services, letting of property).

All employers established in Belgium must submit a quarterly return to the DSS or DSSPLPS. The amounts of the social security contributions due are calculated on the basis of DSS and DSSPLPS returns. From the information stated in these returns, it is possible to calculate the compensation of employees (D1).

In some branches of the service activities, the wage bill is used to estimate the value added of companies with no annual accounts and NPIs placed in the non-financial corporation sector (S11).

3.2 Calculation of the value added of non-financial enterprises

The calculation comprises two stages:
- compilation of a production account and a generation of income account for each branch (NACE 3 or 4 digits) and institutional sector in accordance with administrative/commercial concepts;
- totalling of these figures to give a higher level of aggregation (SUT branches) and conversion to concepts and valuation methods of the national accounts (ESA 95).

The output and income are estimated *simultaneously and in an integrated manner*. This ensures that the consistency between value added and its components (compensation of employees, non-product-linked taxes on production, non-product-linked subsidies and gross operating surplus) is monitored right from the start of the calculations.

3.3 Calculation of 'administrative' aggregates

In the first phase, the administrative aggregates are calculated in detail via the characteristics recorded in the repertory. Calculation at detailed level also permits quality checks at this level, and the correction of any anomalies.

Non-financial corporations (S11)

The figures are calculated at NACE 3 or 4 digit level by totalling the results for the underlying sub-populations (categories):

Category	Description
A1	Large enterprises filing "full format" annual accounts
A2	Large enterprises without usable[13] annual accounts
B1	SMEs using the abbreviated format and stating turnover and purchases
B2	SMEs using the abbreviated format without turnover and purchases
B3	SMEs without usable annual accounts
H	Non-profit institutions (NPIs) included in S11

A1) Large enterprises with "full format" annual accounts

All relevant variables are available for large enterprises in category A1:

Operating income:

Code, annual accounts	Description
70	Turnover
71	Change in stocks of produced goods (increase +, reduction -)
72	Own produced fixed assets
74	Other operating income
740	Operating subsidies
741/9	Miscellaneous operating income[14]

Operating expenses:

Code, annual accounts	Description
60	Consumption of merchandise, raw materials and auxiliary materials
600/8	Purchases of merchandise, raw materials and auxiliary materials
609	Changes in stocks of purchased goods (increase -, reduction +)
61	Purchases of services and miscellaneous goods (not recorded under 600/8)
62	Remuneration, social security charges and pensions
64	Other operating expenses
640	Business taxes
641/8	Miscellaneous operating expenses
649	Operating expenses capitalised as restructuring costs (-)

---

[13] Annual accounts are regarded as not usable (for further statistical processing) if the financial year does not coincide with the calendar year <u>and</u> the financial year data cannot be converted to calendar year data. Corporations with annual accounts which are "not usable" are treated in the same way as corporations with no annual accounts.

[14] 741/9 means the sum of accounts 741 to 749.

The following 'administrative'[15] aggregates can be derived from this:

Aggregate	Code, annual accounts
Production	70 + 71 +72 + 74 – 740
Intermediate consumption	60 + 61 + 641/8
Gross value added	70 + 71 + 72 + 74 -740 -60 -61 -641/8
Staff costs	62
Net business taxes	640-740
Gross operating surplus	70 + 71 +72 + 74 - 60 - 61- 62 - 640/8

A2) Large enterprises without usable annual accounts

In the case of large enterprises belonging to category A2, we know the turnover (and purchases) according to the VAT returns and wages calculated on the basis of the DSS records. The wage data are taken over as they stand. The other items are estimated either via turnover (this applies to the majority of branches) or via wages (in the case of a number of service branches)[16].

B1-B3) Small and medium sized companies (SMEs)

In the case of SMEs there is less detailed information:

Code, annual accounts	Description
70	Turnover (*optional information*)
60/61	600/8 + 609 +61 = consumption of goods and services (*optional information*)
62	Remuneration, social security charges and pensions
640/8	640 + 641/8 (other operating expenses including business taxes)
70/61	70 +71 + 72 + 74 - 60 - 61 : if the gross margin is > 0
61/70	70 + 71 + 72 + 74 - 60 - 61 : if the gross margin in < 0

In the case of SMEs using the abbreviated format stating turnover and purchases (population B1), the most important items (particularly turnover and consumption of goods and services) are known. The missing items are derived from the known items or estimated on the basis of structural ratios known for large enterprises in the same branch.

The data for SMEs using an abbreviated format, without stating turnover and purchases (population B2), are estimated by taking the B1 figures and multiplying them by the ratio of gross margin B2/gross margin B1. The wage figures stated in the annual accounts are used.

The data for SMEs without usable annual accounts (population B3), and for NPIs included in S11 (population H), are estimated either via the VAT turnover or via the DSS wages on the basis of the structure of B1+B2. The DSS wages calculated for this category are taken as they stand.

---

[15] These are intermediate aggregates/balances which in this phase are still entirely in accordance with the conventions and valuation rules of commercial accounting as specified in the legislation on accounting.

[16] The structure of A1 is transferred to A2 using the ratio of VAT turnover A2/annual accounts turnover A1, or the ratio of DSS wages A2/annual accounts wages A1.

The populations A2, B3 and H for which no annual accounts are available and the activities of which have to be estimated via other sources represent only about 9% of the total value added of S11.

Enterprises without legal personality included in the household sector (S14)

Depending on the activity, various sources are used to estimate the value added (and mixed income) of self-employed persons.

The calculations for *agriculture, forestry and fisheries* make use of specific sources such as the statistics of the Centre for Agricultural Economics[17].

For *self-employed persons registered for VAT,* value added is estimated via the VAT returns.

For *self-employed persons not registered for VAT* and heads of businesses (directors and business managers), personal income tax returns are used. The disadvantage of this source is that the final data do not become available until late (final data for income year t are available at the end of t + 2.). For the medical professions, data from the National Institute for Sickness and Disability Insurance are also used.

Housing services (rent and imputed rent) are estimated according to the stratification method prescribed by a European Union decision. An econometric method is used to calculate the rent paid, for the stock of rented housing, as a function of the housing characteristics (type of housing, age, location, amenities). The total output of housing services can be calculated by applying the rent paid to all housing within a housing stratum.

The value added of *private households with employees* (NACE 95) coincides with the wages paid by households to workmen, gardeners, cleaning ladies, etc. Since most of these services are performed without being declared, official sources are little if any use.

3.4 Conversion from administrative aggregates to the national accounts aggregates

By definition, an exhaustive estimate of GDP is obtained by applying the ESA 1995 definitions correctly. For the estimates from the output side, this is achieved by means of a detailed estimate of all transitional components between the administrative aggregates and the aggregates according to the ESA 1995.

To achieve exhaustiveness, specific adjustments are made for: wages in kind, tips, and the black economy .

Non financial corporations (S11)

In the first phase, the administrative aggregates are calculated by branch (NACE 3 of 4 digit level) and by sector. These interim results are then totalled at a higher aggregation level (120 SUT branches).

---

[17] This source is also used to estimate the aggregates for agricultural enterprises operating in the form of a corporation (S11).

In the second phase, the administrative variables are converted to ESA 95 aggregates for each SUT branch (and separately for S11 and S14). The gross value added (B1g) and gross operating surplus (B2g) are also obtained from this as a balance.

Administrative aggregates		ESA 1995 aggregates	
70+71+72+74-740	->	Output	P1
600/8 + 609 + 61 + 641/8	->	Intermediate consumption	P2
62	->	Compensation of employees	D1
640	->	Other taxes on production	D29
740	->	Other subsidies on production	D39

The adjustments for the purpose of calculating the ESA 95 aggregates from the administrative aggregates concern among other things: merchandise, basic price adjustment, elimination of capitalised research and development from output and investment, recording of non-capitalised expenditure on software as investment, elimination of current gains and losses from operating income and expenses, property rent paid, transfer of some bank costs to intermediate consumption, discounts for cash payment, non-life insurance premiums and benefits, wages in kind, tips, grossing up of commission work, and estimated additions for the black economy.

There is a 'contra' entry for all adjustments and reclassifications, which may appear in the production or generation of income account or elsewhere. This ensures that the budget identity is maintained at the global level of the sector account.

The information needed to calculate these adjustments is available either from the annual accounts, or from the structural survey, or as exogenous data in the accounts of general government (S13) (taxes on production and imports, and subsidies) and financial corporations (S12) (insurance premiums received and claims paid).

Households (S14)

The administrative aggregates are also converted to ESA 95 aggregates for sole traders and self-employed persons. Since there is far less information on such operators, adjustments are only calculated on account of merchandise, banking costs, insurance premiums, tips and the underground economy.

3.5 Estimate of the underground economy

In practice, there is some overlap between hidden labour and tax evasion. A registered enterprise may commit fraud by using undeclared labour through overtime performed by registered staff, or work performed by staff not registered by the enterprise. A non-registered enterprise which (by definition) uses only hidden labour is simultaneously committing tax evasion. Note that it can be assumed that the VAT fraud committed in this case is purely VAT fraud with complicity. If the VAT fraud were committed without complicity and the purchaser were entitled to reclaim the VAT, the underground enterprise would run the risk of being discovered [18].

---

[18] Conversely, it is not necessarily true that all VAT fraud with complicity is committed by clandestine enterprises.

In practice, is not possible at present to make a separate estimate of VAT fraud and tax evasion exclusive of VAT fraud. The two types of fraud are combined: income related to VAT fraud is not declared by the producers.

Since no information is available permitting a separate adjustment for value added resulting from unregistered labour, under-declared taxable income and VAT fraud without complicity, an overall adjustment is estimated per SUT branch[19].This overall adjustment per SUT branch is calculated by applying percentages to turnover and purchases for S11 enterprises and S14 enterprises separately, in accordance with the NACE classification deemed relevant within an SUT branch for a differentiated adjustment per activity. If SUT branch is composed of NACE branches for which different percentages are applicable in respect of the underground economy, the percentage for turnover and purchases respectively for the SUT branch is calculated as a turnover/purchase-weighted average of the NACE components. For some branches (e.g. construction), both turnover and purchases are adjusted, for others (e.g. legal services) it is only necessary to adjust the turnover. For most branches, turnover and purchases are adjusted by the same percentage (as producers who commit fraud ensure that the ratio between declared turnover and purchases remains acceptable to the tax authority).

As in most other European countries, the underground economy is most developed in the branches which supply the major part of their output to individuals. This applies, for instance, to the construction industry (especially building installation and finishing work), the retail trade, maintenance and repair of motor vehicles, hotels and restaurants, and services to individuals. In SUT branches 45D1 (building installation) and 45E1 (building completion), part of the total adjustment relates to non-registered labour.

A major revision has been undertaken in Belgium during 2005. The National Accounts series published in September 2005 reflect this revision. The revision had only a small positive impact on the estimates for the black economy. The following adjustments were made:

- hidden wages paid out by employers sectorised in S14 sector (5% of official wages); in order not to diminish mixed income, output went up with the same amount as the hidden wages (99 million Euros in 2002);
- wages in kind produced by employers in the car assembly industry and in the hotels, restaurants and cafes industry (62 million Euros in 2002);
- black output in the fishery industry (5 million Euros in 2002);
- percentages used for grossing up official sales and/or purchases in order to capture the hidden activity were adjusted in some industries.

3.6 Integration in the supply-and-use table

An integrated calculation of GDP from the output, expenditure and income sides takes place in the framework of the SUT, which covers 120 branches and 320 products. The SUT is compiled for the reference years 1995 and 1997, and for each year from 1999.

In view of the integration of data from various sources, the supply-and-use table is the most appropriate method of obtaining an exhaustive estimate of GDP. The efforts to improve exhaustiveness will therefore be developed further primarily within this framework.

---

[19]   Note that, since all producing units are registered, an adjustment for hidden labour corresponding to the adjustment for clandestine enterprises is not relevant.

In some countries, the calculation of GDP is more or less based on employment data; on the basis of these data the value added for a number of enterprises is extrapolated for the branch as a whole. Research on the consistency between employment data in the surveys used to calculate value added and in specific employment statistics (labour force survey, population census, etc.) therefore offers a crucial test of the exhaustiveness of GDP.

In the Belgian national accounts, employment plays no role in the calculation of value added. The results obtained are therefore tested only indirectly against the employment figures obtained from the employment statistics, namely by assessing the value added per employee and/or self-employed person for each branch (in future, per full time equivalent). By examining the consistency between output, compensation of employees and employment, any problems could be tracked down.

Alternative estimates were produced by applying a monetary method, for instance. However, the general assumption is that the results of these studies are too dependent on macroeconomic assumptions. Moreover, they do not provide the amounts by branch required for compiling the national accounts.

A tax audit which attempted to estimate the adjustment ratios for the underground economy did not produce any usable results in Belgium. In investigating tax evasion, the tax authority does not aim to derive any ratios which might be representative for a complete NACE category, and which could therefore be used to estimate the underground economy.

The selection of the enterprises to be inspected takes no account of representativeness by NACE category, and is also dependent on fluctuating political sensibilities.

4. Implications and effects on national accounts and GDP estimates

The exhaustiveness adjustments applied for 2002, before integrating the SUT, are summarised below.

The value added figure was increased by 5.803 million Euros in the non-financial corporations sector (S11).

For households (S14), an explicit adjustment of 3.932 million Euros is made. The calculation of the value added for the SUT branches 01A1 agriculture, 02A1 forestry and 05A1 fisheries is based on detailed quantity and price data obtained from the Centre for Agricultural Economy, so that the adjustment for the underground economy is implicitly included. For SUT 95A4 private households with employees, an average hourly wage is applied to an estimated number of hours' work, so that here too, an adjustment for the underground economy is implicitly taken into account.

To allow for wages in kind, turnover was increased by 56 million Euros in sector S11 and by 5 million Euros in S14 for produced goods and services. Intermediate consumption was reduced by 712 million Euros so that purchased goods and services made available as wages in kind could be transferred to wages.

In some branches (hotel and catering, hairdressers, taxis) turnover is increased to take account of tips. In S11 and S14, the figures used are 286 million Euros and 108 million Euros respectively.

The total correction made for the underground economy, after balancing the supply-and-use table, is estimated at between 3% and 4% of GDP.

BRAZIL

1. Sources and estimation methods

The estimation of the non-observed economy (NOE) includes the production of all productive units that are not covered in economic statistics and administrative records. There are three categories of non-observed production: underground, informal and illegal.

Using 1985 as the base year, the adjustments for non-observed production were estimated by comparing the number of employed persons from the National Household Sample Survey (NHSS) and the number of employed persons in the Economic Census. An imputed per capita production value was applied to the new figure of employed persons by activity, which was similar to labour productivity of small enterprises included in the Economic Census.

Estimation of the non-observed production within each branch is made separately from the estimation for the formal sector. Non-observed output is estimated by means of double extrapolation. The volume index used is the annual variation of employment, assuming implicitly that there is no increase in productivity in this sector. The price index used is the annual variation of average income.

The main source of the volume and price indexes is the NHSS. Data from the Monthly Employment and Income Survey are used for quarterly accounts.

2. Implications and effects on National Accounts

The table below presents the current values of non-observed output as an absolute value and as a percentage of Brazil's GDP.

Table 1. NOE Adjustments (Total)

Years	Per cent of GDP	Million Reals
1996	14.75	114.879
1997	14.57	126.871
1998	14.13	129.210
1999	13.74	133.800
2000	13.11	144.322
2001	12.84	153.925
2002	12.65	170.239
2003	12.79	198.968

BULGARIA

1. Introduction

The work on exhaustiveness of National Accounts (NA) in Bulgaria aims at achieving compliance with ESA 95 and improving the quality and reliability of the regular statistical process underlying the NA. The information provided below is based on the results of Eurostat's projects on Exhaustiveness and adoption of the ESA 95 methodology.

The annual GDP compilation in Bulgaria is done according to the production, expenditure and income approach. The production and expenditure approaches provide independent GDP estimates both in current and constant prices of the previous year. The growth rates are chain linked using the previous year as a base. The compilation of the generation of income account is not independent as its data sources originate from the production side. The balancing of the accounts for GDP and its components is achieved through the annual supply-and-use tables. The officially published annual data for GDP are based on the production approach, including additional items for unbalanced amounts in the final use components.

2. Estimation Methods

2.1 Output Approach

The output approach plays the leading role in making exhaustiveness adjustments. However, it is also important to ensure that the adjustments on the expenditure and production side of GDP are consistent. The estimated values of specific transactions on the production side are directly linked to the related categories of final demand; such as production of households for own final use, and own-account construction of residential buildings. Some data from the demand side are used to determine the adjustments for production; for example, household budget survey (HBS) data on expenditures on consumables (usually food commodities) are used to adjust the output of relevant producers and retailers.

N1- Producers deliberately not registering

As part of the Phare 2004 project, the NA Division of the National Institute of Statistics (NSI) has developed estimation procedures for non-registered units. A small sample survey was conducted in 2000. The results show that nearly 4 per cent of active small-scale business units are not registered. A more comprehensive survey will be carried out in 2006 under the National Phare Project.

Small-scale enterprises where there is little distinction between capital and labour are usually classified as the informal sector.

N2 - Illegal Production

The adjustments for illegal activities are not incorporated in the GDP estimates. In the framework of Eurostat's Pilot Project on Exhaustiveness, drug distribution and consumption have been investigated on an experimental basis. The results show that the illegal production, distribution and consumption of drugs have a possible impact of 1.3 per cent on GDP.

N3 - Informal sector production

Informal sector activities include households' own account production and processing of agricultural products including those used for own consumption. Within agricultural households, a distinction is made between market and non-market output instead of separating the units producing goods exclusively for own final consumption. In practice, households engaged informally in agricultural activity produce both for the market and for their own final consumption.

These households are not formally required to register as long as they are not covered by social insurance. The most important source of information for estimation of crops, livestock breeding and food-processing activities of households are the agricultural balances by types of crops and animal products. The balances are broken down by type of units, distinguishing the units belonging to the household sector. Informal activities of households are estimated by using the commodity-price approach.

Household production for own final use

The estimate of own account construction of households is based mainly on administrative information on planning permissions for individual construction of dwellings. The HBS is an additional data source for estimating the main repairs on dwellings done by households.

N4, N5 - Legal persons (units) and entrepreneurs not surveyed

This part of the formal economy is not covered in regular NA compilation because of the problems with updating the Statistical Register. The active and non-active units in the register are distinguished according to information derived from the last annual observation. However, small units have high mobility and annual frequency is not enough for correctly defining active and non-active units.

It is not possible to undertake any economic activity in Bulgaria without registration. Therefore, units that are not registered because they are below the registration thresholds are not considered to be under-covered.

Self-employed persons, such as lawyers need to apply only for a tax number and are not registered in the administrative register of economic units (BULSTAT). The estimation of their output is based on the information from administrative data sources such as their annual income declaration and data from the lawyers' union.

2.1.5 N6 - Producers deliberately misreporting

The adjustments for under-reporting of economic activities that are legal are made via indirect methods. These can be summarized as follows:

- investigation of input-output ratios among the units within a chosen homogeneous group of economic units at the micro-level, to estimate the degree of over-reporting of intermediate consumption and under-reporting of gross output;
- labour input method (explained in detail in section 3);
- use of demand-side data sources (mostly from the Household Budget Survey) to evaluate the underestimation in retail trade activities and some manufacturing activities (sales and output). Traditionally the HBS shows a bigger amount of expenditures for food consumption than registered retail sales of food. Therefore, the turnover of the retailers and some wholesalers, and the output of related producers are adjusted.

N7 - Other statistical deficiencies

Non-response

The subject matter divisions of the NSI use specific techniques to treat non-response. The adjustments are made at the three digit level of NACE and involve the identification of the number of non-responding units, their activities and number of employees. The average revenue from sales per employee is calculated from the data on responding units with similar activities and number of employees. The obtained ratio is then used to estimate the activity of non-responding units. The non-response adjustment accounts for 5 per cent of GDP.

Wages and salaries in kind

The estimates of wages and salaries in kind are structured both according to NACE classes and to Classification of Expenditure According to Purpose (COICOP). The figures are balanced between the production, expenditure and income approaches. As the calculation of gross output is based on the receipts from sales, it does not include the goods and services provided as wages and salaries in kind to employees: the latter is additionally added to output. At present, estimates are based on information from the annual labour report and number of employees in different activities. The following items are recognized for NA purposes:

- free food products for the employees of enterprises producing pasta products, meat, milk, oil, alcohol, beer etc.;
- clothes;
- coal for employees of mining companies;
- detergents;
- free tickets for the employees of the National Railway Company, free transport to and from work, free airplane tickets etc.;
- free telephones;
- free food for people working in restaurants, snack bars etc.;
- meals and drinks consumed while travelling on business.

Tips

Explicit estimates of tips have not been recorded in NA up to now.

2.2 Expenditure Approach

The GDP expenditure approach is applied independently of the production approach. In general, the estimates derived from the expenditure approach are about 1 - 2 per cent larger than those from the production side.

The main exhaustiveness adjustments concern income-in-kind, households' agricultural production and own-account construction. The exhaustiveness adjustments by expenditure approach are linked to the adjustments made at the production side.

Household final consumption expenditure

Since 1997, household final consumption expenditures are calculated according to COICOP at the four digit level. Balance of payments data is used to adjust the total household final consumption expenditure for net tourism as required by the national concept, which has been followed since 1996.

A comparison of estimates of household final consumption expenditures by COICOP items reveals some discrepancies, mainly concerning food commodities. The HBS estimates constantly exceed retail trade figures. In order to analyze this, the regular HBS questionnaire was extended with questions specifying the type of outlet where the household purchases are made. It was found that the main reason for the discrepancies is that households purchase food not only from the retail trade system but also from other outlets and producers such as households, producer-enterprises, wholesale trade outlets, and open air stalls.

Household production for own final consumption includes the agricultural products produced by households, sub-divided into processed and not processed (fresh) agricultural products. The valuation of processed agricultural products is classified as output of unincorporated (secondary) activities and is estimated at basic prices. The value of non-processed agricultural goods is estimated at average selling prices using data from the agricultural balances.

For the estimate of "consumption of fresh products", national accountants use the information provided by the HBS regarding the indicator "resources and distribution of food products". For the estimation of its components, NA also uses information from the Agricultural division. In the estimate of GDP by final use, the produced agricultural products for own final consumption are adjusted for the internal turnover and for the part that is sold directly on the market or between households.

The purchases of private households based on retail trade data are adjusted for purchases for business purposes following the commodity flow approach.

The estimates of wages and salaries in kind are balanced between the production, expenditure and income approaches.

Gross fixed capital formation (GFCF)

GFCF is measured by expenditure on acquisition of fixed assets (the actual expenditure on construction, improvements of existing assets, on delivery and mounting of fixed assets, including non-finished construction paid by customers) less the disposal of existing fixed assets.

Informal or household sector investments, especially for construction, are estimated on the basis of information from construction permits for newly initiated projects, which give indication of expenditures.

Exports and imports of goods and services

The exports and imports of goods are valued 'fob' (free on board) and are calculated on the basis of customs declarations. These data are provided by the External Trade Statistics Division of the NSI at the eight-digit level of the Combined Nomenclature, which has a transition key to the National CPA and NACE. The same figure is included in Balance of Payments (BoP). However, the adjustments are essentially made to bring the data in accordance with national accounts methodology, that is an adjustment of imports (8 per cent) to put them on a fob basis rather than 'cif' (cost, insurance and freight). A special investigation of the basic data sources was done within the framework of a bilateral project between the Bulgarian NSI and Statistics Norway in order to establish the procedure for proper calculation of cif/fob adjustments on imports data, especially with respect to allocation of resident transport services related to the external trade turnover. The results show that for 2002 and 2003, resident transport constitutes the biggest part of the cif/fob difference, almost 65 per cent.

No adjustments are made for 'shuttle trade' in spite of an expected impact on macro aggregates. Under the National Phare 2004 project, the NA Division is investigating shuttle trade, possible indirect data sources and development of adequate estimation procedures.

3. Sources

3.1 Statistical business register

The Unified Register of Economic Units in Bulgaria (BULSTAT) is used as a common sample frame for all enterprise surveys. It consists of all legal entities including foreign-owned ones, natural persons registered as sole proprietors, partnerships, budgetary units and non-profit institutions serving households (NPISH). According to the law, all units have to register with BULSTAT.

The register contains information about the main activity according to NACE, name, address, and legal status. BULSTAT contains three levels of units: enterprise, sub-division (for establishments with complete bookkeeping) and local units (only wages and salaries are observed). It does not cover secondary self-employed activities, temporary and occasional activities, etc.

The Statistical Register is derived from BULSTAT and keeps track of currently registered units for statistical purposes. In addition to the identification characteristics, the Statistical Register contains information about the main activity, the number of employees and total employment as well as the turnover and long-term tangible assets. As many of the new registrants are not necessarily in operation, the main source of information on whether the new firms are actually operating or not is the tax authorities, specifically for information regarding firms that have registered for inclusion in the VAT system. Information from the tax authorities and from the local court authorities is also used for determining whether enterprises in their respective areas are still trading.

Self-employed such as advocates and judges have to apply for a tax number and are registered in a special tax register. Individual registrants (physical persons) do not require judicial decisions and register directly with BULSTAT.

For all agricultural producers, including private households, a special additional register is being created now on the basis of the Register of the Ministry of Agriculture and Forestry, Social Insurance Register and the last Census on population, housing and agricultural farms.

Other registers used for cross-checking purposes are the Social Insurance Register and VAT register. The VAT register contains only units registered under VAT Law. Since 2003, the threshold for VAT registration has been diminished from 75000 to 50000 Levs. This will increase the number of units in the VAT register and might improve the exhaustiveness of NA estimates.

3.2 Data sources

The largest source of information for national accounts compilation is the information provided directly by enterprises. The statistical surveys are conducted on the basis of the register of statistical units. Statistical reports are available from the whole enterprise as well as from local subdivisions. The questionnaires are differentiated by activities and also for units using double- or single-entry bookkeeping.

The main statistical surveys conducted by NSI and used for National Accounts purposes are as follows:
- annual bookkeeping statement, provided by all public and private enterprises with double-entry bookkeeping, including statistical annexes for production, employment, wages and salaries, investments and more detailed description of the assets;
- annual statistical report on revenues and expenditures, provided by private firms with single-entry bookkeeping;
- annual report of insurance enterprises, collected by NSI and based on the specific accounting standard of insurance undertakings;
- annual report of non-profit institutions based on the specific accounting standard and allowing output to be split between market and non-market output;
- annual report of investment funds;
- annual report of pension funds;
- PRODCOM Survey;
- agricultural balances in the methodological frame of Economic Accounts for Agriculture, containing detailed information about the supply of goods and their use in both quantity and value terms, compiled by type of production unit: state and co-operative agricultural farms, private farms and households;
- annual labour statistics on the average annual number of employees under labour contract, employed persons, wages and salaries and hours worked;
- labour force survey;
- material balances in quantity and value terms for about 200 commodity groups, realized/consumed in production process of enterprise and sub-division;

- household budget survey with the information on the expenditures by COICOP groups, incomes from wages and salaries, social security, own production, preserved and processed food products etc.;
- monetary and banking statistics provided to NSI by Bulgarian National Bank (BNB). They include the annual balance sheets and income statements of BNB and commercial banks with more detailed breakdown of indicators;
- Balance of Payments;
- annual detailed information on the government budget, by separate budgetary units and functions;
- customs statistics;
- income declarations collected by Ministry of Finance;
- tax authorities' information about the accrual of VAT and excise duty.

3.3 Employment data reconciliation. Value added due to unregistered employment

During 2002-2003, NSI took part in the Eurostat pilot project on Employment Data Reconciliation organized under the Phare 2000 Multi-Country Statistical Cooperation Programme. Besides the work done in the Project on the compilation of tables on employment (employment, hours worked and compensation of employees) according to the definitions of ESA 95, it also focused on the reconciliation of employment data derived from two flows:

- labour supply: the number of employed persons is obtained from the quarterly Labour Force Survey;
- labour demand: the number of employed persons is obtained from the quarterly labour report of enterprises.

For certain activities additional sources were used to supplement the LFS data:

- Farm Structure Survey: used for determining the number of self-employed in the agricultural sector (ESA branches A+B).
- Population Census: used for determining the number of self-employed in C and E classes and for consistency checks.

Statistical sources used for measuring employment

The *Quarterly Labour Report* provides information on the average quarterly number of employees with labour contracts, the time worked by them, their earnings and other labour. The survey covers all registered units with at least one employee. It is exhaustive for public sector enterprises and private enterprises with more than 50 employees. A stratified random sample is used to observe the private sector enterprises with 1-50 employees. The average number of employees is derived as a simple average. The persons working half day, half week, half month or less than four hours per day are included in the average number of employees after the transformation to full time equivalents is made.

The *Labour Force Survey* is carried out on a quarterly basis. It collects data from a sample of population 15 years and above, living in non-institutional households. The sample used includes 24 000 households. It is a two-stage stratified cluster sample, designed by regions, separately for urban and rural populations. The clusters in the first stage are the enumeration districts and in the second are households.

All data on employment are prepared on a quarterly basis. Yearly data are calculated as an average of the four quarters in a reference year.

Employment, domestic concept

The LFS and Labour Statistics (LS) data are adjusted and combined in order to achieve one general employment number compliant with the domestic concept. Data are prepared separately for employees and self-employed.

Data on employees are calculated as a sum of two components: employees working under labour contract and employees working with other than labour type of contract (as civil non-labour contract) or without any contract.

Except the NACE activities A, B, C and E, the data on the self-employed are estimated by mainly using the corresponding LFS data, adjusted in the same way as is described above for the employees by other type of labour contract.

For the estimation of self-employed in classes C and E, data from the March 2001 Population Census are used and applied for all 2001 quarters. Their number is small and the LFS could not provide reliable estimates.

A different approach is used for the estimation of self-employment in agriculture (A). Data are derived from Farm Structure Surveys (FSS), conducted by the Ministry of Agriculture and Forestry. As with persons producing agricultural goods for their own consumption, these data mostly fit the NA concepts, whereas they are not entirely covered by the LFS or the Population Census. The disadvantage is that the information available from the FSS is relatively limited on the distinction between main and secondary jobs. For the purpose of the Project, data on full-time equivalents (FTE) is used – the number of annual working units (AWU), calculated for natural persons. Quarterly estimates are prepared on the basis of quarterly distribution of self-employed data in agriculture, in accordance with LFS.

Hours worked

Data on hours worked are prepared on a quarterly basis. Yearly data are calculated as a sum of the four quarters of the year. Generally data from quarterly LS on hours worked, employees and earnings and LFS are combined for the preparation of final data, with the exception of hours worked in agriculture. Data are prepared separately for employees and self-employed.

The LS was chosen as the main source for data on hours worked by employees (although such data are also available in the LFS) due to better coverage and more reliable NACE breakdown of the survey. Data on hours worked by employees working by other type of contract or without contract are obtained from the LFS. In order to meet the National Accounts general concepts, data on hours worked by employees from LS as well as data from LFS are adjusted in the same way as for employees and self-employed.

For the estimation of hours worked by self-employed in activities C and E, the average number of LFS hours per self-employed person in the activity is used and multiplied by the number of self-employed, derived from the March 2001 Population Census.

Data on hours worked in agriculture are based on the Farm Structure Survey, conducted by ministry of Agriculture and Forestry. The number of annual working units (AWUS) is multiplied by 1856 (1 AWU = 1856 hours). Specifically for agriculture, quarterly distribution of hours worked by self-employed persons is made according to the estimated quarterly distribution of the number of self-employed persons and their average hours worked provided by LFS.

Employment according to the national accounts

The national accounts procedure for estimating employment has led to an estimated total of 3 229 118 employed persons of whom 7.3 per cent were unregistered (without employment contract) in 2001. Unregistered employment is more widespread among employees in activities like manufacturing, trade, hotels and restaurants. In agriculture, the relevant presence of unregistered employment is related to the seasonal character of the harvest.

Table 1. shows the reconciliation of data from different sources and the final estimates.

Table 1. Estimation of total employment and hours worked – 2001
(millions)

NACE		Employees NA estimates	Self-employed NA estimates	Total employment NA estimates (c1+c2)	Hours worked by employees	Hours worked by self-employed	Hours worked in total employment (c4+c5)
A+B	Agriculture, hunting, forestry and fishing	107.7	676.3	784.0	190.1	1 255.2	1 445.3
C	Mining and quarrying	36.4	0.0	36.6	59.6	0.3	60.0
D	Manufacturing	614.9	36.9	651.8	1 022.4	67.2	1 089.6
E	Electricity, gas and water supply	61.3	0.0	61.4	103.6	0.2	103.8
F	Construction	120.2	11.7	131.9	205.2	19.0	224.2
G	Trade	288.0	122.0	410.0	501.1	223.3	724.5
H	Hotels and restaurants	90.8	22.7	113.6	158.5	43.7	202.2
I	Transport and communications	179.3	18.4	197.7	301.8	32.2	334.0
J	Financial intermediation	29.7	1.1	30.7	50.9	2.4	53.3
K	Real estate	110.2	18.6	128.7	186.0	33.8	219.8
L	Public administration	242.2	0	242.2	441.6	0	441.6
M	Education	205.0	1.3	206.3	319.9	1.8	321.7
N	Health	136.6	10.0	146.6	223.8	19.5	243.3
O	Other community, social and personal	73.4	13.7	87.1	126.4	19.5	145.9
P	Private households with employed persons	0	00	00	0.8	0	0.8
Total		2 296.2	932.9	3 229.1	3 891.8	1 718.2	5 610.0

Adjustment to value added due to unregistered employment

In order to estimate missing production due to unregistered employment, the number of employed persons used for current GDP calculations (2 968 069) is compared with the standardized employment derived as a result of the project (3 229 118). The analysis of jobs/persons is made at a very detailed level of economic activity. Jobs are considered to be equal to the persons and FTE for regular employment from the demand side, as the Labour Statistics require the enterprises to report the number of employees as FTE. On the basis of hours worked, LFS data for self-employed, employees with second jobs and employees without labour contract are transformed into FTE. The difference of 121 006, except in the NACE class L (armed forces, security and conscripts) is interpreted as the number of persons employed in the hidden economy. Recalculated in FTE, the number of employed persons decreases by around 17.5 per cent. The activities for which the reconciled employment data exceed the data used in national accounts calculations are trade, manufacturing, hotels and restaurants and agriculture. The adjustment in agriculture is related mostly to an increase of compensation of employees rather than the upward adjustment of the gross output, respectively gross value added, as the output is obtained through commodity by price method.

For estimation of underground activities (where producers are deliberately misreporting) due to the irregular employment, the following steps are taken:

- the employed from the two sources are disaggregated by activities and employees/self-employed are additionally separated by the size of the enterprises:
    - enterprises with less than 10 employees;
    - between 11 and 50 employees; and
    - more than 50 employees;
- unpaid family workers are regarded as self-employed persons;
- on the base of hours worked, the employed persons are transformed into full time equivalent and full time irregular employment is subsequently derived;
- the estimates of output per unit of labour input and value added per unit of labour input are obtained for registered employment;
- for every activity, by size of the enterprises and number of employees/self-employed, an assumption is made that the ratios of registered and irregular employment are equal;
- estimation of the output/value added per unit of irregular labour is made by applying the ratios from the previous step;
- then estimated gross output/gross value added of irregular employment is integrated into actually measured gross output/gross value added.

The implementation of the labour input method lead to the adjustments of GDP indicated in Table 2.

4. Summary of adjustments

The types of adjustments incorporated in the published national accounts, according to the approaches adopted for ensuring the GDP exhaustiveness are shown in Table 3.

The overall exhaustiveness adjustment is 10.2 per cent of GDP. The largest adjustments are made to the GVA of manufacturing, construction, trade, hotels and restaurants and transport and communications. The impact of the adjustment for wages and salaries in kind (increase of gross output) on GVA and respectively on GDP is 0.4 per cent. Among the various types of adjustments, the most significant is related to under-reporting of output and over-reporting of intermediate consumption. Together with hidden labour these add 7 per cent to the GDP.

Table 2. Exhaustiveness adjustments due to irregular employment, part of N6 - 2001

NACE Groups		Type of non-exhaustiveness adjustment			
		in GVA - million Levs		Per cent of GDP*	Per cent of GDP*
		N6 current	N6 experimental	N6 current	N6 experimental
A-B	Agriculture, hunting, forestry and fishing	0.4	0.4	0	0
C	Mining and quarrying	0.3	0.2	0	0
D	Manufacturing	29.1	273.9	0.1	0.9
E	Electricity, gas and water supply	0.2	0.3	0	0
F	Construction	21.3	37.1	0.1	0.1
G	Trade	50.4	237.5	0.2	0.8
H	Hotels and restaurants	16.3	158.2	0.1	0.5
I	Transport and communications	9.0	36.4	0	0.1
J	Financial intermediation	1.0	0.9	0	0
K	Real estate	5.0	12.9	0	0
L	Public administration	0	0	0	0
M	Education	0.8	6.6	0	0
N	Health	0.9	8.3	0	0
O	Other community, social and personal services	4.1	17.9	0	0.1
	Total adjustments	138.7	790.6	0.5	2.7

*GDP – 29709 million Levs

Table 3. Adjustments to GDP

		Informal & households own final use (N3)	Underground (N1, N4, N5, N6, N7)	Total	Informal & households own final use (N3)	Underground (N1, N4, N5, N6, N7)	Total
		Million Levs			Per cent of GDP		
A	Agriculture, hunting, forestry	639.2	31.6	670.8	2.2	0.1	2.3
C	Mining and Quarrying		318.0	8.0		0.0	0.0
D	Manufacturing		770.5	770.5		2.6	2.6
E	Electricity, gas and water supply		0.3	0.3		0.0	0.0
F	Construction	94.3	361.2	455.5	0.3	1.2	1.5
G	Trade		277.6	277.6		0.9	0.9
H	Hotels, restaurants		40.9	40.9		0.1	0.1
I	Transport, Communication		507.1	507.1		1.7	1.7
J	Financial intermediation		1.5	1.5		0.0	0.0
K	Real estate		133.3	133.3		0.4	0.4
M	Education		46.9	46.9		0.2	0.2
N	Health		25.5	25.5		0.1	0.1
O	Other community, social and personal services		84.7	84.7		0.3	0.3
	Total adjustments	733.5	2 289.2	3 022.7	2.5	7.7	10.2

CANADA

1. Introduction

In 1994 Statistics Canada published a study highlighting the potential size of the Canadian underground economy. The study was undertaken after the Goods and Services Tax (GST), a form of value-added tax, was put in place in Canada and there was speculation that a large proportion of the economy had been driven underground. The approach of the study was to establish a statistical range of what may be missing from GDP due to underground activity and to compare it to previous work done on the same basis. The results of this study are included in the 2003 UNECE Survey of the National Practices in Estimating Non-Observed Economic Activities in National Accounts. Since that time, Statistics Canada has not published any official estimates of the size of the underground economy (UE).

However, some in-house work has been underway since 2002 to establish a time-series of UE estimates starting from 1991. Subsequently the publishing of the OECD *Handbook on Measuring the Non-observed Economy* enhanced Statistics Canada's new effort to examine the issue of measurement of non-observed economic activity. The goal of this study is also to see if the importance of the non-observed economy is growing and whether or not point estimates for underground activity could be generated.

2. Definitions and scope of the study

In the Canadian System of National Accounts (CSNA), the underground economy is examined using the expenditure based approach, that looks at the components of expenditure based GDP with special emphasis on personal expenditure on goods and services, residential construction, imports and exports in order to identify and assess potential underground economy problem areas such as construction, 'skimming', sales of alcohol and spirits, tobacco and cigarettes, rent, childcare, tips, etc. The definition of the underground economy employed in the current study consists of market-based economic activities whether legal or illegal that escape measurement in the official GDP due to the hidden, illegal, or informal nature of the activities. The study will utilize a framework analogous to the one outlined in the OECD handbook and attempt to provide estimates for each of the three UE sectors (that is, hidden, illegal, and informal sectors).

Estimates of the hidden sector represent productive activities that are unreported due to intentional under-reporting of gross output, or over-reporting of intermediate inputs in order to understate value added and to avoid: a) payment of value added or other taxes; b) payment of social security contributions; c) having to meet certain legal standards such as minimum wages, maximum hours, safety or health standards; d) complying with certain administrative procedures, such as completing statistical questionnaires or other administrative forms.

In the CSNA, survey under-coverage problems are not considered to be a major issue given the strength of the survey system coupled with the integrated nature of the SNA. As a result no estimates will be generated for survey under-coverage.

Estimates produced for the illegal sector will represent the production of goods and services whose production, sale, distribution or mere possession is forbidden by law, such as prostitution or the production and sale of narcotic drugs, as well as productive activities which are usually legal but become illegal when carried out by unauthorized producers, such as illegal manufacturing of wine and smuggling of tobacco.

Estimates of the informal sector represent activities associated with establishments that are not registered with fiscal or social security authorities because they are not required by law to register with such authorities. As a result, these businesses are also missing from the Canadian business register (BR). The informal sector is characterised as consisting of units engaged in the production of goods or services with the primary objective of generating employment and incomes to the persons concerned. These units typically operate at a low level of organization and on a small scale, with little or no division of labour and capital as factors of production. Labour relations – where they exist – are based mostly on casual employment, kinship or personal and social relations rather than contractual arrangements with formal guarantees. Beyond the scope of this study is the measurement of household production for own final use and measures of the hidden sector resulting from survey non-response, non-updated or non-registered businesses.

3. Analytical framework

The work that is currently being undertaken at Statistics Canada follows the Italian agency ISTAT's analytical framework for measuring the underground economy, in that the various underground activities are classified by UE sector and sub-sector or component as depicted in Figure 1. Measures for all components of the underground economy with the exception of hidden production due to statistical reasons will be pursued.

4. Implementation and data sources

Statistics Canada is closely following the implementation plan as identified in the OECD Handbook. Consultation has begun with the user community and Canadian national accounts advisory board as well as identifying current UE adjustments made when compiling the national income and expenditure tables. Once this work has been completed the areas which are weak or where estimation methods need to be extended will be identified.

Statistics Canada has also begun exploring availability of additional data sources that can be used in the measurement of the hidden, illegal and informal sectors of the underground economy. The current focus is on the use of household expenditure survey data used to measure the hidden and informal sectors, tax audit data to measure the hidden sector, and police records and related survey data on criminal activities to come up with measures of illegal activities. Data development activities in other countries are followed. The final stage in the process will be to develop estimates for non-observed economic activity and incorporate these new measures when undertaking the next NA revision in 2010.

Analytical framework for measuring the underground economy

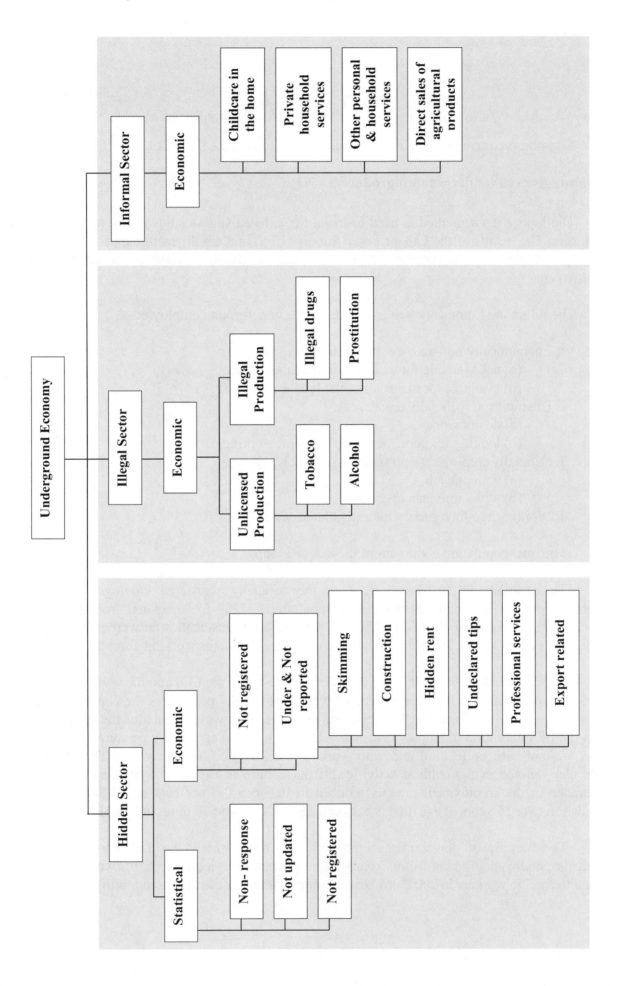

CROATIA

Non-observed economy in Croatia is estimated following the Eurostat tabular framework.

1. Non-registered (underground) producers - N1

The labour input method is used to make the exhaustiveness adjustments for non-registered producers. The results of the Labour Force Survey (LFS) and employment data from the Financial Agency's (FINA) annual statistical report are used to calculate GDP produced by registered employment.

The following framework was used to estimate underground employment:

    1. Economically non-active population:
            (a) not available for inclusion in the labour force;
            (b) available for inclusion in the labour force.
    2. Unemployed (officially registered):
            (a) do not work;
            (b) looking for permanent employment, working part-time.
    3. Officially employed (with social insurance):
            (a) with one job;
            (b) with more than one job.
    4. Working age foreigners with unregulated status.

The total population is the sum of these four groups.

To establish the difference between the officially registered employees and actually employed persons, the number of resident population (4 184 677 persons) from the Census of Population has been used. To this number are added the non-residents who were present in Croatia at the time of the Census, and are deducted the number of residents working abroad.

The difference between the number of employees from the LFS and the registered number of employees is significant. It ranges between 4.0 per cent and 4.7 per cent of the population above 15 years of age, or 150 thousand to 175 thousand employees. However, much of the difference stems from the LFS definition of employment, whereby an employed person is a person who was paid for their work in cash or in kind and who worked at least one hour per week. This difference is particularly noted in agricultural activities. If agriculture is excluded from the calculation, the difference in the employment rates is reduced to between 0.6 per cent and 1.8 per cent of the population over 15 years of age, that is between 25 thousand and 70 thousand employees.

The number of non-residents employed in Croatia should be added to the number of residents employed. According to Croatian Employment Service data, 5791 work permits were issued to foreign workers in 2001, primarily in shipbuilding, construction and tourism.

In order to establish the total income of this non-exhaustiveness type on the basis of the labour force methodology, it was also necessary to compare productivity and working hours of employees.

Employment structure data were used, distinguishing between full-time and part-time employees. For part-time employees, an employment figure was obtained based on full-time equivalents.[20]

Additionally, the number of employees by activity from the LFS has been compared to the number of employees from annual statistical reports used in GDP calculations, which were also based on full-time equivalents. The difference is assumed to be non-registered employees. Since the results of the survey are only reliable at the level of activity (NACE letter level), reliable comparison is possible at this level only. The value of gross output, intermediate consumption and value added per employee generated by small entrepreneurs in the same activity has been applied to the number of non-registered employees.

This method has been applied to all the activities apart from agriculture and public administration. The official number of employees (FINA's annual statistical report) is incomplete in public administration and defence, compulsory social security (military employment not included, even though the compensation of employees is included in GDP). Therefore the assumption is that there are no unregistered persons employed in this activity.

Table 1. Differences between the total number of employees according to the regular statistical reports and the Labour Force Survey

	Activities according to NACE	1998	2000	2002
A	Agriculture, hunting and forestry*	-	-	-
B	Fishing	0	0	0
C	Mining and quarrying	100	245	217
D	Manufacturing	12 984	28 336	25 103
E	Electricity, gas and water supply	224	466	432
F	Construction	11 349	5 945	6 027
G	Wholesale and retail trade, repair of motor vehicles, motorcycles and personal and household goods	32 668	16 895	7 292
H	Hotels and restaurants	10 268	5 297	5 356
I	Transport, storage and communication	11 672	2 952	2 611
J	Financial intermediation	1 046	411	599
K	Real estate, renting and business activities	5 966	0	0
L	Public administration	0	0	0
M	Education	3 846	1 368	1 537
N	Health and social work	14 017	7 522	5 808
O	Other community, social and personal service activities	9 377	2 091	167
	Total	**113 516**	**71 528**	**55 148**

* The method cannot be used for agriculture due to the different employment definition.

---

[20] The described example will explain the applied method: if in one activity there are 1000 full-time employees working 40 hours per week, and 500 employees who work less than full time (for example 20 hours per week), then the number of employees according to the full time equivalent is 1250: 1000+(500*20/40).

Table 1 shows that the difference between official number of employees and the number of employees from the LFS has been continuously decreasing. Industry, especially manufacturing, is the only exception to this trend. The decrease has been especially remarkable in trade but is also significant in health, transport, and hotels and restaurants. There are practically no differences between official data on the number of employees and the LFS data in services (real estate, business activities and other community, social and personal service activities) and financial intermediation.

In addition, illegal employment has decreased since the year 2000, as confirmed by data of the State Inspectorate of Croatia.

The differences in the data on total number of employees by activity have been multiplied by average value added per employee. The obtained results give the estimate of unrecorded income of underground producers by activity (Table 2).

Table 2. Unrecorded income by underground producers (N1), per activity

	Activities according to NACE	1998	2000	2002	1998	2000	2002
		Million HRK			Share of total unrecorded income (per cent)		
A	Agriculture, hunting and forestry	0	0	0	0	0	0
B	Fishing	0	0	0	0	0	0
C	Mining and quarrying	10	17	12	0.1	0.3	0.2
D	Manufacturing	1 061	2 570	2 862	13.8	39.3	50.8
E	Electricity, gas and water supply	20	34	50	0.3	0.5	0.9
F	Construction	689	596	574	8.9	9.1	10.2
G	Wholesale and retail trade, Repair of motor vehicles and motorcycles	2 414	1 613	810	31.4	24.7	14.4
H	Hotels and restaurants	446	392	446	5.8	6	7.9
I	Transport, storage and communication	1 298	350	326	16.9	5.4	5.8
J	Financial intermediation	164	138	149	2.1	2.1	2.6
K	Real estate renting and business activities	529	0	0	6.9	0	0
L	Public administration	0	0	0	0	0	0
M	Education	131	91	75	1.7	1.4	1.3
N	Health and social work	438	329	287	5.7	5	5.1
O	Other community, social and personal service activities	502	408	45	6.5	6.2	0.8
	Total	**7 701**	**6 538**	**5 636**	**100**	**100**	**100**

In accordance with the employment differences, the total unrecorded income by underground producers in the Croatian economy has been decreasing in the observed period, falling by 27 per cent over five years. In 2002 it totalled 5.6 billion HRK.

The unrecorded income by underground producers increased in the industrial sector. The greatest share of unrecorded income was in the manufacturing industry, reaching more than half of all unrecorded income by underground producers in Croatia in 2002.

2. Illegal producers – N2

Illegal production is included within the production boundary defined by the System of National Accounts 1993 (SNA93). However, there are practical difficulties to obtain data on these activities.

Since these activities are illegal, it is not possible to measure them using standard statistical methods. Special efforts have been made to obtain relatively reliable estimates. Data on criminal activities from various sources have been used, such as statistical data from the Ministry of Internal Affairs, the Croatian National Institute of Public Health, the findings and reports of the State Inspectorate of Croatia and expert estimates in criminology, medicine, software distribution, discography etc.

The income from illegal activities has been estimated for the following activities: narcotics distribution, human trafficking, abuse of copyrights and corruption. More detailed descriptions of these estimates are provided in the publication *Estimation of the total non-exhaustiveness value in the coverage of NA in the Republic of Croatia.*

The drug distribution income estimates are based on data on the confiscated quantities of drugs by type, estimates of police efficiency and prices of narcotics at the entry in Croatia and on sale to the final users. It is estimated that the police confiscate 20% - 33% of the total amount of narcotics distributed on the black market. It is assumed that the estimated purchasing price for the imports of greater quantities of narcotics in Croatia is on average 20% of the same drug on smaller quantities to the final users. The remaining 80% of the retail price value represents the narcotics distribution income on the Croatian market. The profit ratio depends on the narcotics type and quantity, the purity of the imported drug in relation to the purity of the final retail product, the origin of narcotics, the means of transport, the time of purchase, the market conditions, the quantity of single buying-selling transactions within the country, the number of intermediaries, import and distribution risk and many other factors.

Income from prostitution is based on an estimate of the total number of prostitutes, number of active days, and average prices. According to expert estimates, 70% of the total of 700 – 1000 prostitutes are full-time prostitutes and 30% are women who have regular jobs, for whom prostitution is an additional source of income. It is estimated that the number of working days for the first group is 250 days annually and for the second group, 100 days annually. The expert estimate for the number of daily services by prostitute is 5 - 6. According to the unofficial estimates, the prices spanned from 200 to 1 000 HRK per service, or 500 HRK on average. The cost of this activity (clothes, accommodation and other expenses) are estimated at 20% of total receipt, the rest being net income.

The income from human trafficking - the illegal transfer of persons across the state border - is estimated on the basis of the number of foreigners who were caught illegally crossing the state border during one year, and the estimated average price paid to the smugglers. Assuming that police prevented 50% of this activity, the approximate number of illegal transfers across the border is twice the number of illegal immigrants found. The estimated income is this figure multiplied by the average price paid per person. The costs are estimated to be 20% of the income. The remaining 80% is estimated as profit.

The income generated through the production and distribution of "pirated" products in breach of copyright is estimated on the basis of the quantity of products confiscated during the analysed period. The price of each medium (video-cassettes, audio-cassettes, CDs, DVDs) depends on a number of factors and has changed over time. It generally varies between 15-30% of the value of the original product. According to the estimates of the Copyright Protection Association, the percentage of "pirate" music sales is around 50%, for films around 30% and for computer software 67%. Given the estimated police efficiency in confiscating illegal pirated materials, it may be estimated that black market sales exceed authorised sales by seven to eight times for audio-cassettes, four to five times for video-cassettes and ten times for CDs and DVDs. Production and distribution costs of these products can be estimated at 15 per cent of the sales price. The earnings represent about 85 per cent of the value generated through the sale of these unauthorised products.

Income from corruption is estimated on the basis of the total number of reported criminal offences, and the value of the gain per offence. It should be noted that the issue is to estimate income from corruption, and not income in the narrow sense (the value of bribes accepted and bribes offered). Furthermore, the data originate from police records and provide only a possibility that a criminal offence has been committed. Only at the end of the criminal proceedings, the court decides whether a crime was committed and the extent of the claimed value. Thus estimates of the value of illegal income through corruption will necessarily be imprecise.

The total average annual income from illegal activities in Croatia amounted to almost 1.8 billion HRK, a little over 1 per cent of GDP in 2000-2003 (Table 3). The most significant sources of illegal income are corruption, narcotics distribution and prostitution.

Table 3. Estimate of the total average annual income generated through illegal activities in Croatia, 2000 – 2003

(million HRK)

Type of illegal income	The value of average annual illegal income (million HRK)	Share of GDP (per cent)
Narcotics distribution	469.2	0.27
Prostitution	328.0	0.19
Trafficking	71.0	0.04
Copyright abuse	17.6	0.01
Corruption	870.0	0.50
Total net illegal income	**1 755.8**	**1.02**

3. Producers not required to register – N 3

The non-exhaustiveness type N3 covers producers who are not required to register because they have no market output. This category includes individual agricultural producers, those producing goods for their own final consumption, and households involved in construction and maintenance of dwellings on their own account. Since the survey on agricultural production comprises all the producers, including those who produce goods exclusively for their own consumption, the adjustments for agricultural income are classified in the category N7 (statistical data deficiencies). In the case of agricultural income, the correction is made based on average price, and not based on numbers of unregistered producers.

The type N3 covers all own account construction of dwellings by households. According to SNA93, if natural persons from the household sector (craftsmen and small enterprises are excluded) carry out own account construction, the estimated total value of construction should be imputed. From this should be subtracted the intermediate consumption (construction costs). The difference gives the imputed income by the household sector from own account construction.

In the calculation of the value of own-account construction, the results from the annual statistical reports in the construction of real estate by private owners have been used. The estimate is that 10 per cent of investments in construction work are by natural persons on their own account. Based on that is estimated the value of gross output of construction by the producers not required to register. The intermediate consumption is estimated on the basis of the share of intermediate consumption in the value of gross output for small entrepreneurs and craftsmen. Table 4 shows the total estimated income from own account residential construction by the household sector.

Table 4. Estimation of income by producers not required to register (N3)
(million HRK)

	1998	**2000**	**2002**
N3 Own account residential construction by households	117.6	180.5	291.4
Share of N3 in official GDP, %	0.09	0.12	0.16

4. Registered legal entities not surveyed– N 4

There is a difference between standard statistical data sources for structural business statistics and annual statistical reports collected by FINA which are used in the GDP calculation. Some registered legal entities are not included in the statistical surveys for the standard structural business statistics. However, the annual FINA reports used in the GDP calculation do achieve full coverage. All legal entities are divided into groups: entrepreneurs, banks and other financial intermediaries, insurance corporations, budget beneficiaries, budget funds and non-profit institutions. The FINA's register is used to check the exhaustiveness of the statistical research carried out by other institutions. The comparison of the number of employees with other administrative sources indicates that the number of active legal entities who do not submit their annual statistical report is negligible.

Additional data sources include the Tax Office statistics on craftsmen's income, the estimation of rent for dwellings and the output of agricultural households. In principle these sources give complete coverage. Since these sources and not the structural business statistics data are used in the calculation of GDP, it is considered that N4 type data deficiencies in Croatia are not significant.[21]

5. Registered unincorporated enterprises not surveyed – N 5

Registered unincorporated enterprises are excluded from the statistical coverage for several reasons. For instance, the administrative register is not always delivered in complete form and in time to the Central Bureau of Statistics. In Croatia, this non-exhaustiveness category would also

---

[21] According to FINA analysis of the period when the payment system was its exclusive responsibility, non-response was recorded only for small entrepreneurs whose annual turnover amounted to less than 1000 HRK per account.

include the income from renting out dwellings, rooms and office space, which is reported to the relevant institutions (such as the Tax Office), and is not included in the calculation of the official GDP data. The Tax Office records are used as the data source for this category. Table 5 shows the non-exhaustiveness adjustments of type N5.

Table 5. Estimation of the income by registered unincorporated producers not surveyed (N5) (million HRK)

	1998	2000	2002
N5: Total generated income from renting out dwellings, rooms and office spaces	380.2	476.7	631.7
Share of N5 in the official GDP, percentage	0.28	0.31	0.35

The data on income from registered craft and freelance activities in the GDP calculation are taken from the Tax Office that provides a complete coverage. Due to the financial penalties that the craftsmen face for not submitting an annual income statement, it can be assumed that this non-exhaustiveness type in Croatia is not significant.

6. Inaccurate reporting by the producers - N6

In order to estimate inaccurate reporting by producers, indicators of revenues and costs per employee and tax audit results are used. The most common form of misreporting is overestimation of incurred costs to reduce taxes. The difference between reported and imputed revenues and costs per employee according to the size of enterprise are analysed. In all activities, small entrepreneurs tend to report a lower gross output and a higher incurred cost per employee.

6.1 Misreporting by legal entities

The starting basis for estimating how much the reported gross output is reduced is the breakdown of gross output, intermediate consumption and value added into 13 groups according to enterprise size and activity.

Within each activity, gross output per employee (on the basis of the full working hours) of entrepreneurs with less than 10 employees was compared with the gross output per employee of the units with more than 10 employees.

When the gross output per employee in the smaller units was lower, it was assumed that the real value for the smaller unit was equal to the average of the reported gross output value in larger units. This model has been applied to all activities except those where there are significant productivity differences (oil extraction, telecommunication, electricity) due to the applied technology.

The next step was to analyse intermediate consumption for the above groups according to activity and size. In activities where the share of intermediate consumption was higher in small units, it was assumed that the share of intermediate consumption is equal to the average reported share of intermediate consumption in larger units.

In addition tax audit results were used to identify the activities where there is higher probability of income underestimation for tax evasion purposes. Table 6 shows the audit results in

2000-2002. More detailed descriptions are provided in the publication: *Estimation of the total non-exhaustiveness value in the coverage of NA in the Republic of Croatia.*

Table 6. Tax evasion per activity (percentage of all tax evasion)

	Activities according to NACE	2000	2001	2002
A	Agriculture, hunting and forestry	4.9	2.8	3.2
B	Fishing	0.3	0.6	0.1
C	Mining and quarrying	0.6	0.3	0.4
D	Manufacturing	16.0	23.2	15.5
E	Electricity, gas and water supply	0.3	1.3	2.3
F	Construction	16.7	15.8	12.7
G	Wholesale and retail trade, repair of motor vehicles, motorcycles and personal and household goods	35.7	30.0	31.9
H	Hotels and restaurants	7.5	6.6	4.0
I	Transport, storage and communication	4.2	4.8	5.6
J	Financial intermediation	0.6	1.0	1.2
K	Real estate, renting and business activities	7.0	10.5	10.1
L	Public administration	0.0	0.0	0.0
M	Education	0.1	0.4	0.8
N	Health and social work	0.6	0.2	0.2
O	Other community, social and personal service activities	5.3	2.5	12.1
	Total	**100.0**	**100.0**	**100.0**

Table 7 shows the levels of underestimated value added by legal entities. For small entrepreneurs the estimate is based on the comparison with large entrepreneurs and tax audit results, while for large entrepreneurs the correction of value added is exclusively based on the tax audit data.

The inaccurate reporting of business results by producers during the analysed period has tripled from 1.7 billion HRK in 1998 to 4.9 billon HRK in 2002.

6.2 Under-reporting of income in the crafts and freelance sector

In order to determine the inaccurate reporting by craftsmen and freelancers, the value added per employee for this sector has been compared with the equivalent indicator for small entrepreneurs (those with up to ten employees). Where the value added per craftsman (including employees) is lower than the value added per employee of small entrepreneurs, the assumption is that the real value added is equal to the weighted average of reported value added (weight 60 per cent) and value added per employee of small entrepreneurs (weight 40 per cent).[22]

Inaccurate reporting by craftsmen has increased during the analysed period, but not as much as for legal entities (Table 8).

---

[22] In the case of craftsmen, only data on income are available from the Tax Office.

Table 7. Inaccurate reporting by producers (N6), legal entities

	Activities according to NACE	1998	2000	2002	1998	2000	2002
		Millions HRK			Share in all inaccurate reporting (percentage)		
A	Agriculture, hunting and forestry	40	296	153	2.3	9.0	3.1
B	Fishing	13	1	29	0.7	0	0.6
C	Mining and quarrying	12	5	18	0.7	0.2	0.4
D	Manufacturing	285	590	668	16.4	18.0	13.5
E	Electricity, gas and water supply	3	11	19	0.2	0.3	0.4
F	Construction	205	317	583	11.8	9.7	11.8
G	Wholesale and retail trade, repair of motor vehicles, motorcycles and personal and household goods	636	1 265	1 887	36.5	38.6	38.1
H	Hotels and restaurants	43	118	155	2.5	3.6	3.1
I	Transport, storage and communication	245	258	322	14.1	7.9	6.5
J	Financial intermediation	34	63	201	2.0	1.9	4.1
K	Real estate, renting and business activities	157	295	610	9	9.0	12.3
L	Public administration	0	0	0	0	0	0
M	Education	18	14	17	1.0	0.4	0.3
N	Health and social work	18	4	12	1.0	0.1	0.2
O	Other community, social and personal service activities	33	43	273	1.9	1.3	5.5
	Total	**1 741**	**3 279**	**4 947**	**100**	**100**	**100**

Table 8. Inaccurate reporting by producers (N6), craft

	Activities according to NACE	1998	2000	2002	1998	2000	2002
		Million HRK			Share in all inaccurate reporting (per cent)		
A	Agriculture, hunting and forestry	52	28	33	2.4	1.1	1
B	Fishing	34	44	77	1.6	1.7	2.4
C	Mining and quarrying	1	0	0	0	0	0
D	Manufacturing	421	483	482	19.8	19.2	15
E	Electricity, gas and water supply	0.3	0	-0.2	0	0	0
F	Construction	271	387	379	12.7	15.4	11.8
G	Wholesale and retail trade, repair of motor vehicles, motorcycles and personal and household goods	478	556	752	22.4	22.1	23.4
H	Hotels and restaurants	63	196	459	3	7.8	14.3
I	Transport, storage and communication	378	340	342	17.7	13.5	10.6
J	Financial intermediation	13	38	21	0.6	1.5	0.6
K	Real estate, renting and business activities	288	334	451	13.5	13.3	14
L	Public administration	0	0	0	0	0	0
M	Education	2	2	5	0.1	0.1	0.2
N	Health	54	10	45	2.5	0.4	1.4
O	Other community, social and personal	77	96	164	3.6	3.8	5.1
	Total	**2 131**	**2 513**	**3 210**	**100**	**100**	**100**

6.3 Unreported income from renting out rooms and dwellings

The N6 type includes unreported income from renting out dwellings or rooms by natural persons. All landlords registered with the Tax Office are included in type N5. The estimation of income from house rentals is based on the Household Budget Survey results. The share of intermediate consumption is imputed from the costs of small rental agencies in order to obtain the remaining value added. Table 9 shows the data concerning the value of unreported income from rent (N6).

Table 9. Estimate of unreported income from rent (N6)
(million HRK)

	1998	2000	2002
Part of N6: Total unreported rent income	991	655	851
Share of total unreported income in official GDP, in per cent	0.72	0.43	0.47

7. Statistical deficiencies – N7

This element of the non-observed economy includes:
- household income from own account agricultural production, corrected by market prices;
- tips;
- wages in kind;
- income of households generated through secondary activities.

The income of agricultural households is calculated on the basis of produced quantities. These result from regular surveys lasting several decades and the total value produced quantities have been well recorded. However, in the calculation of the individual agricultural household income, purchasing prices are used which are significantly lower than potential market prices. For each group of agricultural items, the breakdown by end use has been estimated (wholesale, own consumption, sales to other households). The purchased quantities have been valued using the purchasing prices while the value of sales to other households is calculated using the average difference between the market price and wholesale purchasing price. The value of products intended for own consumption is calculated using the average of wholesale purchase price and market price.

The value of tips has been estimated for hotels and restaurants in accordance with the Eurostat approach. The estimation is based on the tourist office information on recommended tips for particular services. The total turnover in restaurants and bars (by type), and the amount of average expenditure and recommended tips have been used.

The data source for wages in kind is the Household Budget Survey. Since the data from this source is not available at the activity level, the total of wages in kind has been allocated according to the structure of value added by activity. The data on income generated through secondary activities of the household sector (paid directly to households) have also been obtained from the

Household Budget Survey and are allocated to the business services activity and personal services activity.

Table 10 shows the statistical data deficiencies (N7). Apart from wages in kind, these corrections are confined to a few activities. In agriculture, this is mainly the corrections of purchasing prices, in the case of hotels and restaurants mainly tips, and in business and personal services mainly the secondary activities of households.

Some particular types of statistical data deficiencies are stable, suggesting the need for improving the methodological basis and data collection.

Table 10. Statistical data deficiencies (N7)

Activities according to NACE	1998	2000	2002	1998	2000	2002
	Million HRK			Share in all statistical data deficiencies (per cent)		
A Agriculture, hunting and forestry	1 074	955	1 088	41.3	34.7	40.2
B Fishing	1	1	1	0	0	0
C Mining and quarrying	2	3	3	0.1	0.1	0.1
D Manufacturing	81	82	88	3.1	3	3.3
E Electricity, gas and water supply	12	12	13	0.5	0.4	0.5
F Construction	26	18	25	1	0.7	0.9
G Wholesale and retail trade, Repair of motor vehicles, motorcycles and personal and household goods	46	40	55	1.8	1.5	2
H Hotels and restaurants	79	65	83	3	2.4	3.1
I Transport, storage and communication	32	38	47	1.2	1.4	1.7
J Financial intermediation	16	18	24	0.6	0.6	0.9
K Real estate, renting and business activities	772	938	731	29.7	34.1	27
L Public administration	39	39	35	1.5	1.4	1.3
M Education	16	20	21	0.6	0.7	0.8
N Health and social work	19	22	23	0.7	0.8	0.8
O Other community, social and personal service activities	386	502	467	14.8	18.3	17.3
Total	2 601	2 752	2 705	100	100	100

8. The estimation of the imputed rent for dwellings and its effect on total GDP

8.1 The method used in the calculation of the gross imputed rent for dwellings

According to SNA93, the services of owner-occupied dwellings (imputed rent) should be included in GDP. The value of these services is calculated on the basis of the market prices or according to the production costs where market prices are not available.

In Croatia, owner-occupancy prevails. As a result of privatization of the housing stock, according to the 2001 Census of Population, 96% of the inhabited dwellings in Croatia are in private ownership, while legal entities own just 4% of dwellings. 2.9% of dwellings are occupied by a tenant with a contract, and 0.9% households are partly rented. Due to this occupancy structure, the indirect "user cost" method has been applied in the calculation of the value of services of owner-occupied dwellings.

The gross output value of housing services (i.e. gross rent for dwellings) consists of the actual rentals for housing paid by the tenants and the value of housing services of owner-occupied dwellings, that is, imputed rent for housing.

The user-cost method of calculation implies that the imputed dwelling rent is equal to the sum of intermediate consumption and gross value added. The intermediate consumption includes the costs of materials and skilled labour for regular maintenance and repairs, as well as the expenditure for dwelling insurance. The value added consists of the consumption of fixed capital, other (net) taxes on production and net operating surplus.

So far, the gross output value of housing services is calculated for the total dwelling stock without breakdown into owner-occupied dwellings and rented dwellings. The dwelling stock includes only the dwellings for permanent residence, while dwellings for temporary residence (e.g. dwellings for vacation, recreation, seasonally used dwellings) are excluded.

Data from 1991 and 2001 Census of Dwellings are used for calculating the dwelling stock. For the years between the Censuses, data from construction statistics on the number and total area of newly built and demolished dwellings are used. The value of the dwelling stock is estimated based on construction statistics: the average prices for new dwellings include the price of the land, construction price, and other costs. In the estimation of the purchasing value of the dwelling stock the construction cost data have been used. Thus in the valuation of dwelling stock a correction is made to include the quality of the existing dwelling stock. In the period 1991 - 2001, a correction was made to account for dwellings demolished due to the war, which amounts to 3.7 million square metres, or 3.3 per cent of total residential stock.

According to the 1991 Census of Dwellings, the majority of residential buildings were constructed after 1960 (around 70%). Therefore the current value of dwelling stock has been calculated on this basis as 70% of the purchasing value of the dwelling stock.

The consumption of fixed capital (of the dwelling stock), used to estimate the gross rent, represents the decrease in the value of dwelling stock due to usage and deterioration. In Croatia the service life of the dwelling stock is set at 77 years, with annual deprecation rate of 1.3 per cent. Intermediate consumption i.e. costs of minor repairs, are estimated as 1.0 per cent of the dwelling stock value at current prices.

In the majority of EU countries the value of gross imputed rent for dwellings represents around 10 per cent of GDP. According to the methodology used so far, the share of the rent for dwellings in 2002 amounts to 6.5 per cent of the GDP of Croatia. It is obvious that the existing methodology significantly underestimates the value of the rent for dwellings. This will become more evident in the future as overall economic activity increases faster than the rent. By maintaining the existing methodology of rent calculation, the share of residential rent in the GDP would decrease below 6 per cent, which is very small. Table 11 shows the data used to calculate the imputed rent for dwellings.

Table 11. Calculation of the imputed rent for dwellings
(according to the existing methodology) 1998 – 2002
(million HRK)

	Rent for dwellings (million HRK)		
	1998	2000	2002
Purchasing value of the dwelling stock	456 483	525 655	588 697
Current value of the dwelling stock	319 538	367 959	412 088
Consumption of fixed capital	5 934	6 834	7 653
Repair and maintenance cost of the of the dwellings	3 195	3 819	4 121
Gross output value (gross rent for dwelling)	9 130	10 653	11 774
Gross domestic product	137 604	152 519	181 231
Share of gross output value f renting dwellings in the GDP (%)	6.6	7.0	6.5

8.2 The Eurostat recommendation for calculation of imputed rent using the user-cost method

The European Commission Decision (95/309/EC) clarifies in detail the methods for the calculation of the rent for dwellings. Eurostat recommends that in those countries where the share of rented dwellings on the market is less than 10 per cent of the total number of dwellings, and where there is a large difference between the market rent and other paid rent, the user-cost method can be applied as the alternative in the case of the owner-occupied dwellings, while the stratification method should be applied in the case of rented dwellings.

Using the user-cost method, the gross imputed rent for dwellings is the sum of the following components:
- intermediate consumption;
- consumption of fixed capital;
- other (net) taxes on production;
- net operating surplus.

To estimate the intermediate consumption, the data from the Household Budget Survey should be used. For the estimation of the consumption of fixed capital, the Perpetual Inventory Method is universally accepted; this method should enable separate estimation for owner-occupied dwellings and privately rented dwellings as well as state-owned dwellings. For net operating surplus, Eurostat suggests applying the fixed rate of 2.5 per cent of the net value of the dwelling stock. This estimation should be reviewed every five years.

Finally, the imputed value of owner-occupied housing services should include the valuation of land on which the dwelling is located. The assumption is that the data sources required for the valuation of the land are available, or estimations can be made and reviewed every five years.

On the basis of the available data and following the Eurostat suggestions, an experimental alternative calculation has been made of the dwelling rent value for the period 1998-2002.

For the calculation of the intermediate consumption, the data from the Household Budget Survey was used. Because of the disparity of HSB data over the years, the average of the ratio of intermediate consumption to gross rent was used, that is 11.5 per cent of gross rent. The net operating surplus was estimated at 2.5 per cent level. Consumption of fixed capital estimation at the level of 1.3 per cent of the dwelling stock purchasing value is considered to be acceptable. Table 12 shows the results of the experimental calculation.

With new alternative value of calculated rent, the share of dwelling rent following the inclusion of non-observed economy in the GDP ranges from 8.8 per cent in 1998 to 8.7 per cent in 2002.

Table 12. The calculation of the gross rent for dwellings
(according to the methodology recommended by Eurostat) 1998-2002
(million HRK)

	1998	2000	2002
Intermediate consumption	1 559	1 811	2 019
Consumption of fixed capital	4 065	46 810	5 242
Net operating surplus (2.5 per cent)	7 988	9 199	10 302
Gross dwelling rents	13 612	15 691	17 563
Gross domestic product (official)	137 604	152 519	181 231
Gross domestic product (adjusted for exhaustiveness adjustments N1-N7)	154 632	170 469	201 333
Share of gross dwelling rents in official GDP (%)	9.9	10.3	9.7
Share of gross dwelling rents in adjusted GDP (%)	8.8	9.2	8.7

9. Summary of adjustments for the non-observed economy

The total of non-exhaustiveness adjustments in 2002 amounted to 20.1 billion HRK with the inclusion of illegal activities, or 18.3 billion HRK excluding illegal activities (Table 13). This amount has increased in absolute terms but the share in the total GVA and GDP declined through the analysed period. Without illegal activities, the share of total non-exhaustiveness adjustments in GDP was 10.2 per cent in 2002 compared to 11.4 per cent in 1998.

The following activities had the greatest shares of non-exhaustiveness adjustments in the gross value added in 2002: hotels and restaurants, real estate and business activities, fishing, construction, other community, social and personal services, and trade (see Table 14).

Among the particular non-exhaustiveness types, the most significant is N6 (misreporting) at 9.0 billion HRK, followed by N1 and N7 (Table 15). Non-exhaustiveness type N6 has generated the greatest increase, while non-exhaustiveness type N1 has decreased. This indicates that the non-observed economy has been moving towards inaccurate reporting while the number of unregistered (underground) producers has been decreasing due to the continuous development of market institutions and more severe penalty systems. In other words, tax evasion methods have become more sophisticated.

Table 13. Total non-exhaustiveness adjustments according to activity

	Activities according to NACE	1998	2000	2002	1998	2000	2002
		Million HRK			Share of non-exhaustiveness adjustments (per cent)		
A	Agriculture, hunting and forestry	1 166	1 278	1 274	7.4	7.8	7
B	Fishing	47	46	106	0.3	0.3	0.6
C	Mining and quarrying	25	24	34	0.2	0.1	0.2
D	Manufacturing	1 849	3 725	4 100	11.8	22.7	22.4
E	Electricity, gas and water supply	36	571	81	0.2	0.3	0.4
F	Construction	1 308	1 497	1 853	8.3	9.1	10.1
G	Wholesale and retail trade, repair of motor vehicles, motorcycles and personal and household goods	3 574	3 474	3 504	22.8	21.2	19.2
H	Hotels and restaurants	1 012	1 248	1 775	6.5	7.6	9.7
I	Transport, storage and communication	1 953	986	1 037	12.5	6	5.7
J	Financial intermediation	228	256	395	1.5	1.6	2.2
K	Real estate, renting and business activities	2 737	2 221	2 643	17.5	13.5	14.5
L	Public administration	39	39	35	0.2	0.2	0.2
M	Education	166	128	118	1.1	0.8	0.6
N	Health and social work	528	366	367	3.4	2.2	2
O	Other community, social and personal service activities	997	1 050	949	6.4	6.4	5.2
	Total (excluding illegal)	15 663	16 908	18 272	100	100	100
	Illegal activities	1 404	1 556	1 830			
	Total (including illegal)	**17 028**	**17 950**	**20 102**			

Table 14. Share of total non-exhaustiveness-adjustments in total GVA of specific activities
(per cent)

	Activities according to NACE	1998	2000	2002
A	Agriculture, hunting and forestry	10.9	11.7	10.1
B	Fishing	19.8	15.8	26.7
C	Mining and quarrying	3.8	2.9	2.9
D	Manufacturing	7.5	13.9	13.8
E	Electricity, gas and water supply	0.9	1.5	1.9
F	Construction	16.9	25.5	21.7
G	Wholesale and retail trade; repair of motor vehicles,	25.9	26.4	19.1
H	Hotels and restaurants	28.3	29.6	33.7
I	Transport, storage and communication	20.0	7.9	6.6
J	Financial intermediation	4.6	4.5	4.8
K	Real estate, renting and business activities	49.3	35.3	31.7
L	Public administration	0.3	0.3	0.3
M	Education	3.4	2.0	1.7
N	Health and social work	9.3	5.1	4.8
O	Other community, social and personal services	37.1	28.0	19.9
	Total, including N2 illegal production (per cent of GVA)	**15.4**	**14.9**	**13.9**
	Total, including N2 (per cent of GVA)	**12.4**	**11.8**	**11.2**
	Total, excluding N2 (per cent of GVA)	**11.4**	**10.7**	**10.2**

Table 15. Total non-exhaustiveness adjustments by type

Non-exhaustiveness types	1998	2000	2002	1998	2000	2002
	Million HRK			Share in total non-exhaustiveness adjustment (per cent)		
N1 Unregistered (underground) producers	7 701	6 538	5 636	45.2	36.4	28
N2 Unregistered illegal producers	1 404	1 556	1 830	8.2	8.7	9.1
N3 Producers not obliged to register	118	181	291	0.7	1	1.4
N4 Registered legal person not surveyed	-	-	-	-	-	-
N5 Registered unincorporated enterprises non surveyed	380	477	632	2.2	2.7	3.1
N6 Inaccurate reporting by producers	4 863	6 447	9 008	28.5	35.9	44.8
N7 Statistical data deficiencies	2 601	2 752	2 705	15.2	15.3	13.5
Total	**17 028**	**17 950**	**20 102**	**100**	**100**	**100**

The Tax Office needs to focus on the inaccurate reporting by producers. On the other hand, there is significant scope for improvement of the exhaustiveness of statistical information, which accounts for 13.5 per cent of the shortfall in the coverage of economic activity in Croatia.

Table 16 shows the shares of specific non-exhaustiveness adjustments according to the non-exhaustiveness types in the total gross value added. At the national level, the share decreased from 15.4 per cent in 1998 to 13.9 per cent in 2002.

Table 16. The shares of adjustments in the total gross value added (GVA)
by non-exhaustiveness type
(per cent)

Non-exhaustiveness types	1998	2000	2002
N1 Unregistered producers (underground producers)	7.0	5.4	3.9
N2 Unregistered illegal producers	1.3	1.3	1.3
N3 Producers not required to register	0.1	0.1	0.2
N4 Registered legal entities not surveyed	0.0	0.0	0.0
N5 Registered unincorporated enterprises non surveyed	0.3	0.4	0.4
N6 Inaccurate reporting by producers	4.4	5.3	6.3
N7 Statistical deficiencies in the data	2.4	2.3	1.9
Share in total GVA	**15.4**	**14.9**	**13.9**

Table 17 shows the values of all required corrections to the GDP, and the effect of the change in the methodology of calculating the imputed dwelling rent.

Table 17. Total GDP including non-exhaustiveness adjustments at current prices
(million HRK)

	1998	2000	2002
Official GDP	137 604	152 519	179 390
All non-exhaustiveness adjustments (N1-N7)	17 028	17 950	20 102
Share of non-exhaustiveness adjustments in official GDP (%)	**12.4**	**11.8**	**11.2**
GDP including non-exhaustiveness adjustments	154 632	170 469	199 492
Share of non-exhaustiveness adjustments in adjusted GDP (%)	**11.0**	**10.5**	**10.1**
Changes due to the new methodology of calculation of dwelling rent	6 391	7 359	8 242
Total adjustments (including new dwelling rent)	23 419	25 310	28 344
Total adjusted GDP (including new dwelling rent)	161 022	177 828	207 734
Share of non-exhaustiveness adjustments in official GDP including the dwelling rent calculated according to the new methodology	**17.0**	**16.6**	**15.8**

CZECH REPUBLIC

1. Introduction

The Czech Statistical Office (CZSO) has been compiling National Accounts since the beginning of the 1990s with the aim of ensuring comprehensiveness of production, income and expenditure-based GDP estimates.

Two kinds of adjustments are made to the national accounts. The first is referred to as methodological and conceptual adjustments and is divided into two categories:
- adjustments due to differences between business and national accounting rules;
- adjustments relating to own-account productive activities, as laid down by ESA 95; refers to adjustments for imputed rent for housing services provided to themselves by owner-occupiers.

The second type of adjustments relate to the non-observed economy. Exhaustiveness adjustments were incorporated in the Czech National Accounts from the very beginning. During the work on the Eurostat Pilot Project on Exhaustiveness (1998 PPE) the process of estimating the non-observed economy (NOE) became more systematic and consistent. It was furthermore improved in the new Project on Exhaustiveness in 2003.

The following description refers to exhaustiveness adjustments, which are classified according to the Eurostat's Tabular Approach.

2. Exhaustiveness adjustments by type: output approach

2.1 N1: Producers deliberately not registering – underground

Type N1 involves small producers who intentionally do not register to avoid taxes and social and health insurance contributions. Unregistered small businesses can be found in the area of small crafts, maintenance, repairs, and building activities in both rural and urban areas. The number of unregistered units in the Czech Republic is rather high. According to observations in the districts of southern Moravia, various forms of unregistered business activities thrive in both rural and urban areas. This is due to high unemployment, out-of-date legislation and overall low efficiency of regulation in the entrepreneurial arena. Craftsmen do not see the advantages in being registered, nor do they feel any necessity to play by the rules. Also, they do not perceive any risk of audits and legal sanctions.

The estimate of the production by producers deliberately not registering (Table 1) was based on the estimates of the number of producers deliberately not registering, intermediate consumption and value added per worker. The estimate of the number of producers deliberately not registering was based on the analysis of results of the balance of labour, LFS and commodity flows in the supply-and-use tables.

Table 1. The estimate of production by producers deliberately not registering - 2000

	NACE	Number of producers deliberately not registering	Value added per worker (thousand CZK)	Gross value added (million CZK)	Intermediate consumption (million CZK)	Gross output (million CZK)
A	Agriculture	2 611	227 5	594	149	743
B	Fishing					
C	Mining					
D	Manufacturing	10 956	140 1	1 535	387	1 922
E	Electricity					
F	Construction	23 671	188 1	4 451	1 146	5 597
G	Trade, repair	3 796	163 6	621	155	776
H	Hotels, restaurants					
I	Transport, communication	3 876	248 2	962	241	1 203
J	Finance					
K	Real estate, business services	3 264	184 7	603	151	754
L	Public administration					
M	Education	1 462	210 7	308	77	385
N	Health, social work	1 272	202 0	257	64	321
O	Other services	4 839	183 1	886	222	1 108
P	Private households	1 468	89 9	132	0	132
	Total	**57 215**	**180 9**	**10 349**	**2 592**	**12 941**

2.2 N2: Producers not registering - illegal activity

Four types of illegal activities are recognized and estimated: prostitution, production and consumption of drugs, sales of stolen goods and smuggling. The estimates of prostitution and sales of stolen goods have long time series and these two types of illegal activities are included in national accounts.

2.2.1 Prostitution

Three independent studies formed the backbone of the assessment: analysis of the Ministry of the Interior; phone survey of home-based prostitution; and the study *Facts, estimation and prostitution trends in Czech Republic*. Based on these sources it was concluded that about 6 300 persons work in prostitution earning a daily income of approximately 2500 CZK. This figure gives an annual amount of 5749 million CZK.

According to expert estimation, 65 % of customers are foreigners, and the rest are Czech citizens. Therefore, 3737 million CZK is reported in the system of national accounts as export of services, and 2012 million CZK as household final consumption.

The costs, such as the purchase of clothes, cosmetics, and taxi expenses are estimated to be 20 per cent and amount to 1150 million CZK, which is reported as intermediate consumption. In total, prostitution accounted for 0.2 per cent of GDP in 2000 (that is 1.985 billion CZK).

2.2.2 Drug consumption

On the demand side, the value of final consumption of drugs is equal to the number of consumers multiplied by the average quantity consumed valued at street prices.

The following data sources are used:
- number of drug consumers – the prevalence estimate of problematic drug users (namely the multiplicative method based on the number of drug-addicts undergoing treatment combined with the capture-recapture method);
- average quantity consumed: after long-term monitoring in the Environmental Health Office, the CZSO determines the average quantity consumed per year;
- street prices are obtained from police statistics and reports.

On the supply side, the value of final consumption of drugs is equal to imports destined for the Czech Republic, valued at street prices, and multiplied by a coefficient to take into account the purity of drugs.

The imports destined for the Czech Republic equal the quantity seized by the police multiplied by a coefficient to take into account the quantity of non-seized drugs, multiplied by the rate destined for the Czech Republic.

Data sources:
- seized quantities – received from the General Directorate of Customs and police statistics and reports;
- street prices – police statistics and reports;
- rate of drugs dedicated for Czech Republic – police statistics and reports;
- seizure rate and import purities and street purities – police statistics and reports.

2.2.3 Sales of stolen goods

Thefts in dwellings, houses, shops, trucks and passenger cars and the resale of stolen goods are a common phenomena. Almost all stolen goods can be assumed to be intended for resale through middlemen. While the act of theft itself is not a productive activity, those of the middlemen are considered a business activity. It can be assumed that financial flows concerning sales from stolen goods are partially picked up in the national accounts. It can also be assumed that some middlemen sell stolen goods legally. The margin of middlemen selling stolen goods was estimated for thefts of passenger cars only. The estimate used crime statistics at the level of 10 per cent of the value of stolen cars (about 0.4 billion CZK for 2000). For the time being, sales of other goods have not been taken into account, because a large part of such sales already passes through legal business activities, permitted by current legislation (when buying stolen goods, the buyer becomes their new owner).

2.2.4 Sales of smuggled goods

The illegal imports of goods for resale is widespread in the Czech Republic today. This is especially true for tobacco products, alcoholic beverages, automotive fuel, clothing, footwear, and second-hand (frequently stolen) cars, where the purchase price is significantly below the price of a comparable legally traded product. Sales of smuggled goods were not estimated explicitly, though crime statistics do provide figures on smuggling and the loss of customs duty. Instead, the CZSO assumes that these sales are part of the sales of small retailers (stall-holders, in particular), for which the CZSO already has estimates of concealed incomes. Another reason for not quoting the estimates of sales of smuggled goods is that crime statistics understate its real value as they are based on the evidence emanating from recorded offences only.

2.3 N3: Producers not required to register

Under type N3, the CZSO made adjustments for the informal sector, individual housing construction and output of agricultural products for own final use.

2.3.1 Informal sector

Only some production activities of households were included in exhaustiveness estimates for the informal sector. Given that non-registered business activities are deliberately placed in N1 and part of secondary gainful employment and contracts of services in N5, there remain only under-threshold occasional production activities in agriculture (i.e. legal activities which households do not report in tax returns because the income provided by these activities does not reach the specified level), and household personnel services in the informal sector.

Small non-reported revenues from sales of agricultural products are estimated at the same level as reported ones. Intermediate consumption is estimated with reference to similar activities reported. The estimate of production associated with household personnel services is based on the number of personnel full time equivalents (Table 2). The data are established by the Labour Force Survey (LFS) assuming a working period of 12 months for CZK 10 000 (approximate monthly net average wage in Czech Republic).

Table 2. The estimation of production of household personnel services - 2000

Number of personnel	2 400
Number of personnel (full time equivalents)	2 280
Income per month	10 000 CZK
Number of months worked	12
Total gross output	274 million CZK

2.3.2 Individual housing construction

Data on construction of dwellings by households is based mainly on annual statistical reports of local construction authorities on completed buildings, in which there is at least one dwelling. Four types of builders are mentioned in the report, with a natural person mentioned under Code 1, where individual housing construction is included. Family houses and extensions to family houses for individual needs fall under individual housing construction, but construction of dwellings for sale does not. From the survey, the total investment costs for construction including planning and technology (e.g. heating) are obtained. Some types of work, such as gas and power distribution, have to be carried out by specialised companies, and there are also highly specialised jobs such as sanitary installation, roof frames construction, and plumbing systems that are normally done by specialised companies. As far as total investment costs for building a family house by natural persons are concerned, about 50-55 per cent (expert estimate) is deducted on average from the costs for work done by specialised companies (depending on whether a family house or an extension is involved) and the remaining 45–50 per cent is allocated to individual housing construction.

The second data source is Household Budget Survey. It is used for evaluating intermediate consumption for individual housing construction, and the volume of reconstruction that is not included in the surveys taken by the planning and building control authorities. In the household budget survey, a special group of expenditures related to construction of family houses is measured. These expenditures are not included in the final consumption of households and applied to two items: (1) goods for construction or reconstruction of a house or dwelling, and (2) purchased services for construction or reconstruction of dwellings.

To the estimated intermediate consumption, own work of builders (households) is added. Consumption is estimated from the ratio of wages (15%) and operating surplus (15%) to intermediate consumption of goods at smaller construction companies. The difference between the total volume of output and individual housing construction is then taken to be the value of reconstruction made individually.

2.3.3 Own-account output of agricultural products

Own-account output of agricultural products is derived from household budget data, Farm Accountancy Data Network (FADN) statistics, forestry statistics and from expert estimates. The output is estimated as the own consumption of agricultural and food products, which is measured separately in household budgets. Intermediate consumption relating to own-account output of agricultural products was estimated for 1995 by experts and is extrapolated for the following years. The family budget statistics have been updated for the year 2000.

The FADN data related to own final consumption is obtained from the Research Institute of Agricultural Economics. This institute maintains the Farm Accountancy Data Network (FADN). The survey was carried out in March 2000 and included 1204 agricultural enterprises. The data acquired via this survey relate only to agricultural households with information on their structure of agricultural products.

The source of forestry data for agricultural own final consumption is the *Report on Forestry of the Czech Republic*, published by the Ministry of Agriculture. It was found that most households collect berries and mushrooms. Experts estimate the proportion of berries collected for own final consumption and the market. Estimates produced by experts on the volume and structure of forest products are presented in Table 3.

Table 4 presents the summary of agricultural products for households own final consumption included in national accounts for 2000. Because the data taken from the family budget include all households, data from FADN are deducted from it.

Table 3. Forest products, 2000
(million CZK)

Forest products gathered by households	Total output	Estimates by experts of the proportion (percentage) destined for own consumption	Output for own final consumption by households	Output destined for the market
Mushrooms	2 007	80	1 606	402
Blueberries	985	50	492	492
Raspberries	219	95	208	11
Blackberries	146	95	139	7
Cranberries	109	90	98	11
Elder-berries	184	10	18	166
Total	**3 650**		**2 561**	**1 089**

Table 4. Self-supplied agricultural products, 2000
(million CZK)

Product	Total	HBS	FADN	Forest products
Pig meat	2 280	2 280		
Beef, other meat, edible offal	581	578	3	
Rabbit meat	2 617	2 617		
Pig meat smoked, butcher goods	722	722		
Canned meat	144	144		
Poultry	957	957		
Lard and bacon	337	337		
Eggs	1 800	1 198	602	
Milk	279		279	
Potatoes	1 303	515	788	
Fresh vegetables	2 624	1 694	930	
Fresh fruit of the temperate zone	4 776	4 630	146	
Other food and drink	2 539	1 607	932	
Grapes	468	202	266	
Spirits and other alcoholic drinks	552	552		
Forest products	2 561			2 561
Total	**24 540**	**18 033**	**3 946**	**2 561**

2.4 N4: Legal persons not surveyed

Timely updating of the statistical registers is most important for all the national statistics. The standard technique adopted in the EU countries is the permanent access to the administrative databases of the income tax, VAT and social insurance contributions by statistical offices. In autumn 2002, the Business Register was updated for the first time with the income-tax payers' database. In doing so, the number of active natural persons was increased by 79667 units and the number of active legal persons was increased by 2550 units for 2000. At the same time, a substantial change in the industrial structure was made. Since the Business Register serves as the base for the grossing up to the complete set of units, a new grossing up was carried out. The result was the reduction of the GVA of natural persons and an increase of GVA of legal persons. The aggregate impact was an increase of output by 2.3% and intermediate consumption by 1.8%.

2.5 N5: Registered entrepreneurs not surveyed

The units having some kind of economic activity, for which they do not need to be registered in the Business Register but are registered elsewhere (e.g. as tax payers, for social insurance) are included under category N5.

Based on the State Statistical Service Act, the Statistical Business Register includes economic subjects (businesses): all legal and natural persons who have the status of an entrepreneur.

There are no limitations on the size of unit or the kind of activity carried out. As a result of the definition of an entrepreneur, natural persons engaged in arts (sculptors, painters, writers), journalists, professional sportsmen, and other less frequent freelance occupations are not registered and therefore not surveyed. Moreover, the law does not stipulate that all natural persons carrying out production activities must be registered. Some natural persons do not have to be registered for paying income tax.

A comparison of the Business Register with the register of health and social insurance contributors does not help in obtaining a complete coverage either because natural persons do not need to register for social insurance if their incomes are only from author's royalty or rent. And there is no need for a natural person to register for health insurance if the natural person's income is from rent only.

The extent and nature of activities not recorded in the Business Register but officially reported in tax returns such as author's royalties, income of artists and sportsmen (§ 7 of Income Tax Act clearly defines the industries: 748 for author's royalties; 923 for artists; and 926 for sportsmen) was obtained based on comparison of data reported in tax returns and in the P4-01 questionnaire. Income from renting real estates and movables (§ 9 of Income Tax Act), from gardens and a number of other similar activities (§ 10 of Income Tax Act) was taken from the tax returns as reported. Intermediate consumption was estimated with reference to similar activities reported.

Table 5. Registered entrepreneurs not surveyed, 2000
(million CZK)

Income Tax Act	Gross output	Intermediate consumption	Value added
§ 7 (incomes of entrepreneurs)	4 561		
§ 9 (income from renting)	21 503		
§ 10 (other incomes)	616		
Total	**26 680**	**5 330**	**21 350**

The estimate (Table 5) does not directly include under-threshold production activities for which it is not obligatory to submit tax returns. Deliberately concealed activities are not included either (see N3 and N6). There are only indirect indications available for estimation. It is presumed that such activities are indirectly included in national accounts via adjustments made in balancing the flow of commodities.

2.6 N6: Producers deliberately misreporting

Under-reporting is widespread in the Czech Republic. Reporting units resort to diminishing their tax assessment bases and social and health insurance contributions. This is most frequent for reporting units where the rate of control is fairly low and the proprietor or management is interested in making savings. In the framework of the pilot survey on "Exhaustiveness of the Czech National Accounts", a special survey focused on under-reporting was undertaken in 1999. Its results were used in national accounts for 1997 to 2000. Within the Eurostat Exhaustiveness project 2002, a new survey was conducted to review the previous survey outcomes. Due to the nature of the phenomenon, the principle of anonymity of respondents had to be adhered to or else the respondents would not have provided true answers for fear of legal recourse against them or their clients. That is why reporting units were not approached, instead experts were asked to make estimates based on their experience. The respondents mostly included accountants, tax and financial advisors and auditors. They responded to a questionnaire, by describing the situation not in their units but by generalizing their experience with clients. This approach gives an objective insight into the subject at hand.

The questionnaire requested that the described units be itemized according to CZ-NACE categories and size categories (there are four categories for numbers of employees: 0, 1-19, 20-99, 100 and more). The extent and reason of under-reporting was also requested against the following five book items and sub-items: concealed sales/revenues, overestimated material costs, overestimated costs of services, concealed wages costs, and concealed capitalization of fixed assets. Respondents were also asked to estimate the tendency to under-report in the last five years.

To ensure wide coverage, chambers of auditors, tax and financial advisers and accountants were contacted. Respondents were identified by conducting an electronic search. The chambers thus contacted provided their members' databases. Consequently, questionnaires were sent out to 3 000 e-mail addresses. Responses could be received either by e-mail or by post.

Average rates of intentional distortion (adjusted for outliers) were calculated by cross categories of the subject of activity (CZ-NACE) and the size of unit i.e. number of employees. They were presented for each accounting item of sales, consumption of material, consumed services, and wages. Due to the small number of responses in the 2003 survey, these rates were calculated without such cross categorisation for that year. The aggregated average rates of intentional distortion of data in 1999 and 2003 are listed in Table 6.

These rates were then applied to the respective categories of statistically observed units (for the 1999 survey, different rates of under-reporting for each size category were applied; for the 2003 survey, same rates of under-reporting for different size categories were applied). The estimate of output was made only for those industries selected by experts, whereas intermediate consumption was estimated for all. The estimate of under-reported output was applied to small and medium-sized private non-financial enterprises (S.11002) and entrepreneurs - natural persons (S.14) only.

Table 6. Rates of intentional distortion of the reported data
(per cent)

CZ-NACE	Revenues		Materials		Services		Wages	
	1999	2003	1999	2003	1999	2003	1999	2003
A+B	12.28	0.00	2.60	0.00	0.54	0.00	3.05	0.00
C+D+E	5.41	1.76	2.98	0.72	3.11	1.92	1.00	0.26
F+I	9.90	7.88	8.42	8.09	8.39	7.82	2.99	6.50
G+H	23.08	8.29	9.50	5.13	12.15	6.91	7.85	6.41
J+K+L+M+N+O	2.56	2.27	5.38	3.55	10.88	5.60	0.34	0.38
Total	**8.74**	**5.12**	**4.40**	**4.08**	**7.69**	**5.06**	**2.63**	**3.29**

The calculation of intentional under-reported or over-reported values by each item is shown in the Table 7. A comparison of the 2003 and 1999 survey results revealed only a small difference in the share of value added of N6 adjustment in the value added of the whole economy: 5.1 per cent (2003 survey) and 4.8 per cent (1999 survey). However, bigger differences were understandably observed for individual industries (or industry groups that were created for the analysis) and for individual items. For example, in the 2003 survey from a total amounting to 30.144 million CZK, 12.813 million CZK or 43 per cent of overestimation of costs of services was ascribable to industries F+I; in the 1999 survey, from a total of 19.189 million CZK, 5.597 million CZK or 29 per cent was ascribable to industries F+I.

Table 7. Estimation of intentional misreporting of data
(million CZK)

CZ-NACE	Gross output P.1	Intermediate consumption P.2		Wages and salaries D.11	Value added B.1g	Operating surplus / Mixed income B.2.3g	Share of total Value Added by NACE
		Materials	Services				Percentage
				1999			
A+B	5 196	604	38	586	5 838	5 252	7.7
C+D+E	6 473	4 887	1 328	1 105	12 688	11 583	2.1
F+I	15 303	4 642	5 597	1 462	25 542	24 080	7.5
G+H	32 606	2 494	6 392	4 699	41 492	36 793	13.3
J+K+L+M+N+O	1 890	1 092	5 833	129	8 815	8 686	1.4
Total	**61 468**	**13 718**	**19 189**	**7 981**	**94 375**	**86 394**	**4.8**
				2003			
A+B	0	0	0	0	0	0	0
C+D+E	2 414	1 329	1 483	42	5 226	5 184	0.8
F+I	23 369	9 133	12 813	1 850	45 315	43 465	13.3
G+H	27 374	3 512	8 731	3 054	39 617	36 563	12.7
J+K+L+M+N+O	2 877	1 570	7 117	56	11 564	11 508	1.8
Total	**56 034**	**15 544**	**30 144**	**5 002**	**101 722**	**96 720**	**5.1**

To improve the exhaustiveness of Czech NA, the Ministry of Finance was contacted to discuss the possibility of use of fiscal audit data in NA. Following the discussion, it was concluded that the manner in which the Ministry of Finance conducts fiscal audit and the form of the final results do not comply with exhaustiveness requirements.

Fiscal audits are conducted with the intention of preventing tax evasion and are targeted at particular areas and firms where high risk of tax evasion can be expected. Such selective results cannot be converted into estimates of exhaustiveness for the entire population of economic subjects. Moreover data on fiscal audits are not provided in any suitable structural form.

2.7 N7: Other statistical deficiencies

Under type N7, wages and salaries in kind and tips are estimated.

2.7.1 Wages and salaries in kind

Types of incomes in kind quantified in Czech National Accounts:
- wages & salaries in kind (taxable);
- meal vouchers;
- contributions from social funds;
- per diem for business trips;
- expenditures on clothing of regular members of the armed forces;
- other social expenditure (covered from costs);
- housing contribution;
- goods at a reduction and provided free of charge;
- remitted interest;
- company cars used for personal needs;
- board and lodging provided free of charge.

Three main data sources are used for quantifying the individual types of wages and salaries in kind: (1) financial and statistical questionnaires of costs and revenues linked with economic activity of institutional units of all residential sectors, (2) the statistical survey of total labour costs (TLC), and (3) some items estimated by experts.

The following items in national accounts are obtained from the **financial and statistical questionnaires**:

Wages and salaries in kind - as a part of taxable wages and salaries.

Per diem on business trips - meals and drinks are estimated as part of surveyed travelling costs (30 per cent as part of wages and salaries in kind, 70 per cent as part of intermediate consumption, in the case of small enterprises with less than 20 employees, 15 per cent as part of wages and salaries in kind and 85 per cent as part of intermediate consumption). Estimation of proportion of per diem on business trips to travelling costs has to be updated. Travelling costs are not surveyed in banks and non-profit institutions serving households. Total value of travelling costs inclusive of per diem for business trips is included in intermediate consumption.

Statutory social cost and other social cost - social costs are tax-liable contributions by employers to employees for (a) running costs of sport, recreation and leisure time facilities, (b) boarding, (c) recreation, (d) culture and sport, (e) exchange action, (f) social assistance, (g) supplementary pension agreements and (h) anniversary gifts. Social costs also include non-taxable contributions such as severance pay. In business accounts the costs cited above are not included under wage costs, instead they are covered under: statutory social costs, other social costs or various operating costs, social fund, fund of cultural and social demands (FKSP) or other company funds or profit.

Statistical reports on total labour costs (TLC)

All industries and all sectors excluding the household sector are covered by the labour costs survey. Sample surveys are used for units with 1 to 499 employees, whereas units with more than 499 employees are fully covered. Most items of income in kind are surveyed by the TLC survey. Exceptions are per diem on business trips, board and lodging provided free of charge or at reduced prices to employees of restaurants, hotels, company's canteens and in agriculture. Most of the aforementioned items are in compliance with the Council Regulation No. 530/1999 on the organization of structural statistics on labour costs.

Wages & salaries in kind - as per the law on wages, part of the wage income can be paid in kind. For tax reasons, the value of goods and services provided to employees (according to Article 13 of the law on wages) are recorded as part of wages and salaries. It is considered a part of effective wage income and not benefits provided to current and former employees and members of their families.

Meal vouchers provided by employers to employees or contributions of employers to operating costs of canteens - these are estimated by calculating the total annual difference between canteen meals' costs and revenues from sale of canteen luncheon vouchers, including also contribution of employees on purchase of meal vouchers.

Contributions from social funds - these comprise finance paid from social funds (created for instance in banks, insurance companies) or Fund for Cultural and Social Needs (created for instance in budgetary organizations). These expenditures are used for motivation, social assistance, programmes to improve employee qualifications, for recreation, cultural and sport events.

Expenditures on clothing of non-civil sections of the Ministry of Defence, the Ministry of the Interior and the Ministry of Justice - since 2001, the TLC survey has covered the non-civil sector as well. All items of income-in-kind surveyed in TLC are included in relevant types of income-in-kind (Prior to 2001 these items were not surveyed separately but reported as one figure). Expenditures on clothing related only to regular members of the armed forces. Income-in-kind for 2000 was adjusted according to the number of regular members of armed forces in 2000.

Other social expenditure - covered under costs of an institutional unit, include expenditures on labour force regeneration such as contribution to rehabilitation, health-care facilities, recreational facilities, pre-school childcare, personal services provided to employees, and contribution for transportation to work.

Housing contributions of the employer - to assist employees and their families with purchase of housing or housing equipment, calculated as the difference between expenditures on maintenance and administration of housing and rent revenues, and allowances granted to employees in connection with housing, installation and moving.

Discount on the company's goods - consists of items sold to employees at a reduced price or free of charge. It is measured as the difference between the cost price and the price at which the products are sold to staff, or the cost price of goods supplied free of charge.

Contribution in the form of remitted interests and reduction of price of company shares - consists of loans provided to employees at reduced or even zero rates of interest, or shares provided to employees for free or below market prices. It also includes finance on the settlement of the difference in interest of corporate savings schemes. Presently, experts' estimates are used to measure this item.

Company cars used for personal needs - tax regulations dictate that an enterprise that provides company cars for personal use shall include a part of its expenses in wage incomes of employees for taxation purposes. The estimate is made on the basis of the number of cars used for personal needs as established by the total labour costs survey. The calculation assumes a monthly depreciation of cars by 1 per cent of input price (according to the Income Tax Act, input price is assumed to the CZK 500 000 for year 2000) and car usage for a period of 12 months (a typical calculation is thus: number of cars * 500 000 * 1/100 (as depreciation)* 12 (months)).

Board and lodging provided free of charge - comprises board and lodging provided free of charge or at reduced prices to employees of restaurants, hotels, company canteens and in agriculture. These are not recorded in business accounting. Estimates in national accounts are based on the assumption that consumption per employee amounts to CZK 50 (estimated average price of a meal in a company canteen) for a period of 100 days, where the number of employees is established by the total labour costs survey. In agriculture, where greater seasonality is expected, only 25% of employees are taken into consideration. Calculations are made for industries 011 to 014 (agriculture) and 551 to 555 (hotels, restaurants and other provisions of lodging).

Estimation of different types of income in kind is arrived at by combining the above mentioned data sources with other data sources available for a particular sector. Final estimates for year 2000 and adjustments made to different items in national accounts are shown in Table 8. "Impl." in the table indicates that the figure is implicitly included in the primary data source and the NA items do not need any adjustments.

2.7.2 Tips and gratuities

CZSO assumes that tips are given to personnel in the following areas: (1) restaurants and bars, (2) hairdressing and other beauty treatment, (3) physical well-being activities and (4) taxis.

Tips are calculated following two methods: (1) final consumption expenditure (Table 9) and (2) numbers of persons receiving tips (Table 10). The first method is based on final consumption expenditures of households and foreign visitors structured according to COICOP. Share of tips in different areas correspond to local practice and depend on quality of services. According to experts, tips vary from 3 to 10 per cent of total payment.

Table 8. Wages in kind and tips: estimation and recording in NA, 2000
(million CZK)

	Type of income in kind	Output	IC	W & S		HPC	Interest
				Total	Added		
	SNA codes	P.1	P.2	D.11	D.11	P.31	D.41
1.	Wages & salaries in kind (taxable)	Impl.		997	Impl.	997	
2.	Meal vouchers	Impl.	-426	9 607	2 152	4 803	
3.	Contributions from social funds	Impl.	-192	3 705	967	3 705	
4.	Per diem for business trips		Impl.	7 923	Impl.	Impl.	
5.	Expenditures on clothing of regular members of the armed forces		-327	327	327	327	
6.	Other social expenditure (covered from costs)		-1 365	1365	1 365	1 365	
7.	Housing contribution	267	-217	484	484	484	
8.	Goods at a reduction and provided free of charge	122		122	122	122	
9.	Remitted interest			130	130		130
10.	Company cars used for personal needs	3 734		3 734	3 734	3 734	
11.	Board and lodging provided free of charge	742		742	742	742	
12.	Tips	3 269		3 269	3 269	Impl.	
Total		**8 134**	**-2 527**	**32 405**	**13 292**	**16 279**	**130**

Table 9. Tips: estimation as percentage of final consumption, 2000
(million CZK)

	Total	Restaurants	Bars	Taxi	Hairdresser	
					For men	For women
Final consumption expenditure of households and non-residents	58 283	27 852	16 875	3 625	1 015	8 916
Percentage of tips		7.0	3.5	5.0	10.0	5.0
Tips (million CZK)	**3 270**	**1 950**	**591**	**181**	**102**	**446**

Table 10. Tips – estimation by number of persons, 2000
(million CZK)

	Total	Restaurants	Bars	Other land transport	Other service activities
Number of persons – total	295 659	112 268	3 850	131 728	47 813
Number of employees	192 926	80 111	2 701	96 365	13 749
Number of working owners of companies	102 733	32 157	1 149	35 363	34 064
Workers with an opportunity to get tips	51 430	22 454	3 850	13 173	11 953
Tips per day		420	650	70	220
Average number of working days		211 65	211 65	201 76	205 88
Tips (million CZK)	**3 253**	**1 996**	**530**	**186**	**541**

The second method is based on numbers of persons active in the areas mentioned above, amount of tips per day and average number of working days per year. For this purpose, two basic data sources are used: Labour Force Survey and average numbers of working persons according to main data sources used for compiling national accounts (data at the CZ-NACE three-digit activity level).

An attempt was made to approximate results from both methods. Based on a comparison of the results of the two methods, tips are estimated to be 3270 million CZK for the year 2000.

CZSO assumes that tipping takes place in non-financial corporations and the household sector. The total amount of tips was included in the output and income calculation according to the number of employees in these sectors.

2.8 Summary of exhaustiveness adjustments: output approach

Table 11 presents all exhaustiveness adjustments made in the value added for 2000.

3. Exhaustiveness adjustments: expenditure approach

All adjustments made in expenditure approach have some relation to output approach as the two approaches, except for household private consumption and exports and imports, have almost the same data sources for gross output and intermediate consumption, and also main adjustments to household final consumption expenditures (HPCE) are made together in both approaches.

Table 11. Summary of adjustments by output approach 2000
(million CZK)

Components	Type of non-exhaustiveness adjustment							Total		
	N1	N2	N3	N4	N5	N6	N7	Absolute	% of item	% of GDP
Gross Output	12 941	6 169	58 001	86 144	26 680	65 787	7 199	262 921	4.9	
Intermediate consumption	2 592	1 234	30 743	53 291	5 330	-29 307	0	63 883	1.9	
GVA	10 349	4 935	27 258	32 853	21 350	95 094	7 199	199 038	10.3	9.3
Per cent of GDP	0.5	0.2	1.3	1.5	1.0	4.4	0.3	9.3		

3.1 Household final consumption expenditure

Many sources are used for adjustment of household private consumption (HPC). The main source is the Household Budget Survey (HBS). The basic sample of HBS includes households of employees, households of farmers (including employees), households of entrepreneurs and households of pensioners. In addition to the basic sample, supplementary samples are also used, which contain information on income and purchases of households with children and minimum-income households. The basic reporting file of the family budgets for the year 2000 consists of budgets of 1 800 households of employees, 300 households of farmers, 450 households of entrepreneurs and 700 households of pensioners.

For HPCE, HBS data are applied to one person in CZK in COICOP classification. The HBS department also processes data on purchases of households according to net income per person. Subsequently, the estimate for 2000 was revised by shifting the general average per capita in the direction of the average of the tenth (upper) decile of households with the highest monetary income.

HBS data are, in some cases, grossed up or replaced by data from other sources or expert estimations, if these are more precise. The size of these adjustments is shown in Table 12.

Estimation of illegal services (N 2) - is based on special research. Prostitution services have been included in national accounts and the part consumed by residents constitutes part of household private consumption.

Production for own final consumption (N 3) - the estimation is based on three data sources: HBS, FADN and a forestry report published by the Ministry of Agriculture.

Private consumption of entrepreneurs (N 6) - is based on calculation of the hidden economy, namely on estimation of over-reported material and service costs. Reporting units who aim to reduce their tax assessment bases and social and health insurance contributions intentionally distort their figures by reporting an increase in their costs. Over-reported costs partly apply to the fictitious costs and partly concern private consumption reported as business costs.

The value of goods and services intended for final personal use of entrepreneurs is estimated at 75 per cent of over-reported material and 15 per cent of over-reported services.

Table 12. Household private consumption by type of adjustments, 2000
(million CZK)

Products (by COICOP)	Correction of HBS Total	Alternative sources (-/+)	Consumption of residents abroad	Consumption in social organisations	Illegal activities N.2	Own final consumption N.3	Personal consumption of entrepreneurs N.6	Wages in kind N.7
1 Food, non-alcoholic beverages	20 972		2 228			18 622		122
2 Alcoholic beverages, tobacco	73 376	71 087	710			1 579		0
3 Clothing and footwear	2 904		2 203				374	327
4a Rents	4 956	4 246	226					484
4b Housing, water, electricity, gas	324		194			-347	327	150
5 Household equipment	6 186		1 599			-115	4 702	
6 Health	483		108			-171		546
7 Transport	11 987		6 032			-166	1 397	4 724
8 Communication	1 600		15				1 585	
9 Recreation, cultural and sport services	26 218	14 800	2 807			1 783	2 515	4 313
10 Education	68		0					68
11 Hotels, cafes and restaurant	13 424		4 934				2 945	5 545
12 Miscellaneous goods and services	24 369	18 076	637	3 644	2 012			
TOTAL	**186 867**	**108 209**	**21 693**	**3 644**	**2 012**	**21 185**	**13 845**	**16 279**
Per cent of total HPC	**16.9**	**9.8**	**2.0**	**0.3**	**0.2**	**1.9**	**1.3**	**1.5**

Consumption of products received as wage-in-kind (N 7) - to estimate the consumption in kind of soldiers, the Czech Statistical Office used the statistical questionnaire of budgetary organizations in 1999. At present, the consumption in kind of soldiers is calculated from the total intermediate consumption of budgetary organizations for defence and security.

Alcoholic beverages, tobacco (N 7) - data for these items are calculated on the basis of the excise duty (consumption tax). Calculations for domestic goods and imports are made separately. Also, average prices are needed to calculate representative expenditures of households for alcoholic beverages and tobacco.

3.2 Final consumption expenditure of general government and NPISH

Exhaustiveness adjustments in the government sector are related to wages in kind only. Expenditure estimates for non-profit institutions serving households are recorded in the Czech national accounts based on a sample survey. Exhaustiveness adjustments in this sector concern wages in kind only.

3.3 Gross fixed capital formation

The treatment of the concept of gross fixed capital formation (GCFC) in Czech National Accounts depends, to a large extent, on the treatment of the concept in business accounting. Mostly the same data sources as those used for the calculation of output and intermediate consumption are used for the compilation of acquisition of non-financial assets. These data are partially supplemented with data on acquisitions of assets from the special statistical questionnaire on investment. For all statistical surveys, grossing-up estimates of non-response are made.

For GCFC, four types of exhaustiveness adjustments are made:

Balancing of acquisitions and disposals and of free of charge transfers of existing fixed assets (N6) - Due to the specific nature of economic development during the transformation process in the Czech Republic (especially the restitution process), and sample surveys of some enterprises, the method of balancing of acquisitions and disposals and of free transfers of existing fixed assets between individual sub-sectors is applied. In addition to statistical questionnaire data, also information from the National Property Fund on free-of-charge transfers is used. When the balancing process is finished, only taxes on transfer of property constitute the difference between acquisitions and disposals of existing fixed assets. This reality does not correspond to the ESA95 methodology, because of valuation of disposals of existing assets at selling prices, i.e. including professional and similar charges. The size of these adjustments in 2000 was 8142 million CZK.

Balancing of commodity flows (N6) - Initial estimates of GFCF are not made within the framework of supply-and-use tables. Results from the supply-and-use analysis are then incorporated in figures of GFCF. After the supply-and-use analysis in 2000, no adjustments to the total value of GFCF were needed.

Business register updating (N4) - The business register is updated based on the information on enterprises activity according to their fiscal statements. This resulted in a change in GFCF by non-financial corporations about 8378 million CZK and by entrepreneurs – natural persons in the household sector – of about 583 million CZK.

Individual housing construction, including reconstructions (N3) - Individual housing construction is recorded in the national accounts under the volume of acquired tangible fixed assets by the household sector. The calculation of individual housing construction is based on two data sources. The first are the statistical reports of the Building Control Department on completed constructions, which provide information on construction by natural persons. The second data source is the household budget survey. In 2000, the total value of individual housing construction amounted to 34830 million CZK.

3.4 Changes in inventories

The calculation of changes in inventories is based on variation of stocks at the beginning and end of the year. To settle the situation in inventories or changes in inventories, Czech statistics exploits data sources used for GDP estimates following the production approach. For changes in inventories, two types of exhaustiveness adjustments are made:

Balancing of commodity flows (N6) - final results of changes in inventories are verified by the process of balancing the supply-and-use tables. In 2000, the supply-and-use analysis did not provide any changes in the total value of change in inventories (indicator P.52).

Business register updating (N4) - new data sources led to some changes in the business register. Due to the updating of the business register in 2000, the value of changes in inventories has resulted in a modification of about 877 million CZK for non-financial corporations and about 753 million CZK for entrepreneurs and natural persons in the household sector.

3.5 Exports and imports of goods and services

To ensure exhaustiveness of exports and imports of goods and services, the consumption of residents working abroad, the consumption of non-resident workers, and exports of prostitution services are estimated.

The estimate of the consumption of the resident working abroad – N 7

The estimation of the consumption of residents working abroad is based on the number of residents working abroad (measured quarterly in the Labour Force Sample Survey) and on annual estimates of consumption of food, manufactured goods and services per person (derived from the household budget statistics).

The estimation of consumption of non-resident workers – N 7

The estimation of the consumption of non-resident workers (N7) is based on the number of non-residents working in the Czech Republic (divided into groups according to country of origin of the non-resident and estimated consumer habits; data on the number of the valid licenses for the foreigners' employment in the Czech Republic provided by the Employment and Wages Statistics Department of the CZSO) and on annual consumption of food, manufactured goods and services per person (derived from the household budget statistics).

3.6 Summary of exhaustiveness adjustments: expenditure approach

All of the exhaustiveness adjustments made in the final version of each of the individual components of final use of GDP for 2000 are shown Table 13.

4. Exhaustiveness adjustments: income approach

Since the income approach of GDP estimates uses the same data sources and non-response estimation procedures as the production approach, the provision of exhaustiveness of national economy by the income approach has the same pros and cons as the production approach. Considering the income approach to GDP compilation, only wages and salaries, net operating surplus and mixed income are influenced by exhaustiveness adjustments. To ensure exhaustiveness of individual income components of GDP, attention was paid to estimates of wages-in-kind and of wages within the framework of intentional distortion of reported data. Table 14 presents a summary of the exhaustiveness adjustments for the income approach.

Table 13. Summary of adjustments by expenditure approach, 2000
(million CZK)

Components	Type of non-exhaustiveness adjustment							Total		
	N1	N2	N3	N4	N5	N6	N7	Absolute	% of item	% of GDP
Household final consumption expenditure		2 012	21 185	0	11 393	14 451	4 866	53 907	4.9	2.5
Purchases of goods and services		2 012				14 451		16 463	1.5	0.8
Production for own final use			21 185					21 185	1.9	1.0
Other HFC components							4 866	4 866	0.4	0.2
Final consumption of general government								0	0.0	0.0
Final consumption of NPISH						978		978	7.3	0.0
Gross fixed capital formation			31 482	9 300		13 369		54 151	9.2	2.5
Changes in inventories				3 929		-16 769		-12 840	-33.8	-0.6
Exports							4 371	4 371	0.3	0.2
Imports							870	870	0.1	0.0
Total		2 012	52 667	13 229	11 393	12 029	8 367	99 697	4.6	4.6
Per cent of GDP	0.0	0.1	2.5	0.6	0.5	0.6	0.4	4.6		

Table 14. Summary of adjustments by income approach, 2000
(million CZK)

	Item	Type of non-exhaustiveness adjustment							Total		
		N1	N2	N3	N4	N5	N6	N7	Absolute	% of item	% of GDP
D.11	Wages and salaries	0	0	272	0	0	8 355	8 339	16 966	2.08	0.66
125 D.12	Employers' social contributions	0	0	0	0	0	0	0	0	0.00	0.00
D.21	Taxes on products	0	0	0	0	0	0	0	0	0.00	0.00
D.29	Other taxes on production	0	0	0	0	0	0	0	0	0.00	0.00
D.31	Subsidies on products (-)	0	0	0	0	0	0	0	0	0.00	0.00
D.39	Other subsidies on production (-)	0	0	0	0	0	0	0	0	0.00	0.00
K.1	Consumption of fixed capital	0	0	0	0	0	0	0	0	0.00	0.00
B.2n	Net operating surplus	0	0	0	0	0	40 996	-66	40 930	5.93	1.60
B.3	Mixed income	12 593	4 026	25 515	0	14 151	55 313	-2	111 596	32.36	4.36
	FISIM (-)	0	0	0	0	0	0	0	0	0.00	0.00
B.1g	Gross domestic product	12 593	4 026	25 787	0	14 151	104 664	8 271	169 492	6.62	6.62
Per cent of GDP		**0.49**	**0.16**	**1.01**	**0.00**	**0.55**	**4.09**	**0.32**	**6.62**	**6.62**	**6.62**

ESTONIA

Definition and concepts

The Statistical Office of Estonia (SOE) participated in the Eurostat Project on Exhaustiveness in 2002. During 2005, the methods of measuring the different types of non-observed economy (NOE) have been revised and improved. Adjustments for some types of NOE, such as illegal economy, have been recalculated according to the new method. The following types of non-exhaustiveness are considered as most important in National Accounts and are currently included in the GDP estimates: adjustments for unregistered underground economy (non-exhaustiveness type N1), misreporting (type N6) and other GDP undercoverage (type N7). Illegal activities (type N2) are also estimated and included in GDP.

The NOE has been estimated mainly in the non-financial corporations and household sector. Minor adjustments are made in the non-profit institutions serving households (NPISH) and financial corporations sector for income in kind. Also, some adjustments are made in the general government sector.

It is assumed that illegal activities, such as prostitution and smuggling of tobacco, alcoholic beverages and fuel, are confined to non-financial corporations sector. The trade of drugs is also included in the calculations for the household sector.

The non-exhaustiveness adjustments to GDP by production approach are made to all institutional sectors and economic activities. The estimates by production approach have been related to the GDP expenditure approach estimates.

Sources and estimation methods – production approach

The main data sources for production approach are: Structural Business Statistics (SBS), the data from Estonian Tax and Customs Board and Estonian Labour Force Survey (ELFS).

Adjustments for unregistered economy (N1)

This type of non-exhaustiveness adjustments is based on the labour input method. The discrepancy between employment data from the supply side based on the ELFS, and the data from demand side (SBS), is considered as hidden employment and is used for estimating the non-observed production. This type of adjustment is made for underground activities of producers in non-financial corporations and household sector. For households sector, the data from Estonian Tax and Customs Board and SBS are used in the calculations.

Adjustments for illegal economy (N2)

The estimations of illegal activities cover prostitution, production and distribution of drugs, and smuggling of tobacco, alcohol and motor fuel. The administrative data, such as SBS, can not be used for illegal economy. The calculations of illegal economy are based on information from the

Estonian Police Board, sociological studies, Estonian Tax and Customs Board (quantities of confiscated products) and the media (research done by journalists).

The estimation of prostitution is made from the supply side based on the number of brothel-clubs and rented apartments. The turnover of prostitution is calculated using the average price of sex service, the number of services per day per brothel and the number of brothel-clubs and apartment-brothels.

The estimation of drugs is made from the supply side based on the police data on seized quantities by type of narcotics, prices of different drugs and the assumption on seizure rates. Based on other countries' experience, it is supposed that the authorities confiscate approximately 5% of the goods circulating on illegal market.

At present, the estimates of smuggling are based on the number of confiscated cigarettes obtained from Estonian Tax and Customs Board and the assumption on seizure rates.

Adjustments for misreporting (N6)

Misreporting of economic indicators by producers is considered as one of the most important types of hidden activities in Estonia. Main reasons for underreporting of turnover, wages and salaries and over-reporting of expenses by corporations are the evasion of value added tax, social security contributions and income tax. The principal aim of underreporting of income by unincorporated enterprises is the evasion of income tax payable by sole proprietors.

Adjustments made for underreporting are intended to cover output, wages and salaries and profits that are not recorded in the business accounts of the enterprises. Data sources and methods used for the estimation of possible underreporting of wages and profits are:
- results of household surveys by the Estonian Institute of Economic Research (EIER) indicating the scope of the payments of "envelope" salaries;
- comparison of the declared per capita wages, salaries and profits between enterprises by strata and by industry, based on data from statistical surveys;
- correction of wages, salaries and profits if data are implausibly lower than the corresponding industry average, based on analysis made by national accountants.

Estimates of output, intermediate consumption and value added of unincorporated enterprises are based on administrative data (i.e. tax declarations on business income of sole proprietors from the Tax and Customs Board). The primary information declared by sole proprietors are regarded as not of very good quality, as producers tend to give inadequate information on their revenues and costs, increasing the costs and hiding business income. Other reasons for poor quality are that: (1) according to the law on bookkeeping, the business accounts of sole proprietors are not required to be audited; (2) due to limited resources, Estonian Tax and Customs Board mostly concentrates on the audits and analyses of the tax declarations of large enterprises.

In National Accounts, the following adjustments for underdeclaration of unincorporated units are made:
- gross output and value added are corrected upwards using the adjustment coefficients for misreporting of small enterprises;
- intermediate consumption is consequently adjusted downwards.

Other GDP undercoverage (N7)

In national accounts, estimates for wages and salaries in kind are based on two sources, administrative data and household budget survey (HBS). Tax and Customs Board data is the starting point in the calculation of income in kind of corporations and NPISH sectors. HBS is the additional source used for the comparisons and further calculations. Administrative data are adjusted to the outcomes of HBS, which is considered to be more exhaustive as respondents may underestimate expenses on fringe benefits in completing the tax declarations to avoid double taxation.

For general government sector, wages and salaries in kind are estimated by using the statement of execution of state and local budgets, where the following payments are treated as wages and salaries in kind: food and housing allowances of employees of certain categories, daily allowances, use of business cars, etc.

Adjustments to outputs are made for the private use of business cars and for goods and services produced by employer and provided to employees cheaper or free of charge. Income in kind is often included as intermediate costs by the enterprises that respond to the SBS survey of enterprises, while they should be counted as compensation of employees according to ESA95. Therefore, the expenditures on goods and services provided to the employees for free are reallocated from intermediate consumption to the compensation of employees.

As the direct primary data for tips are not available, the calculations are based on experts' estimates using all available information. Estimates for tips are made in hotels, restaurants and taxi services. Average amount of tips was estimated by taking into account the location and size of the unit.

Exports and imports

Imports are taken into account in the calculations of illegal economy. On the basis of available data, it is estimated that imports exist for smuggling and the trade of drugs. The Statistical office does not give estimation on exports due to the lack of data.

Table 1 gives an overview of the figures of NOE by economic activities in 2000.

Table 1. Summary of NOE adjustments by economic activity in 2000
(million EEK)

NACE activity	Type of non-exhaustiveness				Total	Per cent of GDP	Per cent of initial value added
	Unregistered economic units N1	Illegal activities N2	Mis-reporting N6	Other under-coverage N7			
A	294.9		29.2	6.7	330.8	0.3	9.3
B	27.1		4.4	0.4	31.8	0.03	13.5
C	4.6		10.6	4.5	19.7	0.02	2.0
D	689.8	68.8	511.3	99.3	1369.2	1.4	9.9
E	0.2		111.5	12.9	124.5	0.1	4.8
F	956.4		277.7	24.0	1258.1	1.3	35.7
G	701.3	423.6	838.2	66.4	2029.5	2.1	23.9
H	184.0		72.9	99.5	356.4	0.4	35.7
I	659.7		562.8	173.8	1396.3	1.5	12.6
J	0.0			50.5	50.5	0.1	1.5
K	138.2		508.5	43.2	689.9	0.7	4.9
L				206.5	206.5	0.2	4.1
M	212.9		9.4	19.6	241.8	0.3	5.8
N	133.6		23.8	9.1	166.5	0.2	6.9
O	43.6	75.0	65.9	12.4	197.0	0.2	9.1
P	0.0				0.03	0.00003	0.1
Total	**4046.3**	**567.4**	**3026.3**	**828.7**	**8468.7**	**8.9**	**11.0**
% of GDP	**4.2**	**0.6**	**3.2**	**0.9**	**8.9**		

FINLAND

1. Introduction

The statistical base for the Finnish national accounts consists of Structural Business Statistics (SBS), Business Tax Register (BTR) and statistical surveys conducted by Statistics Finland. These sources, together with the use of the Business Register and other basic statistics provide a good base for GDP estimates.

The Finnish national accounts are mainly compiled using the production approach. The main source data for calculations i.e. the Business Register and Structural Business Statistics are complete in their coverage of registered economic units. Though these sources provide comprehensive coverage, there can be some problems due to random errors and for other reasons.

The following activities may not be covered by the main sources:
- non-reported data from registered units that are not captured using the normal methods;
- casual (or small) units, and units that remain unregistered for the purpose of tax evasion.

The above activities are targeted in the estimation of the non-observed economy in the national accounts. Estimates are made using special studies, employment comparisons between the Labour Force Survey (LFS) and the national accounts and tax audit data. On the basis of such studies, it is found that the underground economy in Finland is not very marked. The sources and methods used to calculate GDP ensure that the parts of the hidden economy attributable to construction and housing services are included in the national accounts. Tax audits give only an indication of the extent of non-observed activity, as the audits are not representative samples.

While aiming for exhaustiveness of the Finnish GDP, Statistics Finland has also made calculations of the discrepancy between theoretical VAT and actual VAT.

Due to the nature of the methods used, an exact assessment of the hidden economy is not feasible. Furthermore, special surveys on the non-observed economy were done ten years ago, thus pointing towards the need for new studies in order to ensure calculations of NOE. The sources and methods used are based on the work done at the end of the 1990s.

Adjustments for activities of the illegal economy are not included in the Finnish national accounts.

2. Sources and estimation methods

The Finnish national accounts use supply-and-use tables (SUT) in the annual compilation of the accounts. The balancing is done using 957 product level. This also gives possibility to check NOE estimates. Time series of SUT are calculated from 1995 onwards and final data is available in

December t+2. The use of SUT does not necessarily determine the exact level of NOE figures. These have to be checked by new studies in the Finnish national accounts in the future.

2.1 The use of tax audit data

Tax audit data have been available from special surveys since 1996. Due to the methods of selection for auditing, the results are difficult to incorporate into the national accounts. The audits have been almost exclusively of companies where taxation irregularities have been revealed. There have been only two cases (taxis and restaurants) where more general audits have been conducted. For other industries, the audit material gives only an approximation of a likely upper limit of the underground economy.

Due to the limitations of the tax audit method, it can only be used to produce a broad estimate. The tax audit data have therefore been used with other sources of information. Tax audits are concerned with three kinds of income: hidden wages, hidden income and the so-called hidden distribution of dividends. The compilation of the Finnish national accounts is mainly based on the production approach. In this approach the most important of these three components is hidden income, because it increases the total income and output. The other two components form parts of the distribution of value added, which are important in the income approach.

2.2 Examples of methods for calculating underground and informal activities

2.2.1 Construction

The output of construction of buildings by households consists of three parts: output of own-account workers, own-account construction, and own-account workers in the so-called hidden economy. Own-account construction is output entirely for own final use. Other household construction is termed market output.

The output of own-account construction is derived from imputed hours worked in the construction industry and hourly rates for construction work. The hours worked are taken from a survey of the hidden economy in construction from 1990 to 1996, carried out by a private consultant. The imputed rate for construction is the average hourly rate for employees engaged in the construction of buildings, excluding employer social contributions and supplemental wage and salary costs. The value added of construction consists of the value of own-account work calculated in the above manner. After 1996, the output of own-account construction was valued by means of the annual growth in the value of single-family house construction and annual repairs. Compensation of employees and consumption of fixed capital are not calculated for construction.

Output is the sum of value added and intermediate consumption, the proportions of which are estimated to be 35 per cent and 65 per cent respectively.

The base year output of hidden economy own-account workers is estimated by applying hourly rates to imputed working hours. The working hours were obtained as residuals from data in the LFS. The own-account worker's income per hour is the same as the hourly wage for own-account construction, and output is calculated as for own-account construction. The intermediate consumption share of output is presumed to be 25 per cent, i.e. output consists mainly of value added, or in this instance the value of work done, because capital consumption is not calculated for hidden economy own-account workers. It is assumed that own-account work is carried out mainly by households, which acquire the building supplies needed. In the national accounts, annual growth of the output of hidden economy own-account workers is calculated in accordance with annual growth in own-account construction.

3.2.2 Wholesale and retail trade

According to experts, the underground economy does not represent a large part of total sales in wholesale and retail trade. The main reason is the concentration of trade around large corporations and the marginal market share of independent small shopkeepers. Based on a 1995 survey by the Federation of Finnish Commerce and Trade, it was concluded that the share of the underground economy in trade is between 1 and 5 per cent.

A consultancy firm has made estimates of the possible size of hidden income and its influence on measured output, on the basis of the Tax Administration auditing data. Concealed income (additions to the income of businesses) is correlated by branch of activity to the turnover of the audited cases. Multiplying the share of turnover for any concealed income in the audited cases by the turnover data for the population of equivalent industries results in the so-called imputed starting value of the industry as a whole. These values produce an estimate, which is too high for undisclosed income since the majority of businesses manage their affairs appropriately. It is presumed that the real undisclosed income, or missing turnover, of the industry is closer to 20-40 per cent of the imputed starting value of undisclosed income.

The share of output attributed to concealed income is high in certain trade sectors (car sales, repairs, outdoor markets, etc.). Bypassing the cash desk is easy in such industries because most of the customers are private individuals. According to the estimates made by consultants (based on Tax Administration auditing), imputed concealed income in the trade sector was 222 – 444 million FIM in 1997. This would amount to roughly 0.3 to 0.6 per cent of output in the trade sector.

4. Implications and effects on national accounts and GDP estimates

Methods of estimating NOE below refer to the work done five to ten years ago. Of the industries mentioned, the percentage of NOE varies between 0 to 5 per cent of output.

4.1 Construction

The hidden economy in construction was estimated to be 2424 million FIM. This estimate was based on better source statistics for the construction activity and the use of comparisons between different basic data sets.

4.2 Trade

Hidden economy adjustments in trade are made for motor vehicle trade and repairs (one third) and retail trade (two thirds). Only 2 per cent of the adjustments were accounted for by the wholesale trade. Changes in the proportions of intermediate consumption are also made. The adjustments are based on broader use and comparison of source statistics, and a consultant's study. Crosschecks for consistency between trade and manufacturing are also made.

4.3 Hotels and restaurants

The main correction for exhaustiveness is made for the restaurant branch, with only about 15 per cent of the adjustment attributed to hotels. Relative shares of intermediate consumption were also changed. Information from tax audits of 35 restaurants in two small coastal towns in 1997 was used in estimating the total hidden economy for this industry.

4.4 Transport and communication (market activities)

Adjustments were made in road transport and taxi traffic, totalling 1.235 million FIM for output. Intermediate consumption is estimated using the stock of vehicles and average costs, so that it includes intermediate consumption resulting from hidden production without any extra adjustments. The estimates were based on tax audits carried out for all taxis and taxi firms (about 230) in three towns in 1996.

5. Summary results

Adjustments for NOE for various economic activities are summarised in Table 1.

Table 1. NOE of output 2002

Industry	NOE (million Euros)	Per cent of output
Construction, buildings	387	2.7
Transport (land, taxis)	238	5.0
Trade	80	0.8
Hotels, restaurants	98	2.1
Business activities	62	0.4

GEORGIA

1. Introduction

The share of the non-observed activities in the Georgian economy varied little until 2003 but recorded a fall in 2004 from about 33 to 28 per cent. However, the level still remains high.

Table 1. The share of NOE in total output of the economy

	2000	2001	2002	2003	2004
Non-observed output of the national economy - %	33.7	33.4	33.2	33.1	28.3
Non-observed output of the business sector - %	57.8	56.2	55.1	54.9	45.6

As the share of non-observed economy is high, it is vital to estimate it as precisely as possible to guarantee exhaustiveness and quality of national accounts.

2. Sources and estimation methods

2.1 General overview

The analysis of NOE shows that inadequate accounting in small enterprises and the informal sector are the most important reasons for non-exhaustiveness of national accounts.

Part of the production in the informal sector is often for own final use. Therefore, determining the actual volume of informal production is one of the most difficult problems in measuring the non-observed economy. The issue is of particular importance for Georgia due to the large share of the informal sector in the national economy.

Table 2. Share of the informal sector in total value added

	2000	2001	2002	2003	2004	I-II Q. 2005
Share of the informal sector - %	38.0	38.0	34.0	36.0	31.0	30.0

The decrease from 38 to 30 per cent is mostly due to the GDP growth; the volume of the informal economy remained practically unchanged.

It is difficult to cover all small and individual enterprises with regular statistical surveys. In these cases, indicators obtained from regular surveys are extrapolated to the whole population on the basis of comparison of employment data from regular surveys of enterprises and data from the Labour Force Survey (LFS). The comparison is carried out by type of activity.

However, often the detailed classifications of the labour force and business surveys do not correspond and the labour force statisticians run into difficulties in allocating relevant codes.

Therefore, the adjustments are made at a higher level of aggregation than desired. In the meantime efforts are being made to improve the quality of the classification and questionnaire used in the LFS. A new and more detailed classification of types of economic activity was completed with additional explanations in 2005.

Balancing the supply-and-use of goods and services is one of the main approaches used to determine the components of NOE arising from incomplete and misreported information on production, incomes, expenditure and other key indicators. The reasons for imbalances are analysed by comparing data from different sources (Business Survey, Household Budget Survey (HBS), Foreign Trade Statistics) and adjustments are made for the components attributable to non-observed activity.

It should be noted, however, that this method is often used only in combination with other adjustment methods. Its use becomes difficult when several institutional sectors contribute to either supply or use, and it is necessary to take account of all components. In such cases it is often impossible to obtain reliable estimates of one or more components based on regular surveys.

2.2 Special surveys

Organising special surveys is an effective method of obtaining adjusted estimates. Such surveys are planned and carried out in specific areas, where either the quality of data obtained by current statistical surveys is low, or there are no data at all and a preliminary analysis indicates a possible high rate of NOE.

A number of special surveys were conducted within the framework of the TACIS programmes, and with the help of national accounts experts from the statistical offices of the Netherlands, Greece and Poland. The surveys enabled essential adjustments to be made in the national accounts, particularly in the production and income accounts.

2.2.1 Survey of tobacco consumption (1999)

The comparison of the results from this survey with business statistics data showed that the value of tobacco imports should be increased 1.2 times, and the value of tobacco production 1.5 times. The estimate for tobacco consumption (242 million Georgian Lari (GEL)) was 4.5 times greater than the figure obtained from the Household Budget Survey. An adjustment of about one per cent was added to the gross output in the production account. Corresponding adjustments were also made in the distribution of income account.

The estimate of increased tobacco consumption added about 3.2 per cent to the total GDP calculated from the expenditure side.

2.2.2 Survey of restaurants, cafes, bars and other similar establishments

Information obtained from the survey on the number of customers and average cost of services indicated that the actual output of these establishments exceeded by 3.8 times the figure reported in the regular statistical surveys. This suggests that 75 per cent of the actual volume of restaurant services is not observed. Corresponding adjustments in the main macroeconomic indicators, based on the survey results, were also made. In particular, the total output of this industry increased 3.4 times. Adjustments were also made to the expenditure side of GDP.

2.2.3 Survey of construction activities

According to a survey carried out in Tbilisi, the total volume of construction and related activities was 145.1 million GEL, more than twice the amount reported in the 1999 regular business survey. The results from the same survey also showed that investment in construction was 197.4 million GEL, which is 2.1 times higher than the figure reported in the regular survey. The results suggest that about 50 per cent of all construction activities were not observed.

2.2.4 Survey of health care services

The results from the survey showed that in the first quarter of 2000, households obtained at least 4.3 times more health services and purchased 3.1 times more medicines and medical appliances than declared in official sources.

The estimate of the quarterly value of health care services was 87.1 million GEL, exceeding by about 6.8 times the same indicator obtained from the HBS. The estimate of household expenditure on medicines was 72.9 million GEL, 3.1 times higher than the figure obtained from the HBS. The comparative analysis of supply and use of medicines showed that the total supply should be increased by a factor of at least two, i.e. imports, exports and production should be adjusted accordingly.

In total, the summary effect of the adjustments on final use categories, obtained on the basis of this survey, equaled 3.4 percentage points. This estimate almost coincides with the adjustments that were made to the GDP compiled using the production approach.

2.2.5 Survey of education services

According to the results of the survey, household expenditures on education were 1.9 times higher than those reported by educational institutions. Household expenditures on schooling items exceeded by 2.2 times (or by 64.8 million GEL) the corresponding figure obtained from the HBS. Moreover the survey also enabled, for the first time, an estimate of households' expenses on education abroad of 45.2 million GEL.

In the production accounts, the adjustments made to output and value added due to the increased volume of education services amounted to 59 million GEL, or 1.0 per cent of GDP in 2000. The total adjustment made to education services, including expenditure on schooling items and on education abroad, was 152 million GEL, equal to 2.6 per cent of GDP in 2000.

2.2.6 Survey of supply and use of tobacco goods (repeated survey), TV sets and other consumer commodities.

According to the survey, the estimate of legal imports must be increased about 3.5 times for the commodity groups under consideration. The registered imports of the commodities covered by the survey in 2001 was 5.8 per cent of the total registered imports (natural gas and electricity included). The actual imports of the considered commodities obtained from the survey makes up 13.2 per cent of the presently adopted adjusted import indicator and 27.3 per cent of the presently adopted adjustment. Due to the survey, the adjustment of the total annual imports of about 100 million US dollars was confirmed at about 3.1 per cent of the 2001 GDP.

The survey also made it possible to adjust the expenditure data on the considered commodities obtained from the HBS. The adjustment made was 4.8 per cent of total household expenditure.

A survey conducted in 2002, showed that consumption of cigarettes increased as compared to 1999. However, the tobacco prices decreased during the same period, thus resulting in a decrease of the total expenditure on tobacco goods.

A comparison of the results of the surveys conducted in 2002 and 1999 shows that in 2002, both unregistered imports and unregistered production increased considerably.

Domestic production of cigarettes sharply increased since 1999. At the same time, the share of non-observed production has also increased.

The results of the surveys mentioned in previous sections affected national accounts compilation process and adjusted corresponding figures in both production and final consumption accounts. Based on the surveys conducted, the overall adjustment to GDP due to changes in production, use, imports and exports was more than 10 per cent.

The special surveys of NOE are very important for the compilation of accurate national accounts. The results of the surveys, combined with additional employment data, provide well-founded estimates of the non-observed economy.

3. Share of NOE by activity types

Table 3 shows estimates of NOE by activity over the period 2000-2004. The share of NOE considerably decreased in 2004 to 28.3% from 33.7% in 2000. This can be explained with the economic changes that took place in the country during that period.

Table 3. Share of non-observed output by main types of economic activity
(per cent)

	2000	2001	2002	2003	2004
Agriculture, forestry, fishing	10.3	9.2	7.7	8.3	9.4
Mining and quarrying	18.9	19.3	19.8	18.6	10.3
Manufacturing	49.4	49.6	41.9	43.4	37.9
Electricity, gas and water supply	22.3	20.7	20.1	19.5	9.1
Processing products by household for sale or for final own consumption	-	-	-	-	-
Construction	60.4	55.4	49.3	39.5	33.5
Trade services, repair services	61.0	70.2	69.3	70.1	60.2
Restaurant and hotel services	69.1	80.5	83.0	82.8	71.6
Transport and storage	45.0	39.4	45.1	45.5	38.7
Communications	20.0	8.0	7.9	14.8	15.0
Financial intermediation; real estate, renting and business activities	4.8	4.8	4.8	4.8	4.8
Real estate, renting and business activities	42.2	45.2	39.5	54.7	48.6
Public administration and defence	-	-	-	-	-
Education	40.2	42.1	47.5	44.8	34.3
Health care and social services	77.5	78.7	78.9	75.7	52.7
Other community, social and personal service activities	21.7	25.3	27.3	23.3	18.6
Private households with employed persons	-	-	-	-	-
Inputted rent of own dwelling services	-	-	-	-	-
Net taxes	-	-	-	-	-
Total output	**33.7**	**33.4**	**33.2**	**33.1**	**28.3**

GERMANY

1. Definitions and concepts

According to the European System of Integrated Economic Accounts (ESA 1995), hidden/informal economic activities are included in the production boundaries and, consequently, have to be included in GDP. Production activities to be covered by GDP therefore include activities performed illegally or conducted without the knowledge of taxation, social security, statistics or other authorities. According to an international convention, own-account housework is not included in production in the context of national accounts.

The Federal Statistical Office (FSO) uses various measures to produce GDP figures that are as comprehensive as possible:

- Explicit imputations are made especially in those areas where large-scale censuses are conducted only at long intervals (e.g. the census of crafts, and the census of distributive trade and the hotel and restaurant industry). Special calculations are also made for own-account construction and tips.
- In many cases, implicit coverage of hidden/informal economic activities is ensured by the calculation method itself. For instance, agricultural production is determined on the basis of areas under cultivation and the relevant average yields. Also, rents are calculated through the stock of dwellings – broken down by size and other characteristics – and the relevant rents per square metre. Whether or not the incomes thus calculated and included in the GDP figure are declared for tax purposes is neither known nor considered relevant for an exhaustive coverage of such production activities.

Therefore, the frequently voiced opinion that the GDP does not include hidden/informal economic activities is incorrect as far as Germany is concerned.

2. Sources and estimation methods

2.1 Major steps to ensure GDP exhaustiveness

Obtaining exhaustive results is a major goal of national accounting. Ensuring the exhaustiveness of gross domestic product (GDP) and gross national income (GNI) measures was a major goal of the national accounts revision undertaken in Germany in 1999 when implementing ESA 95. Within the scope of the 2005 major revision of national accounts, the exhaustiveness of the GDP compilation was further improved by integrating the results of the latest large-scale censuses and other multi-annual surveys as well as by refining some special estimates and adjustments. The various measures are summarised below for the production and expenditure approaches.

2.1.1 Comparison of employment data

When implementing ESA 95, a large-scale project was carried out with the goal of checking the exhaustiveness of GNI on the basis of employment data. Extensive comparisons were performed between employment data from population statistics and those from surveys for specific industries (where they are included in GDP calculations), in order to identify possible under-coverage. In the 2005 revision process, the compilation of employment data was based on the existing but methodologically improved statistics as well as on new sources like the monthly telephone survey on employment status.

2.1.2 Comparison with turnover tax statistics

To further improve the basis for the calculations, comparisons were made with turnover tax statistics for all areas of the GDP production approach. A problem with this method is that it is not always possible to compare data, due to differences in industry classifications used in the data sources.

2.1.3 Integration of large-scale censuses

Generally, GDP exhaustiveness was improved by integrating the results of various large-scale censuses and other multi-annual surveys at the time of the latest national accounts revision. They included, for instance, the 2001 census of energy and water supply, the 1999, 2000 and 2001 censuses of distributive trade and the hotel and restaurant industry, the microcensus 2002 (which was used for the recalculation of the housing stock) and new results of the time budget survey, the services statistics and the agricultural accounts.

Moreover, GDP exhaustiveness has been improved by implementing new statistics which were developed in the last few years. These are the structural business statistics (SBS) for small enterprises (with 1 to 19 employees), the business register and the statistics on long-term nursing care.

2.1.4 Comparison with household budget surveys

As part of the work undertaken to study the use of household surveys for national accounting, the final consumption expenditure of households was checked for exhaustiveness. To that end, in the 1999 benchmark revision a first detailed comparison was performed between the data from household surveys (sample survey of income and expenditure) and the data obtained from the supply-sector approach (sales to households as derived from economic and taxation statistics). This exercise was repeated during the 2005 major revision. Results from that comparison were used to make adjustments, especially in the area of the distributive trade and the hotel and restaurant industries.

2.1.5 Comparison with investors approach

The product-based estimates of gross fixed capital formation in construction and in machinery and equipment were compared with the results based on investment data from investors, leading to adjustments in some cases. Since in recent years various statistics were either newly introduced or refined (e.g. structural business statistics for small enterprises in industry and construction, and particularly services statistics), most of the data missing in the investors' approach, which in previous years had to be estimated, are now available from SBS.

2.1.6 Production-turnover comparison

As part of calculating fixed capital formation in machinery and equipment by the commodity flow method, checks are made to determine whether any investment services have to be included in addition to the production covered by production statistics. Such additions are based on a comparison between production and turnover statistics.

2.1.7 Checks and special calculations

In addition to the above mentioned checks for exhaustiveness, separate exhaustiveness studies were performed for many areas of both the production and expenditure approaches, particularly by comparison with specific, and in part non-official, data sources. Calculations included those regarding own-account construction, prostitution, private lessons, tips and income in kind. Also, supplementary estimations are made for data not collected due to cut-off limits. Finally, valuation at purchasers' prices was done on the basis of computed turnover tax rates.

2.1.8 Input-output integration

Revisions also arose from integrating information obtained from input-output computations of previous years, which generally are not available early enough to be included in current-year GDP calculations. The results of the input-output data for 2000 were incorporated in the 2005 benchmark revision. Corrections affected the output and intermediate consumption.

As a consequence of the exhaustiveness checks, imputations for undercoverage are calculated for various GDP aggregates. Explicit imputations covered various kinds of undercoverage such as own-account construction, tips and remuneration in kind, evasion of taxes and levies and statistical cut-off limits. As all relevant information was not available, a further breakdown by individual causes was not possible.

2.1.9 Separate estimation of hidden/informal economic activities

The Federal Statistical Office does not compile separate estimates of hidden/informal economic activities as part of national accounting for the following reasons:
- The main goal of national accountants is to capture as exhaustively as possible economic activities according to ESA 95 concepts. For GDP exhaustiveness, it is irrelevant whether or not a specific economic activity is legal or illegal or otherwise hidden;

- There is no international definition of the hidden/informal economy. Sometimes this just refers to un-invoiced sales and repairs or own-account construction, and sometimes to illegal criminal activities, i.e. those activities liable to prosecution. In addition, the existence of cut-off limits in statistical surveys reduces the coverage of that part of the economy;

- To the extent that hidden/informal economic activities are covered implicitly by the calculation methods already in place, it would be necessary to remove these from independent estimates to avoid double-counting. However, information on their volume is not available.

Therefore, the Federal Statistical Office does not intend to publish a separate estimate on the size of the hidden/informal economy. The FSO considers that the issue of separately identifying the non-observed economy is subsumed by the need for overall reliability, objectivity and scientific verifiability in official statistics.

Notwithstanding this general guideline, the FSO is currently working on a feasibility study to investigate whether drug trafficking and production, and smuggling of cigarettes and alcohol can be estimated in a sufficiently reliable way for national accounts purposes.

3. International comparability of GDP data

After the EU Commission had, for various reasons, questioned the exhaustiveness of the national income data of the Member States in 1992, Member States thoroughly revised their national accounting systems. Since then, the exhaustiveness questions have been given particular attention at least in the course of a major revision. In Germany, the 2005 benchmark revision resulted in a data-related increase of the GDP from 1991 to 2004 by 0.7 per cent in nominal terms.

HUNGARY

1. Introduction

In Hungary, various estimates of the size of illegal activities and the underground economy have been published by researchers and research institutes. The investigations have usually defined these phenomena in a much broader sense than the SNA 93. However, the estimates derived from these research works cannot easily be incorporated into the national accounts, as they do not conform to the standard industry, sector and transactions classifications of the SNA. In addition, the estimation methods cannot be repeated regularly as is required for official statistical publications.

2. Definitions and concepts

In principle, the definitions related to concealed production and underground economy are based on SNA 93 par. 6.34-6.36, and on the definitions and classifications in the OECD *Handbook on Measuring the Non-Observed Economy*. The concept of the non-observed economy (NOE) is a broad one, defined as all productive activities that are likely to be excluded from the basic statistical data collection programme.

The current description refers to the results of the second Eurostat Pilot Project on Exhaustiveness and uses the N1-N7 types of NOE.

3. Sources and estimation methods

The main methods to estimate GDP in Hungary are the production and the expenditure approaches. The income approach is less developed and is not independent from the production approach.

Output estimates of GDP are based on the following data sources:
- annual survey of economic statistics;
- annual tax declarations and financial reports of enterprises with legal entity and partnerships without legal entities;
- personal income tax declarations on unincorporated enterprises and private households' activities;
- for central and local government and social security bodies, budget data and the individual annual reports of the budgetary institutions.

In general, the Hungarian Central Statistical Office (HCSO) considers the output estimate as the most reliable measure of GDP in Hungary. Generally there is no reason to change the production estimates, as the data used are common to other approaches. The national accounts department has an electronic cross-checking system to ensure data quality.

The expenditure data is compiled using a number of sources. Household budget surveys (HBS) and retail trade data are used for private household consumption expenditure (PHC); government consumption expenditure makes use of annual reports of general government units and budget data; gross fixed capital formation (GFCF) and changes in stocks are based on the HCSO surveys and on various additional information on households. Exports and imports of goods are obtained from customs declarations and services from the Balance of Payments (BoP). To a large extent, the information comes from the same sources as for the output approach.

The GDP according to the income approach is not considered as an independent estimate. The estimates for the compensation of employees, operating surplus, mixed income, taxes and subsidies on production use information from the same or similar sources as for the output approach. Consequently, both approaches practically coincide.

The discrepancy between the output and expenditure approaches is shown explicitly in the annual publications (it is small; usually 2 per cent of GDP). Balancing procedure has recently been done at an aggregated level. There is no detailed reconciliation procedure, using for example, annual input-output tables or supply-and-use tables. Some modifications have been introduced to NA estimates when new estimation was made for 2000 as a new base year.

3.1 Output approach

The output approach for compiling national accounts is the most important in Hungary. The main data sources for the estimation of output vary according to the institutional sector:

- general government sector: the main data sources, which consist of taxation and other administrative reports, are collected and controlled by the Ministry of Finance and by the Treasury;
- financial corporations sector: the Central Bank and the supervisory bodies of the units concerned (financial institutions, insurance companies and security dealers) collect data and forward it to the HCSO. It is not considered necessary to check the exhaustiveness of general government and financial corporations data because all units in these sectors comply with their obligations to submit their reports to the supervisory entities;
- non-financial corporations sector: the main data sources are: registers, administrative data in the form of tax declarations, and statistical survey results.

3.1.1 Statistical underground (N1 and N2)

The Business Register contains every unit with a tax number. No specific criteria are applied (for activity, revenue or work force) to be included in the Register. The Business Register is based on statistical and administrative sources. Among statistical sources there are two questionnaires:

- for enterprises which are obliged to register with the Commercial Court;
- for enterprises which receive the questionnaire from the tax authorities.

Since 2000, Register data have been updated with an interim questionnaire as part of the National Statistical Data Collection Programme. This questionnaire is received by almost 40 000 organizations every year and is distributed five times a year. Every quarter, almost 8 000 organizations are considered as data suppliers. The units for which no statistical or tax data have been available since their creation are asked to provide information to the HCSO on the activities for the last two years. The fifth distribution of the questionnaire is a special case, with 8 000-10 000 respondents. This survey is normally focused on a concrete area of the national economy, for example, agricultural, financial organizations or those units that were affected by the 2002-2003 changes in main activity.

The results of several surveys in economic statistics, especially the integrated surveys, affect the Register data. The statistical sources primarily modify data housed by strata and the activity codes that affect data collections.

The Business Register is updated based on the systematic database of the Tax Office every week. The HCSO also takes monthly data from the Hungarian State Treasury where the budgetary institutions are recorded. In the "one-window" system 100 000 new organizations are recorded in the Business Register every year, while the number of those closing down is 80 000 on average. Annually, 400 000 changes are recorded together with the Tax Office data transmission.

The tax declaration of personal income is one of the main data sources used for calculating the production of sole proprietors with a licence or other permission. Although it records sales and costs of the enterprise, tax data are considered unreliable either for gross output or for intermediate consumption. On the other hand, the number of tax declarations is used for the estimation of the number of production units, considering that the Register is unreliable in this regard. Taking the number of tax declarations as the base, there is an equation for the "full-time equivalent number of people involved in the production" of sole proprietors with licence or other permission. Coefficients in this equation are mainly expert estimates.

It is assumed that:
- some entrepreneurs do not fulfil their obligations to present tax declarations;
- the numbers of employees declared as supplementary data on the personal income tax declarations are not reliable, and as a consequence they are replaced by the number of employees from the Labour Force Survey;
- some entrepreneurs and their employees do not work full-time (e.g. those for whom it is a second job, pensioners).

Considering the data for gross output (GO) and intermediate consumption (IC), adjustments are needed to obtain acceptable national accounts data for GO, IC and gross value added (GVA) generated by this sub-sector. Because of the low quality of personal income tax data, the output per employee and the coefficients IC/GO are substituted by corresponding data derived from those of the small enterprises. It is assumed that the ratio of IC/GO should be lower than that of the reference group. Based on expert estimate, it is assumed that corporations work with higher overhead costs. Information from the Ministry of Finance (i.e. the report on the minimal level of income of entrepreneurs by counties and professions) is used in the territorial and professional breakdown of GVA. The estimations are made at the four digit level of the classification of activities (370 activities) for 20 counties.

For the estimation of illegal activities related to drugs and prostitution, a benchmark estimate was made for 1999 and was updated for 2000 taking into account the price movements in these activities. Estimations are made by the NA department. In the case of prostitution, according to the estimates, about 25 per cent of GVA is already included in the official GDP data. The work on the estimation of illegal activities started recently and is made independently from other non-exhaustiveness adjustments. Therefore, no reliable information is available for the time being about which industries are affected by these estimates. Only those parts which are not included in official GDP estimates are counted under N2.

The estimation of illegal activities is being expanded to other areas. For the smuggling of tobacco a considerable amount of information from newspapers, research, and criminal records was accumulated. This work is a first attempt in a difficult field and is considered very experimental. In spite of the quantity of information collected, the picture seems rather controversial. It seems that this activity does not affect production but export, import and consumption figures. There is evidence on the incidence of both exports and imports. According to the information processed, illegal exports is higher than imports. Therefore, household consumption seems to be overestimated for tobacco.

3.1.2 Economic underground (N6)

For NOE type N6 (under-reporting), the methods used differ according to the size and legal form of the enterprises concerned.

For non-financial corporations, two types of corrections are made in national accounts. For small enterprises with double-entry bookkeeping, an adjustment is necessary because enterprises declare much less value for their output than they really produce. The estimation is based on expert opinion. According to this, the smaller an enterprise, the simpler the economic form in which an enterprise operates, and the greater the possibility for trying to avoid tax. The calculation is made on the basis of expert estimations. Hence, the gross output data of small-scale enterprises is increased.

Corrections are also made for single-entry bookkeeping enterprises, because enterprises declare more costs than they actually have. The correction is based on a hypothesis according to which companies applying single-entry bookkeeping can account – because of the more simplified regulations in accounting – some final consumption items as intermediate consumption with the intention of avoiding tax. The calculation is made by expert estimation, which is based on data of small enterprises applying double-entry bookkeeping.

In the case of entrepreneurs, neither the number of personal income tax returns nor output and intermediate consumption seem to be reliable. Therefore, the data are estimated according to industry-specific adjustment and using the ratio method (by sector size, industry and county) described in the previous section.

3.1.3 Informal economy (N3)

Informal economy covers household production activities for which no registration is required, e.g. private lessons of teachers, letting of rooms, and other services.

3.1.4 Other adjustments (N7)

Tips

Giving tips for certain service activities is typical in Hungary. In the interest of exhaustiveness, output has to be increased by the estimated value of tips. The basic source for estimating the tips was the household survey conducted in 1997. The adjustment is made for four activities:
- hairdressing and other beauty treatment,
- taxi operation,
- restaurants,
- bars.

Gratuities

There is widespread and tolerated illegal payment in the Hungarian health care system, called gratitude money, which is a donation from patients to doctors. Gratitude donations are not covered by social security insurance, and involve tax-avoidance. Thus this phenomenon is actually part of the hidden economy.

Calculations for the amount of gratitude money is based on a Social Research Institute study published in 1999. This study summarizes the outcome of a sample survey of 1000 doctors and 1400 patients about the amount and the frequency of both assumed and received gratitude money.

The data starting from 1998 are revised annually using certain health statistics.

Wages in kind

- Social welfare (cultural, health and social) services provided to employees

Enterprises provide various social welfare services to their employees, either at reduced prices or for free (for example kindergarten, subsidised meals). The subsidy on these services is valued as compensation of employees. Therefore, output for total cost of social welfare services provided to employees is increased less the charges paid by employees.

These data are not directly available in the tax files, but they are available in the Labour Cost Survey. For enterprises covered by Labour Cost Survey, data from the statistical survey are used. On the basis of the figures reported, it is possible to estimate the data of other enterprises by using personal income tax figures declared to the Tax and Financial Control Office on wages in kind.

- Own products given to employees

According to ESA95 regulation, the value of own products and services given to employees are also accounted as part of gross output and wages in kind (for example free passes at transport companies or free beer in breweries).

These data are not directly available in the tax files, but they are available in structural business statistics (SBS). For enterprises covered by SBS, data from the statistical survey are used. On the basis of the figures reported, it is possible to estimate the data of other enterprises by using personal income tax figures declared to the Tax and Financial Control Office on wages in kind.

- Purchased goods and services given to employees

In business accounting, material costs and the costs of contracted services contain the value of those benefits-in-kind, which are purchased and then given to the employees by the enterprise. These items are subtracted from intermediate consumption and added to the compensation of employees.

In the same way as own products given to employees, these data are not directly available in the tax files, but are estimated based on SBS.

■   Value of the use of passenger cars for personal purposes

Enterprises account outlays related to company cars within the costs (material costs or costs of contracted services). However, these cars are used for personal purposes too, which are regarded as benefits-in-kind according to ESA95 regulation. Consequently, the estimated costs of personal use are subtracted from intermediate consumption, and added to the compensation of employees. The estimation is made with the help of relevant personal income tax items.

3.2 Expenditure approach

3.2.1 Household final consumption expenditure

Several sources are used for estimating the household final consumption expenditure. The two main sources are the Household Budget Survey and the Retail Trade Survey. According to the PHARE 2000 Project on Household Final Consumption, the adjustments made by the NA department on Household Budget Survey data are not considered as exhaustiveness adjustments. However, there are some important areas where it is necessary to make other adjustments in order to achieve exhaustiveness.

One of these areas is alcoholic beverages and tobacco. For alcoholic beverages, supply-and-use tables are used. With the new supply-and-use tables for 1998 and 1999 (at current prices) and for 2000, it was possible to cross-check the estimates of alcoholic beverages and tobacco.

Tipping is a widespread phenomenon in Hungary, especially in health services. Until now, estimation on tips (or gratitude money) was based on the Household Budget Survey and the personal income tax declarations data. In January 2003, the first health satellite accounts were published. Based on the satellite accounts data, a detailed model was established for estimating the gratitude money for health services. This model uses the number of different kind of treatments, the likelihood of payment and estimated amount of gratitude money by type of treatment. The result of this new type of estimation was used for the final calculation of 2001 data and the revised data of 2000.

For tips given for several other types of services, a new estimation was made during the finalisation of 2001 data after revising 2000 data using the results of a survey on tips carried out in 1997.

With regard to illegal activities such as drugs and prostitution no adjustments are made, although a pilot study was carried out in 2000. For this study, two models were established for estimating the production, expenditure and income from these activities. The models were based on non-statistical information, but used administrative sources and publications.

The models used several indicators, like the number of cases cleared up, the estimated price of a case, and the estimated percentage of cleared-up cases and hidden cases. There are no immediate plans to use these estimations in the Hungarian national accounts, although checking and improving these models remains a priority.

In the case of final consumption expenditure of NPISHs and government no adjustment are made for exhaustiveness.

3.2.2 Gross fixed capital formation

The units engaged in production are all considered to be subject to gross fixed capital formation (GFCF) estimation. The data collection system currently provides GFCF data for the units working with five or more employees. Available supplementary information is used to estimate the non-observed part in their annual GFCF. The data collection covers all the required asset categories and transactions covered by GFCF. For the non-observed part of the economy some GFCF items are not dealt with in the estimation process, mainly because of their small magnitude and the uncertainty of the estimation results. Transactions with second-hand assets affecting the household sector, and the value of investments in intangible fixed assets carried out by the non-observed units, are not estimated at all.

3.2.3 Changes in inventories

The calculation of changes in inventories is not fully based on statistical surveys, because small enterprises are not requested to report this information. The method used for the surveyed enterprises is to calculate the difference between the closing stocks of two consecutive years. Adjustments between the production and demand sides are also included in this item.

3.2.4 Exports and imports of goods and services

HCSO does not make any adjustment to ensure exhaustiveness for the exports and imports of goods and services figures. This is because data on exports and imports of goods are taken from customs declarations, which are considered as a full scope data source, and data on exports and imports of services are taken from the balance of payments. Corrections for shuttle trade, smuggling and illegal activities have not been incorporated in the Hungarian national accounts as yet.

3.8 Income approach

3.8.1 Compensation of employees

Wages and salaries are calculated from surveys conducted with respect to the different sectors. Three types of sources are used: fiscal data, the Annual Survey of Economic Statistics for Enterprises, and data from the Labour Force Department. Because of discrepancies between the different sources, the average of the data from the three sources is sometimes used for estimates related to private enterprises.

Adjustments are made for unincorporated enterprises, where a comparison with the salaries paid by corporations of similar size and activity indicate that the data for these enterprises are underreported. In such cases, the average salaries of the corporate sector are used for the unincorporated units. Different methods are used for the following cases:

- enterprises with employees: adjustments are introduced which reclassify intermediate consumption to wages and salaries;
- own-account workers: intermediate consumption is reclassified to households' final consumption;
- incorrect figures in fiscal declarations: ratios from the Labour Force Survey are used.

4. Implications and effects on national accounts and GDP estimates

The adjustments and imputations related to the improvement of the exhaustiveness of the national accounts are an integral part of the estimation process, and the methods used do not normally enable the explicit identification of those related to the non-observed economy. The adjustments made for 2000, as a result of the work done within the framework of the 2002/03 Eurostat PPE project, are shown in the Table 1.

The plans for improving the estimation of underground and informal activities in the national accounts of Hungary involve:
- continuous monitoring and improvement of the methods used;
- development and improvement of global methods to ensure exhaustiveness: these are the employment method; reconciliation of final estimates using SUT; and use of registers;
- improving estimation of the illegal economy.

Table 1. Summary of exhaustiveness adjustments by type (legal activities), 2000
(billion HUF)

	Billion HUF	Million Euro[23]	Per cent of GDP
N1	362.9	1 451.6	2.8
N2	180.0	720.0	1.4
N3	16.6	66.4	0.1
N4	0	0	0
N5	0	0	0
N6	879.5	3 518.0	6.7
N7	125.1	500.4	0.9
Total	**1 564.1**	**6 256.4**	**11.9**

---

[23] Exchange rate used: 1 Euro=250 HUF.

IRELAND

1. Definitions and concepts

In the Irish national accounts, two independent estimates of GDP are compiled using the income and expenditure approaches. The compilation system is designed to ensure that all relevant transactions are captured and included at their appropriate value in the two estimates. Illegal activities are not covered but the accounts are designed to include items which, while legal in themselves, are not reported to the fiscal authorities. The description below summarises some of the principal methods used to ensure that such activities are captured.

2. Sources and estimation methods

When a data source is partial or incomplete, adjustments are made to include figures for the missing elements. Although every effort is made to ensure the reliability and comprehensiveness of the income- and expenditure-based figures, the two approaches still produce different results. The estimates therefore still include coverage and measurement errors, some of which are probably the result of transactions being recorded at different times on the two sides of the account. Since there is no reason to believe that one or other of the estimates is superior or more comprehensive, the average of the two results is taken to give the definitive version of GDP.

In the Irish accounts, most of the explicit adjustments made to ensure the exhaustiveness of GDP are made on the income side of the account because the data sources used for the income estimates are considered to be less complete than those used for the expenditure- based measure. All the adjustments made to ensure comprehensiveness were reviewed and updated in 1998 as part of a special work programme undertaken to ensure the exhaustiveness of the national accounts. The relevance and adequacy of the existing adjustments were verified and a number of new adjustments were introduced when data sources were found to be inadequate. The net impact of the changes made on that occasion was to increase the level of GDP by about 4 per cent. GDP estimates back to 1988 were recalculated to incorporate the new adjustments. In this report, the figures relate in the main to a special examination of the 1996 national accounts and are given in Irish pounds (IR£). In 1996, GDP was estimated at 45.7 billion IR£.

2.1 Final balancing procedure

The income and expenditure estimates, incorporating the adjustments described in later sections, are compared and the average is taken as the definitive version of GDP. The income-based estimate is generally lower than the expenditure-based figure but not in all years. On balance, the primary data sources and estimation procedures used for the expenditure-based estimate are considered more comprehensive and should not be subject to the same degree of understatement or evasion as some of the components in the income based estimate. Nevertheless, there is ongoing concern about the potential impact on the expenditure-based GDP measure of even small errors in the measurement of the External Trade statistics, given the scale of the gross flows involved.

In Ireland, the combined value of imports and exports is equivalent to about 150 per cent of GDP and even small discrepancies in the trade data can therefore generate significant errors in the overall GDP. It is therefore considered best practice to take the average of the income and expenditure based measures to be the definitive version of GDP. A balancing adjustment equal to half the difference between the two measures of GDP is then included in both the income and expenditure measures.

2.2 Verification of the transactions of large companies

As an additional check on the reliability and comprehensiveness of data for large exporting companies, a special unit within National Accounts compares on an ongoing basis, the consistency of all the data for those companies that are used in the national accounts. The returns which are the subject of this exercise include:

- imports and exports of goods (Intrastat and SADs);
- turnover (monthly industrial turnover inquiry);
- service imports (Balance of Payments inquiry);
- profits (Balance of Payments inquiry);
- profits (taxation returns used in estimating gross operating surplus);
- census of industrial production;
- index of industrial production (monthly inquiry).

A limited number of variables are compared each quarter but the more detailed examinations are only possible on an annual basis since the detailed Census of Production results and tax accounts for each company are available only yearly.

The majority of the large companies are exporters and also import most of their raw materials. It is therefore possible to build up a coherent picture of each company, equating (a) turnover with exports; (b) purchases with imports; (c) research and development costs, royalties and other large service payments with Balance of Payments service imports, through to (d) value added and (e) operating surplus. This exercise helps ensure the exhaustiveness and consistency of the import and export data and related components of the GDP estimate.

The companies, whose transactions are individually validated for correctness and consistency each year, account for over half of all exports, over a third of imports and about half of the operating surplus of corporations.

2.3 Income-based estimates

The income-based estimate of GDP is calculated by estimating and combining the separate components of income, namely compensation of employees and operating surplus. Adjustments are made to ensure the exhaustiveness of these two income elements.

2.3.1 Compensation of employees

Use of the Quarterly National Household Survey based employment totals

In the Irish accounts, compensation of employees is calculated by assigning a wage to all employees in the Quarterly National Household Survey (QNHS, previously the Labour Force Survey). This survey is considered to be a reliable source of information on employment. This was confirmed in a special one-off exercise undertaken as part of the Labour Force Survey in 1996, which was designed to make an objective assessment of the employment status of persons officially registered as unemployed. A 1 per cent sample of persons on the official unemployment register (the Live Register) was added to the LFS sample and the standard survey questionnaire was also completed for these additional households. The results showed that about 20 per cent of persons officially registered in social security records as unemployed had full-time or part-time jobs and were recorded as such in the LFS. Table 1 shows the ILO based employment status of the Live Register sample.

Table 1. ILO Employment status of the Live Register based on a sub-sample of the LFS, 1996

ILO Economic activity status	Number	As per cent of the total
Employed, full time	167	11.4
Employed, part time:	146	10.0
Not underemployed	107	7.3
Underemployed	39	2.7
Unemployed	724	49.5
Marginally attached to the workforce	66	4.5
Others, not economically active	359	24.6
Total	**1 462**	**100.0**

The estimates of employee numbers from the QNHS are based on the International Labour Organization (ILO) definition of employment. This definition captures all persons who were at work for one hour or more during the week prior to the survey. The QNHS questions concerning the ILO definition ask for information on hours worked in main jobs (full-time or part-time) and in second jobs. This allows the conversion of part-time main jobs and of second jobs to full-time equivalents (FTE).

The calculation of FTE from the QNHS is carried out for each activity branch. However, the information on FTEs can only be used in the remuneration calculations for a branch, provided that the basic remuneration data are reported on a FTE basis, or alternatively that the data source distinguishes between full-time and part-time work and earnings.

The statistical surveys used as the sources of the earnings information are being systematically updated to include this split. Sources with the required breakdown include:
- Census of Industrial Production;
- annual Services Inquiries;
- direct returns for the education and health branches;
- annual national accounts National Income Survey.

Adjustments to capture all elements of remuneration

Every effort is made to ensure that the remuneration allocated to each individual in the QNHS is appropriate and complete. The industry group to which the individual is classified in the QNHS determines the remuneration rate that is assigned. Information on average remuneration rates in the different industry groups is collected primarily in the statistical surveys of businesses undertaken by the Central Statistics Office (CSO). Some of these surveys collect full details covering almost all of the components of compensation of employees. However, some are less detailed and only collect information on basic wages and salaries. Elements of remuneration such as benefits in kind will therefore not be covered. In such cases the information collected is adjusted upwards to include the missing remuneration elements. These additions are estimated also from statistical surveys and especially from the four-yearly Labour Costs survey that provides details of all elements of remuneration paid by employers.

One element of remuneration not captured in the adjustments described in the previous paragraphs is gratuities or tips, which are associated with employment in certain industries. These are not paid directly by employers and they will not be included in adjustments based on the Labour Costs Survey. The scale of tipping is assumed to be between 5 per cent and 10 per cent of sales depending on the activity. This represents a much higher proportion of wages and salaries.

2.3.2 Operating surplus and mixed incomes

Estimates of operating surplus in the Irish National Accounts are largely based on the income and corporation tax records of the self-employed and companies. However, statistical surveys are used in preference to tax files to estimate the operating surplus of financial enterprises located in the International Financial Services Centre (IFSC). In the case of the Agriculture and Rents of Dwellings branches, value added is estimated using the output-based approach and tax records are not used.

Considerable adjustments are required in order to calculate operating surplus from the tax-based information. These include the conceptual adjustments that are needed to ensure that the definition of operating surplus complies with that in the ESA95. In addition a number of adjustments are needed because the basic sources are sometimes incomplete and the reported incomes may be understated. These latter adjustments which are needed to ensure the exhaustiveness of the operating surplus estimates are described in the following paragraphs.

Use of the QNHS employment totals for self-employed

Employment numbers from the QNHS are used as the control totals for numbers of self-employed in the calculation of mixed incomes. Since QNHS-based control totals are also used to calculate employees' remuneration, this means that an income is effectively assigned to each person classified as at work in the QNHS.

In the case of the self-employed, tax files are used to calculate an average value of mixed income for each of the industry groups. These average incomes are then applied to the numbers of self-employed in each industry, as estimated from the QNHS (or its predecessor the LFS, back in 1996). In aggregate, the total numbers recorded as self-employed in the survey exceeded those on the tax files by around 37 000 (30 per cent) in 1996.

Including tax-exempt activities and excluding double counting

Certain activities and incomes are exempt from income and corporation tax and some special adjustments are, therefore, also made to ensure that these incomes are captured in the national accounts. There are also some small overlaps and double counting between tax files and the output-based value added estimates for agriculture and these have to be removed.

The 1998 exhaustiveness study included a detailed examination of the Corporation and Self-employed Income Tax systems in order to identify any relevant enterprises and incomes that were missing from the tax system and not captured elsewhere in the compilation process. It was discovered that a small number of enterprises and activities were being omitted. These included entities such as charities, credit unions (essentially mutualised personal savings clubs) harbour authorities and amateur sports bodies.

It was also found that certain incomes were being missed. These included items such as employment grants that were exempt from tax. Some farming incomes were also being omitted from GDP. To avoid duplication, the profits of self-employed persons classified in the Agriculture Branch were being excluded from the estimates of self-employed incomes derived from the Income Tax files. However, the profits thus omitted included some non-farming income such as tourism revenue, which was not included in the output-based estimate of agricultural income.

The integration of the tax-based estimates with the output-based estimate of farming and fishing also gives rise to some double counting. While farmers and fishermen are excluded from the tax-based estimates of mixed income, some company farms and fish farms are included in the Corporation Tax based estimates of operating surplus so there is some duplication of income with the output-based estimates.

Adjustments are made to ensure that these omissions and double counts are corrected for. In 2003, the additions and deductions to the income based estimate of GDP were as shown in Table 2:

Table 2. Operating surplus & mixed income of tax exempt activities and incomes, 2003

2003	Euro (million)
Adjustment for employment grants which are exempted income for tax purposes	32
Adjustment for operating surplus of corporate bodies exempted from Corporation tax:	
Charity Shops	4
Credit Unions	-180
Housing Finance Agency	1
Commercial Sports	Now captured in Corporation Tax file
Amateur Sports Bodies	7
Irish Intervention Agency	0
Other exempt corporate bodies not covered elsewhere including National Rehab lottery, Irish Horseracing Authority etc.	3
Adjustment for non-agricultural income of farms	97
Farm income	-10
Fish farms	-13
Total	**-58**

Under-reporting of incomes

Adjustments are also made for under-reporting of incomes in the tax files. In the case of the self-employed the uplifts are applied to mixed incomes net of capital consumption of fixed assets. The adjustment rates are based on evidence from the Revenue Commissioner's programme of audits supported by comparisons with income information from the CSO's Household Budget Survey (HBS).

The incomes reported by larger companies to the tax authorities are considered reliable and are used in the accounts without adjustment (apart from the conceptual adjustments needed to convert the tax-based definition of profits to operating surplus). However, the accounts of smaller companies are sometimes not audited and they are therefore thought to be liable to the same degree of understatement as the incomes of the self-employed. An upward adjustment for understatement of incomes is therefore also made to the smallest companies.

2.3.3 Comments on specific industries

Agriculture and fishing

In Ireland, the Agricultural and Fishing industries consist mostly of unincorporated enterprises. Many of these are small and are not liable for the payment of tax. The tax records are therefore not a good basis for estimating operating surplus in these two industries.

Value added in Agriculture and Fishing is estimated instead using an output-based approach. The estimates of gross output in agriculture are considered reliable. Sales of the principal agricultural products tend to be calculated from the demand side so they are independent of information provided by farmers. For instance, the output of milk is estimated using information on milk intake by dairies, supplemented by information on the value of milk consumed on farms without sale. The gross output of the fishing industry is calculated mostly using information on fish landings. This information is provided by the enterprises engaged in fishing and is grossed up by one third to allow for under-reporting.

Rents of dwellings

An output-based method is also used to calculate the value added of the Rent of Dwellings branch. The methodology used imputes a rent and value added to owner-occupied accommodation. Estimates for a benchmark year are based on a full enumeration of both rented and owner-occupied accommodation and are therefore fully comprehensive. This complete enumeration is conducted as part of the Census of Population and is repeated every ten years.

Construction, distributive trades and hotels, restaurants and catering

The black or hidden economy is likely to be more prevalent in some industries than in others. The three branches Construction, Distributive trades, and Hotels, restaurants and catering are generally recognised as being especially difficult to record comprehensively in GDP. As part of the exhaustiveness exercise undertaken in 1998, the income-based estimates of value added for these three branches, for a number of years in the mid-1990s, were compared with a number of alternative measures. These included output-based estimates of value added. These had to be especially constructed by the CSO since an output-based measure of GDP is not yet routinely compiled.

The checks undertaken for these branches generally confirmed the reliability of the income-based value added estimates. A few minor amendments were made to the methodology used for the income-based GDP calculations, including an increase in the per centage adjustment made for the under-reporting of income in the self-employed tax files.

Childcare

In the Irish GDP calculations, a specific adjustment is made to include income earned for childcare services that would otherwise not be captured in the compilation system. In Ireland, a considerable amount of childcare is arranged informally and the resulting employment and income may not be captured in official records. An adjustment is made to the estimates of mixed income to cover babysitting and care in the childminder's own home. These are the situations most likely not to be captured elsewhere in the compilation system. The adjustment made is calculated on the basis of the estimated household expenditure on these two services. Expenditure on babysitting services is based on the Household Budget Survey results. The value of mixed income is taken to be equal to expenditure since intermediate consumption is negligible. Estimates of the expenditure on childminding in the carer's own home were also made using the HBS.

However, alternative estimates, which were slightly higher, were available from a dedicated survey of childminding services undertaken by the Economic and Social Research Institute (ESRI) in 1996. The average of the two estimates was taken to be the definitive figure. In calculating the related income, the intermediate consumption is again assumed to be zero. However, some part of this activity will be captured in the tax system. In calculating the adjustment, it is assumed that some 90 per cent goes unrecorded. Childcare services for 2003 amounted to 253 million Euros.

Correction for VAT fraud

The final explicit adjustment made to the income-based estimate of GDP is in respect of income corresponding to VAT fraud without complicity. This is intended to cover the case where a trader collects VAT from a customer but does not pay the VAT to the Tax Office. This results in higher operating surplus for the trader and this extra income would not have been specifically captured in the under-reporting adjustments described above. A special calculation is therefore made each year to estimate the amount of VAT fraud without complicity, using a methodology set out in EU legislation.

The methodology involves calculating the theoretical amount of VAT that should have been collected on all transactions recorded in the national accounts and comparing this with the actual amount of non-deductible VAT paid to the tax authorities. The difference between the two is an estimate of VAT evasion. This then has to be split into cases where both parties to the transactions agreed to avoid VAT and cases where traders actually collected VAT but never forwarded it to the Tax Office. The assumption is made that in the latter case the traders will be registered for VAT whereas traders evading VAT with the mutual agreement of customers will not be on the tax files. In calculating the adjustment in the Irish national accounts, it is assumed that VAT evasion with the agreement of customers relates to self-employed traders recorded as employed in the QNHS, but not making self-employed Schedule D income tax returns. In 1996 an amount of 50 million Ir£ was included as an estimate for VAT evasion without the purchaser's agreement.

2.4 Expenditure-based estimates

When compiling the expenditure-based GDP measure, every effort is made to ensure that all relevant economic activity is captured. The explicit exhaustiveness adjustments that are made to the expenditure-based GDP components are not as extensive as those needed on the income side because the primary basic data sources and compilation procedures used, result in more complete coverage of the economy. Most of the basic data on which the estimates are based will already have been edited and checked for completeness. For instance, all statistical surveys will have been grossed up to ensure that estimates cover the entire population. The following paragraphs outline some of the checks and adjustments made to ensure that the various elements of the expenditure-based GDP estimate are comprehensive.

2.4.1 Final consumption expenditure of households

Estimates of household consumption expenditure are calculated using commodity flows based on production and trade information, fiscal data reported by the tax office, the Household Budget Survey and administrative data and direct surveys.

Most of the basic information from statistical surveys used in the household expenditure estimates will already have been checked for reliability and exhaustiveness by the compiling branches before it is incorporated into the national accounts. For example, Household Budget Survey results will have been grossed up to ensure that the estimates cover all private households. This grossing corrects for differential non-response. The reliability and comprehensiveness of the production and external trade data that are used in the commodity flow estimates will also have been checked and verified by the compilers of the basic statistics. The adjustments made to the basic statistics include an upwards adjustment to the merchandise imports corresponding to about 3 per cent of EU arrivals. Specific aspects of the household expenditure calculations designed to ensure exhaustiveness include the following:

Rents of dwellings

A figure is imputed for rents paid for owner-occupied accommodation, in compliance with ESA95. This is based on the rental levels payable for similar types of rented accommodation. The rent levels are calculated from the Census of Population and the Quarterly National Household Survey. The Census of Population is used to benchmark the rent calculations every ten years and collects comprehensive information on all rented and owner-occupied accommodation. This includes details of actual rents paid and information on the size, location and amenities of both rented and owner-occupied accommodation (e.g. number of rooms, availability of central heating). Estimates for years between Censuses are compiled by projecting forward the estimate for the benchmark year to take account of changes in the volume of the housing stock and in the levels of rent. Information on rent levels is collected in the QNHS.

Repair work on dwellings

As mentioned above, the construction sector, particularly the part covered by small firms, is one of the activities generally considered to be most difficult to cover comprehensively in the national accounts. Household expenditure on everyday repairs and maintenance can be understated because of this. However, in Ireland, a special monthly survey carried out by the Economic and Social Research Institute (ESRI) captures household spending on both current and capital type repair and maintenance. Households are asked for amounts spent on all minor repairs and maintenance in the previous two months, and on all major work undertaken in the last 12 months. Comparisons were made between the results of this survey and the 1994-95 HBS. The expenditure estimates in the ESRI survey for day-to-day repair and maintenance of dwellings were considerably in excess of those in the HBS. The ESRI survey showed 565 million Ir£ compared to 300 million Ir£ in the HBS. On this basis the ESRI survey was regarded as comprehensively covering the small construction companies and has been used as the basis of the household expenditure estimates from 1996 onwards, in preference to the HBS.

Nursing Homes

Estimates of expenditure on private nursing homes are obtained from the Department of Health, as this type of expenditure would not be covered in the Household Budget Survey.

Childcare services

This figure is based on the 1999 HBS figure for childcare services equivalent to 134 million Euros. Annually, this figure increases with the growth in the number of women at work with children under 12 (from the QNHS) and by the CPI for "Other Services".

Service charge for pension funds

The amount is calculated as 1% of the residual pension fund. This is the pension fund amount not covered by the Insurance Industry "Blue Book" – the difference between the total amount as calculated by the Irish Association of Investment Managers (IAIM) and the pension amount in the Blue Book. There is also an allowance made for pension funds not managed by IAIM members and this is from the CSO's Balance of Payments division. In 2004, the total amount was 526 million Euros.

The administration charge for pension funds in the Blue Book is captured as part of the administration fee for insurance.

Consumption of home grown produce on farms

The Agriculture Division of CSO estimates the value of produce produced and consumed on farms without sale. These estimates are based on information collected in the Household Budget Survey and the National Farm Survey conducted by Teagasc, a state-sponsored agricultural research institute. All produce is valued at farm gate prices. The value of these items in 2004 is shown in Table 4.

Table 4. Farm produce and fuel consumed without a process of sale, 2004

Product	Value (million €)
Meat	18.0
Milk, cheese & eggs	17.0
Fruit & vegetables	7.0
Potatoes	3.0
Other preserves	0.5
Fuel	30.0
Total	**75.5**

2.4.2 Private non-profit institutions (PNPIs)

Separate estimates for PNPIs are not compiled in the Irish national accounts. Final consumption expenditure of PNPIs is instead combined with Household Consumption Expenditure. Specific entries are included for final consumption on that part of the output of PNPIs which corresponds to the compensation of employees (COE) working in these organizations. Values are based on the estimated values of COE calculated in the income-based account. Indirect allowances are also made for final consumption on that part of the output of PNPIs which corresponds to their intermediate consumption. For instance, estimates based on the HBS are grossed upwards, usually by about 3 per cent, to cover the intermediate consumption of PNPIs.

2.4.3 Government final consumption expenditure (GFCE)

By definition, the Central Government Sector consists of public units that are mostly financed and answerable to Government. As part of the exhaustiveness study undertaken during 1998, the employment figures underpinning the remuneration element of GFCE were compared with independent employment data from the Labour Force Survey. Because of definitional problems, valid comparisons were not possible in all cases. However, the comparisons that could be made largely confirmed that the coverage of public units in the General Government Sector was complete. The one exception was in the area of Public Health where it was discovered that a large number of voluntary agencies funded by the State had been excluded with the result that their output was not included in GFCE. This omission was corrected and the estimates of GFCE are now considered to be fully comprehensive. This employment comparison will be repeated regularly to ensure the ongoing comprehensiveness of the results.

2.4.4 Capital formation

The basic estimates of capital formation are also considered to be reasonably comprehensive. The main sources used in the compilation of GFCF are administrative and fiscal data, surveys, direct information and trade and production data in the commodity flow method. The Department of Environment and Local Government (DELG) produces a Construction Industry Review and Outlook (R&O) each year that is used to estimate GFCF on building and construction in the State. For the most part, these estimates are not based on information provided by builders and are considered to be reasonably reliable and comprehensive. For instance, new house construction is based on the number of house completions. These are estimated using information on new electricity connections. Expenditures by households on capital type improvement works, such as extensions, are measured using the special household survey undertaken by the ESRI as described above. The estimate of capital formation also includes the value of transfer costs incurred in the sale of land and buildings. The total value of transfer fees on land and buildings in 1996 was 321 million Ir£.

2.4.5 Imports and exports

Merchandise imports and exports are compiled mostly using the Intrastat surveys for trade with EU member states and customs declarations for trade with countries outside the EU. Estimates of trade in services are compiled mostly from Balance of Payments direct surveys. The following paragraphs describe adjustments made for exhaustiveness.

Intrastat

In Ireland, the full Intrastat system applies to traders whose exports to EU countries in the previous year exceeded £500 000 or whose imports from EU countries exceeded £150 000. About 95 per cent of the traders surveyed respond and these also account for 95 per cent of total EU trade.

Results for large traders are verified against other information available from the statistical records and tax files of these companies. The results are also grossed up to include estimates for non-respondents and below threshold traders. All traders are required to record the total value of goods imported from and exported to other EU member states on their VAT returns and this information is used to estimate total EU trade for traders below the Intrastat thresholds and for non-respondents above the thresholds. These VAT returns are also used for maintaining the register for the Intrastat survey.

Traders not registered for VAT and private individuals who move goods within the EU have no obligations under the Intrastat system and their trade is therefore not included in the statistics. However, an overall upward adjustment is made to imports in order to compensate for these and other imports missed in the Intrastat system. This under-coverage adjustment is equivalent to almost 3 per cent of Intra-EU arrivals. Experience with the Intrastat system suggests that imports tend to be understated and that some upward adjustment is needed to the reported figures. The level of adjustment applied in Ireland was determined after an examination of mirror statistics and macro-economic trends soon after the introduction of the Intrastat system. It has been retained pending the completion of a more up-to-date supply-and-use table, which will permit additional analyses.

SAD Trade System

The SAD (Single Administrative Document) Trade System captures all imports and exports that are subject to the normal customs declarations. These cover most of the trade with non-EU countries. However, the statistics have to be supplemented with estimates for certain special categories of trade not covered by the normal customs regime, namely parcel post, non-EU low-value transactions, and the imports and exports of companies operating in the Shannon Free Zone.

Other unrecorded trade

A largely conjectural estimate is included for net unrecorded trade and smuggling. Cross-border shopping by Irish residents in Northern Ireland and vice versa has been a feature for many years. The levels and direction of such activity can vary from year to year depending on the underlying price levels, differences in indirect taxes and changes in exchange rates. The effect of this adjustment in 1996 was to add a net 60 million Ir£ to Imports.

Exports and imports of services

Exports and imports of services are largely based on the Balance of Payments statistics, which are also compiled by the CSO. The estimates are based on direct surveys conducted by the Office and are generally comprehensive. Whenever necessary, the survey results are grossed upwards for non-response or non-coverage.

ITALY

1. Introduction

In the early 1990s the European Commission promoted research on the harmonisation of gross domestic product among member countries.[24] In this context, the Italian national accountants adopted methodologies to assist in identifying the so-called "underground economy". The underground economy represents legal production that is not directly observed due to economic or statistical reasons. These definitions are in accordance with the SNA 93 and ESA 95.

2. Definitions and concepts

2.1 General overview

In Italy, the part of the underground economy attributable to economic reasons is identified as resulting from the use of unregistered labour, the under-reporting of legal production and the over-estimation of intermediate costs by enterprises. The underground economy that is due to statistical reasons occurs largely from the difficulties in maintaining the coverage and updating of registers of a large number of small production units, and the growing participation in the production process of freelancers and othe producers who are difficult to find with the usual enterprise-based survey techniques.

The approaches used for measuring the statistical and economic underground are mainly the following: a) survey techniques that make it possible to measure the significance of unregistered work; b) correction of the under-reporting of income by enterprises, through adjustments to the per capita production and value added values declared mainly by small production units (fewer than 20 employees); and c) checks of consistency in economic aggregates through the balancing of resources and uses made at the industry level. The first two approaches are identified with the labour input method that was pioneered by ISTAT during the 1980s and now recognised at the international level (see box 1).

2.2 ISTAT framework for the non-observed economy (NOE)

The ISTAT framework was elaborated at the end of the 1980s and was further developed in the 1990s within the European Union during technical assistance activities in transition and developing countries.[25]

The framework shows the relationship between NOE problems and associated statistical measurement problems. In the framework, the eight types of NOE are classified into three broad categories: unregistered units, non-response, and under-reporting. According to ESA 95, in addition to legal productive activities, those classified as illegal and informal fall within the production boundary. No specific estimates of illegal production activities are included in the national accounts till now.

---

[24] EC Council Directive 89/130 Euratom.
[25] A detailed description of the Italian framework is provided in the OECD Handbook (2002).

Box 1

> The <u>labour input method</u> is considered the most effective supply-based procedure. Three important steps are at the core of the Italian method:
>
> - Estimates of the supply of labour inputs to GDP are obtained for selected industries and enterprise size classes, from a household Labour Force Survey and/or other demographic source (e.g. the Population Census);
> - Using regular or special purpose surveys, estimates are derived of output per unit of labour input, and value added per unit of labour input, for similar industry and size classes;
> - The labour input estimates are multiplied by unit ratios to compile output and value added classified by industry and size of production units.
>
> Further, this method serves to meet two basic aims:
>
> - Minimising the problems of identifying active enterprises and their structural changes that are the main cause of statistical underground, and re-allocating this area to the observed economy;
> - Identifying the economic underground if the household survey data give more complete coverage of labour input to GDP than do the enterprise survey data.

3. Sources and estimation methods

3.1 Employment measures

The approach used for quantifying the input of labour within the national income statements consists of extrapolating base year estimates by surveys and administrative data. The base years for the employment series have been 1981, 1991 and 2001, that is the years of Business and Population Censuses.

With respect to the above years, reconciliation was carried out on employment data from administrative, sampling and census records. The reconciliation took into account who provided the information (enterprises, institutions or households). As noted above, the base-year employment levels are updated with information from ISTAT surveys and administrative sources.

3.1.1 Method of estimation

Through the use of consistent definitions of employment in labour surveys and in other national accounts surveys that also provide employment estimates, differences between the measures produced by each type can be quantified and analysed.

3.1.2 Unregistered employment

The Italian approach to the estimation of the total labour input consists of calculating full-time equivalent jobs for legal labour (defined as registered with appropriate authorities), unregistered resident labour, and registered and unregistered non-resident labour. Estimates are made by comparing the various available data sources.

Estimates of labour input are designed to achieve exhaustiveness in the national accounts by ensuring that all productive labour is taken into account. The principle steps in obtaining a comprehensive measure of full-time equivalent employment inputs are:

- harmonisation and integration of the different sources of employment information from the supply and demand of labour, with respect to concepts and definitions, in order to obtain a first estimate of jobs;
- comparison of separate estimates of employment from the demand and supply sources of information to identify a first estimate of labour input and obtain indicators of the various types of employment, such as registered and unregistered multiple-job-holders;
- use of additional sources such as special surveys and administrative records to capture data not collected in the standard data sources of the categories of employment not directly observable from the sources of information;
- conversion of jobs data to a full-time equivalent basis.

Harmonisation of data sources

To ensure consistency in comparisons across aggregates at the geographic, industry and institutional level, international definitions are used for domestic employees, jobs and full-time equivalent units.

The definition of domestic employment is different from that of national employment since domestic employment does not include residents who work in producing units not located in the domestic economic territory, while it does include non-residents working in resident producing units. The concept of national employment includes all resident people employed in both resident and non-resident producing units, and excludes non-resident workers.

The concept of employment used in household surveys is very close to that of national employment. The full harmonization of the definition of employment in the Labour Force Survey (LFS) with the national accounting definition also requires the inclusion of workers permanently in an institution, conscripts and the military forces. Table 1 shows the steps taken in the derivation of total employment for national accounts purposes from the LFS. If consistent definitions and time periods are used across the data sources, comparisons of the results will enable the identification of the same registered employment in each source. The remaining difference will then be indicators of the amount of employment not captured in the standard surveys.

Integration of labour input data

In estimating labour inputs, both the labour supply and labour demand are integrated and then compared.

For labour supply, the main data sources are the Population Census and the quarterly household Labour Force Survey. The major information sources for labour demand statistics are the Industry, Services and Institutions Census, the Agriculture Census, and Ministry of Finance VAT data. Other periodic surveys are used to supplement the basic information or fill in gaps in the data.

Table 1. Derivation of domestic employment for national accounts purposes

	Number of employed people (Labour Force Survey, annual average)
+	Foreign workers present on the national territory for a period longer than one year, but not included in the population register
+	Seasonal foreign workers that work in the country for a period less than one year, not included in the population register
+	Members of the country's armed forces in the rest of the world
+	Conscripted forces
+	Staff in charge of national embassies located abroad
+	Resident workers living permanently in an institution
-	Resident frontier workers that work in non-resident establishments
+	Non-resident frontier workers that work in resident establishments
+	Trainees not paid within enterprises
+	Employed individuals with an age of less than 15 years
+	Workers employed in underground productive activities not covered by the Labour Force Survey
+/-	Integration with other sources
=	Number of domestic workers in national accounting (annual average)

Data from households are usually in terms of persons employed while data from enterprises are usually in terms of jobs. A person can have more than one job. Thus, in order that data from the two sources can be meaningfully compared, they must be converted to the same standard units of labour input, represented by full-time equivalent employment.

The aim of the integration of sources of data from the labour demand (enterprises and institutions) is to produce exhaustive estimates of the registered employment covering primary and secondary jobs.

The aim of the integration of sources of data from labour supply (households) is to obtain an exhaustive estimate of registered and unregistered workers. There are two reasons to suppose that this is likely:

- household surveys pick up labour inputs to enterprises that are not included in enterprise surveys, for example because these enterprises are too small to be registered in the files from which the survey frames are constructed, or because they are too small to be included in the survey;
- individuals may declare their employed condition to household surveys whereas enterprises may conceal those same inputs in order to evade taxes or administrative regulations.

Comparison of labour input data

Comparisons of numbers of jobs are made at a detailed level of economic activity by region, separately for employees, self-employed and unpaid family workers. Three cases are distinguished:

- registered workers with a main job, when the number of jobs registered by enterprise surveys is equal to the number of workers registered by the household surveys;
- unregistered full-time workers, when the number of workers registered by the household surveys exceeds the number of jobs of the enterprises surveys;
- registered multiple jobs, when the number of jobs exceeds the number of workers.

Additional data sources

To complete the information on labour input, various administrative sources provide direct estimates of employment, when the procedure of integration and comparison described above fails to provide an exhaustive estimate of the input of labour by industry (in particular, in the following industries: agriculture, construction, hotels and restaurants, transport and domestic services).

Other typologies of employment require indirect estimation methods because they are not covered in the standard data sources; unregistered foreign workers and multiple unregistered jobs fall in this category. Table 2 shows the sources used to estimate the numbers and categories of employees.

Full-time equivalents

For the purpose of measuring the input of work as a factor of production, ESA95 suggests estimating the total number of hours worked or, as an alternative measure, the number of the full-time equivalent units. The total of full-time equivalent units is obtained by the sum of (primary and secondary) full-time jobs and part-time jobs, transformed into full-time units. Part-time jobs (primary and secondary) are transformed into full-time equivalents by means of coefficients based on the ratio of hours worked in part-time jobs to hours worked in full-time jobs.

3.2 Output measures

In order to meet the objectives of the analysis of the underground economy within national accounts, it is very important not to limit attention to value added alone, but also to evaluate explicitly the two amounts that generate it, i.e. output and intermediate consumption.

It is also important to emphasise that according to the NACE Rev.1 industry classification, each industry may or may not be destined for market. It is possible to identify the following institutional sectors for national accounts purposes[26]:
- market enterprises;
- market public administration institutions;
- non-market public administration institutions;
- market non-profit institutions serving households (NPISH);
- non-market NPISHs.

The presence of an underground economy is not envisaged in the *non-market* units of production. However, it does not mean that the presence of the underground economy is not considered within a specific industry. On the contrary, the calculation method followed to ensure

---

[26] For the sake of completeness, it is necessary to mention another sector comprising the production of goods for own final use. This kind of activity is present in the following industries: agriculture, construction, renting of buildings, and domestic and live-in services with families. This production is included in market enterprises.

the exhaustiveness of the estimates does not permit the breakdown of the supplements similar to that used for the other industries of the market enterprises segment.

Table 2. Main sources of information for the estimation of labour input

Sources	Typology of Information	Data for base years	Data for current years
Households and enterprises			
1 Population Census	Resident employed individuals and per working place	•	
2 Labour Force Survey	Resident employed individuals	•	•
3 Multi-purpose Survey	Employed persons in private households		•
4 Industry, Service and Institutions Survey	Registered employment, main and secondary activities	•	
5 Agriculture Census	Agricultural sector, main and secondary jobs	•	
6 Tax Register	Enterprises and employed individuals with VAT	•	•
7 ISTAT Register of Productive Enterprises (A.S.I.A.)	Number of people employed at industry level		•
8 Social Security Institute (data on employees and family workers)	Employees from households and enterprises, part-time registered workers, registered foreign workers	•	•
9 ISTAT surveys of the accounts of enterprises	Up to 19 employees, 20 or more employees, more than 500 employees		•
10 Balance sheets for specific business sectors	Energy, tobacco, railways, post offices, telephone and communications, credit, insurance	•	•
11 Periodical ISTAT surveys of sectors prone to underground production	Ordinary and extraordinary maintenance of homes	Case-by-case	
12 Administrative data and statistical surveys on specific typologies of employees	Non-resident foreign workers, temporary lay-off workers	•	•
13 Administrative data for specific business sectors	Road transport of goods and passengers, research and development, private education	•	•
Institutions			
14 State General Accounting Office, ministries and other public institutions	Data on employees and on hours worked in the General Government sector	•	•
15 ISTAT surveys of public institutions	Municipalities, mountain communities, provinces, regions		•
16 Social Security Institute data for Private Social Institutions (NPHI)	Private non profit institutions	•	•

The procedure for estimating output and value added by industry is summarised by the following formula:

$$Y = \sum_{b=1}^{m} \sum_{c=1}^{n} X_{bc} \cdot U_{bc} + \sum_{b=m+1}^{z} YM_b + \sum_{b=1}^{z} YP_b + \sum_{b=1}^{z} YN_b$$

where: Y = overall estimate of the aggregate (i.e. value added)

    b = indicator of industry (for $i = 1, \ldots, m, \ldots, z$)

c = indicator of the size of the establishment (for $c=1,....,n$)

X = average per capita value of the aggregate derived by business surveys

U = fulltime equivalent units

and where the following are values of the aggregate not estimated using the labour input method:

$\sum_{b=m+1}^{z} YM_b$ = value of the aggregate referring to market services

$\sum_{b=1}^{z} YP_b$ = value of the aggregate referring to public administration institutions

$\sum_{b=1}^{z} YN_b$ = value of the aggregate referring to non market services of public administration institutions and NPISH

Average per capita values of the aggregate are estimated on the basis of annual surveys of enterprises' budgets, with adjustments for under-reporting as described below. The above ratios are multiplied for exhaustive estimates of full-time equivalent units. This procedure can be expected to give a more exhaustive coverage of production if the household survey data give more complete coverage of labour input to GDP than do the enterprise survey data.

In conclusion, for each industry broken down by size of enterprises using the labour input method, the labour input estimates provide the weighting factors by which to inflate enterprise survey based estimates of output and value added to totals.

3.3 The underground economy in the output estimates

The preceding section focused on estimating total employment in the economy, with a view to compiling comprehensive accounts for the macroeconomic aggregates. This type of process results in final estimates that take account of the statistical and economic underground, including that arising in the informal sector.

While such processes assist in obtaining more accurate total supply estimates, they do not necessarily result in more accurate accounts at detailed levels. In order to measure correctly the contributions of the various factors of output and value added, it is necessary to carry out in-depth reconciliation, by way of input-output analysis, of the resources and uses.

Adjustments to reported values

The adjustments made to initial national accounts estimates to account for non-observed production can be summed up by the following equation:

$$NA = SUR + \Delta CLA + \Delta RE + \Delta UNR + \Delta ESA + \Delta BAL$$

where: NA = final aggregate estimated in the framework of national accounts (that is output or value added)

SUR = value added and production from standard surveys

ΔCLA = adjustments for understatement of the aggregate by registered employment (1)

ΔRE = adjustments for understatement of revenue or overstatement of costs (2)

ΔUNR = adjustments for costs and output associated with unregistered labour (3)

ΔESA = adjustments for other under coverage, such as self-developed software and payments in kind (4)

ΔBAL = adjustments arising from balancing supply-and-use in the input-output framework

(1) – Compiled by multiplying total registered full-time equivalent employees by estimates of per capita adjusted aggregate for each industry. Adjustments for undeclared incomes of owners is described below.

(2) – Based on relationships between output and intermediate input in each activity. Costs and revenues are also adjusted in accordance with the results of income and output analysis referred to in (1) above.

(3) – Based on per capita output and wages for unregistered employees. Costs and value added are both adjusted.

(4) – These items are estimated from special data collections.

4. Quantifying the underground economy

Using the above methodologies, experimental estimates of the lower and upper bounds of the value of the underground economy are made. In doing so, it is assumed that the main reason for the existence of the economic underground is the desire to evade taxes.

Mechanisms created for tax evasion may be particularly complex and, very often, involve a combination of factors. However, there are three main ways in which tax evasion is carried out:
- concealment of all production;
- understatement of sales revenues;
- overstatement of costs.

Concealment of production is accounted for by the adjustments to intermediate inputs, output and value added attributable to unregistered labour. This method implicitly assumes that production is hidden through the non-declaration of some or all employees and therefore no declaration is made on the production or costs associated with the unregistered employees.

The understatement of sales revenues and the overstatement of costs are adjusted in two ways: the revaluating of turnover and the balancing of supply-and-use statistics. However, the adjustments resulting from the balancing process will inevitably include elements of both the economic and statistical underground.

Per-capita output and value added collected by business surveys are adjusted for under-reporting turnover. The underlying hypothesis is that income of a self-employed worker of an enterprise should at least equal the highest wage of the registered employees by stratum. Each stratum is identified by job position, legal status, size of enterprise and duration of enterprise activity. The income of self-employed workers is obtained by taking the value added reported by the enterprise and subtracting the compensations of employees, the capital consumption and other components in accordance with the SNA 93. When income, thus computed, is less than the highest wages of employees by stratum, it is adjusted upwards to be the same as the identified wage. The comparison, in order to be conducted correctly, must be based on hourly income; this means that the wage of the employees are corrected with a coefficient on ratios of average hours worked by owners to average hours worked by employees.

In the methodology used, the adjustments for non-declared output, overstated costs or understated revenue, and output of unregistered employment are designed to account for the economic underground (i.e. deliberate actions on the part of producing units for the purpose of evading tax or other social contributions). Adjustments arising from the input-output balancing process on the other hand include both the economic and statistical underground (i.e. non-observed production due to non-response to surveys and deficiencies in registers used for survey purposes). It can be assumed therefore, that the former estimates represent the lower bound of the likely size of the non-observed economy, while the latter represent an upper bound.

Figure 1 shows the estimates of the lower and upper bounds as a percentage of Italian GDP from 1992 to 2003. In 2003 the lower bound was around 14.8 per cent of GDP, while the upper bound was about 16.7 per cent.

Figure 1 – Share of adjustments for the underground economy in GDP
(Per cent)

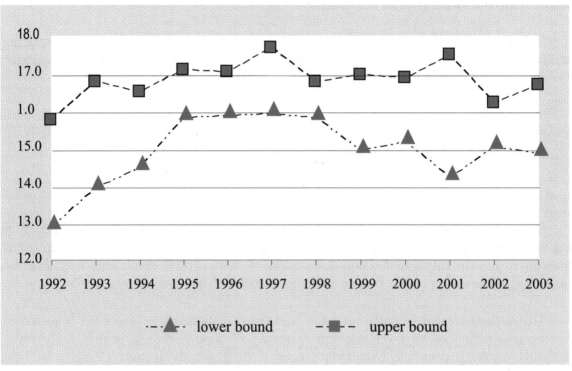

KAZAKHSTAN

1. Principles of estimating the non-observed economy

The Agency on Statistics of the Republic of Kazakhstan (ASRK) produces regular national estimates of the hidden and informal economy. The methods applied at the macro- and micro-levels correspond to the general rules developed by international organizations, namely:

- calculations should be carried out in accordance with the definitions of the system of national accounts, to ensure comparability of the results with other indicators of economic statistics;
- the results should be taken into account in compiling GDP; they should be linked to other indicators of the system and should not contradict them.

Production in the household sector is carried out by unincorporated enterprises. This category includes households, family unions or associations, and individual entrepreneurs. The informal sector includes the hidden activities of these enterprises. The following problems exist in this field:

- under-reporting or data by registered enterprises;
- a large number of unregistered enterprises;
- unregistered employed persons in the formal sector.

2. Sources and estimation methods

Generally, there are three methods for statistical estimation of the non-observed economy : direct methods, indirect methods and combined methods.

Direct methods use data from sample surveys and administrative sources. The following surveys are used:

- surveys of volumes of production in the households sector;
- surveys of enterprise activities;
- surveys of informal markets;
- surveys of working time at enterprises;
- study of the results of taxation, financial and other (legal) checks.

The preferred direct method is a household survey. This method is used on a regular basis to study different aspects of the population's activities: living standards, employment, poverty, consumption trends, income and expenditure structures.

The household surveys are used:

- in industry – to calculate household production of processing foodstuffs grown at individual household plots;
- in trade – for specifying trade turnover (expenditure of households for the purchase of goods);
- in agriculture – to compare the production and consumption of food products;
- in SNA – as indicators for comparisons or adjustment.

In addition, special household surveys are currently conducted to study the labour market (utilization of labour force, employers and self-employed, labour expenditure, time use). The study of the labour market helps to determine:

- scale of unregistered economic activities;
- informal employment in the households sector;
- volume of work carried out in hidden economy with breakdown by status in employment – employees, employers, self-employed;
- work done by persons registered as unemployed;
- income of employees engaged in the unrecorded sector of the economy.

Indirect methods are used to make estimates based on the analysis of all available information. Indirect methods include the commodity flow method, balancing labour supply and use, and using the population census results.

The combined method mixes the direct and indirect methods and expert estimates. The choice of the method depends on the specific character of a given branch, available sources of information, the possibility of conducting additional surveys, etc.

Adjustments are made in two stages, at the branch level and at the level of national accounts compilation. Adjustments made at the branch level include:

- adjustments for non-response;
- adjustments for informal activities;
- adjustments for under-reporting.

Adjustments for non-response are made by grossing up the average values of the enterprises which have submitted their reports to those enterprises which have not reported.

A special quarterly sample survey of production is the main source used to estimate the informal activities of households. The survey provides indicators of the industry structure of households' activities. The volume of production per household in each industry is estimated and the results are grossed up according to the industry structure.

3. Methodology applied at the branch level

3.1 Industry

Non-observed economic activities in industry include:
- under-reporting of production by registered enterprises;
- non-licensed production of goods and services;
- illegal production;
- production by unincorporated enterprises belonging to households;
- irregular and individual activities.

With respect to officially accounted activities, the adjustments are made for all enterprises (large, medium, small, non-industrial organizations, individual entrepreneurship), as well as for volumes of output underreported by legal entities in order to evade taxes, compliance with legislation, etc. With respect to informal activities, the production of goods by the household sector is adjusted. Expert estimates of the production of selected goods are made by comparing indicators of production per capita for the given periods.

The volume of production in the informal sector is adjusted on the basis of the results of quarterly household surveys. Calculation of volumes (separately for urban and rural areas) are made according to the following formula:

$$V_{hh} = (V_{budget\ survey} : n) : Fam \times Pop.$$

where V_{hh} = volume of products produced in households;
$V_{budget\ survey}$ = volume of production from budget survey;
n = number of surveyed families;
Fam = average size of a family;
Pop = number of resident population.

The balances of production and distribution of most important kinds of raw materials, industrial goods and consumer goods are compiled on the basis of data on production reported by industrial enterprises, consumption of raw materials, fuel and energy, reported data on trade, merchandise and combined markets, as well as the customs data. Statistical discrepancies in the supply-and-use of selected goods reveal the hidden production or hidden consumption.

3.2 Construction

The balancing method is used to determine the volumes of hidden and informal activities in construction. The volumes are determined as the difference between the use of resources and the data reported by enterprises.

Resources comprise construction and other materials used in construction and mounting and repair works. Estimated volume of hidden activities in construction (contract works) is determined on the basis of used resources according to the following formula:

$$V_{contracts} = V_o \times (1-d)$$
where
V_o = estimated volume of executed construction and repairs;
d = share of own-account construction works.

The volume of hidden and informal construction activities is determined as the difference between the estimated volume of contract work and the data reported for small enterprises.

The value of hidden and informal construction activities is distributed by region in proportion to the level of under-reporting of data by construction enterprises, and similar data reported by customers.

3.3 Agriculture

Output in agriculture is determined with combined methods, which implicitly include the estimates of non-observed economy. Output of crops is calculated on the basis of data on sowing areas, by type of crop and their average yield. Output of livestock products is calculated on the basis of the number of livestock and its average weight. The adjustments for informal activities concern the products produced on individual household plots. Hidden activities of enterprises are determined by the residual method; the volume of household output and the reported data of enterprises are excluded from the total volume of production.

3.4 Transport

Individual entrepreneurs provide almost all transport services in Kazakhstan. The rent of transport vehicles by them from transport enterprises is also included. Therefore, it is not possible to collect objective information directly from individual entrepreneurs and calculations are made indirectly. The basis for the calculations are data of the State Automobile Inspection on the number of lorries, buses, and taxis owned or rented by citizens. Also data on average mileage, load and profitability of cargo transportation are used. Calculations of passenger transportation by taxis are made in the same way on the basis of the data on issued licenses.

3.5 Trade

Estimation of non-observed trade includes adjustments for retail turnover. First, adjustment for non-response is made. To this end, the volume of retail turnover of all types of enterprises for which retail trade is the main or secondary activity is determined on the basis of data from regular statistical observations. The turnover per enterprise is calculated and extrapolated to those enterprises that have not submitted their reports. Data of the sample survey of trade at the markets and by individual entrepreneurs are added to the received value. The turnover calculated in this way is compared with the data from the survey of population expenditure on food and non-food products. This enables to determine the concealed volumes of sales of goods by enterprises.

3.6 Market services

The volume of hidden and informal market services provided to the population is determined mainly by indirect methods.

The size of under-reporting is estimated by comparing the volumes of services and sales of enterprises with similar staff and service profiles. The results of statistical bodies' checks on primary bookkeeping documents are also used. The actual volume of market services provided and adjustment coefficients for each kind of service, are determined on the basis of the data reported by enterprises on the volume of market services provided and the sum of revealed unrecorded earnings.

Concealed volume is then determined by extrapolating the adjustment coefficient to the overall volume of market services provided by all enterprises which presented their reports to the statistical office. Primary criteria for determining the volume of market services provided in the informal sector are:
- the number of individual entrepreneurs engaged in providing market services;
- their labour productivity (volume of services per entrepreneur).

The average volume of market services provided by small enterprises per worker is taken as an indicator of the labour productivity of entrepreneurs. This is applied to the number of individual entrepreneurs and the volume of services provided by them is determined.

An additional method for calculating the volume of services provided by individual entrepreneurs is based on households' statistical observation data, which help to calculate the average number of individual entrepreneurs in each area of the consumer services market. Data on the annual average number of individuals providing market services, grossed up to the total population, must be compared with the data of tax office on the number of officially registered individual entrepreneurs. If, for certain types of activity, the data of tax offices exceed the figures received from household surveys, the tax data are used.

4. Adjustment of enterprises' data on the basis of their financial reports

Adjustment of primary data for unreliability is made by comparing and analyzing interrelated indicators presented by enterprises in their financial reports. The structure of the reports makes it possible to compare indicators of production (gross output, intermediate consumption, gross value added) at the enterprise level with the data of different statistical reports. Gross value added is determined by two methods: on the basis of output; and on the basis of the expenditure for its components. Here one condition is observed, namely, if an enterprise has paid income tax, profit should not be negative. Otherwise, profit should be taken as equal to profitability for the given branch. Figures for intermediate consumption are calculated on the basis of information on the enterprise's expenditure and are not adjusted. The estimates of gross value added are compared and the larger amounts are used in the calculations. After that the output is adjusted correspondingly.

5. Methodology applied at the level of national accounts

At the next stage, in compiling national accounts, estimates of the non-observed economy are made to ensure the completeness, reliability and coherence of SNA indicators and GDP. This requires adjustments for non-observed economy both on the part of production of goods and services, and of generation and use of incomes. Goods, services and incomes concealed at the production stage can be covered by regular statistical observation when they are used, and the adjustments at the production and consumption stages may not coincide.

After comparing the output of goods and services adjusted by branches with the figures of output received by adjusted financial reports, a decision is made what data will be used to calculate gross value added for each type of activity. Then the production estimate of GDP is made.

In order to ensure reconciliation of the estimates of produced GDP with those of consumed GDP, analysis is made of the components of gross value added. Assuming that the Ministry of Finance data on taxes are reliable and gross profit is estimated by a residual method, the comparison is made on the basis of compensation of employees. To calculate the compensation of employees in the SNA framework the following information is used:

- reports on the number of employees and total wages by type of economic activity;
- bank reports on incomes and losses (National Bank);
- reports of insurance companies and pension funds;
- reports on the implementation of state budget (Ministry of Finance);
- reports on the activities of small enterprises;
- main indicators of the labour market.

The compensation of employees is calculated in several stages. It is assumed that the data from the Ministry of Finance and the National Bank are reliable, and that all adjustments are made for the non-financial sector.

At the first stage, the reported data on the number of employees are compared with those taken from the population survey. Adjustments are made by grossing up average wages per employed person, calculated for each kind of activity to the number of uncovered employed persons.

Average wages per employee, calculated on the basis of the data contained in the report on the activities of small enterprises, are used to adjust the compensation of employees of small enterprises. After grossing up this value to the number of employees taken from the population survey, the wages for small enterprises are determined.

Data on the number of employees taken from the bulletin *Main indicators of the labour market in the Republic of Kazakhstan* are used to estimate the value of adjustments for farmers' households. Data on average wages in agriculture are taken from the report on the activities of small enterprises. Then the percent of compensation of employees in gross value added by branches is determined, and compared with a similar indicator in the report on production and financial activities of enterprises. These shares are used to estimate the compensation of employees; the difference between this and the reported figure shows the needed adjustment for hidden compensation of employees. Along with this, the analysis of dynamics of other gross value added components is made (profit, taxes).

Adjusted compensation of employees is distributed by components (wages, actual contributions of employers for social insurance, imputed contributions of employers for social insurance) according to the structure, received from the reported number of employees by economic activities.

For the expenditure-based estimate of GDP, adjustments are made for final consumption of households, exports and imports. Data for exports and imports adjusted for 'shuttle traders' (the method is described above) and 'transit residue' is presented by the National Bank. The sources of information to estimate household expenditures for final consumption are: retail trade statistics, household budget surveys and balance of agricultural products.

The data for 2004, calculated using the NA framework and household budget survey, are given in Table 1.

Table 1 shows that data on final consumption of households according to the SNA exceed the results of the household surveys by more than one and a half times and constitute 36.8 per cent of GDP (21.2 per cent according to the family budget survey). Most discrepancies fall in the category of expenditure on services.

Comparison of data at different levels leads to various adjustments. Many of them are connected indirectly with hidden and informal activities, not included in primary data sources. That is why the non-observed economy included in the estimates of national accounts cannot be determined and shown explicitly. However, the values of adjustments can be obtained from comparisons with primary data. The dynamics of the non-observed economy for 1990-2003 are shown in Figure 1.

Table 1. Data calculation using the SNA framework and household budget surveys

| | 2004 | | | |
| | GDP billion tenge | Expenditure according to household surveys | Share in the household final consumption expenditure | |
			According to NA framework	According to household surveys
Total goods	**1 381.0**	**950.7**	**63.7**	**76.3**
Food products	739.2	577.6	34.1	46.3
Non-food and other products	642.9	373.1	29.6	29.9
Total services	**785.4**	**294.8**	**36.3**	**23.7**
Health care	139.2	11.6	6.4	0.9
Education	174.1	44.5	8.0	3.6
Culture	78.7	6.1	3.6	0.5
Transport and communications	281.0	84.2	12.9	6.8
Communal services	98.5	139.2	4.5	11.2
Banks, insurance	7.3	0.0	0.4	0.0
Other	6.7	9.19	0.3	0.7
Total expenditure	**2 166.5**	**1 245.4**	**100.0**	**100.0**

Figure 1. Share of non-observed economy in GDP of the Republic of Kazakhstan
(Per cent)

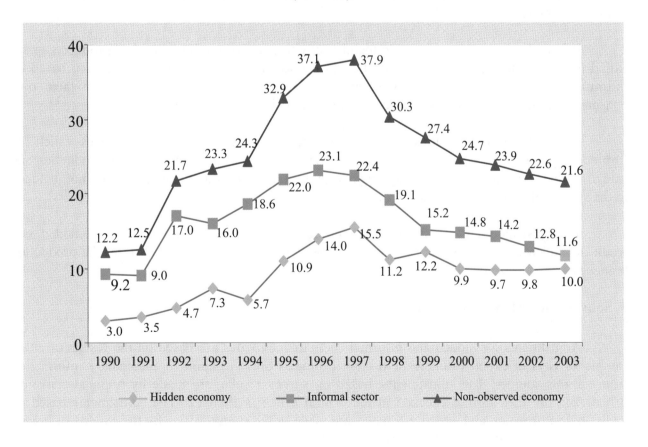

KYRGYZSTAN

1. Introduction

The existence of underground economy in the Kyrgyz Republic is an accepted fact. The hidden (non-observed and non-recorded) economic activities significantly affect most important macroeconomic indicators, such as GDP. Without taking account of hidden economic activities it is impossible to make an objective estimate of the size of the national economy and especially of some of its components that are particularly prone to non-observed activity, such as trade and services.

2. Concepts and definitions

In the Kyrgyz Republic, the statistical definition of the term "non-observed economy" includes both hidden and informal activities.

Hidden economy includes economic activities which are being hidden or underreported by enterprises, with the purpose of avoiding taxes, social security or other administrative obligations, as well as non-submission of administrative forms or statistical questionnaires. These activities may be carried out in all branches of the economy.

Hidden activities mainly consist of two different kinds of activities: activities that are deliberately concealed or the activities which are not registered due to deficiencies in the statistical information system.

Informal economic activities are mainly activities carried out by individual producers or so-called unincorporated enterprises, which belong to individuals or households. They are based on informal relations and produce goods and services completely or partially for their own consumption. Informal activities often constitute a secondary employment.

Illegal economic activities cover the production of those goods and services which are forbidden by law. Such activities include production and sale of drugs, unauthorised production and sale of weapons, prostitution and smuggling. At present, illegal economic activities are not included in the system of national accounts.

To adjust the GDP calculated by the production method, an estimate of value added as a result of hidden or informal production was made. This estimate is included in all the production branches.

3. Sources and estimation methods

Adjustments for hidden and informal economic activities are based on the results of either sample surveys or expert estimates and other estimates drawing upon supplementary information from various sources. The adjustments, based on survey results, are made by regional statistical offices and are then further checked in the central office in Bishkek. The adjustments based on additional information and expert estimates, are made in the central office by the experts of branch divisions or of the national accounts division.

In production-based estimates of GDP, the adjustments are made for the indicators of industrial output, construction, transport, trade, and marketed consumer services, including financial services. To a certain extent, adjustments are made to the indicators for all main branches producing market goods and services. Informal production in agriculture is also estimated but is not included in the total figures of hidden or informal production.

4. Adjustments for hidden and informal activities by industry

4.1 Industry

The adjustments for informal and hidden output in industry are not very large. They mainly concern handicraft production carried out by households. These activities are largely concentrated in the food industry and to a lesser extent in clothing, jewelry and some other industries. Data for the adjustments are obtained from issued licenses and a special survey. In general, this type of production is confined to the informal sector, and there is a degree of hidden production that results from some handicraft producers deliberately not reporting income in order to avoid taxes. For example, because of their low price and high quality, hand-made clothes can compete in the local market and also be supplied to the CIS countries.

Apart from that, adjustments by the regions for concealed production of flour and bread are made by the balancing method, using the data from household budget surveys on consumption of these products by the population.

4.2 Construction

Some construction activities in Kyrgyzstan are carried out not by professional and formally organized building firms but by informal and temporary construction teams or directly by residents. These activities are taken into account by collecting data on the registration of constructed buildings and dwellings from the local authorities. Such activities are included in the informal sector. The information obtained in this way is sufficiently reliable to accurately reflect the physical volume of new construction.

However, the value of many structures may be understated at the time of registration. In the opinion of experts, the value of premises for office use is understated considerably and systematically. A similar situation applies with individual housing construction.

For example, the actual value of one square meter of housing in Bishkek is estimated by experts to be 150 to 300 US dollars, whereas the recorded value per square meter does not exceed 300 to 600 soms, which is about 10-15 times lower. Apart from that, adjustments for individual builders are made on the basis of the licenses issued.

4.3 Trade

Hidden economic activities are mainly concentrated in trade. Trade is also the second largest branch, after agriculture, in which households' informal activities are concentrated. It is very difficult to check the reliability of reported trade data, especially when it relates to the activities of small enterprises or individual entrepreneurs (households).

Hidden economic activities include trade and catering enterprises that have not been duly registered. The data for these enterprises are adjusted on the basis of branch averages obtained from special one-off surveys. Additional surveys and checks are conducted to correct for misreporting by trade enterprises that, for example, over-report intermediate consumption.

Informal trade activities are studied by carrying out systematic sample surveys of all types of markets throughout the country. These surveys are carried out professionally and their results are considered sometimes more reliable than the data of the sample Household Budget Survey. Data from surveys of informal markets are widely used, not only for calculating trade as a branch of the economy, but also for calculating households' consumption of consumer goods and services.

In addition, reconciliation of the balance between supply and use is also employed with respect to certain consumer goods, such as alcohol, cigarettes and petroleum products. The level of recorded sales is compared to reasonable consumption levels for such goods and, where necessary, adjustments are made. In accordance with established practice, the entire volume of market sales is assigned to the informal sector.

4.4 Transport

Individuals provide a significant share of transport services in Kyrgyzstan. Since the collection of objective information directly from individual entrepreneurs is not possible, calculations are based on indirect information. For example, based on the data from the State Motor Vehicle Inspectorate on the number of serviceable lorries and buses owned or hired by private individuals, details of average distance travelled, average loads carried, and average earnings from transport operations. Calculations for passenger transportation by taxis are made using a similar method on the basis of data for licenses issued. The adjustment is allocated entirely to informal activities.

4.5 Services

The volume of produced market services is estimated on the basis of data from the statistical observation of enterprises providing services to the population, expert estimates of the volume of services provided by individual entrepreneurs and data from sample surveys of selected kinds of market services. Apart from that, adjustments for the activities of currency exchange bureaus, pawnshops and other market services are made on the basis of the reports of enterprises and the number of employed persons. The estimate received in such a way enables an adequate judgement of the scope of the hidden economy with respect to individual services.

4.6 Foreign trade

Foreign trade transactions undertaken by persons engaged in 'shuttle trade' are recorded on the basis of customs documents. Individuals exporting or importing goods in large quantities (e.g. by lorry or charter flight) fill up a cargo customs declaration. These data are regularly included in total figures for foreign trade. 'Shuttle traders' bringing goods into the country and taking goods out in small quantities by railway, air and automobile transport fill in a simplified customs declaration.

5. Estimation of non-observed economy from the production side

The estimates of hidden and informal production for the period 1995-2003 are presented in Table 1.

Table 1. Size of the hidden and informal economy according to the production approach

	1995	1996	1997	1998	1999	2000	2001	2002	2003
Million soms	1 353.9	2 203.3	31 67.3	4 073.6	6 451.8	8 535.6	10 687.7	12 469.8	14 228.9
As per cent of GDP	8.4	9.4	10.3	11.9	13.2	13.1	14.4	16.5	17.0

The share of the non-observed economy is increasing both in nominal terms and as a percentage of GDP. This is attributable mainly to the increased role of the households sector in production. In 2003, the share of non-observed economy in the households sector amounted to 15.1 per cent, against 13.3 per cent in 2001 and 12 per cent in 2000.

The biggest volume of non-observed (underground) economy is traditionally observed in the sphere of trade and services. In 2003 their share in GDP constituted about 13 per cent. Table 2 below shows the structure of the non-observed economy in 2003 by type of economic activity, in output and gross value added.

Table 2. Structure of non-observed economy by kind of economic activities in 2003

	Total million soms		Share of NOE in GDP (per cent)	Share of NOE by branches (per cent)	
	Gross output	Gross value added		In gross output	In gross value added
Mining industry	2.0	0.3	0.0	0.3	0.1
Manufacturing industry	4 287.5	1 678.3	2.0	9.5	15.1
Construction	1 362.7	468.5	0.6	19.0	19.1
Transport	1 826.3	856.5	1.0	31.0	32.2
Trade, repairs of automobiles, domestic articles and personal goods	16 624.4	10 556.6	12.6	79.5	83.0
Hotels and restaurants	298.5	163.7	0.2	12.1	13.3
Real estate activities, renting and providing services	108.2	39.2	0.0	2.9	1.7
Financial activities	58.9	47.1	0.1	2.9	9.4
Health care and social services	212.7	113.7	0.1	9.0	7.9
Education	342.5	155.8	0.2	7.0	4.6
Communal, social and personal services	286.4	149.2	0.2	13.6	16.5
Total	**25 410.1**	**14 228.9**	**x**	**14.4**	**17.0**

6. Estimation of non-observed economy through the labour expenditure method

The work on using the labour expenditure method to estimate the non-observed economy is carried out at present by the National Statistical Committee of Kyrgyzstan within the framework of the TACIS project *Non-observed economy*. The resources of labour expenditure on the production of GDP by type of economic activity are estimated on the basis of the Labour Force Survey or another demographic survey.

Data on working time are obtained directly from households rather than from enterprises. Data on average output are obtained from all types of enterprises, including small enterprises. Multiplying the indicators of time actually worked by average output allows to determine the actual output.

Successful implementation of this method requires reliable data. The hours worked should be recalculated into an average working day, especially to be able to take into account the second job (often part time). Enterprises should provide high quality data on the output per standard unit of employment, that is, per standard working day.

Different methods can be used to determine the size of the non-observed economy based on the above mentioned data:

Calculations on the basis of the discrepancy between the actual and officially registered level of employment.

The actual level of employment is estimated from the data of the household survey (Labour Force Survey). After grossing up the sample data to the general population it is possible to estimate the total number of persons actually employed. The difference between officially determined figures and the results of the sample survey will show with some error the number of persons employed in the underground economy. From the number of persons employed in the underground economy and average labour productivity can be calculated the extent of underground economic activity.

Calculations on the basis of the discrepancy between actual and officially registered working time during a week.

In the sample household survey, the actual time worked during the survey week is identified, including the time worked at the main and additional job, as well as the time worked to receive additional wages. GDP from the sample data is calculated as follows:

$$\text{GDP}_{\text{sample survey}} = (T_{\text{hours}}/T_{\text{persons}}) * T_{\text{persons}} * W,$$

where:

$(T_{\text{hours}}/T_{\text{persons}})$ - the total number of hours worked during the year per one employed person (according to the sample);

T_{persons} – officially registered number of employed persons;

W – productivity of labour calculated by GDP.

Discrepancy between the estimated and official GDP characterises the size of hidden economy of the studied type. Both methods of estimation give similar results.

7. Calculation of indicators

For the first time, in November 2002, the National Statistical Committee of Kyrgyzstan conducted a Labour Force Survey in the framework of the project entitled *Development of Statistics in Support of the Comprehensive Framework of the Kyrgyz Republic Development/National Strategy of Poverty Reduction*. It was financed by the United Kingdom Department for International Development. Comparisons of the results of this survey with the data of current statistics made it possible to determine some parameters of the underground economy.

According to the survey data, 219 600 persons were employed in trade, repairs of automobiles and domestic articles, whereas according to the data of the annual balance of labour resources the figure totalled 194 300 persons, including individual entrepreneurs. The official number of persons employed in the sector of non-financial corporations for this branch comes to 26 600. Hence, the difference of 193 000 persons can be attributed to those employed in informal and hidden (non-financial) sectors.

At the next stage, on the basis of actual data, the data were calculated for small enterprises employing up to four people to show gross output in trade, repairs of automobiles and domestic articles per person (90 300 soms), intermediate consumption (49 900 soms) and gross value added (40 400 soms).

By using the data on the number of employed persons in the non-observed economy and the data on gross value added per person employed in trade, repairs of automobiles and domestic articles, the value of non-observed gross value added in this branch was estimated at 7.8 billion soms (193 thousand persons * 40.4 thousand soms), or 10.6 per cent of total GDP (data for 2001). As mentioned in the explanation to Table 1, the estimates of the non-observed economy according to the methodology used at present amounted to 10.4 per cent in 2001. Practically the same outcome was arrived at using the labour force method.

8. Estimate of non-market agricultural output

A survey of farmers' households and private subsidiary plots for 2005 has been conducted in the framework of the Non-observed economy component of TACIS Statistics - 7 project to estimate non-market agricultural output. In all, 2000 farmers' households are included in the survey. Individual consumption of production and use of products produced at private subsidiary plots are also observed. The questionnaire includes such questions as total annual production, volume of individual consumption, quantity of products used for processing and intermediate consumption. An important indicator in this survey is the availability of stocks at the beginning and at the end of the year in order to follow the changes in stocks of unincorporated agricultural producers.

The results of the survey will show production and consumption separately by farmers' households and private subsidiary plots of the general population. It will allow to analyse the results of the latter with the data from the sample household budget survey and to use the received indicator for five to seven years. However, these indicators will be representative only at the country level because of the small samples both with respect to farmers' households and private subsidiary plots of the population.

LATVIA

1. Exhaustiveness adjustments: output approach

1.1 Introductory remarks

This report presents information on exhaustiveness adjustments in the national accounts of Latvia for the year 2000. The methodology of the adjustments, in general, has remained unchanged since 1997 when the previous pilot study was undertaken.

The results of the adjustments are presented in accordance with the classification of non-exhaustiveness used in Annex C of Eurostat's General Guidelines for the Candidate Country Exhaustiveness Project. At times the distinction between the different types of non-exhaustiveness was not clear, in which case the whole adjustment was allocated to the type of non-exhaustiveness that was dominant.

The calculation of the gross domestic product starts with the production approach and includes the results of all economic activities involved in the production of goods and provision of services. Calculations are based on the information from various statistical surveys and administrative data sources. To ensure full coverage, indirect calculations and special surveys are conducted. Indirect calculations are made by analysing data from statistical surveys and using labour input data.

1.2 Data sources used for calculation of production account and for adjustments

In calculating production account aggregates, attention is paid to ensure full coverage of all economic activities, including the results of those activities which are not registered and not surveyed. Table 1 presents information on data sources used for the calculation of gross output, intermediate consumption and gross value added by kind of activity, as well as for exhaustiveness adjustments by kind of activity.

Adjustments of non-registered economic activities are based on the employment method. This method compares the total number of employed persons with information on employment from enterprise surveys. The main data source for calculation of total number of employed persons is the Labour Force Survey (LFS).

The numbers of employees from enterprise surveys are compared with the number of employees from the LFS in total and by branch. For a few branches (public administration, electricity, gas and water supply) more reliable data are available from the enterprise surveys, but in agriculture the data from LFS can be considered more reliable.

Table 1. Data sources for production account compilation and adjustments

NACE code	Data sources for NA calculations	Adjustments made to survey data according to non-exhaustiveness types	Adjustments for non-registered activities
A01	Surveys of large enterprises, sample surveys of private farms	no	no
A02	Annual surveys- budgetary data	N6	N1, N4
B	Annual survey - quantity data	N6	N1, N4
C	Annual survey	N6	no
D	Annual survey- special register	N4, N6	N1, N4
E	Annual survey- quantity data	N6	no
F	Annual survey-special register survey, special household budget survey	N4, N6	N1, N4
G	Annual survey- special register survey, special household budget survey	N4, N6, N7	N1, N4
H	Annual survey - special register survey, special household budget survey	N4, N6 , N7	N1, N4
I	Annual survey - special register survey , special household budget survey	N6, N7	N1, N4
J	Profit and losses accounts of banking institutions and insurance companies -annual survey	N6	no
K	Annual surveys - budgetary data	N6	N1, N4
L	Annual surveys - budgetary data	N6	no
M	Annual surveys - budgetary data	N6	N1, N4
N	Annual surveys - budgetary data	N6	N1, N4
O	Annual surveys - budgetary data	N6, N7	N1, N4

Experts from each statistical branch are involved in evaluating the results. Estimations are made based on the development during the year, as well as all additional data sources (surveys).

1.5 Identification and adjustment by non-exhaustiveness type

1.5.1 N1: Producers deliberately not registering – underground

This category includes the production of households not registered in the enterprise register. In order to acquire the status of a legal entity and to start business activities in accordance with the Latvian legislation, all producers must be registered in the *Register of Enterprises of the Republic of Latvia.* If individual producers are not in the Register, they can also work with licenses or perform small activities without registration. For the year 2000, the results of production activities of persons working with licenses were not available and therefore the type N1 adjustment were calculated together with the results of non-registered activities of private persons using the labour input method. It is assumed that the production of all non-registered self-employed persons and half of the non-registered employed persons are in the households sector. Valuation of this non-registered private labour input (except agriculture) is based on small enterprises survey data and also on special household budget survey data collected especially for quantification of the consumption of non-registered goods and services.

1.5.2 N2: Producers deliberately not registering – illegal

This section describes the results of a simple estimation of trade in drugs and prostitution. For the trade of drugs, the starting point is an estimation of drug consumption. These calculations are based on information from health authorities and media about potential drug users and quantities of drugs consumed. Police authorities provide information on average prices. A comparison of the levels of street prices and prices paid by drug traders leads to the assumption that the trade margin is around 50%. Thus, output of trade in drugs is estimated as half of drug consumption.

Output of prostitution is calculated in a simple way using information from the police about average number of persons working as prostitutes and their likely earnings from this activity.

Intermediate consumption for illegal activities is not calculated because there are indications that part of intermediate consumption of prostitution could be included in national accounts calculations implicitly. It is possible that small private businesses registered in the Administrative Enterprise Register performing legal activities (for example hotels or saunas) could provide prostitution services as some kind of secondary activity. In this case, incomes shown in surveys and tax declarations consist of legal income only but expenditures cover also an illegal part.

Furthermore, expenses related to private flats (rent payments, heating and communal services) used in this kind of business are included in private consumption expenditures. Therefore, corresponding corrections have to be made in private consumption expenditures but there are no plausible estimations of the expenses.

Although the output of illegal activities is estimated, it is not included in the official GDP estimates.

1.5.3 N3: Producers not required to register

It was not possible to distinguish this type of non-exhaustiveness from that associated with N1 and it is thus included within the total for N1. When more information from the State Revenue Service on incomes of private persons working with licenses is available, corresponding adjustments will be made.

1.5.4 N4: Legal persons not surveyed

The adjustment for this type of non-exhaustiveness consists of two types of adjustments. The first one (N4-1) - adjustment for non-registered employment - is based on labour input method. Half of the non-registered employed persons that are assumed to be working in non-financial corporations, are missing in the surveys, and the output of these activities is compiled using the number of non-registered employees and productivity data on small enterprises.

The second type of adjustment is for legal persons that are not surveyed (N4-2) and is based on special register survey data. Newly created enterprises and enterprises that have been identified as active ones from the register survey, are not included in the list of surveyed enterprises for the current year. For such units, a special list of surveyed enterprises is prepared, in addition to the general list constructed on the basis of regular information for that year. The enterprises included in the special list are surveyed using regular survey forms. Strictly speaking, such additional collection of statistical information should not be treated as an adjustment. However, in the calculation of quarterly indicators, the output produced in enterprises not included in regular surveys is adjusted taking into account the results for the previous year.

1.5.5 N5: Registered entrepreneurs not surveyed

No special adjustments are made for this type.

1.5.6 N6: Producers deliberately misreporting

This type of non-exhaustiveness relates mainly to small enterprises employing less than 50 persons, as these enterprises are not checked by auditing and the data they provide to surveys are not always of good quality. Furthermore, activities of small enterprises are becoming more and more significant in Latvia.

Using an approach based on the Italian experience, quantification of possible under-reporting of wages and profits in small units is based on checks as follows: if average wages per month are under the lowest level permitted by law, it is treated as under-reporting and the data are adjusted assuming that average wages are equal to the lowest level permitted by law; profit after taxes should be, at least, equal to the amount of average wages of employees in this kind of activity in small companies. Thus, survey data showing under average wages of employees are adjusted.

For the 2000 year estimations, more than 5500 profit and loss accounts and surveys on labour and wages were analysed and individual adjustments were grossed up using a coefficient for each kind of activity.

1.5.7 N7: Other statistical deficiencies

This category includes adjustments for tips, for which calculations are made using turnover data from surveys of enterprises in the following activities:
- maintenance and repairs of motor vehicles (NACE 502),
- repair of personal and household goods (NACE 527),
- other provision of lodgings (NACE 5523),
- restaurants (NACE 553),
- bars (NACE 554),
- taxi operation (NACE 6022),
- other service activities (NACE 93).

Tips are assumed to be 5% of the net turnover of enterprises. This share is based on expert assumptions and information from restaurants where tips are included in the bills. The share of service charge in these restaurants is between 5%-12%. The lowest is chosen taking into account that service charge is partly included in bills. Besides, in Latvia it is not customary to pay high tips, and often the amount of payment is rounded to full Lats.

1.6 Summary of adjustments and future work

The results of the adjustments to the production account aggregates are presented in Table 2.

In Table 2, the adjustments are dominated by those based on labour input method. That is why methods of refinement of these adjustments are still being researched. At present, the new Labour Force Survey provides regular data on non-registered labour input on a quarterly basis and provides information not only about employed and non-employed persons, but also on working hours. It allows making adjustments for non-registered labour input using information on hours worked. Besides, present Labour Force Survey gives the possibility to make adjustments based on labour input data on a quarterly basis.

Table 2. Adjustments to production account aggregates by types of non-exhaustiveness (million Lats)

Type of non-exhaustiveness	Gross output	Intermediate consumption	Value added	Per cent of GDP	Per cent of total NOE adjustments
N1. Producers deliberately not registering –underground	674.6	361.3	313.3	7.2	47.8
N2. Producers deliberately not registering - illegal	63.5		63.5	1.5	9.7
N3. Producers not required to register	-	-	-	-	-
N4. Legal persons not surveyed of which:	537.2	316.2	220.9	2.5	16.9
4-1 non-registered employment	327.2	178.7	148.5	3.4	22.7
4-2 enterprises not surveyed	210.0	137.6	72.4	1.7	11.1
N5. Registered entrepreneurs not surveyed	-	-	-	-	-
N6. Producers deliberately misreporting	52.9		52.9	1.2	8.1
N7. Other statistical deficiencies	4.9		4.9	0.1	0.7
Total	**1 333.0**	**677.5**	**655.5**	**15.1**	**100**

Equally important for making the adjustments to ensure the exhaustiveness of national accounts aggregates is the co-operation with the State Revenue Service with regard to the detailed data on entrepreneurs' activities.

2. Exhaustiveness adjustments: expenditure approach

The calculation of GDP by expenditures is based on completely different data sources from those used in the production approach. The calculations based on the two approaches are compared, discrepancies are analysed and results are reconciled. Reconciliation starts with an evaluation to identify less reliable calculations due to changes in data sources that were used by comparing with data from the previous year. For example, if there were changes in survey or sampling methods for the calculation of one particular aggregate, it should be taken into account.

At present, supply-and-use calculations are finalised with three years delay as compared with national accounts calculations, but in some cases supply-and-use tables are used as the basis for compiling national accounts.

Data sources used for calculation of main aggregates of GDP by expenditures and the reasons for adjustments are presented in Table 3.

Table 3. Data sources and adjustments to expenditure aggregates

Expenditure aggregates	Data sources used for calculations	Indications and data sources for exhaustiveness adjustments
Private consumption expenditure of households	Household budget surveys, data of main producers of particular goods, retail trade data	Volume data of consumption of alcoholic beverages, numbers of private cars registered first time, special survey of households on consumption of non-registered services
Final consumption expenditure of NPISH	Annual survey	No exhaustiveness adjustments are made
Final consumption expenditure of general government	Budget data, data on imports of services financed by international organisations	No exhaustiveness adjustments are made
Gross fixed capital formation	Statistical survey on investments	Quantitative data on investments in households sector
Changes in inventories	Annual survey data	No exhaustiveness adjustments are made
Exports of goods	Customs documents	Differences in prices in customs warehouses
Imports of services	Information on transactions without customs declarations	Information on transactions without customs declarations

When retail trade data do not provide comprehensive and detailed information for private consumption expenditure calculations, household budget survey data and data from large producers of particular goods are treated as the main data source. Retail trade data are an additional source for calculating the consumption of particular goods. For estimating the expenditures related to the use of non-registered goods and services, a special survey in addition to the regular LFS is developed. The results of this survey also allow the indication of unrecorded incomes because the expenditures for non-registered services for some kinds of private services exceeded total expenditures of families recorded in the regular HBS. In accordance with the methodology, one family member was asked about the expenditures for non-registered goods and services.

2.1 Identification and adjustment by non-exhaustiveness type

2.1.1 N2: Producers deliberately not registering – illegal

This category includes the estimation of drug consumption and the expenditures of households on prostitution. The estimation of the expenditures on prostitution services is based on the adjustments for the production of these services. The adjustments for production of and expenditure on illegal services are based on the same data sources and are done simultaneously. Consumption of drugs is calculated using all available data sources - number of regular and occasional drug users, quantities and kinds of drugs used from health authorities, street prices of drugs from police authorities.

2.1.2 N5: Registered entrepreneurs not surveyed

These include the estimation of the investments made in households sector including investments in private agricultural farms. Investments in buildings, based on adjusted output in construction, are done using data on square meters of newly constructed private dwellings and average construction prices. An adjustment for construction of private agricultural farms is based on changes in volume indicators of these farms and construction prices. Investments in machinery are estimated using volume indicators (for example, changes in number of tractors and other machinery in private ownership). For estimating these changes, average prices of imported machinery are used.

Adjustments for imports are done to cover goods imported without customs declarations, for example goods for private use bought via sales catalogues and repairs of ships owned by non-residents.

2.1.3 N6: Producers deliberately misreporting

This category includes adjustments for exports of goods to compensate for underestimation of exported goods produced in Latvia, which are stored in customs warehouses and are subsequently exported. A comparison of average prices from customs declarations for goods entering customs warehouses with the prices of the same goods exported to the CIS countries through customs warehouses, revealed significant difference in prices. According to customs documents, the values of many goods were reduced in the customs warehouses by three times and more. Taking into account that export prices are considerably lower than producer prices, it is assumed that customs documents do not show real payments. To eliminate this under-reporting, goods exported through customs warehouses to the CIS countries are valued at the prices they had upon entering customs warehouses.

2.1.4 N7: Other statistical deficiencies

This category includes adjustments for unmeasured purchases of goods and services for private consumption. The adjustments are based on volume indicators for consumption of alcoholic beverages and tobacco. They are calculated using production data sources and involve various expert opinions including those of the health service authorities. The share of non-registered consumption is calculated by comparing this consumption data with the level of consumption that is calculated using registered data. This amount is estimated at prices, which are around two times lower than the retail trade prices.

The adjustments for consumption of services like maintenance and repairs of dwellings, operation of personal transport equipment, personal care etc. are done using a special household budget survey. The questionnaire is elaborated in addition to the regular Labour Force Survey. The main purpose of the survey is to estimate the consumption of excised goods and the share of the hidden part in the total economy. A household member, between the age of 15-74, is interviewed for this survey. The interview records total purchases of excised goods (spirits, alcohol beverages, wine, beer, cigarettes, petrol, diesel fuel) and the part of the goods, which were purchased without a bill or cash register cheque.

Questions concerning "without a bill or cash register cheque" reflect expenditures in cash made without a bill or cash register cheque or other document, which confirm the corresponding payment. For instance, if a car, TV set, or apartment is repaired by an officially registered atelier, but the customer paid for the service without a bill or cash register cheque, the transaction is shown as payment of non-invoiced service. Payments of various repair services to private persons who are not employed by ateliers but provide repair services, are also included here.

Purchases of products from private persons, who do not have a license for retail trade services are included in purchases of non-invoiced goods. Purchases of goods and services in shops, repair ateliers for household appliances are also registered as non-invoiced purchases when a deal is made without a bill or cash register cheque.

The results of this questionnaire are grossed up and used for adjustments for the production and the private consumption of specific kinds of services.

3. Summary of adjustments and future work

The adjustments made to the expenditure-based GDP, are summarised in Table 4.

Table 4. Summary of adjustments to the expenditure-based GDP

Expenditure aggregates	Adjustments (million Lats)	Per cent of GDP
Private consumption expenditure of households	235.5	5.4
of which included in published data	148.0	3.4
Gross fixed capital formation	60.9	1.4
Imports of goods	31.1	0.7
Exports of goods	120.2	2.8
Total	**447.8**	**10.3**
of which included in published data	**360.3**	**8.3**

At present the published GDP data include only adjustments related to the coverage of production and consumption of legal goods and services. Illegal activities are estimated but not included in the published data.

LITHUANIA

1. Definitions and concepts

The treatment of non-observed economy (NOE) in Lithuanian national accounts is in compliance with the latest requirements of Eurostat and follows the recommendations given in the OECD *Handbook on Measuring the Non-observed Economy*. Like the other new Member States of the EU, Lithuania participated in the Pilot Projects launched by Eurostat aiming to improve the exhaustiveness of GDP calculations and to measure the share of NOE in GDP. Two pilot studies of NOE were carried out by Statistics Lithuania in that respect; results of the first described the situation on NOE for 1997-1998, the second - for the year 2001. The results of the second study are presented in Table 5 below.

2. Sources and estimation methods

In 1995–1996, Statistics Lithuania carried out a comprehensive study of the non-observed economy in cooperation with the World Bank and other international organisations. The results were applied to adjust and revise the national accounts indicators. The main achievement of this study was an elaboration of a compilation scheme of how national accounts data obtained from the primary sources have to be adjusted. The adjustment coefficients derived from the special surveys in 1995 were used as the benchmark for the measurement of the non-observed part of the particular GDP component. Since the Statistical Business Register (SBR) was not developed enough and sampling methods were not applied at that time, the statistical reasons made up a significant part of the total GDP adjustment for exhaustiveness. The economic underground (under-reporting of income) was assessed on the basis of a survey on the opinion of experts from the State Tax Inspectorate (STI) on hidden income of enterprises.

In practice, the adjustments were made to the GDP output components at the detailed level, taking into account the kind of activity, type of ownership and size of the unit. GDP expenditure (household consumption expenditure, gross fixed capital formation) and income components were also adjusted accordingly.

As a result of the development of SBR and statistical surveys based on it, the underestimation of national accounts indicators due to statistical reasons was minimised during the last decade.

In addition to the special surveys, an analysis of the income and costs by the size classes of enterprises was made regularly. The analysis was based on the information of the Structural Business Survey. The results of the comparison of income and costs components by size groups allowed disclosing possible under-reporting in some particular parts.

Labour Force Survey (LFS) data on employment by kind of activities and by type (employees, self-employed) were used for the analysis. The discrepancies revealed in supply and demand of employment were also taken into account. However, the frequency and level of detail in LFS data were not sufficient to allow to use them as the basis for comprehensive calculations in national accounts.

It should be mentioned that illegal activities were also investigated in the course of previous studies and experimental estimates were made in Lithuania. However, their results were not incorporated in the official GDP estimates.

The latest observations of NOE in Lithuanian national accounts evidenced that the under-reporting of income by registered units makes up the most significant part of NOE and should be a subject for further investigation.

In 2002–2003, new non-observed economy studies were initiated under the auspices of the national PHARE programme. Similar to the previous studies, aspects of the non-observed economy directly related to GDP estimation were examined. Since the production approach of GDP calculation is considered as the main method, and the under-reporting of income of enterprises as the most significant in the NOE estimates, the surveys focused on this issue. In addition, informal employment and earnings, some specific aspects in retail trade and construction were also analyzed. The value added generated by illegal activities was also considered.

In Lithuania, a big proportion of enterprises do not report all the earned income (turnover) in their financial statements and statistical reports. This was observed during the 1995 survey and repeatedly proven in the 2003 studies and estimations, which were based on the interviews conducted among the State Tax Inspectorate (STI) officials as well as on official statistical data sources.

The regional STI inspectors expressed their opinion on the share of income not declared by enterprises in 2002 in their official financial and statistical reports. Having summarised the collected information, the share of the non-declared income was broken down by economic activity, type of ownership and size of enterprises. Such data, expressed in the form of coefficients (ratios), are suitable for adjustment of the national accounts indicators.

A survey of the STI experts' opinions showed that private enterprises, particularly entrepreneurs, frequently do not declare all income from sales. The survey disclosed that for the declared sales in 2002, statistical estimates should be adjusted almost in all economic activities: at least by 1 per cent in energy to 25 per cent in textiles, 35.6 per cent in forestry and 50 per cent in fishery. The 2002 survey revealed that the non-financial enterprises (including sole proprietors) on average did not declare about 14.3 per cent of their income (Table 1).

Within the manufacturing sector which generates about 20 per cent of the country's gross value added, the highest share of non-declared income was identified in textiles (25.2 per cent), publishing and printing (17.8 per cent), sewing of clothing and dressing of furs (16.5 per cent), manufacture of furniture (15.4 per cent), food products and beverages (13.3 per cent) and wood and wood products (except furniture) (13.2 per cent). The share of non-declared income in other manufacturing activities that have not been mentioned is estimated to be below 10 per cent, while on average for the entire group it is between 8 to 11 per cent. The managers of manufacturing enterprises and associations were also interviewed in order to enrich the survey based on STI inspectors' opinions. They virtually confirmed the estimates of the STI experts.

Table 1. The share of non-declared income by kind of economic activity in 2002
(per cent)

Kind of activity	Share
Forestry and logging	35.6
Fishery	50.0
Manufacturing	9.1
Electricity, gas and water supply	2.8
Construction	18.3
Wholesale and retail trade	15.0–16.5
Sale, maintenance and repair of motor vehicles	22.7
Repairs of personal and household articles	26.6
Hotels and restaurants	20.3–21.1
Road transport	19.2
Real estate operations	24.1
Rent of machinery and equipment without operators and personal appliances	29.9
Other business activities	35.9
Education	15.1
Health and social care	25.0
Sewerage and waste disposal activity	10.7
Recreational, culture and sports activity	10.3
Other service activities	32.9
Total (average)	**14.3**

Within the analysed sector, the share of non-declared income is estimated differently depending on the forms of ownership of the units. For example, the share of the non-declared income of individual (sole) proprietors engaged in the manufacturing of chemicals, chemical products, and rubber and plastic products is estimated to be 28.5 per cent and 11.7 per cent, while in public companies and public and private joint-stock companies it equals zero. However, the mentioned activities are an exception.

In general, within the prevailing economic activity in Lithuania, which is manufacturing, only minor differences in the share of the non-declared income by type of ownership have been traced (see Table 2).

Table 2. The share of non-declared income in manufacturing in 2002
(per cent)

	Public and private joint-stock companies	Sole proprietors
Manufacture of food products and beverages	13.3	13.9
Manufacture of textiles	24.9	32.5
Manufacture of clothing	16.3	17.8
Manufacture of wood and wooden products (except furniture)	12.8	15.6
Manufacture of furniture	15.0	20.0

It should be emphasised, that the survey did not cover enterprises engaged in agricultural production and services, and financial and public administration services because of peculiarities in the calculation of their production and value added in national accounts.

Based on the conducted surveys, the bulk of the non-declared income was observed in enterprises engaged in fishery (under 50 per cent) and forestry (under 35.6 per cent). However, value added generated in these economic activities made up just 0.1 per cent of the country's gross value added. Meanwhile, the share of non-declared income in retail and wholesale trade, repair of motor vehicles and trade in gasoline, and construction was 17.9 and 6.4 per cent respectively and is estimated to range from 15 per cent in wholesale trade to 18.3 per cent in construction and 22.7 per cent in repair of transport vehicles and trade in gasoline.

The Association of Trade Enterprises of Lithuania conducted a survey among the experts of the largest trade enterprises who submitted additional information about the situation in trade. After analyzing the information and comparing it with the inquiry carried out among tax inspectors, it was found that the official data sources in 2002 did not count over 1.6 billion LTL (or 14.6 per cent) of the non-declared retail trade turnover. The survey confirmed that small enterprises hide a larger share of the turnover than the large ones (Fig. 1).

**Figure 1. The share of non-declared turnover in total turnover
of retail trade enterprises in 2002 (per cent)**

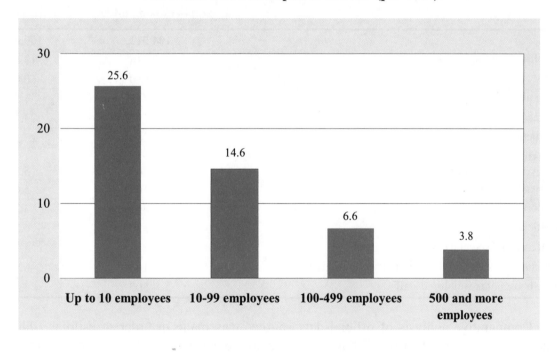

The share of non-observed turnover in trade of second-hand cars was estimated separately. Results drawn from interviews in car markets as well as expert estimates showed that in 2002 the share of non-observed turnover amounted to between 20 - 30 per cent (about 500 million LTL).

Considerably high shares of non-declared income were found in enterprises providing all types of market services. This is characteristic for many small enterprises, regardless of whether services are rendered to businesses or individual customers. These units show higher shares for non-declared income.

In addition to the previously covered areas, health care and educational services were included in the current survey to estimate unofficial earnings for health treatment services rendered by public health care institutions, and additional non-estimated earnings of teachers providing unofficial tutors' services. The survey demonstrated that employees in the public health institutions could unofficially earn approximately 59 million LTL, while persons in the educational system providing unofficial tutors' services could earn about 27 million LTL. These amounts had to be included in the GDP.

One part of the survey was devoted to analysis of unofficial employment and earnings. Based upon comparisons with official statistical data sources, attempts were made to estimate and ascertain the number of non-registered employees. The results demonstrated that in 2002, the number of non-registered employees was reaching 104 000 (Table 3). The largest share was for construction and manufacturing enterprises (23 per cent for each group of enterprises) and slightly less for agriculture, hunting and forestry (20 per cent). The estimation of unofficial employment confirmed the results of the parallel non-declared income survey, as the two parts of the non-observed economy are directly related.

Table 3. Distribution of non-registered employees by kind of economic activity

	Number of employees	Share, per cent
Total	**104 512**	**100.0**
Agriculture, hunting, forestry	20 518	19.6
Fishery	0	0.0
Mining and quarrying	1 543	1.5
Manufacturing	24 190	23.1
Construction	24 383	23.3
Wholesale and retail trade, repair of motor vehicles and motorcycles, rent of personal and household appliances	5 463	5.2
Hotels and restaurants	3 102	3.0
Transport, storage and communications	3 452	3.3
Education	6 326	6.1
Health care and social work	3 818	3.7
Other communal, social and personal service activities	7 100	6.8
Private households with hired staff	4 507	4.3

Comparative analysis of official data sources was made in order to estimate the share of non-declared earnings. The results showed that economic entities in 2002 did not declare at least 23 per cent of the wages and salaries paid to their employees.

Statistics Lithuania does not include value added generated by illegal activities when estimating GDP. However, such estimations are made to identify the likely GDP level. The project was envisaged to improve the methodology for estimating illegal activities as well as widening the coverage of the illegal types of activities. The analysis, assessment and adjustments related to the value added generated in 2002 covered the following activities:

- illegal production and sales of alcoholic drinks;
- production and sales of drugs;
- sexual services;
- sales of stolen cars;
- production and sales of illegal copies of audio, video and other recordings as well as computer games.

The gross value added of the illegal activities was estimated to amount to 435 million LTL or about 0.9 per cent of the country's GDP in 2002. However, as already mentioned, for purposes of international comparison of GDP, the value added of the illegal activities is not included in the official GDP so far. Further discussions were held on this particular issue by the GNI Committee in order to decide which types of illegal activities should or should not be included in GDP.

3. Implications and effects on national accounts and estimates of the size of NOE in the GDP estimates

The results of the conducted surveys and estimations were used in estimating the GDP. To estimate the value added in certain economic activities, adjustment coefficients determined during the surveys or certain elements of the non-observed value added were used. The years when specific studies on NOE were conducted were used as a benchmark for the following year's estimates. This allows the production of time series of estimated NOE share in GDP. The results are presented in Table 4.

Table 4. Share of NOE in total GDP
(per cent)

	1997	1998	1999	2000	2001	2002
Total adjustments	21.0	17.9	17.7	18.0	18.3	18.9
Due to economic reasons	17.0	15.3	15.7	16.8	17.5	18.2
Due to statistical reasons	4.0	2.6	2.0	1.2	0.8	0.7

However, the split of NOE data by components is available only for the years when the Eurostat projects were conducted (Table 5).

Table 5. Summary of GVA adjustments: output approach for reference year 2001
(million LTL)

Sectors	Type of non-exhaustiveness adjustment							Total as included in published GDP	
	N1	N2	N3	N4	N5	N6	N7	Absolute	% of GDP
Non-financial corporations						5 713.3	127.7	5 841.0	12.3
Financial corporations									
General government									
Households	214.1	274.2				2 586.4	12.1	2 812.6	5.9
NPISH							26.8	26.8	0.1
NACE Groups									
A	0.7					226.0	0.0	226.7	0.5
B	0.0					17.9	0.0	17.9	0.0
C	0.0					35.6	0.2	35.8	0.1
D	33.5	236.2				1 538.3	57.9	1 629.7	3.4
E	0.0					0.7	33.6	34.3	0.1
F	4.2					972.7	0.0	976.9	2.1
G	60.0	14.1				2 527.3	4.2	2 591.5	5.5
H	2.9					353.7	10.6	367.2	0.8
I	0.0					1 403.4	21.9	1 425.3	3.0
J									
K	2.0					528.7	0.2	530.9	1.1
L									
M	20.3					172.6	0.1	193.1	0.4
N	0.0					50.4	0.3	50.7	0.1
O	46.9	23.9				472.4	37.7	557.0	1.2
P	43.6							43.6	0.1
Total	**214.1**	**274.2**				**8 299.7**	**166.6**	**8 680.5**	**18.3**

MEXICO

1. Introduction

Non-observed economic activities include the underground economy, illegal activities and the informal sector, which have been measured since 1993 in the national accounts of Mexico. Every year, the results of the production account of the informal households sector are published as a satellite account of the system of institutional sector accounts. Illegal activities such as sexual services are estimated and included there.

2. Implications and effects on national accounts

In 2003, the measured component of the informal economy represented 12.1% of the total value added in Mexico. Within this sector, other services contributed 33.6% of informal production; manufacturing industries 32.7%; transport 17.9%; and construction 7.1%.

Estimates of the underground economy, i.e. hidden activities by enterprises are not included. Furthermore, the following illegal activities are <u>not</u> included:
- national production and distribution of narcotics;
- illegal copies of software, cassettes, videos, compact discs and books;
- profiteering;
- ticket office resale;
- unauthorised medical operations (surgery);
- trade and transport of illegal goods;
- street car washers;
- domestic servants and street vendors;
- homemade food as a secondary activity.

In addition, hidden activities that are performed as a secondary activity are not included, such as car attendants that perform valet parking in discotheques, hotels and public offices.

MONGOLIA

1. Introduction

The non-observed economy is not yet covered adequately in Mongolia. The first major study of the informal sector was conducted by the National Statistical Office (NSO) with the assistance of the World Bank in Ulaanbaatar in 1997. The second study was conducted in 2000 with the assistance of USAID. The last informal sector survey conducted among 15 business sectors in 6 *aimags* and Ulaanbaatar estimated the size of the non-observed economy at about 117 billion Tugrigs, which represents 13.3 per cent of GDP. Another study conducted by the National University for Demography estimated the size of the informal sector at 30%. It is estimated that retail trade contributes 62.0 per cent of hidden economy, while the transport sector contributes 23.3 per cent. Goods and services produced in informal economy amount to 92.5 billion Tugrigs. These are included in the GDP estimates for the year 1999.

The term 'informal sector' in Mongolia is used to denote small-scale economic and business activities that are 'hidden' or 'off the books', i.e. not registered in official statistics. While informal sector businesses tend to remain relatively small-scale, the overall size of the informal sector can have a significant effect on private sector statistics and National Income accounts. The informal sector concept is related to but not identical to the 'shadow economy', which includes illegal activities such as prostitution and gambling. For the purposes of this study, the following definition was adopted:

The **informal sector** consists of small-scale, usually family-based economic activities that may be undercounted by official statistics and may not be subject, in practice, to the same set of regulations and taxation as formal enterprises.

2. Sources and estimation methods

In the design phase of the survey of informal sector, the research team identified more than 30 types of economic activities within five main sectors: retail trade, services, financial services, transport, and manufacturing. The list of 30 was subsequently narrowed down to 17. The main selection criteria included size of the activities (based on previous studies), the number of units registered in each activity, which was of particular importance to the NSO in terms of gauging value added for inclusion in the national accounts. The final list thus comprised:

1. Retail Trade
- Kiosks
- Stalls
- Chemists
- Containers

2. Financial services
- Pawnshops
- Money changers

3. Transport
- Taxis
- Trucks

4. Services
- Cobblers
- Canteens
- Barbershops
- Video game arcades
- Home-cooked meals

5. Manufacturing
- Baked goods
- Soft drinks

A separate survey questionnaire was developed for each economic activity, to cover the period from December 1998 to December 1999. The researchers used Anderson's 1997 survey as a general guide, but amended it, particularly in the area of measuring value added. Questions were designed to assess: a) the size of the informal sector (e.g. value added and employment); b) characteristics of informal sector workers (their age, sex, education levels and the number of people they support); c) characteristics of the sector itself (e.g. seasonality, dynamics, financing); and d) the relationship between the informal sector and the government (including licensing and taxation). Pilot surveys were carried out on a few economic units in each of the 17 activities, resulting in amendments and improvements. A data-entry program was developed and modified at the same time. The questionnaire was eventually approved by the Methodology Board of the NSO.

Sampling was carried out in close cooperation with the NSO. The sample design used the three-stage stratified cluster technique. The primary sampling units were Ulaanbaatar and the *aimags* (localities), the secondary sampling units were Ulaanbaatar city districts and *aimag* centres, and the tertiary sampling units were the individual informal economic units within the economic activities.

The individual units of the study within each economic activity were determined using NSO data on economic units under single ownership, engaged in one kind of economic activity at a fixed place of business. This resulted in an initial list of 25 282 informal economic units in Mongolia, excluding taxis.

Creating a sample from the total population of taxis had to be approached in a more creative manner, given the assumption that every privately owned vehicle on Ulaanbaatar's roads is potentially an informal taxi, at least part-time.[27] The total number of cars owned by individuals was obtained from Annual Technical Inspection data.

It is reasonable to assume that the number of vehicles registered is very close to the actual number of vehicles in operating condition. Recognizing that some cars owned by individuals are never used as taxis, the total population of taxis is a subset of all cars. The research team considered two ways of adjusting for cars never used as taxis. The city traffic police estimate that 5 to 7 per

---

[27] This assumption was not used for *aimag* centres, however. The residents of *aimag* centers know how many cars there are and which ones operate as taxis. Therefore, it was fairly simple to ascertain accurately the population of taxis in *aimag* centers.

cent of individual cars are never used as taxis.[28] Anderson's study resulted in an upper-bound figure of 12 per cent. The EPSP research team opted for Anderson's estimate, given its statistically sound methodological basis. The population of interest, 16 320 individually owned vehicles, includes both full-time taxis that work more than 25 hours per week and part-time taxis that work less than 25 hours per week (and sometimes as low as one or two hours per week).

In the course of conducting the survey, a new sector was added to the original list, which is referred to in the tables as "home cooked meals". This covers the work of people who prepare simple meals at home, usually various forms of meat pies, noodles or dumplings, and sell them to the workers at shops, counters, kiosks, etc. Surveyors asked additional questions to estimate the volume of this service used by the retail businesses that were surveyed. This practice is widespread, and the amount of business it generates is substantial. The total population of the selected activities in urban Mongolia is presented in Table 1.

Table 1. Total population of the activities used in the study

	Ulaanbaatar population		Aimag population		Total population	
	Total	Share (%)	Total	Share (%)	Total	Share (%)
TOTAL	**33 851**	**100.0**	**9 851**	**100.0**	**43 702**	**100.00**
Retail trade	**13 664**	**40.4**	**7 497**	**76.1**	**21 161**	**48.4**
Kiosk	1 948	5.8	1 700	17.3	3 648	8.4
Counter	10 520	31.1	5 224	53.0	15 744	36.0
Container	1 097	3.2	490	6.0	1 587	3.6
Drug store	99	0.3	83	0.9	182	0.4
Financial services	**481**	**1.4**	**57**	**0.6**	**538**	**1.2**
Pawnshops	412	1.2	57	0.6	469	1.1
Money change	69	0.2	0	0.0	69	0.2
Transport	**17 174**	**50.7**	**1 043**	**10.6**	**18 217**	**41.7**
Taxi	15 624	46.2	696	7.1	16 320	37.3
Tracks	325	1.0	0	0.0	325	0.7
Minibus	1 196	3.5	347	3.5	1 543	3.5
Car parking	29	0.1	0	0.0	29	0.1
Services	**2 412**	**7.1**	**1 104**	**11.2**	**3 516**	**8.1**
Shoe repair	93	0.3	74	0.8	167	0.4
Canteen	619	1.8	267	2.7	886	2.0
Barbershop	154	0.5	116	1.2	270	0.6
Games	46	0.1	47	0.5	93	0.2
Home-cooked meals	1 500	4.4	600	6.1	2 100	4.8
Manufacturing	**120**	**0.4**	**150**	**1.5**	**270**	**0.6**
Bakery	51	0.15	92	0.93	143	0.33
Soft drinks	69	0.20	58	0.59	127	0.29

---

[28] These estimates are rough but are based on vehicle inspections. The Ulaaanbaatar Tax Administration regularly cooperates with city traffic police to conduct random checks of cars that appear to be carrying passengers. Drivers are required to show proof that they have paid taxes according to the *Informal Sector Income Tax Law*.

Six out of a total of 22 *aimags* were selected as primary sampling units. Following the standard division of Mongolia into six regions, one *aimag* was chosen from each. Table 2 presents the regions and the *aimags* chosen as primary sampling units:

Table 2. Regions of the country and their representative aimags

Region	Aimags in the region	Representative aimag
Far Western	Bayan-Olgii, Uvs, Khovd	Uvs
Western	Zavkhan, Govi-Altai, Khovsgol	Zavkhan
Central-2	Arkhangai, Bulgan, Ovorkhangai, Bayankhongor	Arkhangai
Central-1	Tov, Orkhon, Darkhan-Uul, Selenge	Orkhon
Eastern	Khentii, Dornod, Sukhbaatar	Hentii
Southern	Dornogovi, Omnogovi, Dundgovi, Govisumber	Dornogobi
Capital city	Ulaanbaatar	Ulaanbaatar

The secondary sampling units were the six Ulaanbaatar districts and the aimag centers (or secondary cities). All informal economic entities within these secondary sampling units were identified from the master list above. In order to locate the tertiary sampling units in the retail trade sector, maps of major markets were prepared.

The size of the final sample was 4 042 informal economic entities, or 12.4 per cent of the population in the secondary sampling units. Within the determined samples, the individual entities to be surveyed were chosen randomly. The final sample is presented in Table 3.

Table 3. Size of the study sample group

	Population	Sample	
		Number	Share (Per cent)
Retail trade	**13 664**	**2 184**	**16.0**
• Kiosks	1 948	325	16.7
• Counters	10 520	1 591	15.1
• Containers	1 097	218	19.9
Financial services	**481**	**300**	**62.4**
• Pawnshops	412	231	56.1
• Money Changers	69	69	100.0
Transport	**17 174**	**1 016**	**5.9**
• Taxis	15 624	448	2.9
• Trucks	325	62	19.1
• Minibuses	1 196	478	40.0
• Garages	29	28	96.6
Services	**1 152**	**481**	**41.8**
• Shoe repair	93	47	50.5
• Chemists	99	50	50.5
• Canteens	619	211	34.1
• Barbershops	154	78	50.6
• Games	46	23	50.0
Manufacturing	**120**	**61**	**50.8**
• Baked Goods	51	28	54.9
• Soft Drinks	69	33	47.8
TOTAL	**32 591**	**4 042**	**12.4**

The third study was conducted through a joint project with the Soros Foundation and the National Statistics Office and the assistance of IRIS of Maryland University, USA. The name of the joint project is Informal Sector Household Survey (ISHS). The survey is the final of three planned data collection exercises associated with the study of the "shadow" economy in Mongolia. It was preceded by a pilot study in Ulaanbaatar in April and a pre-test in June 2004 that took place in Selenge, Khovsgol, Dornogovi, and Ulaanbaatar.

The initial data collection exercises investigated alternative approaches to asking questions about a sensitive activity, and the development of the final survey instruments are a result of what was learned in these exercises. The survey was conducted in nine *aimags* across the five regions of Mongolia that include the West, Khangai, Central, East and Ulaanbaatar and covered 13 900 households.

The primary objective of the ISHS is to generate national and regional measures of value added in the small-scale shadow economy. In addition to determining value added, the survey gathers data on personal characteristics and on the business environment in order to understand the causes and consequences of participating in the shadow economy. For comparative purposes the survey will interview a small number of individuals, both business owners and wage earners, who operate in the formal economy. In addition, the National Statistical Office is conducting an informal sector survey among service sectors in six *aimags* and Ulaanbaatar to estimate the size of the non-observed economy.

MONTENEGRO

1. Introduction

The published estimates of the GDP of Montenegro at current and constant prices for the years 2000 to 2002 have been compiled following the production and expenditure approaches in line with the definitions, concepts, classifications and accounting rules of the SNA 93 and the ESA 95. They cover all legal activities within the production boundary defined by these accounting systems. But they do not cover illegal activities that are included in the production boundary, such as the production and selling of narcotics, prostitution, poaching, smuggling, and the production and selling of pirated DVDs, CDs, videos and software. A number of adjustments for non-exhaustiveness because of incomplete or misreported basic data are included in the estimates. As a result of the adjustments, value added for the whole economy was increased by 8.8 per cent in 2002.

2. Sources and estimation methods

The basic data used to compile the GDP estimates came from different sources: the Statistical Office of Montenegro (MONSTAT), Tax Authorities, Central Payment Institute and financial statements. The principle source of data for non-exhaustiveness adjustments was the Labour Force Survey supplemented by data on wages and salaries. The opinion of experts was mainly based on these sources. The non-exhaustiveness adjustments that are included in the GDP estimates are defined in line with the classification of non-exhaustiveness types followed by Eurostat in its tabular approach.

2.1 Non-exhaustiveness type N1

This type covers producers engaged in legal activities but deliberately not registering as a legal entity to avoid taxes, social security obligations, health and safety regulations, etc. It is particularly prevalent among hotels and restaurants (NACE H) in Montenegro.

Tourism is significant for Montenegrin economy but is not fully covered in the national accounts. This is the view shared by Ministry of Tourism and the expert who helped MONSTAT compile its GDP estimates for 2000-2002. Research undertaken by the World Travel & Tourism Council in co-operation with Ministry of Tourism concluded that the share of hotels and restaurants in GDP was 14 per cent in 2004. According to national accounts estimates the share of hotels and restaurants in GDP was 2.5 per cent in 2002.

Many persons in the private sector renting rooms and beds during the tourist season are unregistered. So the number of rooms and beds they rent are unreported or under-reported. The number of accommodated guests is undercounted and the gross output of hotels and their value added are underestimated. This was confirmed by a statistical survey of accommodation services in private sector. The survey also concluded that the degree of under-reporting fluctuates from year to year.

MONSTAT increased the original estimate of value added by hotels and restaurants in 2002 by around 10 percentage points.

2.2 Non-exhaustiveness type N3

This type covers producers not required to register as a legal entity because they have no market output or their market output is below the level at which they are expected to register. This type of non-exhaustiveness is identified in agriculture, hunting and forestry (NACE A), construction (NACE F), and real estate, renting and business activities (NACE K).

In Montenegro a large number of households produce agricultural products for their own consumption. Part of this is sold either from home or in the open market. Sales are not registered and all the sales income goes to the seller's private budget.

In construction, as a general rule, workers hired to build private houses are not registered.

There are two kinds of activities related to real estate: the renting of dwellings and the renting of business (commercial) premises. Many owners renting dwellings or business premises are not registered and do not report their incomes from renting to the Tax Authorities.

MONSTAT adjusted upwards its original estimates of value added in 2002 by 18 per cent for agriculture, hunting and forestry, 3 per cent for construction, and 5 per cent for real estate, renting and business activities.

2.3 Non-exhaustiveness types N4 and N5

These types cover producers that are registered but not surveyed. N4 refers to incorporated enterprises or other legal persons. N5 refers to unincorporated enterprises and entrepreneurs. N5 is the principal type in Montenegro.

Entrepreneurs are not included in the Administrative Register of MONSTAT and therefore are not covered by statistical surveys. They are, however, registered in the Central Register of the Commercial Court and reported by the Municipal Secretaries (Departments) for Economy. There are plans to include them in the Administrative Register in 2006.

Additionally, some registered non-governmental organizations and sport associations engage in economic activities.

MONSTAT increased its initial estimates of value added in agriculture, hunting and forestry (NACE A) for 2002 by 3 per cent.

2.4 Non-exhaustiveness type N6

This type covers producers that are surveyed but who misreport to avoid taxes and social security contributions. This type of non-exhaustiveness is identified in most economic activities pursued in Montenegro and required by far the largest adjustment of value added for 2002 – some 8.5 per cent overall.

Misreporting is common both to statistical surveys conducted by MONSTAT and the obligatory statistical reports required from registered enterprises. It mainly consists of under-reporting of wages and salaries, numbers of employed persons and gross output.

Misreporting is particularly prevalent in wholesale and retail trade and repair services (NACE G). MONSTAT increased its initial estimate of value added in this activity for 2002 by 30.5 per cent.

3. Conclusions

The estimation of adjustments for non-exhaustiveness is a new task and needs further refinement. In this respect, MONSTAT will implement the methods recommended by the OECD experts engaged in the Eurostat-OECD project on measuring the non-observed economy in the Western Balkan region. This will include among other things the adoption of the user cost approach to estimating rentals of dwelling services.

While it is clear that MONSTAT has to improve the quality of its GDP estimates, it is impeded by a lack of resources, particularly human resources. No alleviation of this situation can be expected in the near future. Improving the exhaustiveness of GDP estimates also requires the co-operation and involvement of other ministries and departments whose data are used in GDP compilation. MONSTAT therefore intends to establish an intra-government group on the non-observed economy that will include experts from these ministries and departments.

Table 1 provides the summary of exhaustiveness adjustments to gross value added in 2002 according to the output approach.

Table 1. Share of non-observed economy in GDP, 2002 (per cent)

Activities by NACE		Type of non-exhaustiveness adjustment (per cent of GDP)							NOE estimate		GDP by branches	
		N1	N2	N3	N4	N5	N6	N7	Absolute (million €)	% of GDP	Absolute (million €)	Share in total GDP
A	Agriculture, hunting and forestry			1.7		0.3			26.4	2.0	148.4	11.4
D	Manufacturing						0.2		2.2	0.2	141.5	10.9
F	Construction			0.1			0.6		9.3	0.7	49.5	3.8
G	Wholesale and retail trade and repair services						2.9		37.4	2.9	160.1	12.3
H	Hotels and restaurants	0.2					0.1		4.3	0.3	31.9	2.5
I	Transport, storage and communication						0.9		11.3	0.9	145.8	11.2
K	Real estate, renting and business activities			0.3					4.4	0.3	98.9	7.6
M	Education						0.2		2.5	0.2	56.0	4.3
N	Health and social work						0.3		3.9	0.3	50.8	3.9
	TOTAL	**0.2**		**2.2**		**0.3**	**5.1**		**101.7**	**7.8**	**882.7**	**67.8**
	Other activities not specified*	..	..	..	..	..	..	..	..	..	418.8	32.2
	GDP										1 301.5	100.0

included FISIM and Taxes on products less subsidies on products

NETHERLANDS

1. Introduction

Statistics Netherlands has a long history in the research of the measurement of the non-observed activities. See for instance Derksen (1939), Begeer and Van Tuinen (1984), Broesterhuizen (1985), Van der Laan and De Waard (1985), Van Eck and Kazemier (1989), Kazemier, Van Eck and Koopmans (1990), Kazemier (1993), Van der Werf and Van de Ven (1996) and Kazemier and Luttikhuizen (2000).

In the Netherlands, informal activities are not very widespread. As far as they exist, they are implicitly included in the Dutch national accounts. Almost all enterprises in the Netherlands, also the informal ones, are registered and therefore are included in the business register of the CBS. Illegal activities are not explicitly accounted for. Part of them will already be included, but to what extent has not yet been investigated.

The text below focuses on the way tax evasion is taken into account and on explicit adjustments made for 'other non-observed activities'. Most of the text is taken from the English translation of the Dutch inventory, prepared for the GNP Committee. Sections 2 and 3 describe the explicit adjustments made because of tax evasion, tips, and income in kind. Section 4 provides an estimate of the total contribution to GNI of the underground activities for taxation reasons.

2. Adjustments for tax-evasion

Underground activities to evade taxation mainly take place (1) in small enterprises, (2) in enterprises in which almost the entire production chain is concentrated in that particular enterprise, (3) in enterprises that use relatively little goods and services (among other things in parts of the construction industry, services) and (4) by means of falsified accounts. Larger enterprises are assumed to have enough opportunities to avoid taxation by legal means.

There are two ways to evade taxation. The first is to under-report turnover, the second is to over-report intermediate costs. Turnover fraud is corrected for by increasing the production estimates (both added value and intermediate consumption). Cost fraud is corrected for by reducing intermediate consumption and increasing value added by the same amount.

Cost fraud is assumed to occur mainly in small enterprises. The expenditure of enterprises with fewer than 10 employees was determined for all industries in which substantial cost fraud is suspected. An initial cost fraud imputation boils down to an amount of over 700 million Euros.

Turnover fraud mainly occurs in the textiles and leather industry, construction, trade and repair, hotels, restaurants and cafes, health care and commercial services.

2.1 Leather and textiles industry

In February 1992, the "Vakraad voor de Confectie-industrie" *[Association for the Textile Industry]* published the report "Illegale Confectie-ateliers, een geïntegreerde bestrijding" *[Illegal sweatshops, co-ordinated counter-measures]*.

It indicates that most of the "concealed" production is sold via the wholesale sector. One of the reasons for the existence of illegal sweatshops in the Netherlands is the change in demand for ready-to-wear clothing. There has been a shift from the traditionally enduring summer and winter collections to rapidly obsolescent fashion, for which demand is unpredictable. To offset lengthy delivery times, the work in question was contracted out to small sewing workshops in the Netherlands.

It is also very likely that the underground production is generated by the wholesale sector. Research shows that outworking wages accounted for a steady proportion (almost 4%) of wholesale textile and clothing purchases during the 1977-86 period. In the past, this work was mainly contracted out to "low-wage countries", but domestic processors have also been used since the appearance of the illegal sweatshops in the eighties.

Since no information is available for more recent years, it was assumed that outworking wages still account for about 4% of the consumption of clothes. This includes both foreign processing payments and domestic wages. Since the early nineties there was a remarkable increase in "unconcealed" textiles and clothing output to the detriment of underground production. This development is confirmed by findings by Zorlu and Reil (1997). They found that after peaking in 1992, the level of activity in illegal sweatshops fell dramatically. The total value added of illegal sweatshops in the Netherlands was estimated at about € 30 million in 1995.

2.2 Construction industry

The data obtained from the production statistics on construction are incomplete. For example, cost fraud is not covered and is therefore estimated separately as above. Separate estimates are also made for private own-home construction by households and concealed home maintenance. Voluntary building activities, which must also be taken into account in the national accounts, are implicitly covered by own-home construction estimates. There are no separate estimates for other voluntary activities such as help with church building because of their negligible scale.

2.1.1 Construction industry: building one's own home

The estimate is based on an investigation into underground activities in the unsubsidised house-building sector in 1991 (Lourens, Kranenborg and Ritmeijer, 1992). The survey was conducted by the Economic Institute for the Building Industry (EIB). The survey made use of CBS statistics on construction permits, such as population figures for unsubsidised dwellings under construction, estimated construction costs and corresponding output estimates. The construction costs quoted in the building permits are checked by local officials with reference to the technical drawings and authorisation is granted if the figures are verified.

This means that the use of underground labour is implicitly covered by the construction costs shown in the planning permission statistics and the corresponding output figures.

A supplementary EIB sample research revealed that, in 1991, about a third of homes were constructed by the actual commissioning party without the involvement of a principal contractor. Among all privately built dwellings, almost 90% involved private individuals (households), with the remainder being constructed by associations providing accommodation for old people and students.

The production value of own-home construction was calculated for the revision year 1995 by multiplying the production value of privately constructed dwellings based on the estimated amount on the building permits by the EIB survey percentages. This gave a figure of about 500 million Euros.

The EIB survey also reveals that concealed payments to subcontractors account for a quarter of this total. The remaining output is accounted for by legally remunerated activity, the individual client or unpaid third-party help (voluntary work). Intermediate consumption was estimated with reference to the production materials quota shown in the production statistics of smaller construction firms. Value added was obtained by subtracting the value of intermediate consumption from output value.

2.1.2 Construction industry: small-scale accommodation maintenance

Small-scale building maintenance is defined as all action to preserve the useful lifetime of buildings. The result is that this form of maintenance is classified as intermediate or household consumption. Underground small-scale maintenance activity is particularly prevalent in the case of households. A report by the Institute for the Scientific Study of Consumer Affairs (SWOKA) (Wilms, 1990) provides the basis for the national accounts estimate.

The 1990 SWOKA survey covered the maintenance expenditure of 850 households. It also sought information on the value of non-invoiced payments to individuals, not employed by an official enterprise or body when maintenance was carried out. The survey treated replies to this question as underground expenditure data and indicated that such expenditure accounted for almost 30% of total maintenance spending. This approximately equals the findings of a CBS investigation of 1981, where about 30% of all labour paid for home maintenance and improvement was paid off the record (Kazemier, 1984).

The total value of average household home maintenance expenditure revealed by the SWOKA survey corresponds to the CBS budget survey figure. This means that the housing maintenance budget survey data also cover underground expenditure. The budget survey, which targeted approximately 2000 households, distinguishes over 100 commodities associated with home maintenance. Spending of less than 500 Euros in a goods or service category constitutes small-scale consumer expenditure on building maintenance. Any higher amount is classified as investment. In 1995, the output value (= added value) of hidden small-scale maintenance was estimated at about 200 million Euros. The national accounts classify the use of building materials for hidden small-scale maintenance as household consumption and impute the associated value added to the construction industry.

2.1.3 Construction industry: large-scale building maintenance

Large-scale building maintenance is defined as action designed to extend the useful life of buildings. This form of maintenance is classified as investment. The household budget survey data are also important for this estimate. The survey distinguishes between large- and small-scale maintenance, pointing out that only owners of dwellings perform the former. Examples quoted in the respondents' guidelines include:

- improved heating insulation, such as cavity-wall infill or the installation of double glazing;
- installation or replacement of a central-heating facility;
- installation of a shower-room or bathroom;
- kitchen modernisation/replacement;
- essential replacement or extension of electrical wiring;
- total or partial replacement of roofs, chimneys, zinc roofing and drains and gutters;
- replacement of windows, doors and frames;
- replacement of joisting and floors;
- damp-proofing;
- external painting (large-scale maintenance).

As no data are available, underground large-scale building maintenance is assumed to account for roughly 30% of total consumer expenditure in this field, like its small-scale counterpart. On this basis, the output value of such maintenance was about 600 million Euros in 1995. Associated intermediate consumption was estimated with reference to the production materials quota revealed by the production statistics of smaller maintenance firms. Value added was obtained by subtracting the value of intermediate consumption from output value.

2.3 Trade and repair

Underground car maintenance and repair activities are covered by a separate estimate. Total maintenance costs are estimated with reference to the service life and average mileage of the existing vehicle stock. The same approach was adopted for repairs. The difference between this estimate and the production statistics totals indicates the extent of concealed activity.

2.4 Hotels, restaurants and cafes

Tax authorities have conducted a variety of special investigations into concealed payments and concealed turnover in the hotel and catering industry since the 1970s. As a result, the authorities now have a vast knowledge on tax-evasion practices in this industry, which has significantly reduced the opportunities for tax-fraud. The special investigations made employers "regularise" their employees' status. Especially in the year following these investigations this was reflected in an "inexplicable" growth of this industry in the production statistics.

Therefore, underground activities have declined in this industry since the end of the 1970s, although it will not be zero. The investigations mentioned indicate that special account must be taken of concealed remuneration, which is hidden from the authorities by not declaring certain turnover or quoting excessively high other expenditure.

Estimates of total underground payments to cafe and restaurant staff are based on "unconcealed" remuneration. Various studies conducted in the hotel and catering sector over the years, both by the tax authorities and the sectoral associations, have limited the extent of concealed activities within the branch. An estimate of 5% for concealed wage payments seems reasonable. (This does not include tips, which are estimated separately). The output associated with these concealed payments is estimated at roughly 3% of the "unconcealed" output, assuming lower productivity on the part of the recipients. The residual value added is classified as mixed income.

In hotels there are less opportunities to pay wages off the record than in cafes and restaurants. Extensive electronic payment in this area (using pin numbers and credit cards) makes it less easy to hide turnover and, consequently, remuneration from the tax authorities. A lower concealed payment figure is therefore applied to hotels, which results in an output value of 1.5% of "unconcealed" output.

Increased output is associated with greater intermediate consumption. This additional consumption is assumed to be equivalent to normal entrepreneurial cost fraud. It is for the entrepreneur to maintain an acceptable balance between output and intermediate consumption. Total adjustments in hotels, cafes, restaurants etc. because of underground activities was almost 300 million Euros in 1995.

2.5 Health care

Although opportunities for additional, hidden earnings exist in the health sector, they are relatively limited. In particular, the tax authorities carefully inspect the tax returns of dentists. In total, mixed income was raised by roughly 100 million Euros, because of underground activities.

2.6 Crèches

In the Netherlands there is a great need for crèches - far greater than can be met through official channels. Unofficial child-minding was estimated on the basis of the 1995 Ancillary Service Use Survey (AVO95) in conjunction with a 1995 working document published by the Institute for Strategic Labour Market Research (OSA) (OSA, 1995) which, among other institutions, covered crèches.

The AVO95 data were compared with the child-minding statistics, which cover "unconcealed" activities and the two sets of statistics showed good correlation as regards official services. The other AVO95 figures were therefore assumed to be sufficiently reliable to provide a basis for estimates in respect of 0-3-year-old children.

These last-mentioned estimates were based on the number of children that are unofficially child-minded, revealed by the AVO95 and the average child-minding costs, excluding kindergartens and day centres, indicated by the OSA report (1700 Euros). The number of 0-3-year-olds unofficially child-minded is 65000. This number was multiplied with the average child-minding cost, resulting in an adjustment of over 100 million Euros.

Since the AVO95 is unreliable for older children, the estimate for 4-12-year-olds was based on the average number of hours of individual child-minding for single- and two-earner families combined as indicated in the OSA working document (1.9 hours/week/child), the number of 4-12-year-olds and the hourly child-minding rate. All the data relate to a 46-week year. The number of such children was obtained from the population statistics, which showed an average of 1 692 053 in 1995. According to the child-minding statistics, the official host family rate was about 1.95 Euros per hour in 1995. Using these figures, the total cost of child-minding for 4-12-year-olds was estimated at almost 300 million Euros.

2.7 Personal services

A significant proportion of personal services are provided outside the normal circuit, for example cleaners, babysitters and the like. Many of these do not, however, involve underground activities, since the amounts in question are below the tax threshold. The supplementary estimate of these informal services does not distinguish between concealed and unconcealed activities.

Two approaches were adopted in order to calculate the output value of this category, with each providing a comparable estimate. The first is based on the 1996 budget survey figures since, by contrast with earlier years, the questions concerning domestic help, child-minders and the like were extremely detailed at that time. The resulting amount is approximately 1000 million Euros in 1995.

The second approach is based on the research conducted by M.E. Homan (1991) and particularly on the statement: *"Approximately 16% of households enjoy domestic help for an average of 4 hours a week at an average cost of approximately NLG 40,- [= Eur 18.15] per week. Domestic help is used relatively frequently by single retired people and active two-income families"*. This statement relates to consumption, which also covers off the record remunerated domestic staff. Data from different years are required for calculations based on the statement. This also produced an output value of approximately 1000 million Euros for 1995.

2.8 Tips

In the Netherlands, tipping is mainly encountered in the hotel and catering industry (hotels, restaurants and cafes). Taxi-drivers, hairdressers, manicurists and the like are also tipped to a limited extent.

2.8.1 Hotels, restaurants and cafes

Estimates of tipping in this sector are based on information obtained from the tax authorities and the relevant branch association. Reference is also made to the documentary evidence in the case concerning compliance with collective agreements in a restaurant[29], which indicates that tipping in restaurants and cafes accounts for 15-20% of gross wages or roughly 4% of output. This percentage is confirmed by recent research at the University of Wageningen.[30] Since, in hotels in particular, payment is frequently made electronically and by credit card, employers cannot conceal corresponding tips from the tax authorities. Any amounts received by employees will be subject to income tax. The amounts also appear in the employer's administrative data and, consequently, in the production statistics. Cash tips are comparatively insignificant, being estimated at 1% of turnover. In the case of campsites and other recreational accommodation there is very little or no tipping. The same is true for canteens and catering. Consequently, a supplementary estimate is not made in respect of these facilities. Total tips are estimated at over 260 million Euros in 1995 and are evenly distributed over wages/salaries and mixed income.

---

[29] The owner of the restaurant in question wanted to deduct total tips received from the collectively agreed wage.
[30] Results of this research can be found in Trouw, 9-1-2003.

2.8.2 Taxis

Total value of taxi services was 515 million Euros in 1995. Approximately 55% of this total was accounted for by normal road journeys, 30% by group transport and 10% by transport of the sick.

Tips are estimated to represent 5% of the value of road and group journeys but only 2% in the case of transport of the sick. On this basis, tips received total at almost 25 million Euros. Approximately two-thirds of taxi tips are attributed to employees, with the remaining third going to (self-employed) entrepreneurs as mixed income.

2.8.3 Hairdressers, manicurists, etc.

Total production of hairdressing services, manicurists and the like was 850 million Euros in 1995. Estimates put the average hairdressers' income accounted for by tips at 2%. This mainly involves the "rounding-up" of the amounts to be paid. On this basis, tips received total circa 20 million Euros.

3. Income in kind

The Netherlands' tax authorities allow only few concessions to employees in the form of remuneration in kind. Tax is payable on almost all forms of such income. This applies, for example, to company provision of meals and beverages, free transport, the private use of a company car or company telephone facility, subsidised child-minding, cut-price purchases (provided these exceed cost price), use of company accommodation, educational subsidies for employees' children and (mortgage) loans provided by the employer below market rates. Virtually all tax matters are negotiated with the employer, with the exception of the private use of company cars, which is not covered by the employer's declaration. In making his income tax declaration, the employer merely indicates an employee's entitlement to use a company car.

The most important sources (annual statistics) on which the national accounts are based explicitly ask for income in kind to be indicated under wages and salaries. It can therefore be assumed that there is no significant underestimation of payment in kind where the national accounts make use of standard CBS annual statistics. It is mainly in the fields of agriculture, financial institutions and government and non-commercial services that these annual statistics cannot be used.

To a large extent, agricultural output estimates are based on physical flows and stocks. This means that any income in kind - in the form of agricultural products - is always included in output value and value added. Consequently, underestimating total wages and salaries to take account of the effects of income in kind will not affect GNI, but only its distribution between wages and salaries and other income.

Whilst use is not made of production statistics in the traditional sense in the government context, the estimates are based on an extremely detailed analysis of government accounts. There is, therefore, no reason to assume that income in kind will not be covered by wage and salary estimates under this heading. There are no particular forms of income in kind associated with non-commercial services.

3.1 Interest benefit to employees

Financial institutions were surveyed in an effort to estimate loan-related interest reductions. In the Netherlands, this possibility is almost exclusively confined to mortgage loans. It was estimated at slightly less than 165 million Euros in 1995. This has no consequences for GNI if booking is in conformity with ESA 95. In the banking sector the increase in gross value added is offset by an equivalent increase in interest margin use. In the insurance sector there is no change in output value and value added, as higher salaries reduce the operating surplus.

3.2 Travel benefits

The transport sector offers limited travel benefits. Free staff travel does not exist, since concessions are always taxable. In all cases, the individual's own contribution is at least 50% of the benefit in question. Estimates are based on surveys of the firms concerned. For railways, urban and local transport (bus, tram, underground) and airlines total travel benefits are less than 10 million Euros.

3.3 Employers' contribution to crèches

Data from 1994 indicate that company subsidies to crèches represent approximately 30% of the total turnover of "unconcealed" childminding services. In 1995, this was equivalent to about 165 million Euros.

3.4 Private use of a company car

In 1995, the Netherlands had approximately 375 thousand company-registered cars, which were also available for private use by employees (sometimes to a limited extent). According to Netherlands fiscal legislation, the possibility of using a company car for private purposes must be notified under taxable income. The increment is 20-24% of the vehicle's catalogue value, depending on the distance to the principal place of employment. Employers must inform the taxation authorities of whether individual employees are entitled to use a "company car".

Both requirements mean that detailed information is available on the number of individuals entitled to such payment in kind. The fiscal-source figures (and particularly the CBS income statistics based thereon) form the basis for the calculation. These data also reveal that the phenomenon of the company car is virtually unknown at government level. The total adjustment is therefore made with reference to company employees.

The total distance privately travelled (in kilometers), including journeys to and from work, is known from CBS data. In 1995, the annual figure was 10800 kilometers (4460 for journeys to and from work, 1000 for holiday use and 5340 for private purposes). Since the number of kilometers travelled per vehicle has hardly changed since 1990, this figure was retained for the following years. The Ministry of Finance has determined the total cost of a private-vehicle kilometer on an annual basis since 1990. This flat-rate cost roughly corresponds to the actual cost price, although it is not based on it. The figure in question must be used for all tax declarations. The calculations for 1998 and 1999 assumed a 3% cost increase. Lastly, the wage cost survey reveals that 40% of employees contribute personally to the use of a "company car".

For calculation purposes, they are assumed to pay 25% of the costs involved. This produces a salary adjustment of almost 1000 million Euros.

4. Effects on GDP estimates

The total amount of explicit adjustments to the value added because of tax-evasion, as presented in section 2, equals about 3000 million Euros or 1% of GNI in 1995. This, however, is not all value added, which was hidden from the tax authorities. There is VAT, which was included implicitly, due to the way the Dutch national accounts are compiled.

An indication for the implicitly included concealed value added can be derived from the difference between the theoretical and actual VAT. The theoretical VAT is the VAT due as calculated from the national accounts. This usually exceeds the actual VAT, which is raised by the tax authorities. Bankruptcies and such cause part of the difference. The main difference, however, is caused by activities, which are included in the national accounts, but that are not reported to the taxman. The average difference over the last years is about 2.5%. The corresponding value added equals to circa 1.25% of GNI.

NORWAY

1. Introduction

In the regular national accounts production process, good care is taken to ensure that the estimates of production are exhaustive by improving the completeness of the sources used, the grossing-up of statistical surveys and the use of the business register. These general approaches are not explained in detail here and can be found in the document "Norwegian National Accounts. New GNI Inventories for ESA 95. March 2004 version" by Erling Joar Fløttum, Statistics Norway. The paper gives a more detailed description of the explicit and implicit adjustments that are made for exhaustiveness in the production and expenditure approach. The checks that are made on the resulting estimates of GDP, and GNI and their components are outlined.

2. Sources and estimation methods

2.1 Production approach

In the 1995 main revision of Norwegian national accounts, a study concluded that total adjustments made to ensure exhaustiveness from the production approach added to 17.4 billion NOK in 1990, or 2.4 per cent of GDP (2.5 per cent of GNI). Adjustments were highest in construction, real estate and other services, accounting for 1.5 per cent of GDP. In other services and construction, adjustments for exhaustiveness contributed to more than 15 per cent of their respective value added. In the remaining paragraphs of this section, the results of this exhaustiveness study are reviewed by industry.

For NACE A - <u>Agriculture, hunting and forestry </u>- most important adjustment for improving exhaustiveness included agricultural production for own use in other households than farmers' households (fresh fruit in particular). Other adjustments made included reindeer production, services from kennel activities not covered by basic data, and services incidental to forestry and logging, like timber scaling, spraying the trees and forestry management planning.

For NACE B - <u>Fishing</u> - adjustments were needed for own consumption of fish, for landings not registered by the sale organizations and unregistered sales of fish. Services incidental to fishing were of minor importance and therefore not estimated.

For NACE C - <u>Mining and quarrying, extraction of crude petroleum and natural gas</u> - adjustment for foreign ownership of border fields with the UK in the North Sea might be considered a problem for exhaustiveness.

For NACE D - <u>Manufacturing</u> - adjustments to include one-man establishments was an improvement for exhaustiveness.

For NACE E - <u>Electricity, gas and water supply</u> - no adjustments to the sources were considered necessary from the exhaustiveness viewpoint.

For NACE F - <u>Construction</u> - adjustments for exhaustiveness of considerable effect were made for own-account construction of buildings, and for one-man establishments.

The former related in particular to existing dwellings (major improvements and the like), but also to own-account construction of new dwellings and on cottages, summer houses etc.

For NACE G - <u>Wholesale and retail trade; repair of motor vehicles, motorcycles and personal and household goods</u> - value added of wholesale and retail trade increased by 35 per cent in the 1995 main revision, part of which might be seen as an improvement in exhaustiveness.

For NACE H - <u>Hotels and restaurants</u> - adjustments were made to improve on canteen and catering services, and to increase scope for camping sites (adding 50 per cent to registered sales).

For NACE I - <u>Transport, storage and communication</u> - adjustments were made to Business Register data in certain areas, in particular for taxi operations, but also for rental services of buses and parking services. Free transport was estimated in railway transport, scheduled motorbus transport, tramway and suburban transport and air transport based on experts' view and other considerations. In water transport, management services were estimated, which were not reflected in the main source of maritime transport statistics.

For NACE J - <u>Financial intermediation</u> - no adjustments had been necessary from the viewpoint of exhaustiveness.

For NACE K - <u>Real estate, renting and business activities</u> - strong increase for dwelling services was made stemming from several considerations - to some extent also exhaustiveness - in particular with addition for secondary dwelling services. For renting and business activities, inclusion of one-man establishments should be mentioned.

For NACE L - <u>Public administration and defense</u> - and NACE M - <u>Education</u> - no adjustments on exhaustiveness were made.

For NACE N - <u>Health and social work</u> - part of the NPISH production has been estimated from exhaustiveness considerations, i.e. for services of catastrophic and aid institutions and part of the ambulance services. Other adjustments made related to income data for dentists (registered too low) and for market hospital services outside National Insurance health plan.

For NACE O - <u>Other community, social and personal service activities</u> - a number of adjustments for exhaustiveness were made due to less satisfactory statistical sources available. These related to various activities of membership organizations, video activities, artistic and literary creation and interpretation, other entertainment activities, news agency activities, certain sporting activities, other recreational activities, physical well-being activities etc.

For NACE P - <u>Private households with employed persons</u> - no adjustment for exhaustiveness was made since household survey data were used directly.

2.2 Expenditure approach

<u>Household final consumption expenditure</u> in the 1995 revision increased by 9 billion NOK, or more than 1 per cent of GDP from the exhaustiveness adjustments. Items under consideration

were: agricultural production for own final use; free transport in railways, air transport and other transportation; adjustments to Business Register data on taxi operation and rental services of buses (split by household and intermediate consumption); addition for secondary dwelling services; adjustment to income data for dentists; and additions from the use side to works of art, other entertainment, other lotteries, hairdressing services etc., and funeral and related services. Minor adjustments to household consumption also involved activities of the reindeer industry; kennel activities; fish for own consumption; inclusion of one-man establishments in manufacturing and in other services; increased scope for other accommodation (camping sites); adjustment for market hospital services outside National Insurance health plan; adjustments to Business Register data on parking services, and addition to other services.

Final consumption of the NPISHs was affected from three items categorized under NACE N and NACE O, which might be looked upon as adjustments of exhaustiveness: services of catastrophic and aid institutions estimated from the use side; part of ambulance services; and communal work for/and sporting services. In sum, these adjustments contributed to 3 billion NOK in 1990, or 16 per cent of total NPISH consumption expenditure.

Gross fixed capital formation has been affected by the adjustments made on including own-account construction of dwellings (new and existing dwellings), and from the inclusion of one-man establishments in construction, after having reallocated a smaller part to intermediate consumption. The effect on gross fixed capital formation from these adjustments was higher than the corresponding effect on GDP, a difference that might be explained by decrease in inventories or increase in intermediate consumption or imports (materials).

Exports were affected through foreign ownership adjustment to oil and gas fields in the North Sea, which raised output, value added and exports by 0.8 billion in 1990. There was also a minor adjustment due to inclusion of management services in ocean transport.

3. Checks to ensure exhaustiveness

Important characteristics of the Norwegian national accounts include an input-output framework integrated on an annual basis, supply-and-use tables built around commodity flows, detailed breakdown of most variables, and the role of national accounts as a long-established tool in integrating and coordinating economic statistics.

Approaches used to calculate GDP are multi-dimensional. The production approach through its strong emphasis on industrial breakdown is regarded as the main approach. The expenditure approach is also much used through the supporting role of the commodity flow approach. The income approach has played a minor role, but will have a more decisive role with the development of complete accounts in integrating accounting approaches by sectors. And most important, the product dimension - with the balancing of supply and uses of each product - is a very strong element in the Norwegian approach to national accounting.

Balancing at both current prices and constant prices at a detailed level has been an important check to ensure exhaustiveness. Balancing at constant prices uses the same framework of integrated supply-and-use tables at current prices, by deflating current values by price indices at the detailed product level. There are two dimensions to the deflation approach:

(i) differentiated by main categories of supply and use (deflating output, imports, exports and implicitly domestic use);

(ii) differentiated through valuation (deflating current values at basic prices by price indices and implicitly determining the other value components, including adjustments against values at purchasers' prices).

Constant-price estimates for aggregates of supply, uses and value added follow through by adding up and balancing constant-price estimates of products. They include aggregates such as output by industry, categories of exports and imports, categories of other final uses, intermediate consumption by industry, value added by industry and GDP. This entails that the principle of double deflation be used through a detailed input-output framework (supply-and-use tables), which is linked to the condition that the individual products are as price homogeneous as possible, with a possibility for adapting to basic statistics available for values as well as prices.

Another important check on the level of GDP is provided by the comparisons of the national accounts estimates of employment and compensation of employees with the same estimates in the labour accounts. This is, to a certain extent, dealt with in the inventory on compensation of employees by kind of activities when reviewing figures on wages and salaries per full-time equivalent employee. Norway is in a favorable position by having labour accounts compilation integrated with the national accounts. This is elaborated below.

4. Employment underlying the GNP estimates and alternative estimates of employment

Employment is one of the key variables for ensuring the exhaustiveness of the national accounts. The process has four steps: (i) defining employment underlying GNP; (ii) standardizing the definition of employment; (iii) assessing the employment comparisons; and (iv) assessing the impact on GNP.

The employment data according to demographic sources should be compared with the employment estimates underlying the GNP (i.e. GNI) estimates. This involves standardizing the definition of employment for the comparison with the domestic occupied population. The demographic data sources used are the Labour Force Survey (LFS) and the Population Census. The rationale behind this comparison is that if the same statistical sources used to estimate production and value added for the national accounts can be used to yield an estimate of employment, then that employment estimate can also be assessed for completeness against the estimates of employment available from demographic sources. If the comparison shows a deficiency in the employment estimates underlying the national accounts, then there may well be grounds for believing that production and value added are also understated in the national accounts. If the comparison shows no such deficiency, then one likely conclusion is that the national accounts cover at least employment exhaustively.

Statistics Norway has more than 15 years experience in constructing Labour Accounts (LA), data from which have been integrated in the national accounts all these years. The LA work has involved validating employment and wages and salaries data altogether in an integrated approach. Through this integrated approach, the Norwegian national accounts estimates are reviewed against both demographic employment data sources, and against vital register data obtained from the employers on wages and salaries as reflecting the actual transactions to be registered with the Tax Authorities.

Consistency considerations play an important role in estimating employment in the Norwegian national accounts. Since the framework generally applied to the compilation of national accounts is the annual supply-and-use tables, detailed employment data by branch (industries) are considered adjacent information of the same format as that of compensation of employees. Furthermore, employment data for employees should be fully consistent with the data on compensation of employees for internal consistency reasons. Therefore, the estimation of employment has been closely linked to the estimation of compensation of employees and to production (output and value added). These are all estimations carried out in the NA unit, thus reviewed and discussed with a view to a best possible consistency.

The Labour Accounts include three basic employment measures: employed persons, full-time equivalent persons and total hours worked. The three types of employment concepts are linked by a set of relationships to a consistent system and are specified according to industry, status (employees or self-employed) and sex. Part-time workers, conscripts and persons temporarily absent from work are included in the employment concepts. This is in line with definitions used in LFS and ESA95.

Several sources and methods are used in the estimation. Basically, there are direct methods or approaches using either industry-based data of the same kind as used for production, or data from the Labour Force Surveys (LFS). Which source to use has been determined by the particular circumstances of each industry, considering the advantages and weaknesses in each case. Implicit methods are also possible, when taking into account wage sums and wage (rate) statistics of better quality than by using employment data directly. The picture of sources and methods throughout the various industries is quite composite and reflects the fact that quality of the data varies considerably from industry to industry. Quality variation also applies to the concepts as such. In general, the estimation of hours worked has been based on more uncertain factors than the estimation of employed persons and full-time equivalent persons, while efforts have also been made over the years to improve the estimates of hours worked.

In the Norwegian system, LFS determines the total number of employed persons in the national accounts. This restriction was introduced because LFS becomes more reliable the more aggregated are the measures, but also to eliminate gaps for certain industries that have not been resolved from using direct information.

The procedure used for the estimation of employment categories and the utilization of information from the LFS may be outlined as follows:

(i)   Basic statistics of different kinds are compiled by branch at detailed industry levels. Inconsistencies between data sources are revealed either directly or indirectly through the use of the conceptual relationships and consequently adjusted.

(ii)   The first-step estimates are aggregated to totals and to a specified intermediate level of aggregation. The total number of persons employed according to the LFS is then compared with these aggregates.

(iii)   Discrepancies lead to feedback adjustments in the detailed estimates, but are not implemented as an automatic procedure. Relevant adjustments are indicated by use of aggregated results at the intermediate level, i.e. at 1-digit NACE level. The feedback adjustment is mostly directed to branches with weak statistical information on employment.

The process of adjustment on details is repeated until the result is considered to be acceptable.

This process of harmonization between LFS and other data sources is conducted separately for employees and self-employed. Some of the conceptual relationships are relevant for employees only, and the data availability at detailed industry level certainly is weaker for self-employed. The data for self-employed and unpaid family workers in the national accounts are however more directly based on the Labour Force Surveys.

At the time of the 1995 main revision, the Population and Housing Census 1990 was the latest population census held in Norway. Its scope comprised all persons who were registered as resident in Norway at the date of the Census - 3 November 1990. The housing census covered all dwellings in which at least one person lived at that date. This means that unoccupied dwellings were not included in the census, nor people temporarily present in these dwellings.

Main totals of population at the census date and of occupational population the year until the census date are shown in Table 1.

Table 1. Population and employment aggregates, 3 November 1990

Total resident population	4 247 546
Resident population 16 years and above	3 393 833
Occupational population 16 years and above	2 124 413
of which: men	1 162 567
of which: women	961 846

A first comparison (Table 2) between the national accounts 1990 estimate of total persons employed and the population census figure of occupational population 16 years and above of the 12 month period before the census date 3 November 1990, shows a discrepancy of 3.4 per cent. It means, NA estimate is 70 000 below the population census figure. However, certain adjustments are necessary in order to have a more standardized comparison.

Table 2. Population census and national accounts, employment 1990

Population census 1990 - occupational population	2 124 413
National accounts - employed persons	2 054 100
Difference in per cent	3.4

A comparison between the population census and the national accounts is undertaken by using the A60 format of the ESA 95 (NACE Rev.1). The population census data compiled by using the former national activity classification based on ISIC Rev.2 have been regrouped at the 3-digit publication level. A few new activity items could not be filled in, with definitional discrepancies remaining here and there. As noted, total difference between the two sources is about 70 000 persons, or 3.4 per cent. Differences above 10 000 are noted for 11 activity items, four of which are negative in the sense that the national accounts show a higher figure than the population census. In two of the latter cases - NACE 61 and 75 - the scope is larger in the national accounts as foreign sailors and conscripts are included. The larger positive differences are in manufacturing, construction and retail trade.

Statistics Norway has conducted quarterly Labour Force Surveys (LFS) since 1972. The concepts and definitions are in accordance with recommendations given by the International Labour Organization (ILO).

A first comparison between the national accounts estimates of total persons employed and the corresponding totals in the LFS for the later years shows small discrepancies in the order of 1 - 2 per cent (Table 3). The LFS totals are however lower than the national accounts estimates, varying from 24 000 to 37 000 in the period 1990 - 2001. The main reason for this kind of difference is that foreign seamen in ocean transport are included in the resident employment estimates of the national accounts, while excluded in the Labour Force Surveys.

Table 3. Labour Force Surveys and national accounts (1000 persons)

	Labour Force Surveys	**National accounts**	**Difference**
1990	2 030	2 054	-24
1991	2 010	2 036	-26
1992	2 004	2 031	-27
1993	2 004	2 041	-37
1994	2 035	2 069	-34
1995	2 079	2 113	-34
1996	2 132	2 156	-24
1997	2 195	2 220	-25
1998	2 248	2 276	-29
1999	2 258	2 294	-36
2000	2 269	2 304	-35
2001	2 278	2 310	-32

LFS data has then been compared with NA estimates by industry using the NACE Rev.1 classification. LFS follows NACE Rev.1, with a detailed breakdown from 1996 and less detailed one back to 1989. The comparison for 1990 was therefore undertaken by utilizing the more detailed 1996 LFS breakdown for those items that needed more detailed LFS data. A slightly more detailed register data for 1992 grouped by former activity classification were utilized as well.

Finally, the various comparisons for 1990 were combined into one where the national accounts (NA) estimates, the Labour Force Surveys (LFS) data and data from the population census (PC) were brought together for comparison (Table 4).

The largest industry differences in 1990 deserve some comments. First, a look at the manufacturing industries. The NA estimate of number of persons employed in total manufacturing was lower than in the LFS and considerably lower than in the population census. Regrouping of LKAUs meant that 8 000 persons employed were moved to non-manufacturing activities using the new nomenclature (NACE Rev.1). This kind of adjustment was already reflected in the LFS and NA estimates above, but not for the population census. Thus, the NA estimate on comparable basis was some 10 000 below LFS and 34 000 below the population census. On the other hand, in the main source for this industry - manufacturing statistics - total number of employed was 276 900 as compared with 294 800 in national accounts, i.e. NA estimate is 18 000 higher (11 000 for employees). For employees in manufacturing, the NA estimates are indirectly derived from using data on wages and salaries obtained in the manufacturing statistics and wage rate data in the wage statistics. Data currently available for employees are the LFS data, the employers/employees register data, and the employment data collected in the annual manufacturing statistics. The NA estimate of employees is between the register and LFS data which are 10 000 - 15 000 higher and manufacturing statistics which are about 10 000 lower.

Table 4. Number of employed, 1990 (1000 persons)

	NACE Rev.1	Population census	Labour Force Surveys	National accounts
01	Agriculture and hunting	98	103	99
02	Forestry and logging	11	7	7
05	Fishing and fish farming	20	20	20
10	Coal mining and peat extraction	0	0	0
11	Oil and gas extraction	18	22	19
12	Mining of uranium and thorium ores	-	-	-
13	Mining of metal ores	2	2	2
14	Other mining and quarrying	4	4	3
15	Food products and beverages	63	49	51
16	Tobacco products	1	1	1
17	Textile products	7	9	7
18	Wearing apparel, fur	3	3	3
19	Footwear and leather products	1	1	1
20	Wood and wood products	22	21	20
21	Pulp, paper and paper products	14	9	12
22	Publishing, printing, reproduction	35	41	37
23	Refined petroleum products	1	2	2
24	Chemicals and chemical products	17	16	16
25	Rubber and plastic products	10	7	6
26	Other non-metallic mineral products	11	10	10
27	Basic metals	22	17	17
28	Fabricated metal products	26	18	18
29	Machinery and equipment n.e.c.	39	28	23
30	Office machinery and computers	..	..	3
31	Electrical machinery and apparatus	19	16	11
32	Radio,TV sets, communication equipment	..	..	5
33	Instruments, watches and clocks	2	3	4
34	Motor vehicles, trailers, semi-trailers	..	..	3
35	Other transport equipment	28	36	34
36	Furniture, manufacturing n.e.c.	14	17	12
37	Recycling	..	..	..
40	Electricity, gas and steam supply	22	22	20
41	Water supply	0	1	1
45	Construction	160	133	135
50	Motor vehicle sale and services	56	46	45
51	Wholesale trade, commission trade	121	107	132
52	Retail trade, repair personal goods	161	163	131
55	Hotels and restaurants	67	57	56
60	Land transport, pipeline transport	60	58	55
61	Water transport	30	22	48
62	Air transport	12	9	12
63	Supporting transport activities	13	25	25
64	Post and telecommunications	50	45	52
65	Financial intermediation	49	47	44

Table 4.(continued) Number of employed, 1990

NACE Rev.1		Population census	Labour Force Surveys	National accounts
66	Insurance and pension funding	14	14	17
67	Auxiliary financial intermediation	..	..	2
70	Real estate activities	11	9	8
71	Renting of machinery and equipment	2	2	3
72	Computer and related activities	..	..	10
73	Research and development	13	12	4
74	Other business services	87	97	92
75	Public administration and defense	143	146	167
80	Education	154	146	151
85	Health and social work	318	316	320
90	Sewage, refuse disposal activities	16	6	6
91	Membership organizations n.e.c.	18	15	18
92	Cultural and sporting activities	30	28	30
93	Other service activities	22	24	21
95	Domestic services	5	10	7
99	Extra-territorial organizations and bodies	0	..	..
	Non-specified	..	5	..
	Total industries	**2 124**	**2 030**	**2 054**

For total manufacturing, the NA estimate of wages and salaries was 68.0 billion NOK in 1996, or 3 - 4 per cent lower than the estimate in the Register of Wages and Salaries (RWS) level of 70.5 billion. On the other hand, the NA level of employment was about 4 per cent higher than in the main source of manufacturing statistics for number of employees. As manufacturing statistics are a NA source in the first case - while not in the second case - it clearly indicates that the quality of manufacturing statistics varies a lot. Data on wages and salaries therein are considered more reliable than the corresponding employment data. Furthermore, the approach taken in the Norwegian NA may be viewed as a compromise between lowering the NA employment estimate to the level of manufacturing statistics and bringing it up to the higher level of LFS and employers/employees register data. If the latter move had been taken and perhaps would have questioned the activity level of output and other economic variables in the manufacturing statistics to be measured too low, it would have brought even more worries with it concerning the continued increases in inventories in the NA.

Given the fact that manufacturing statistics are the basic source for production estimates, the NA estimate at first sight is significantly above the employment underlying GNP. However, this should not lead to indicate that the present NA employment estimate should be replaced by the lower employment underlying GNP. It has been argued that the quality of the source material is such that the employment data in manufacturing should not be used directly. There is reason to believe that employment data in manufacturing statistics underestimate short-term employment. There are indicators that point in that direction: LFS and employment register data that are considerably higher and above the present NA level; RWS register data on wages and salaries that are higher than wages and salaries in manufacturing statistics which together with wage statistics data used should tend to give an even higher employment estimate.

Some comments on other differences in Table 4:

45   Construction
NA estimate of persons employed is much lower than in the population census, but is in accordance with LFS. Construction is one of the largest industries in the total economy, and is thus regarded as a target for adjustment made necessary for keeping total employment according to the LFS. In scrutinizing the estimates to maintain conceptual and other relationships, the final estimates in construction are influenced by various divergent considerations.

51,52 Wholesale and retail trade
NA estimate is in line with LFS, while the distribution is different. The employment level is lower than in the population census, but again higher than in the wholesale and retail trade statistics and register data that both tend to under-estimate short-term employment.

75   The public administration and defense
The employment estimate in NA is much higher than corresponding data in LFS and Register of employers. It is indirectly estimated from wage and salaries data in government accounts and wage rate statistics. Despite this, RWS data are clearly above wages and salaries in the government accounts. In the 1995 revision, a new approach was discussed for future revision for this NACE group.

In the 2002 revision, new employment estimates - for all three concepts - were made by industry that were consistent with the revised estimates of compensation of employees and wages and salaries. Main results pointed to a re-distribution within services and construction industries, while the primary industries, oil and gas extraction and manufacturing remained more or less as before. Employment in other business services (NACE 74) was revised upwards (by 23 000 more employed in 1997), while employment in wholesale and retail trade and in health and social work was revised downwards. Total number of employed persons and total hours worked were both slightly revised upwards (by 0.1 - 0.6 per cent for years 1991-1996). Differences to LFS totals are within the margins of errors in LFS when NA is adjusted for foreigners in ocean transport.

It should also be borne in mind that another population and housing census was carried out in 2001. Similar comparisons to the ones made for the 1990 population census have not been made in this inventory. From a recently published study in Statistics Norway, it could be seen that for some of the aggregated industry groups, such as wholesale and retail trade, hotels and restaurants, and for public administration and defense and education, health and social work etc., the difference between the census data and LFS data was larger than the margins of error in LFS (partly due to non-response in LFS). The difference for the total was small, however. Further analysis might be needed.

5. Income in kind and tips

As a main rule, income in kind is taxable in Norway. There are tax exemptions, however (small size, gifts etc.). The Register of Wages and Salaries (RWS) originally developed for administrative purposes by the Norwegian Directorate of Taxation, comprises all types of payments from employers to employees recorded by the tax authorities. There are items that discern to employers' social contributions in particular, also taken into account for the treatment in NA.

Despite using RWS as a main source, it is not possible to separate some types of payments in kind from payments in cash (daily allowances in travel, deductible expenses on use of company cars, etc.). The borderline problem for wages and salaries in kind is basically against recording as intermediate consumption. In order to determine which of the two transaction flows to follow in each case, the principles of SNA/ESA have been used as a criteria. It is a well-known problem to draw the borderline between these categories in this area, i.e. whether to allocate to employees or employers. More specific information is needed for the composition of each of these items. Therefore, the convention adopted in the national accounts is to allocate 50 per cent to wages and salaries in kind and 50 per cent to intermediate consumption (applying to main groups of 600, 700 and 800 of the RWS). These are all deductible items related to food and accommodation (600-series), use of cars (700-series) and other deductible expenditures (800-series). It should be noted that items altered in the RWS source from one year to the next are duly corrected. Nevertheless, these alterations constitute a big problem for the estimation.

In effect, the national accounts estimation of wages and salaries in kind is organized in three parts, of which the first two are built from the RWS source, while a third part consists of additions in terms of free travel for employees in transport industries. This latter part has been estimated separately in connection with the estimation of output in these industries (using the expenditure approach). The RWS parts consist of source items that fall into two categories. The first part consists of items that are fairly easily allocated to wages and salaries in kind, while the second part consists of items of expenditures that - for the time being - are considered in half as wages and salaries in kind and half as intermediate consumption.

Wages and salaries in kind are estimated at NOK 15.4 billion in 2000 (8.1 billion in 1990), which is slightly over 1 per cent of GDP. The composition of the three compilation categories is illustrated by 1993 figures in Table 5.

Table 5. Wages and salaries in kind, 1993
(billion NOK)

I RWS items fully allocated	4.0
II RWS items 50 per cent allocated	5.6
III Additions for free travel	0.7
Total wages and salaries in kind	**10.4**

The detailed treatment of 10 items of income in kind in the Norwegian NA is described in the following paragraphs.

The first item is <u>business cars used for private purposes</u>. The income approach is used for the NA estimation. Rather than the car purchase as such (purchased by employers for the purpose of at least some business driving), it is the services (use) of cars being offered free or at reduced prices that is relevant here. For the largest item of the group (RWS code 118) - in fact - it is the value of advantage from private use of employer's car that is assessed for taxation. Other items of the RWS are also taken into account (Table 6). This adds up to become the most important item - 53 per cent - of income in kind in the Norwegian NA (5.5 billion or 0.7 per cent of GDP in 1993).

Table 6. Treatment for income in kind items: business cars, 1993

Register of Wages and Salaries title	Percentage taxable	Category	Billion NOK
Free services of vehicles - as advantage of private use of employer's car	99.5	I	2.5
Services of vehicles - private use of company cars etc. (non-taxable part)	0	II	2.5
Free services of vehicles and boats - fixed taxable amount	100	I	0.5
Free services of vehicles - taxable part based on actual driving distances	100	I	0.1
Minor items in addition: additional allowances for passengers and trailers, compensation for use of cars, and adjustment item on free services of vehicles	..	..	..
Income in kind from personal use of business cars			**5.5**

Employers' contributions to the running costs of canteens address at least two problems: whether economic activities of canteens are covered or not in NA, and when they are, to reallocate the uses of such services partly to household consumption expenditure to reflect the advantage to employees through employers' contributions to the running costs of canteens resulting in price reductions (free or subsidized canteens). The first problem pertains to the secondary output of employers, provided that these canteens are run by the employer and do not constitute separate economic units. (In the latter case, their contributions to output etc. are made through the restaurant industry.) A separate estimate is not made for such a secondary output, as no direct sources are available. However, as such costs (intermediate consumption for representation, meals etc.) are not VAT-deductible, an effort has been made to identify and calculate these costs for the theoretical VAT calculations in the national accounts. Employers' costs of canteens are thus included in intermediate consumption in terms of an aggregated item of unspecified products (inter alia, purchased food for own canteens). Although secondary output is not explicitly estimated, there is reason to believe that it is embodied in some other outputs and thus covered in the total output of the respective units. Thus, this aspect of exhaustiveness is most likely taken care of, while ideally a reallocation of outputs might have been opted for to have full identification on the supply side as well.

The final use vs. intermediate consumption problem addresses the income in kind item of this heading. A separate estimate based on the income approach has not been possible as no direct sources are available. Nonetheless, it is reasonable to state that exhaustiveness of the GDP estimate has been ensured. First, specific information on sales in the government (fees of various kinds) has been reviewed and has to a substantial extent been allocated to this kind of expenditure and thus accounted for in terms of household consumption expenditure. In Norway, main government services in areas like education, health and social work are still provided free to a very large extent; thus, expenditures for meals, sales of goods in kiosks etc. have a relatively large share of incidental sales from government.

Apart from household consumption expenditure recorded directly on this basis, household consumption expenditure has been given a thorough review to ensure that a reasonable estimate for the total is arrived at on the basis of available information. This total review takes into account the various sources, and uses the method of commodity flows and the expenditure approach in combination. Based on this review, no further adjustment is deemed necessary to reallocate from intermediate consumption to household consumption expenditure and a separate adjustment for employers' contributions to the running costs of canteens is made.

Meal vouchers provided by employers to employees also pertain to goods and services bought by the employer to provide them free or at reduced prices as income in kind. While this is believed to be a minor item in Norway, the income approach and the RWS source have been used to tackle this item. Two RWS items with small amounts have been included, i.e. administrative board and board when working overtime. Pay to armed forces (conscripts) is treated as wages in cash, not wages in kind.

The next item pertains to food and accommodation provided free of charge or at reduced prices to employees in hotels, catering establishments and agriculture. In a somewhat broader scope than this, the income approach is used to estimate income in kind as part of compensation of employees. Daily allowances are recorded including or excluding accommodation, pertaining to food, drinks and/or accommodation services provided free or at reduced prices to employees as income in kind, which are mostly in connection with travel abroad or inland travel. These are all RWS items that so far have been split conventionally on a 50-50 basis for intermediate consumption (employers) and wages and salaries in kind (benefits of employees). In 1993, the total value of this item has been calculated at 2.2 billion NOK or between 0.2 and 0.3 per cent of GDP (Table 7).

Table 7. Treatment of income in kind items: food and accommodation, 1993

Register of Wages and Salaries title	Taxable percentage	Category	Billion NOK
Daily allowances, incl. accommodation - for inland travel - central government rates	0	II	0.9
Daily allowances, incl. accommodation - for travel abroad - central government rates	0	II	0.6
Daily allowances, excl. accommodation - for inland travel and travel abroad - central government rates	0	II	0.4
Daily allowances, incl. accommodation - for inland travel - other rates	0	II	0.1
Daily allowances, excl. accommodation - for inland travel and travel abroad - other rates	0	II	0.1
Daily allowances - lodgings/barracks	0	II	0.1
Daily allowances, incl. accommodation - for inland travel on special duty	0	II	0.1
Minor items in addition: daily allowances to foreign workers in Norway; daily allowances, incl. accommodation for travel abroad, other rates; and for long-lasting stays; daily allowances for travel abroad to air transport personnel, incl. accommodation; and excl. accommodation; accommodation allowance in lodgings/barracks; daily allowances incl. accommodation for travel abroad to long distance truck drivers; daily allowances for students and their families in certain areas.	..	..	..
Income in kind from daily allowances			**2.2**

The item of rent-free dwellings and dwellings let to employees at below-market rents also pertains to secondary output of employers and self-employed. In Norwegian NA, renting services are provided by the various participating industries, typically as secondary production of renting services of non-residential property. No such part is recorded for residential purposes. Only two minor items (free housing for foreigners in business, housing or accommodation allowances to foreign workers in Norway, in total 40 million in 1993) have been included in this context using the income approach. Military dwellings probably are underestimated in this context.

The value of the interest foregone by employers when they provide loans to employees at reduced, or even zero, rates of interest pertains to financial assets bought, issued or granted by the producer. When loans are provided by a bank to its employees, the interest foregone should be included in calculating output of the bank and in compensation of employees. When provided by a producer other than a bank, it should also be included in the compensation of employees. The income approach is used for this purpose, as the RWS source includes one item on advantage for employees from cheap loans from their employers. It should also be recalled that Norway has a system of State banks that provide subsidized loans, treating the grants as subsidies to those producers benefiting from them, or as social benefits to households as consumers. The 1993 value is 160 million or 0.02 per cent of GDP (99.5 per cent taxable and category I).

The expenditure approach and the income approach are both used to estimate the item of travel tickets supplied free of charge or at reduced prices to employees. The expenditure approach has been applied to special groups of employees in certain transport industries and mostly geared to long-distance travel. Employees in transport via railways, in tramway and suburban transport and in air transport - and their families - can enjoy the benefit of free travel. This expenditure item is estimated primarily from the household budget surveys, but is also based on experts' opinions and considerations related to the estimation of compensation of employees. In the case of railways, total use of railway transportation services is also taken into account. The total estimate of free travel is 0.7 billion NOK in 1993 or less than 0.1 per cent of GDP, more or less half split between air and railway transport. The income approach has been applied to cases of short-distance travel (commuters etc.) and other special cases (special conditions for foreigners etc.), recorded from the RWS source and a number of minor items as well. The RWS part is 0.2 billion or less than 0.05 per cent of GDP in 1993.

The item of electricity and coal supplied free of charge or at reduced prices to employees is not important for Norway, i.e. there are few arrangements whereby an electricity or coal company supplies electricity or coal free of charge or at reduced prices to their employees or others. When such arrangements occur, they have been recorded in wages and salaries in cash (main item 111-A) of the RWS.

The income approach is used to estimate free telephone (at home). Two RWS items - telephone allowance (non-taxable) and free telephone - are recorded under this heading. The latter item sets a fixed subscriber fee plus a threshold to number of telephone calls. In 1993, these two RWS items add to 255 million NOK or 0.03 per cent of GDP.

The item of traders' consumption from their own traded goods and services and other items of income in kind is miscellaneous income in kind, and is calculated according to the income approach. There are only a few examples of traders' consumption from their traded goods and services. In this respect, a final use vs. intermediate consumption problem is faced similar to what is described under the item on canteens. For the same reasons as given above, it is believed that no further adjustment is deemed necessary to reallocate from any intermediate consumption part to household consumption expenditure. The miscellaneous income in kind consists of a fairly long list of RWS items. In 1993, these items added to 1.3 billion NOK or 0.2 per cent of GDP.

The list of examples from ESA95 and SNA93 also contain items that have not been explicitly dealt with here. Also, some RWS items are unspecified and termed miscellaneous. One such ESA95 item is car parking. No explicit estimate is made for this item, part of the reason being that car parking provided free for employees and paid for by employers is not widespread (mostly confined to the Oslo metropolitan area). Ad hoc travel pattern surveys for the Oslo area have revealed that as much as 90 per cent of car parking is in fact free parking, and has also been a motive behind employers' relocations to the outskirts over recent years. This applies to shopping malls also; in these cases the cost of parking has been transferred into higher prices.

The Norwegian national accounts - before the 2002 revision - included no explicit adjustment for tips received. In practice, tipping is not widespread in Norway. At least in the past, only in rather exceptional circumstances were tips given, and they tended to be small. However, two areas often mentioned are restaurants and taxis. In the restaurants industry, studies have been conducted in which national accounts estimates have been compared against special tourist household surveys. From these comparisons a conclusion might be drawn that tipping in the restaurants in Norway is not very extensive. In the RWS, there is a sub-item on tipping concerning restaurant personnel whose remuneration is percentage based. This is an indication that tipping in restaurants to some degree is included with the estimate of wages and salaries in cash in the restaurants industry. For taxi operations, it should be noted that the revised estimates of output and value added now are considerably higher than before the revision, partly due to considerations related to exhaustiveness.

Household consumption expenditure in restaurants, cafes etc. and for taxi services - was 14.2 billion NOK in 1990 or just 2 per cent of GDP. Although some experts tend to take the view that tips are low and even decreasing in importance in recent years, there might still be cyclical fluctuations, i.e. people tend to tip more in good times. In the 2002 revision, the issue of tips in Norwegian NA was addressed and estimates were made in the two areas mentioned. Tips in restaurants are explicitly estimated at 0.1 billion in 2001 or less than 0.3 per cent of output in hotels and restaurants. The estimate is based on the tax authorities' estimate of 3 per cent addition to registered wages for waiters and waitresses who do not report tips. For taxi operations, tips are estimated, on the basis of survey results from the mid-1990s, to add 3 per cent. This would mean a similar small amount as with tips in restaurants.

6. Using fiscal data to validate GNP

In Norway, information from fiscal audits is not used in the national accounts to increase the exhaustiveness. During the revisions in 1995 and 2002, Statistics Norway considered a more thorough effort to explore the possibilities in this field. The results from fiscal audits, however, have been considered difficult to use, mainly due to non-randomness concerning the units that are being sampled.

7. Other considerations

Household final consumption expenditure is estimated from a composite set of sources and methods. Improving exhaustiveness when searching for a best choice of sources and methods involve a review of the sources that are available, and steps are taken accordingly to improve the estimation. For instance, household budget survey data are not utilized when there is an evident loss of coverage, such as for alcoholic beverages, tobacco and for some other consumption goods. Exhaustiveness has also been influenced by the revised estimates of trade margins and the use of wholesale and retail trade statistics. Improvement in exhaustiveness thus has been achieved through the revised estimates of both household consumption and output of wholesale and retail trade.

More specifically, annual household budget survey data has been utilized in a better and more comprehensive way than before. In the benchmark estimates, wholesale and retail trade margin rates have been dealt with explicitly and distributed on all relevant commodity flows. Searching for best choice of sources and methods also involve the use of direct volume information and the information embodied in the commodity flow system, which in itself include a number of adjustments for improvements as obtained in the balancing process each year. In this context since the supply estimates are usually considered to be the stronger, balancing usually affects the expenditure side, and changes in inventories in particular.

Government final consumption expenditure has not been affected by considerations for improved exhaustiveness, since government accounts are used as sources without taking into account adjustments of this kind. However, a number of adjustments or amendments are implemented due to changes of definitions from the old to the new system of national accounts. One of these changes is the addition to government final consumption expenditure of non-government output purchased by government as social transfers in kind for the benefit of households.

Final consumption expenditure of NPISHs has had a weak source and is mainly estimated from indirect use of government accounts, such as distributive flows of grants etc., with due account taken of fees from households and others. More accounting data and a direct approach was attempted in the 2002 revision. Possibilities should be explored for estimating final consumption expenditure of NPISHs in a more direct way, and in this process, adjustments for improving exhaustiveness would also have to play a key role.

Gross fixed capital formation most often has an industry-related source, which means there is some resemblance with the estimation process of the different industries with respect to other items such as output and intermediate consumption. In the next phase, the commodity flow approach plays a substantive role. Altogether, therefore, adjustments for improving exhaustiveness play a key role here as well. In particular, the service industries sometimes lack adequate sources for the estimation of gross fixed capital formation and thus necessitate adjustments for exhaustiveness.

Changes in inventories used to have no reliable source as a basis for estimation, meaning that adjustments have been and still are made to the NA estimates in the balancing process and thereby serve to ensure better exhaustiveness. While the source situation may have improved, better methodology is also foreseen from new studies and will form a research agenda for consideration in the years to come.

Exports and imports are estimated from the external trade statistics, foreign exchange statistics, and in combination with maritime transport statistics, oil and gas activity statistics and some other sources. The close integration between national accounts and balance of payments is important to ensure exhaustiveness. Foreign exchange statistics (ITRS) as a source has been relatively reliable in Norway - at least until recently - and as such serve to ensure exhaustiveness. Adjustments are nonetheless made for exports and imports in certain respects, notably in the area of ocean transport. Here there are two competing sources - foreign exchange statistics and maritime transport statistics - that have resulted in adjustments to both of them, but in such a way that output and intermediate consumption have been adjusted by more or less the same amount. The output adjustment is recorded for exports. ITRS is however, about to be replaced as key source in Norwegian NA and BOP. Hopefully a situation of continued reliable estimation should nonetheless prevail in the future.

The intrastate problem has not been a serious problem in Norway. This is due to the fortunate and stable situation with good administrative data obtained through the customs declarations, which are a sound basis for establishing reliable statistics of exports and imports of goods. However, there are adjustments to be made, as described above.

POLAND

1. Definitions and concepts

The Central Statistical Office (CSO) of Poland has adopted Eurostat's classification of non-exhaustiveness types (N1-N7) used in the Phare 2002 Project on Exhaustiveness. Adjustments are made for both production and expenditure side for the year 2002.

2. Sources and estimation methods

2.1 Production approach

2.1.1 N1: Producers deliberately not registering – underground

Estimation of employment in the hidden economy

Non-registered work is estimated using the <u>labour input method</u>. The CSO applies two methods to estimate the number of persons employed in the hidden economy. Three sources of information are used: the Labour Force Survey (LFS); employment statistics based on the records of enterprises; and data on registered unemployment obtained from labour offices.

The <u>first method</u> compares the number of employed persons according to the LFS with the number of employed persons reported in enterprise statistics, which cover only persons formally employed. Employment in the hidden economy is calculated as the difference between the LFS estimate and the number derived from enterprise statistics.

In practice, the application of this procedure is complicated by differences in the scope of the two information sources. The LFS is conducted exclusively for private households and does not cover working population living in collective households. Neither does the LFS include persons working abroad for Polish employers. However, the LFS counts apprentices undertaking on-the-job training as employed, providing they receive payment, and also includes persons working on commission agreements. Therefore, before estimating hidden employment by this method, the LFS data are adjusted to make them consistent with the reported enterprise data.

The <u>second method</u> arises from the common conviction that a part (perhaps even the majority) of those registered as unemployed with the labour offices are in fact employed as hidden labour. According to legal regulations in Poland, a person registered as unemployed can work and still remain on the unemployed register if the income from work does not exceed 50 per cent of the minimum wage. This category of unemployed will not be captured in the LFS, which uses the ILO definition of unemployed persons as those who do not engage in any work.

The differences between the definitions of unemployment in labour office data and the LFS form the basis for estimating the number of unemployed who work in the hidden economy. This is possible as the LFS also collects information on persons registered as unemployed in labour offices.

According to the second method, the number of persons working in the hidden economy in Poland was almost three times higher than the number obtained using the first method. This is convincing evidence of the difficulties encountered in estimating the size of the hidden labour market.

Survey on unregistered employment

The CSO developed an additional module on non-registered work in the LFS to obtain information on unregistered employment. The special survey was conducted in August 1995 and 1998 and in the fourth quarter of 2004 (results available end October 2005). This section describes the modular survey for the latest available data from 1998.

Design of the survey

The main goal of the survey on unregistered employment was to gauge the effect of labour market conditions on the hidden economy. Information was obtained on the scale of unregistered employment, the range of services provided by persons performing unregistered work, and employment by households. Unregistered employment was defined in the survey as:
- work performed without entering formal labour relationships between the employer and employee, regardless of the sector in which the enterprise is classified;
- own-account work where financial obligations to the state are not paid (e.g., taxes).

A distinction was also made between persons who worked only in the hidden economy, and those for whom unregistered employment was in addition to their main employment.

From January to August 1998, at least 1 431 000 persons were employed in the hidden economy. Compared to the results of the survey of unregistered employment conducted in 1995, a significant decrease in the unregistered labour market was observed in the 1998 survey. Employment in the hidden economy dropped by 2.8 percentage points from 7.6 per cent to 4.8 per cent of total employment, while the number of persons who admitted to holding unregistered jobs fell by 768 000.

The distribution of the type of work performed in non-registered employment was also covered. Results showed that the largest share of employment in an individual activity attributable to the hidden economy was in gardening and agricultural activities (20.3 per cent of its total), partially as a result of the seasonal nature of such jobs (Table 1).

Unregistered employment takes two forms: persons employed without a formal contract in the formal sector of the economy, and casual employment, as occurs in the informal (or household) sector. In Poland, households have a relatively high demand for unregistered labour.

In 1998, over 1.4 million households were engaged in unregistered employment, i.e. 12 per cent of the total number of households. This phenomenon was observed more frequently in rural areas (16.8 per cent of households) than in urban areas (9.5 per cent of households).

The types of jobs and services performed informally for households differed in rural and urban areas. In urban households, unregistered labour was most in demand for construction and installation and maintenance and repairs (47 per cent of households employing non-registered labour).

Table 1. Persons employed in the hidden economy, by type of activities
(per cent of total employed in each activity)

Type of activities	Total employed	Men employed	Women employed	Urban employment	Rural employment
Trade	5.8	2.9	12.6	7.8	3.7
Construction services	15.9	22.4	0.7	17.2	14.5
Construction repairs and maintenance	14.5	20.5	0.7	16.0	13.2
Car repairs and maintenance	5.3	7.6	..	5.6	5.2
Transport services	5.2	7.1	0.7	4.9	5.5
Repairs of electrical and technical devices	1.2	1.7	..	1.4	1.0
Medical and nursing services	1.4	0.1	4.4	1.7	1.1
Hairdressing and beauty services	0.7	0.1	1.9	0.7	0.6
Tourist and catering services	2.5	1.1	5.8	3.8	1.3
Accounting and legal advice	1.3	0.6	3.0	2.1	0.6
Private lessons	3.2	1.8	6.5	4.9	1.5
Translations	0.1	..	0.2	0.1	..
Tailoring services	4.4	0.4	13.7	5.1	3.6
Housekeeping	3.8	1.2	9.8	5.8	1.7
Child/elderly person care	4.5	0.2	14.4	5.3	3.7
Security services	0.6	0.8	0.2	0.8	0.4
Gardening and agricultural activities	20.3	22.2	15.6	11.8	29.0
Manufacturing	3.3	2.6	4.9	3.5	3.1
Neighbourhood services	17.3	19.5	12.3	11.9	22.6
Other activities	3.2	3.9	2.5	3.1	3.5

Table 2. Persons employed in the hidden economy: share by type of employer

Type of employers	Total	Men	Women	Urban	Rural
Total	**100.0**	**100.0**	**100.0**	**100.0**	**100.0**
Individual	68.9	69.1	68.4	63.9	74.0
Private company or co-operative	16.8	16.7	17.0	20.4	13.2
Public or municipal company	1.7	1.7	1.9	2.4	1.0
Own-account work	12.6	12.5	12.7	13.3	11.8

The next largest share was accounted for by housekeeping, which accounted for 22 per cent of unregistered jobs performed for households. The third most important area was in childcare or elderly person care (18.8 per cent of households employing non-registered labour). Rural households most often sought gardening and agricultural activities (68 per cent of households hiring informally), neighbourhood services (about 43.2 per cent of households), followed by construction, installation and maintenance and repairs (21.4 per cent).

Estimation of income from non-registered work

The estimated number of persons working in the hidden economy is converted to full-time equivalents and allocated to activities in accordance with the shares of non-registered employment shown in Table 1 (apart from gardening and agriculture which is estimated separately).

Estimates of income generated by non-registered employees are calculated by multiplying the estimated number of working days within the year by average remuneration rates for each type of activity. Different rates are used for persons whose unregistered employment is their main occupation and those for whom it is secondary employment.

Table 3 shows the number of employed persons and gross value added from non-registered work, estimated using the labour market survey method.

Table 3. Gross value added from non-registered work, 2002

NACE Sections	Persons employed (thousand)	Gross value added (million zlotys)
Total	**302**	**26 560.3**
Industry (C, D, E)	9	1 089.4
Construction (F)	94	9 052.8
Trade (G, H)	62	8 850.8
Transport (I)	13	1 818.7
Real estate and business activities (K)	9	738.0
Other sections (A, B, M, N, O, P)	115	5 010.6

2.1.2 N2: Producers deliberately not registering – illegal

Estimates of illegal production have been made for the production and sale of drugs, prostitution, theft, fencing and smuggling of goods. The estimates should only be regarded as experimental. So far they have not been incorporated into the officially published GDP figures.

Drugs

Since the beginning of the 1990s, increasing consumption of drugs has been observed in Poland. Some of the drugs are imported but production of 'Polish heroin' and raw materials – poppy straw and cannabis plants - also takes place. The scope of activities includes producing, trading and smuggling of drugs. In accordance with national accounting practice, the following transactions should be estimated: output (production and trade margins), intermediate consumption (consumption in production and trade), salaries (of traders and smugglers), gross operating surplus (income of organisers of the production and trade), imports, exports and consumption.

Information included in a document titled 'National programme against drugs 1999-2001', prepared by the Ministry of Health and Social Assistance and 'Drug addiction in Poland in 2001 and 2002', prepared by the Institute of Psychiatry and Neurology, together with information from the police, Internet, radio, TV and newspapers form the basis for estimation of the value of activities associated with drugs.

Number of drug users

In estimating the number of drug users, two groups are identified: regular drug users and occasional users, depending on the quantity of drugs used. According to estimates of the Ministry of Health and Social Assistance, there are about 25-40 thousand regular drug users. For the purposes of estimation, the total number of addicts was assumed to be about 120 000 in 2002.

The number of addicts, by kind of drugs used, was established by reference to number of persons treated in hospitals in 2002. The number of occasional users was estimated on the basis of a sample taken in 2002 among adults in Warsaw who had admitted to taking drugs during the previous year. Data on age structure among users and regional differences in patterns of drug consumption were collected.

Supply and prices

Police statistics on the quantity of confiscated drugs, the number of illegal drug manufacturers and illegal poppy and cannabis plantations were used to estimate supply.

Data on drug prices were obtained from the police. An average of the lowest and the highest prices recorded in 1997 was used as a base for estimating prices, which were then estimated for the next years (up to 2002) by using the consumer price index.

Value of production

The supply of drugs (domestic production and imports) and demand for them (household consumption and exports) were estimated, and balanced in quantity terms. Values were then estimated from the information on prices. The final estimates for six groups of drugs are shown in Table 4.

Table 4. Main drugs transactions, 2002
(Current prices in million zlotys)

Specification	Output	Intermediate consumption	Gross value added	Salaries	Gross operating surplus	Imports	Household consumption	Exports
Total	1 925.6	100.6	1 825.0	354.5	1 470.5	1 557.3	681.3	2 801.6
Polish heroin	158.9	3.0	155.9	15.9	140.0	0	119.1	39.8
Marijuana and hashish	311.2	15.6	295.6	49.1	246.5	180.0	190.2	301.0
Heroin	538.2	26.9	511.3	108.5	402.8	546.3	40.9	1 043.6
Cocaine	733.2	47.7	685.5	148.2	537.3	748.8	77.9	1 404.1
Amphetamine	92.4	1.5	90.9	9.2	81.7	0	79.3	13.1
Ecstasy	69.4	4.5	64.9	18.5	46.4	67.7	137.1	0
LSD	22.3	1.4	20.9	5.1	15.8	14.5	36.8	0

Prostitution

For national accounts purposes, the relevant aggregates are output (value of services provided by domestic prostitutes), imports (value of services provided by non-residents in Poland) and consumption. Information on such services is obtained from newspapers, media and police reports. For 2002, the approximate number of prostitutes in Poland was estimated to be 22 000 and it was assumed that 40 per cent were non-residents.

The annual supply of prostitution services was estimated based on assumptions for the services provided per day, and the number of working days each month. No distinction was made between resident and non-resident workers. The estimated supply of services was compared with estimates of demand.

Information on prices in 2002 was obtained by interview. The results of the estimation are shown in Table 5.

Table 5. Estimate of the value of prostitution services

Specification	2002
Total number of services available per year	13 802 400
of which:	
resident	8 281 440
non-resident	5 520 960
Price per service (zlotys):	
resident	220
non-resident	30
Value of services (output in thousand zlotys):	1 656 300
Imports (thousand zlotys)	165 600
Households' consumption (thousand zlotys)	1 821 900

Smuggling

Smuggling mainly concerns alcohol products, cigarettes, cars and drugs. The aggregates for national accounts purposes are trade margins of intermediaries and traders in the domestic market; intermediate consumption; gross value added; salaries; imports; households consumption and exports.

Estimates for smuggled goods were compiled from Central Customs Office data, Border Guards data and from newspaper reports. As a starting point, data on customs seizures of cars, alcohol, cigarettes, drugs and other goods were obtained. In the absence of any other information, it was assumed that seizures represent 10 per cent of smuggled goods (based on customs experience of seized goods).

Trade margins on imports and exports of smuggled goods were estimated using customs statistics and information from enterprise surveys. As the prices of smuggled imports do not cover customs duties, other border taxes, VAT or excise tax, the trade margins tend to be higher than for legally traded imports.

Customs statistics and survey data indicate that the expected trade margin is about 50 per cent for cars (compared with the official trade margin of 11 per cent), 70 per cent for alcohol (official trade margin is 11 per cent), 85 per cent for cigarettes (official trade margin is 9 per cent) and 50 per cent for other goods. The same margins were applied to exports.

Incomes arising from the smuggling of goods comprise income of persons directly involved in smuggling and bribes made to customs clerks responsible for border controls. For the purposes of estimation, it was assumed that the value of bribes amounted to 8 per cent of the value of smuggled goods. It was assumed that incomes accruing to other persons involved in smuggling were about 2 per cent of the value of the goods. Total incomes were therefore estimated at 10 per cent of the value of smuggled goods. In the absence of information about intermediate consumption, it was assumed to be zero (Table 6).

Table 6. Trade margins and value added for smuggled goods

Specification	2002 (million zlotys)
Trade margin	684.6
• on imports	670.7
cars	189.5
alcohol	175.7
cigarettes	244.8
others	60.7
• on exports	13.9
alcohol	1.2
cigarettes	12.3
others	0.4
Intermediate consumption	0
Gross value added	684.6
Salaries	105.6
Gross operating surplus	579.1
Imports	715.8
Household consumption	1 386.5
Exports	37.5

Theft and fencing

Theft is difficult to measure in national accounts. The value of stolen goods should be recorded as 'other flows' (i.e. changes in the value of assets) rather than as transactions if they pass from one institutional sector to another or when it is a monetary transaction. No values for theft are recorded in the households sector accounts.

Estimates of the value of theft were made on the basis of data from the Statistical Yearbooks of Poland, police statistics, payments of insurance claims, information from newspapers and data on prices. Due to the lack of information, it was necessary to make assumptions about the percentage of thefts that are not reported and the average prices of some types of goods.

Values for stolen vehicles were calculated using data on the number of vehicles taken, numbers of vehicles recovered, type of vehicle (passenger cars, lorries, vans, buses, and microbuses) and average prices for each type. The values estimated were compared with claims paid in respect of stolen vehicles by insurance companies.

Estimates of the value of theft for other goods were made separately for private and public property, using data on the number of thefts and average prices.

To estimate trade margins and value added, it was assumed that those responsible for theft retain all of the value of stolen vehicles and money stolen from banks, and 20 per cent of the value of the remaining theft, with 80 per cent transferred to traders (Table 7).

Table 7. Estimates of the value of sales arising from theft

	Specification	2002 (million zlotys)
1.	Total value of sold goods coming from thefts (2+5)	4 506.3
2.	Stolen cars	*1 457.3*
3.	from which destined to market • domestic (50 per cent)	*728.6*
4.	• foreign (50 per cent)	*728.6*
5.	Other thefts	*3 049.0*
6.	Trade margin (7+8+9)	486.9
7.	• on sold cars on domestic market (10 per cent)	*72.8*
8.	• on sold cars on foreign market (15 per cent)	*109.2*
9.	• on sold other goods (10 per cent)	*304.9*
10.	Intermediate consumption	0
11.	Gross value added (6-10)	486.9
12.	Salaries (10 per cent of trade margin of sold cars)	18.2
13.	Gross operating surplus (11-12)	468.7
14.	Consumption	1 750.6
15.	Exports	541.4

Summary

The consolidated results of estimates by type of illegal activities are shown in Table 8.

Table 8. Value of illegal activities (all types), 2002
(million zlotys)

Specification	Total	Drugs	Prostitution	Smuggling of goods	Theft and fencing
1. Output	4 753.4	1 925.6	1 656.3	684.6	486.9
2. Intermediate consumption	100.6	100.6	0	0	0
3. Gross value added	4 652.8	1 825.0	1 656.3	684.6	486.9
4. Salaries	478.3	354.5	0	105.6	18.2
5. Gross operating surplus	4 174.5	1 470.5	1 656.3	579.0	468.7
6. Imports	2 438.7	1 557.3	165.6	715.8	0
7. Consumption	5 640.3	681.3	1 821.9	1 386.5	1 750.6
8. Exports	3 380.5	2 801.6	0	37.5	541.4

2.1.3 N5: Registered entrepreneurs not surveyed

This estimate concerns persons employed by private households. They are not registered by REGON (administrative register of units) but are in the register of taxpayers.

The output of households' services produced by employing paid staff is valued by the compensation of employees paid. The compensation is calculated by multiplying the number of employed persons by average wages and salaries by one employed person. The number of persons is taken from the register of taxpayers.

2.1.4 N6: Producers deliberately misreporting

Concealed production

The direct method is used to estimate concealed production of registered units (Table 9). An evaluation of concealed production of small economic units (up to 9 persons) and of medium size private enterprises (excluding co-operatives) where the number of employed does not exceed 49 persons is conducted. In the Polish national accounts, small units are included in the households sector and medium units are included in the non-financial corporations sector.

Table 9. Gross value added created by concealed production in 2002

Sections of NACE	Data according to:		Difference 2-1 = hidden economy	Share of concealed production 3/2
	Statistical surveys	Direct method		
	(million zlotys)			(per cent)
	1	2	3	4
All units (small and medium)				
Total	195 451.6	252 222.5	56 771.0	22.5
Industry (C, D, E)	31 926.0	33 403.8	1 477.8	4.4
Construction (F)	17 984.0	24 162.2	6 178.2	25.6
Trade (G, H)	77 153.0	109 587.7	32 434.7	29.6
Transport (I)	13 682.2	15 577.9	1 895.8	12.2
Real estate and business activities (K)	28 862.8	40 325.3	11 462.5	28.4
Other sections (A, B, M, N, O)	25 843.6	29 165.6	3 322.0	11.4
Small units				
Total	142 061.5	197 303.4	55 242.0	28.0
Industry (C, D, E)	15 594.2	17 072.0	1 477.8	8.7
Construction (F)	10 845.0	16 726.1	5 881.1	35.2
Trade (G, H)	59 875.2	91 733.8	31 858.6	34.7
Transport (I)	11 106.5	13 002.2	1 895.8	14.6
Real estate and business activities (K)	21 347.3	32 154.0	10 806.7	33.6
Other sections (A, B, M, N, O)	23 293.3	26 615.3	3 322.0	12.5
Medium sized units				
Total	53 390.1	54 919.1	1 529.0	2.8
Industry (C, D, E)	16 331.8	16 331.8	0.0	0.0
Construction (F)	7 139.0	7 436.1	297.1	4.0
Trade (G, H)	17 277.8	17 853.9	576.1	3.2
Transport (I)	2 575.7	2 575.7	0.0	0.0
Real estate and business activities (K)	7 515.5	8 171.3	655.8	8.0
Other sections (A, B, M, N, O)	2 550.3	2 550.3	0.0	0.0

The direct method consists of obtaining expert estimates of the average sales and the average remuneration. These estimations are used for gross output, intermediate consumption and gross value added. This method was elaborated by experts from the Kielce Statistical Office and is known as the 'Kielce method'. It is based on the following general assumptions:

- average labour productivity should be at a level that ensures the profitability of a given activity;
- small enterprises can adapt to changes in the market;
- wages and salaries paid to persons employed in these enterprises are essentially the same as the average received within medium-sized enterprises in the same branch of the economy and in the same locality;
- the income of the owner is higher than the average wage.

Elaboration of the 'normative tables' had been preceded by the detailed and in-depth analysis of labour productivity, levels of wages and their percentage share in the revenues with distinction of the public and private sector as well as the size of the respective units.

When calculating revenue estimates for small firms, for every section (or group of sections) of the NACE nine levels, normative revenues per employed person were established.

The highest level of revenues per employed person was assumed for 1-person enterprises, based on the expectation that in this case almost all those employed are owners (or co-owners) and that their productivity is higher than that of the salaried staff, they usually work longer hours, and adapt their working hours to local needs. A somewhat lower level of revenues per 1 person was assumed for the enterprises employing 2-5 persons and the lowest one for the group 6-9. The obtained estimates of the monthly normative revenues and the level of wages per employed person were then checked by the experts of the fiscal and social insurance agencies. To take into account the specific features of individual provinces (voivodships), 19 tables of revenues were constructed for groups of similar voivodships.

Within the population of economic units employing more than 9 persons, estimation of revenues was also carried out by sections, kinds of localities and the number of persons employed. Consequently, nine levels of normative revenues were obtained for all sections (up to 49 persons employed per establishment).

The results, achieved by this method are compared with data acquired from enterprises' reports for small and medium units. Finally the data from Kielce method are taken into consideration to include estimates for non-response.

Following experimental studies, a special regular survey was introduced in 1998 in order to update the 'normative tables'.

VAT fraud

In Polish national accounts, calculation of VAT fraud follows the Commission Decision of 24 July 1998 on the treatment for national accounts purposes of VAT fraud.

The calculation of the theoretical VAT is based on the value of transactions exempt from VAT. For calculations of the theoretical VAT, the transactions in household consumption, intermediate consumption and gross fixed capital formation are considered. Initial data are obtained from national accounts and structure by products from the use table. Data from national accounts are transformed into transactions subject to non-deductible VAT and then estimated by groups of products with different VAT rates. The value of transactions by products is multiplied by the relevant products' VAT rates.

Household consumption is compiled in accordance with COICOP (Classification of Individual Consumption by Purpose). The reclassification of data from COICOP to Polish Classification of Goods and Services is made on the basis of cross-classification. Next, data from national accounts are obtained to estimate the value of household consumption subject to non-deductible VAT taxation. For this purpose, the following transactions are subtracted: purchases in market places, natural consumption in private agricultural households, purchases of Polish people abroad, hidden economy on purchased goods and services, imputed rents. The following transaction has been added: purchases of foreigners in Poland.

For calculation of intermediate consumption and gross fixed capital formation, exempted sectors and exempted types of activities are identified. Exempted sectors include general government sector, non-profit institutions sector and other institutional sectors (non-financial corporations sector, the financial and insurance institutions sector and the households sector). Exempted activities include those that do not pay VAT because they produce services that are exempt from VAT.

In the case of intermediate consumption and gross fixed capital formation, it is necessary to calculate the value of these transactions per non-taxable output. This is done using the share of non-taxable output employed separately for intermediate consumption and gross fixed capital formation for exempted sectors.

Total value of the non-taxable intermediate consumption and gross fixed capital formation has been split into groups of goods and services with different VAT rates. The estimation is made on the basis of structures from use table elaborated according to 465 groups of products.

Table 10 shows the results of calculation of VAT evasion "without complicity" in Polish National Accounts (PNA) for 2002.

Table 10. Calculation of VAT evasion "without complicity", 2002
(million zlotys)

Theoretical VAT	70 390.5
Actual VAT	57 441.7
Time differences	587.4
Insolvencies	78.7
Missing revenue	7 547.5
Evasion "without complicity"	4 735.2

2.1.5 N7: Other statistical deficiencies

Two types of exhaustiveness adjustments are made in type N7: not all required data are collected and non-response.

N7a: Not all required data are collected

This includes estimates of tips which are made for small units in the households sector as a percentage (0.1 %) of consumption of households and allocated to the following kinds of activity: transport, hotels and restaurants, health and social work and other community, social and personal services (hairdressers, nurses, cosmetics services). The same value of tips is included in output (output approach), consumption of households (expenditure approach) and in wages and salaries (income approach).

N7b: Non-response

Non-response is calculated in large and medium units of the non-financial corporation sector. The method is based on labour input. For estimation purposes, the following data were used:

- number of non-responding units from business register and reports on completeness of statistical reports;
- number of employed persons in non-responding units;
- data on value of income from sales from similar units (according to size, industries, type of ownership) shown on statistical reports.

The value of income from sales for the non-reporting units is estimated by multiplying the average income from sales (by one employed person) of the reporting units by the number of employed persons in the respective activity in the non-reporting units. The work is done according to kind of activity, size of units and type of ownership. An estimate of gross output, intermediate consumption and gross value added is then made for these units.

For estimating intermediate consumption of the missing units, the ratio of intermediate consumption to gross output was used in the same units which were used to calculate gross output. The ratio of intermediate consumption was estimated on the basis of a financial report that contains elements of costs, which were grouped into intermediate consumption and elements of gross value added. The ratio of intermediate consumption was differentiated according to kind of industry.

The value of the adjusted gross value added concerning non-response was 29 513.8 mln Polish zlotys, that is 3.8 % of GDP (Table 11). The non-response appears mainly in manufacturing, trade and construction (Table 12).

**Table 11. Value of adjustments concerning non-response by NA components
in the non-financial corporations sector**

	Value (million zlotys)	Relative size (in per cent)		of GDP
		of the component		
		Sector	Total economy	
Gross output	80 166.2	8.6	5.2	10.3
Intermediate consumption	50 652.4	8.2	5.9	6.5
Gross value added	29 513.8	9.4	4.3	3.8

2.2 Expenditure approach

2.2.1 Household Final Consumption Expenditure

N1: Producers deliberately not registering – underground

The consumer survey method is used to estimate the size of the hidden economy that cannot be evaluated by the direct method or the labour market survey. The consumer survey collects information about households' expenditure on services from the hidden economy (defined as services paid for without invoices). The CSO carried out a consumer survey of around 4 000 households in October 1998. The questions asked related mainly to households' expenditure on services commonly rendered by the hidden economy, such as construction and renovation of houses, garages and other farm buildings, the renovation of apartments and emergency repairs, automobile servicing and repairs, tailoring services, tourist services, the cleaning of dwellings, baby-sitting, and the renting of houses and apartments.

Table 12. Value added adjusted for non-response by industries in the non-financial corporations

	Value (million zlotys)			Per cent of GDP
	Public sector	**Private sector**	**Total**	
A	0.0	63.4	63.4	0.0
C	136.8	85.1	221.9	0.0
D	129.8	7 757.8	7 887.6	1.0
E	28.9	124.8	153.7	0.0
F	71.5	3 775.8	3 847.3	0.5
G	397.9	9 383.0	9 780.9	1.3
H	32.5	1 140.9	1 173.4	0.2
I	53.6	1 210.8	1 264.4	0.2
K	116.7	4 188.3	4 305.0	0.6
N	0.0	300.0	300.0	0.0
O	0.0	516.2	516.2	0.1
Total	**967.7**	**28 546.1**	**29 513.8**	**3.8**

The study also sought information from self-employed persons, i.e. owners of private establishments who, in their professional capacity, have a good knowledge of the operations of the hidden labour market. They were asked for their estimation of likely income from hidden work.

Table 13 shows household final consumption as measured in the official statistics and the adjustments for the hidden economy based on the consumer survey.

Table 13. Household expenditure on services created by the hidden economy, 2002

Specification	Data according to		Difference = hidden economy	Share of the hidden economy (per cent)
	consumer survey	official statistics		
	(million zlotys)			
Household final consumption	225 120.9	235 627.4	10 506.5	4.7

N2: Producers deliberately not registering – illegal

Adjustment methods are described in the section concerning production approach.

N3: Producers not required to register

This type of adjustment has been made for residents' household expenditure abroad and purchases of foreigners in Poland. The method of estimation is based on a survey of border traffic and expenses of foreigners in Poland and Poles abroad (see N3 adjustment – exports and imports of goods).

The adjusted balance item between resident households' expenditure abroad and foreigners in Poland was 7 343.7 million PLN, which created 0.9% of GDP.

N6: Producers deliberately misreporting

The adjustment is connected with misreporting of production in the output approach. The under-reporting of income from sales of small and medium sized units is taken into consideration. Adjusted value was 5 060.7 million Polish zlotys, which is about 0.7% of GDP.

N7: Other statistical deficiencies

N7a. Not all required data collected

This adjustment has been made for tips. The same value of tips is included in output, consumption of households and wages and salaries.

2.2.2 Gross fixed capital formation

N1: Producers deliberately not registering – underground

Adjustments of gross fixed capital formation for this kind of producers are treated together with the adjustment for N6. Because the method applied is based on supply-and-use tables, the separation of the producers deliberately not registering was not possible and is included under the type that played a more important role.

N6: Producers deliberately misreporting

Supply-and-use methods are used for balancing the estimates in the national accounts. Adjustments to data on gross fixed capital formation (and associated intermediate consumption) are based on data comparison in the supply-and-use tables. Where units wish to hide income, capital formation is typically underreported, while costs are over-reported.

Data are compared from two sources of information on capital formation: financial statistics on investment, and production statistics that form the basis for supply-and-use tables. The results indicate that the value of gross fixed capital formation is higher than that obtained from financial statistics. On the other hand, intermediate consumption is lower than reported in financial statistics. Results from the direct method described earlier, which also addresses the value of intermediate consumption, are taken into account in these estimates.

Table 14 compares the value of capital formation obtained from financial statistics with that obtained using the supply-and-use method. The difference is taken to represent the value of non-observed gross fixed capital formation.

Table 14. Gross fixed capital formation in the hidden economy, 2002

Specification	Data according to		Difference = hidden capital formation	Share of the hidden economy (per cent)
	financial statistics	supply-and-use tables		
	(million zlotys)			
Total economy	122 238.1	148 337.6	26 099.5	17.6
Non-financial corporations sector	73 893.2	78 123.1	4 229.9	5.4
Households sector	14 261.7	36 131.3	21 869.6	60.5

2.2.3 Exports and imports of goods and services

N2: Producers deliberately not registering – illegal

Adjustments for illegal activities have not been included in officially published national accounts. The value of adjustments for illegal imports is 2 438.7 million PLN. This sum accounted for 0.3 % of GDP. Adjusted illegal exports are 3 380.5 million PLN and created 0.4% of GDP. The most important imports and exports concern cars, alcohol, tobacco and drugs.

N3: Producers not required to register

The following types of adjustments for non-registered imports and exports are made:
- goods bought by tourists for resale; the estimates contain goods that do not need to be reported to customs;
- purchases of tourists made for their own needs;
- goods exported without any customs declarations (hidden economy).

These adjustments concern goods exported in large quantities without customs declaration, for instance vegetables, fruits, furniture, shoes and clothes. This arises as customs declarations in exports are less carefully controlled than for imports because of a lack of customs charges for exported goods.

In national accounts, the values of exports and imports are calculated on the basis of information from customs declarations, Balance of Payments statistics from the National Bank of

Poland, and the Tourism Institute. The number of Polish people and foreigners crossing the border was taken from the Tourism Institute.

Purchases made by tourists are estimated on the basis of a survey of border traffic and expenditure of foreigners in Poland and Poles returning from abroad. Foreigners travelling by car also provide the number of persons crossing the border in each car, the distance of their residence from the border and the distance from the border where they made their purchases. Information collected by Border Guards on number of foreigners by country and by means of crossing the border is also used.

Estimates based on the survey are used to extrapolate the value of expenditure for all foreigners leaving Poland and Polish residents returning from abroad.

3. Implications and effects on national accounts and GDP estimates

3.1 Output approach

Total adjustments for non-observed economy, made on the basis of output approach accounted for 15.7% of GDP in 2002 (Table 15). The most important adjustment for output approach is misreporting (7.8% of GDP), followed by non-response (3.9% of GDP) and non-registered work (3.4% of GDP).

The exhaustiveness adjustments have been made for two institutional sectors: non-financial corporations and households. No adjustments are made for other institutional sectors.

Table 15. Share of the non-observed economy in GDP by institutional sectors in 2002, production approach (per cent)

	N1 Underground producers	N2 Illegal producers	N5 Registered entrepreneurs not surveyed	N6 Misreporting	N7 Other statistical deficiencies	Total
Non-financial corporations sector				1.2	3.8	**5.0**
Households sector	3.4	0.6	0.0	6.0	0.1	**10.1**
VAT fraud				0.6	-	**0.6**
Total	**3.4**	**0.6**	**0.0**	**7.8**	**3.9**	**15.7**

For non-financial corporations only two types of adjustments have been made: N6 and N7. They are included in official GDP estimates and account for about 5.0% of GDP.

The adjustment estimates for households sector created 10.1% of GDP. In this sector the highest estimates concern N6 and N1. The under-reporting in household sector created 6.0 % of GDP and non-registered work 3.4% of GDP.

By industry the most important adjustments were made in trade (7.1% of GDP), construction (2.5%), real estate (2.1%), manufacturing (1.5%) and other services (1.3%), and are shown in Table 16.

Table 16. Share of the non-observed economy in GDP by industry in 2002
(per cent)

	N1 Underground producers	N2 Illegal producers	N5 Registered entrepreneurs not surveyed	N6 Misreporting	N7 Other statistical deficiencies	Total
Industry (C,D,E)	0.2	0.0	-	0.2	1.1	**1.5**
Construction (F)	1.2	-	-	0.8	0.5	**2.5**
Trade (G,H)	1.1	0.4	-	4.1	1.5	**7.1**
Transport (I)	0.2	-	-	0.2	0.2	**0.6**
Real estate and business act. (K)	0.1	-	-	1.5	0.5	**2.1**
Other sections (A,B,M,N,O,P)	0.6	0.2	0.0	0.4	0.1	**1.3**
VAT fraud	-	-	-	0.6	-	**0.6**
Total	**3.4**	**0.6**	**0.0**	**7.8**	**3.9**	**15.7**

3.2 Expenditure approach

The share of the non-observed economy measured using the expenditure approach was 7.8% of GDP in 2002 (Table 17). The expenditure components of the hidden economy relate to household consumption, gross fixed capital formation, and exports and imports.

Table 17. Share of non-observed economy in GDP in 2002, expenditure approach
(per cent)

	N1 Underground producers	N2 Illegal producers	N3 Producers not required to register	N5 Registered entrepreneurs not surveyed	N6 Misreporting	N7 Other statistical deficiencies	Total
Household consumption	1.3	0.7	- 0.9	0.0	0.7	0.1	**1.9**
GFCF					3.3		**3.3**
Exports and imports		0.1	2.5				**2.6**
Total	**1.3**	**0.8**	**1.6**	**0.0**	**4.0**	**0.1**	**7.8**

3.3 Impact of the estimates of illegal activities on Gross Domestic Product

Table 18 shows the value of GDP at current prices, the estimated value of illegal activities, and the share of illegal activities in GDP. Both the value and the growth rates of GDP were little affected by the inclusion of illegal activities in the estimates.

Table 18. GDP and the estimate of illegal activities
(million zlotys)

Specifications	2001	2002	Index 2001=100
GDP without illegal activities	**760 595.3**	**781 112.4**	**102.7**
Total illegal activities	**3 735.9**	**4 652.8**	**124.5**
Drugs	1 212.3	18 250.0	150.5
Prostitution	1 500.1	1 656.3	110.4
Smuggling of goods	535.1	684.6	127.9
Theft and fencing	488.4	486.9	99.7
Share of illegal activities in GDP	**0.49**	**0.59**	**120.4**
Drugs	0.16	0.23	143.8
Prostitution	0.20	0.21	105.0
Smuggling of goods	0.07	0.09	128.6
Theft and fencing	0.06	0.06	100.0

REPUBLIC OF MOLDOVA

1. Sources and estimation methods

The estimation of NOE in Moldova covers the following activities:
- informal sector;
- household production for own final use;
- hidden activity of formal sector (the economic underground);

The National Bureau of Statistics (NBS) of the Republic of Moldova does not currently estimate illegal production.

Both direct and indirect methods are used for the estimation of the elements of the non-observed economy. The *direct method* involves the investigation of quantity and/or value indicators, used directly for the calculation of production. The *indirect method* consists of analysis and comparison of data obtained from various information sources. The following sources are used for the indirect methods:
- Household Budget Survey (HSB);
- Labour Force Survey (LFS);
- Structural Business Survey (SBS);
- information from other (financial, tax) institutions;
- administrative sources (State Land Register, Ministry of Internal Affairs, etc).

The estimation of the elements of the non-observed economy is also made on the basis of information on the flows of goods and services in the supply-and-use tables.

2. Informal sector

The informal sector represents a significant part of the economy and labour market. The sector includes productive institutional units, characterized by a low level of organisation, little distinction between labour and capital, and informal relations. These units belong to the households sector. Estimates are made for:
- non-registered enterprises;
- enterprises of own account workers, unpaid family workers and members of cooperatives;
- household enterprises with market production.

2.1 Non-registered enterprises

A special problem faced by almost all transition countries is the quick rate of change of enterprises, which has an impact on the quality of the statistical register. The economic units that are missing from the registers are not included in the statistical surveys and in the GDP calculations.

To eliminate the effects of the absence of economic units from the statistical files, the labour input method is used. Data on labour force supply and demand obtained from business statistics are compared with the data from LFS to find the number of persons occupied in the hidden economy.

The comparison is made for all activities, even for those that are poorly represented in business statistics. The structure of enterprises (regarding size, type of activity, gross output, and so on), is taken into account to arrive at a more accurate estimation of production.

The Structural Business Survey is carried out in two groups: an exhaustive survey of units with 20 or more employees, and a sample survey of units with up to 19 employees. The registered employers with 0 employees are considered as enterprises of own account workers. The calculations for the non-registered employers are presented in Table 1.

Table 1. Non-registered units and employees

Number of employees in the unit	1-10 employees				11-19 employees				20 and more employees			
Industry	Units		Employees		Units		Employees		Units		Employees	
	2000	2001	2000	2001	2000	2001	2000	2001	2000	2001	2000	2001
Agriculture, fishery	343	372	1 087	2 208	66	318	1 328	5 799	194	434	52 179	70 707
Manufacturing	543	99	1 767	545	..	127	..	2 012	105	244	8 265	18 537
Construction	192	121	1 126	649	..	..	..	..	..	49	..	2 964
Trade, retail and wholesale	3 707	2724	12 927	9267	..	166	..	2 735	76	59	2 817	2 580
Hotels and restaurants	358	248	1 135	1 171	34	121	425	1 456	74	84	5 063	5 372
Transport, storage and communications	137	176	201	151	46	..	590	..	..	..	..	..
Business services	808	307	1 942	1 089		144		2 745	8	129	526	4 310
Total	6 088	4 047	20 185	15 080	146	876	2 343	14 747	457	999	68 850	104 470

For each economic activity, a comparison and analysis of all the available sources was made separately.

The next stage consisted of determining the share of production corresponding to the hidden labour force. Taking into account that the incomes of the employers are higher than those of employees, their production was estimated by multiplying the output per worker (employers plus employees) obtained from the SBS, and the number of non-registered employers. This method was used for all non-registered units, grouped by size and economic activity. For the calculation of gross output it is assumed that the productivity of the persons formally employed is the same as that of the non-registered persons.

The production of employees of the non-registered units was calculated based on the average monthly salary for the given economic activity, the number of non-registered employees and the months worked per year. Analysing average salaries, it was concluded that salaries in the private sector are likely to be underestimated in order to pay lower social security contributions. Therefore, the average public sector salary (excluding health, education and culture, where the average salary is higher in the private sector) was used to estimate gross output for employees, as it is considered more reliable.

Intermediate consumption for non-registered employers and their employees was estimated using the share of intermediate consumption by corresponding economic activities from official statistics. The results are presented in Table 2.

Table 2. Gross value added estimated for the non-registered units
(million lei)

Economic Activities	1 to 10 employees		11-19 employees		20 and more employees	
	Gross value added		Gross value added		Gross value added	
	2000	2001	2000	2001	2000	2001
Agriculture, hunting, forestry and fishery	2.9	21.0	2.3	13.5	87.7	131.8
Manufacturing	7.5	7.6	..	13.2	26.2	61.5
Construction	6.6	2.8	..	..	..	8.9
Trade, retail and engross	86.4	64.3	..	19.1	11.8	17.7
Hotels and restaurants	3.1	4.2	0.8	4.5	10.5	14.7
Transport, storage and communications	10.9	10.2	2.9	..	..	..
Business services	10.6	11.8	..	15.1	3.8	14.4
Total	**128.1**	**121.8**	**5.9**	**65.4**	**140.0**	**249.0**
of which non-agricultural	**125.1**	**100.9**	**3.7**	**51.9**	**52.3**	**117.1**

2.2 Enterprises of own account workers, unpaid family workers, and members of cooperatives

The Labour Force Survey provides data on both the main and secondary activities of own-account workers, unpaid family workers and members of cooperatives. The secondary activities were recalculated into full-time equivalents. Gross value added for all these worker groups was estimated based on their numbers by economic activity, the average monthly salary (obtained using the same method as for non-registered employers) and the number of months worked per year (assuming that one month is annual leave).

For the estimation of intermediate consumption, the shares of intermediate consumption for micro-enterprises from official statistics were used. Furthermore, the production for unpaid family workers is not affected by intermediate consumption, as this category of workers does not bear production expenditures. The results are presented in Table 3.

2.3 Household enterprises with market production

The informal sector of the economy includes the production of households for the market, that is production of goods and services sold or exchanged. It mainly consists of production and processing of agricultural products.

Agricultural production. In the process of reforming agriculture, three groups of producers have appeared:

- agricultural enterprises, including state owned enterprises or holdings, farms with 50 hectares or more of agricultural land (1300 enterprises, of which 350 are farms);

Table 3. Gross value added estimated for the own account workers and unpaid family workers and members of cooperatives

(million lei)

Economic activities	Own account workers, unpaid family workers				Members of cooperatives			
	Persons		Gross value added		Persons		Gross value added	
	2000	2001	2000	2001	2000	2001	2000	2001
Agriculture, fishery	517.1	546.1	1 513.6	2 039.6	2.1	4.4	6.2	19.9
Manufacturing	5.4	5.5	41.9	50.0	0.2	1.1	1.9	12.0
Construction	11.0	12.1	64.4	105.0	0.1	0.3	0.8	2.6
Trade, retail and wholesale	41.3	43.0	452.5	571.7	0.6	0.6	6.9	8.0
Hotels and restaurants	0.6	0.5	2.7	4.3	..	0.1	..	0.4
Transport, storage and communications	4.6	5.8	40.6	73.0	0.3	1.2	2.9	13.0
Business services	11.3	6.7	57.4	23.8	0.1	2.3	0.6	21.4
Total	**591.4**	**619.8**	**2 173.2**	**2 867.5**	**3.6**	**9.9**	**19.4**	**77.1**
of which non-agricultural	**74.2**	**73.7**	**659.6**	**827.8**	**1.4**	**5.5**	**13.2**	**57.2**

- households with up to 50 ha of agricultural land; persons owning plots of at least 2 ha, who are not registered (approximately 500 000);
- households who perform agricultural activities on plots near the houses, in gardens in and outside of their village (approximately 1 000 000 households).

For the first group, the volume of production is calculated based on exhaustive statistical information, adjusted according to the agricultural production of the enterprises for which agriculture is the secondary activity, and according to the volume of production estimated for fiscal evasion (the method of estimation is presented in Section 4: *Hidden economy in the formal sector*).

Agricultural production for the households sector is estimated based on statistical survey questionnaires of small agricultural producers. These farms and households account for about 70 per cent of total agricultural production. The standard questionnaire covers household characteristics concerning area of land used, sown area, harvest, sale of own products, livestock and poultry increase, livestock rearing, livestock production, and the weight of livestock and poultry.

In order to obtain more detailed and representative information on small farms owned by individuals, in addition to the regular survey, supplementary data are obtained from a sample of farms with an area up to 50 ha. Two surveys are organised: in June on the area sown for crops, and in December on the yield obtained.

Data is extrapolated separately for households and for farms, by applying calculated weight coefficients, taking into account the area of land of the surveyed households and the total area of respective sectors by village, district and region. For the data extrapolation on sown areas and harvests, information from the June and December surveys is used, as well as information from external sources (Land Register and statistical reports presented to local authorities) on the total surface of plots, gardens, agricultural land and livestock and poultry.

Gross output for every category of households is calculated by taking into account the quantities produced and average prices of the main agricultural products for the reference period.

Processing of agricultural production (Manufacturing industry). Processing of foodstuffs by households also belongs to the informal sector. The calculation of the production of goods is based on data from the Household Budget Survey for wines, dairy products, canning of fruits and vegetables, meat products and sunflower oil. The calculations are made as follows:

- products obtained as a result of processing of raw agricultural material, in natural quantities;
- average size of families;
- price per unit;
- average number of population.

The estimation of the production for market purposes for agriculture and manufacturing are presented in Table 4.

Table 4. Production for market: agriculture and manufacturing industry
(million lei)

	Gross value added	
	2000	**2001**
Agriculture	578	582
Manufacturing (food processing)	19	22
Total	**597**	**604**

3. Production of households for own final use

According to the decision of the 15th International Conference of Labour Statisticians, the production of household unincorporated enterprises for their own final use is not included in the informal sector. This includes agricultural production, processing of agricultural products, construction of individual houses, imputed rent and the services of personnel hired by individual households.

As the same household unincorporated enterprises are engaged in both market production (for sale) and non-market production (own final use), the information sources and estimation methods of agricultural production and processing of agricultural products for own final use are identical to those used for the calculation of agricultural production and processing of agricultural products for sale.

It is important to mention that the GDP for the informal agriculture sector and the production of households for their own final use were included in the production data obtained through the surveys of small agricultural producers. This information is therefore more precise than other information sources.

Construction of individual houses. The information on the construction of individual houses is collected from special statistical reports. It is based on data from the protocols of acquisition and supply of dwellings and implementation of construction projects. The reports are presented separately for urban and rural areas and contain information on the living area of the houses and their value, and are divided into basic construction and extensions. The underestimated value was assessed by comparing real price paid for the house at the time of registration and the market price per square meter.

Imputed rent (real estate transactions). Those living in their own houses and apartments are treated as unincorporated enterprises producing housing services for their own final use. For the capital and big cities, this activity is estimated based on the surface area of private property and the market price obtained from a survey of rental agents. For the rural area this activity is estimated taking into account the area and current expenditures such as payment of communal services, costs of the material and labour for repairs, land and real estate taxes and consumption of fixed capital.

Services of personnel hired in individual households. This category covers the activities of personnel hired by households, such as housemaids, cleaners, servants, gardeners, drivers, baby sitters, tutors. The numbers are obtained from the Labour Force Survey of households. Gross value added (equivalent to production) for this category was estimated based on the average salary for the economy and the number of these persons.

The estimates of the production for own final use are presented in Table 5.

Table 5. Production for own final use
(million lei)

Economic activities	Gross value added	
	2000	**2001**
Agriculture	2 471.72	2 452.93
Manufacturing industry	121.32	197.96
Construction	20.07	22.29
Real estate transactions	312.75	319.07
Activities of the personnel hired by households	42.11	22.72
Total	**2 967.96**	**3 014.98**

4. Hidden economy in the formal sector

4.1 Under-reporting of production by the enterprises in the formal sector

This category covers hidden (underground) production of registered economic units who misreport financial results with the purpose of fiscal evasion. Payments in kind are often accounted as production expenditure of the enterprise in order to decrease the tax and social security payments. To identify all activities that are not covered by the statistical or financial-accounting observations, the State Tax Administration (STA) provides the statistical office the data on all units registered with the tax authorities.

The State Tax Administration *Report on Control Activity* is based on the decisions taken, data of corresponding registers, control plans, personal files and other information available in the fiscal authorities. It includes the data concerning taxes, compulsory payments and fines and penalties. Moreover, the report indicates the number of contributors checked by all fiscal bodies, and accordingly, those with violations of fiscal legislation, broken down by legal and natural persons. From the number of contributors presented by STA (Table 6), persons who do not pay product and import taxes were subtracted, and from the total amount of additionally calculated taxes and payments, only those products and imported goods were selected which are proportional to the value of goods and services produced, sold or imported by residents.

The STA cannot currently present the above-mentioned information by economic activity. Hence, it is distributed according to the number of active enterprises from the National Register of Statistical Units (RENUS) (Table 7).

Table 6. Information on tax contributors and value of extra taxes due, 2001

	Persons
Number of contributors surveyed	**28 855**
of which:	
• legal persons	15 434
• natural persons	13 421
Number of contributors with violations	**20 155**
of which:	
• legal persons	9 947
• natural persons	10 208
Taxes on products and import additionally calculated (thousand lei)	**68 849**
of which:	
• legal persons	62 829
• natural persons	6 020

Table 7. Number of enterprises by economic activities, according to the number of active enterprises from the National Register of Statistical Units, 2001

Economic activity	Companies	Persons	Total
Agriculture, hunting, forestry and fishery	1 200	1 987	3 187
Industry	2 812	2 839	5 651
Construction	1 229	496	1 725
Wholesale and retail trade; maintenance of road vehicles	10 016	26 745	36 761
Hotels and restaurants	531	1 295	1 826
Transport, storage and communication	1 256	2 280	3 536
Other collective social and personal services	3 510	2 741	6 251
Total	**20 554**	**38 383**	**58 937**

In the future, after the signing of a collaboration agreement between NBS and STA, the latter will compile a database of the tax contributors checked (also shown in RENUS). This database will provide an update to economic activities that will lead to a more precise estimation of tax evasion and a better analysis of the results by economic activity.

The Value Added Tax (VAT) in Moldova is calculated at 20 per cent of net market prices. For providers of commodities and services, under-reported VAT is calculated on the taxable amounts which were neither included in the taxed volume nor presented in the documents for VAT payment.

After calculating the taxable amount and the corresponding VAT share, the hidden production for misreporting enterprises is calculated. This amount is extrapolated for all the active economic units.

By applying the share of intermediate consumption, calculated for the corresponding economic activity in the official statistics, a final estimate for gross value added was obtained. The results are presented in Table 8.

Table 8. Gross value added estimated for all economic units, 2000 – 2001
(million lei)

Economic activities	2000			2001		
	Companies	Individuals	Total	Companies	Individuals	Total
Agriculture, hunting, forestry and fishery	27.09	1.55	28.64	5.98	2.46	18.45
Manufacturing	24.62	1.14	25.76	21.50	2.02	23.52
Constructions	12.76	0.23	12.99	12.52	0.47	12.99
Trade, retail and wholesale	187.38	16.16	203.54	157.55	28.44	185.99
Hotels and restaurants	7.61	0.39	8.01	6.39	1.45	7.84
Transport, storage and communications	14.66	1.04	15.70	15.34	1.59	16.93
Business services	61.48	2.49	63.98	58.63	3.18	61.81
Total	**335.60**	**23.01**	**358.61**	**287.91**	**39.61**	**327.52**

The separate calculations for legal and natural persons contributed significantly to the improvement of the calculation of gross value added. 75 per cent of all legal economic units are checked; this equals 53.5 per cent of all economic units. The total of taxes undeclared by legal economic units constitutes 91.3 per cent of the total undeclared taxes. Taking into account that the share of checked economic units from the National Register is quite significant (49 per cent in 2001), the decision to extrapolate estimated production to all economic units was considered valid.

4.2. Estimation of "black-market" employment

A widespread phenomenon is the non-declaration of the actual number of employees by officially registered enterprises. Thus, the difference between the total employees and those officially declared is treated as so called "black-market employees".

Different information sources and indirect methods are used for the measurement of "black-market employees" and their output. The Labour Force Survey provides significant information. The number of employees from LFS is compared with the number from enterprise surveys (Labour Statistics). In the LFS, a distinction is made between permanent and temporary employees. The latter group is of special interest as they can sometimes provide proof of existence of non-declared economic activity. Currently, many enterprises (especially those with over 20 employees) are not active or work at less than full staff capacity, as part of their employees are on enforced leave (in 2000 – 99 757; in 2001 – 83 280 employees). This staff is not paid, but is declared in the official records of enterprises. Although the Labour Force Survey raises specific questions in order to identify these employees, the majority of them are classified as unemployed or as employed in activities other than those reported by the surveyed enterprises.

In other words, the employees on enforced leave should be extracted from the number of employees of the enterprises with 20 or more employees. As a result, they were added to the category of "black-market employees".

The total number of "black-market employees" was compiled by comparing (1) the number of (permanent and temporary) employees from the Labour Force Survey, (2) those from statistical reports (collected on an exhaustive basis) and (3) the number from the labour force from enterprise statistics, excluding those on enforced leave, (4) and the employees of non-registered employers. The results are presented in Table 9.

Table 9. Black-market employees (2000 - 2001)
(thousand persons)

Economic Activities	2000					2001				
	Labour Force Survey	Employees of the non-registered employers	Labour force in enterprise reports (excl. those on forced leave)	Black-market employees		Labour Force Survey	Employees of the non-registered employers	Labour force in enterprise reports (excl. those on forced leave)	Black-market employees	
Agriculture and fishery	287.1	54.6	154.2	78.3		248.1	78.7	145.7	23.7	
Manufacturing	160.1	10.0	112.9	37.1		158.1	21.1	114.3	22.6	
Constructions	33.8	1.1	19.5	13.1		30.8	3.6	18.4	8.8	
Trade, retail and wholesale	101.8	15.7	66.0	20.1		98.6	14.6	64.6	19.5	
Hotels and restaurants	16.9	6.6	8.1	2.2		18.2	8.0	8.1	2.1	
Transport, storage and communications	59.0	0.8	46.0	12.1		57.3	0.2	45.8	11.4	
Business services	292.3	2.5	284.9	5.0		288.1	8.1	278.8	1.2	
Total	**950.9**	**91.4**	**691.6**	**167.9**		**899.2**	**134.3**	**675.7**	**89.2**	
of which non-agricultural	**663.8**	**36.8**	**537.5**	**89.6**		**651.1**	**55.6**	**530.0**	**65.5**	

5. Illegal production.

Up to now, estimation of illegal activities has not been possible because of the lack of reliable data sources. However, in 2002, the Government set up a working group to improve the estimation of informal sector, household production for own final use and illegal production. The representatives of the Centre for Economic Crimes and Corruption, the Ministry of Internal Affairs, and the Customs Department, together with the National Bureau of Statistics are currently working on the formation of the information base necessary for the estimation of illegal production.

6. Implication and effects on national accounts and GDP estimates

A summary of the estimates of the different elements of the non-observed economy is presented in Table 10.

Table 10. Non-observed economy: a summary of estimates
(million lei)

Economic activities	Informal sector		Household production for own final consumption		Hidden economy in the formal sector		Total non-observed economy	
	2000	2001	2000	2001	2000	2001	2000	2001
Agriculture, hunting, forestry and fishery	578.4	588.0	2 471.7	2 452.9	28.6	19.7	3 078.8	3 060.7
Industry	96.4	165.9	121.3	198.0	379.0	336.4	596.8	700.3
Construction	71.7	119.3	20.1	22.3	89.6	132.2	181.4	273.8
Wholesale and retail trade	557.6	680.7	..	..	355.5	403.6	913.2	1 084.4
Hotels and restaurants	17.1	28.0	..	..	17.7	23.9	34.8	51.8
Transport, storage and communication	57.4	96.2	..	..	123.5	157.2	180.8	253.4
Other commercial and trade activities	72.3	86.5	354.9	341.8	131.2	182.5	558.4	610.8
Total	**1 451.1**	**1 764.7**	**2 968.0**	**3 015.0**	**1 125.2**	**1 255.4**	**5 544.21**	**6 035.1**
of which non-agricultural	**872.7**	**1 176.62**	**496.2**	**562.0**	**1 096.5**	**1 235.7**	**2 465.4**	**2 974.4**

The adjustments for the different elements of the non-observed economy constituted 34.6 per cent and 31.6 per cent in 2001.

The main adjustments were made for agriculture and trade (retail and wholesale): in 2000, 19.2% for agriculture and 5.8% for trade; in 2001, 16% for agriculture and 5.7% for trade.

As indicated in Table 11, the share of household production for own final use in GDP is significant – 18.5 per cent in 2000 and 15.8 per cent in 2001. This activity of households is encouraged by state authorities in order to decrease the burden on the "food market". The increase in volume of the production of households is a positive indicator as the population satisfies a part of its necessities from own production. However, it also has a negative impact on the scale of production and general structure of the economy.

The informal sector represents a significant part of GDP (9.1 per cent in 2000 and 9.2 per cent in 2001). The non-registration of enterprises means that a large number of producers in this sector (own account workers, unpaid family workers, members of cooperatives) do not pay taxes, which affects the incomes of the state budget.

The hidden activity in the formal sector represented 6.6 per cent of GDP in 2001, the major part being concentrated in industry (1.8 per cent) and trade (2.1 per cent). This is explained by the fact that those who operate in these branches have a higher tax burden, which leads to fiscal evasion.

Table 11. Share of the non-observed economy in GDP
(per cent)

Economic activities	2000				2001			
	Informal sector	Household production for own consumption	Hidden economy in formal sector	Total	Informal sector	Households production for own consumption	Hidden economy in formal sector	Total
Agriculture, hunting, forestry and fishery	3.6	15.4	0.2	19.2	3	12.9	0.1	16
Industry	0.6	0.7	2.4	3.7	0.9	1.0	1.8	3.7
Construction		0.1	0.5	1.1	0.6	0.1	0.7	1.4
Wholesale and retail trade	3.5	..	2.2	5.8	3.6	..	2.1	5.7
Hotels and restaurants	0.1	..	0.1	0.2	0.1	..	0.1	0.2
Transport and communication	0.4	..	0.8	1.2	0.5	..	0.8	1.3
Other commercial and personal services	0.4	2.2	0.8	3.4	0.5	1.8	1.0	3.3
Total	**9.1**	**18.5**	**7.0**	**34.6**	**9.2**	**15.8**	**6.6**	**31.6**
of which non-agricultural	**5.5**	**3.1**	**6.8**	**15.4**	**6.2**	**2.9**	**6.5**	**15.6**

Figure 1 shows the share of GDP of each element of the non-observed economy in 2000 and 2001.

Figure 1. Structure of Non-Observed Economy, 2000-2001

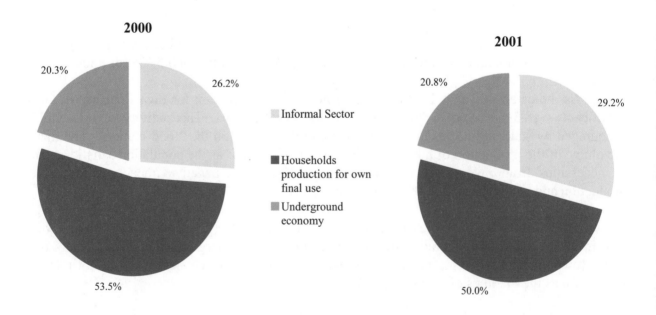

Contribution (in per cent) of the different elements of non-observed economy for 2000 and 2001 to the formation of Gross Domestic Product is presented in Figure 2.

Figure 2. Contribution of different elements of the non-observed economy to GDP, 2000 – 2001

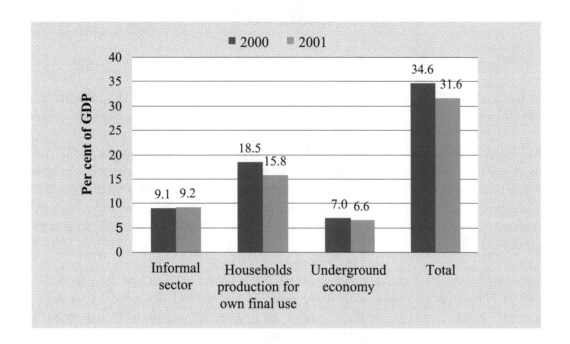

ROMANIA

1. Introduction

For the identification of the NOE in Romania, the whole economy is split into two sectors: formal and informal.

The formal sector in Romania includes corporations, quasi-corporations and public institutions. They are productive units recognised as legal entities and established according to law. The following units belong to the formal sector: government owned units which are independent in decision making (quasi-corporate enterprises such as those engaged in energy, railways, metro, etc.), enterprises, banks, insurance companies, trade unions, political parties, religious organisations and various other NPISHs.

According to the Law of Accounting no.82/1991, all these units are required to keep a full set of accounts. This law also applies to those units which are not independent legal entities and which have their headquarters in another country, or have headquarters in Romania but belong to natural or legal persons from abroad. In general, the accounting statements for corporations and quasi corporations cover the profit and loss account, the balance sheet assets and liabilities by type, and certain annexes covering inventories, provision for losses, assets and liabilities and distribution of profit. The accounting statements are submitted to the Ministry of Finance. These cover information at the enterprise level. The Ministry of Public Finance compiles aggregated accounting statements by ownership and by sector, at the two-digit level of CANE (Classification of Activities on the National Economy).

All units from the formal sector are registered in the Fiscal Register (maintained by Ministry of Public Finance) and Statistical Register (maintained by the National Institute of Statistics).

The informal sector includes family associations and self-employed according to a specific law. They submit annual income declarations to the Ministry of Public Finance. These declarations cover gross income, taxable income and income tax by activities and by regions. The data are aggregated by the Ministry of Public Finance, first at a regional and then at the national level. These units are registered in the Fiscal Register and in the Statistical Register.

The non-observed economic activities in Romania can be classified into the following three types:

a) Non-registered units

Undertaking any economic activity in Romania requires a registration in the Fiscal Register and Trade Register. Therefore, non-registered units, carrying out a legal activity can exist only in the informal sector. This category includes: dressmakers, tailors, workers who repair cars, house painters, teachers giving private lessons, and people who rent out their houses during the holiday time.

b) Under-reporting

In both sectors (formal and informal), registered units can under-report their activities in order to avoid taxes, social security contributions, etc. A specific methodology is used to estimate this important part of the non-observed economy.

c) Non-response and lack of updated information

The Statistical Register is the unique source for providing unit nomenclatures in order to carry out the surveys. The main characteristic of the Statistical Register (REGIS) is its full compatibility with the other registers used in the economy (Trade Register and Fiscal Register). The Statistical Register is updated on a monthly basis.

2. Sources and estimation methods

The National Institute of Statistics in Romania has been estimating non-observed economic activities since 1996. The methodology used has been improved every year, as new data sources become available. The share of underground economy in GDP in the year 2002 is presented below:

Table 1. The share of NOE in GDP
(billion Lei)

NACE group	Formal sector		Informal sector		Total sectors
	billion Lei	%	billion Lei	%	%
Industry	96 726.2	6.4	13 320.8	0.9	7.3
Construction	10 294.9	0.7	9 293.8	0.6	1.3
Trade, hotels and restaurants	22 569.5	1.5	36 541.1	2.4	3.9
Transports and communication	36 610.6	2.4	6 467.2	0.4	2.8
Other services	19 958.6	1.3	15 851.4	1.0	2.4
TOTAL	**186 159.8**	**12.3**	**81 474.3**	**5.4**	**17.7**

2.1 Under-reporting

The estimation of under-reporting of value added by registered institutional units has two components:
- hidden labour;
- value added tax evasion.

2.1.1 Estimation of hidden labour

The activities which are under-reported are estimated on the basis of labour input, the procedure recommended by SNA 93. Using this approach, it is possible to estimate informal labour within the production process and under-declaration of production by formal labour.

The method is based on the comparison between the labour force supply and demand in order to identify undeclared persons conducting legal activity in the formal sector.

Labour force supply

The estimation of labour force supply is made using data from the Labour Force Survey and other administrative sources on participation of the population in the labour market. The survey offers information about the number of persons who declared that they had been paid for undertaking an activity in the reference time period, the number of persons who worked full or part time, those who have a second job by branches of activity, by kind of enterprises or by professions, and on persons who worked occasionally.

The estimation of the labour force supply is made by homogeneous branches of activity at the two digit level of CANE (compatible with NACE-Rev.1.1), excluding agriculture and public administration. Agricultural production is compiled using quantitative data. For general government, it is assumed that under-reporting does not occur in this institutional sector.

Labour force demand

An estimation of labour force demand is made on the basis of information from the annual Structural Business Survey (SBS). The SBS, also called Enterprise Annual Survey, is the main source of annual structural data on enterprises in Romania.

In order to compile the labour force demand, various data are used from the SBS, such as the average number of employees, by activity, at the CANE 4 digit level. The survey also provides information on the number of persons who worked part time, or occasionally, and those who worked on the basis of an assistant agreement. For part time activity, the only information available is the number of people who worked half time and quarter time; the adjustment to convert into full time is made directly, without any other assumptions.

Estimation of hidden labour

In order to estimate hidden labour, the demand and supply of labour force are compared by branch of activity (see Table 2). The difference between the number of people declared as working in an enterprise and those declared by enterprises represents "black" labour.

Table 2. The production, intermediate consumption and value added by hidden labour

	Industry	Construction	Trade, hotels and restaurants	Transport and communication	Other services	Total
Hidden labour -difference between LFS and SBS (thousand persons)	226.4	60.80	129.0	110.7	67.5	**594.5**
Compensation of employees (thousand lei per person per year)	67 700.3	58 320.2	46 408.7	94 286.4	66 876.2	
Total compensation of employees (billion lei)	15 328.9	3 546.9	5 988.9	10 436.6	4 514.2	**39 815.5**
GVA (billion lei)	**44 690.7**	**7 763.8**	**19 299.0**	**26 746.4**	**13 582.3**	**112 082.3**
Per cent of GDP						**7.4**
Intermediate consumption (billion lei)	21 419.8	3 210.7	4 158.2	7 283.3	4 722.7	**40 794.7**
Gross output (billion lei)	66 110.5	10 974.5	23 457.2	34 029.8	18 305.0	**152 877.0**

Intermediate consumption is determined based on the share of intermediate consumption in the production of small enterprises in the respective branch of activity. "Black" labour is estimated using the same components, such as average gross wages, and social security contributions.

2.1.2 Estimation of VAT fraud

One part of VAT fraud represents the VAT for underground economy already estimated using the methods presented above. The other part represents VAT fraud of reported turnover. For the total VAT, tax evasion is calculated as the difference between the theoretical VAT and the actual amount received by the State Budget. Theoretical VAT is calculated for intermediate consumption, final consumption of households, final consumption of general government and GFCF based on VAT rates and by products, defined by the law.

Table 3. Estimation of VAT fraud, 2002

NACE group	Total non-observed economy based on VAT fraud (billion Lei)
Industry	52 340.7
Construction	2 585.3
Trade, hotels and restaurants	3 270.5
Transports and communication	9 864.2
Other services	6 016.9
TOTAL	**74 077.6**
Per cent of GDP	**4.9**

2.2 Informal sector

The estimation of informal sector covers all activities performed by family associations and self-employed. Data on these activities are available from the Ministry of Public Finance. The estimation concerns not only under-reporting, but also unregistered units and lack of statistical surveys. Self employed and family associations are not covered by the SBS because they are considered as belonging to the informal sector.

Information on the number of persons who work in family associations and self-employed is obtained from the LFS. The estimations are based on the assumption that income earned by non-paid workers (from family associations and self-employed) cannot be less than the average wage earned by employees of small units, carrying out the same activity. The income declarations of registered self-employed and family associations are compared with these calculations. Consequently, incomes are adjusted (Table 4).

Another part of non-observed economy is represented by activities conducted in non-registered units, such as: dressmakers, tailors, car mechanics, hairdressers, house painters, plumbers, teachers providing private lessons, and people who rent out their houses during holidays. For such activities, a distinct valuation is undertaken using specific assumptions and available data sources from the statistical system. These data sources are specific to each kind of activity.

Table 4. Estimation of gross value added in informal sector

	Industry	Construc-tion	Trade, hotels and restaurants	Transport and communi-cation	Other services	Total	Per cent in GDP
Hidden labour							
Persons	34 908.6	5 354.4	97 221.2	7 596.8	26 040.9	**171 121.9**	
Average gross salaries - million lei	65 096.6	56 077.1	43 851.9	85 780.7	53 138.5		
GVA -billion lei	10 539.5	1 625.4	20 001.0	2 553.5	5 086.7	**39 806.2**	**2.6**
Family associations and self-employed							
GVA -billion lei-difference	3 219.6	2 321.8	3 056.3	3 370.8	6 896.2	**18 864.6**	**1.2**
Tips - billion lei		246.3	1 930.3	548.7	1 211.1	**3 936.4**	**0.4**
Non-reporting		5 346.6	9 983.8		3 536.8	**18 867.1**	**1.2**
Total informal sector	**13 759.1**	**9 540.0**	**34 971.4**	**6 473.0**	**16 730.8**	**81 474.3**	**5.4**

Hotels: it is assumed that the number of non-registered tourists is equivalent to 1/3 of total registered tourists. The average values of accommodation for a night, considering 15 holiday nights per year, is then multiplied by the number of non-registered tourists to calculate output. The intermediate consumption is estimated by using the IC/output ratio of the formal sector.

Construction: it is assumed that 75% of the total self-employed persons registered in this activity also carry out a non-registered activity. This number is multiplied by the average gross salary in construction to calculate GVA. The GVA/output ratio of the small construction enterprises from the formal sector is used to calculate production.

Education: it is estimated that half of the pupils registered in the last year of secondary school, as well as those on the last year of high school take private lessons. Their numbers are multiplied by the average value of a lesson, by the frequency of the lessons per week and the number of weeks in a year.

Table 5. Estimation of national accounts aggregates for unregistered units
(billion Lei)

Industries	Gross value added	Intermediate consumption	Total output
Construction	5 346.6	943.5	6 290.1
Trade, hotels and restaurants	9 983.8	8 168.6	18 152.4
Other services	3 536.8	437.1	3 973.9
Total	18 867.1	9 549.2	28 416.4
Per cent of GDP	1.2		

3. Summary of exhaustiveness adjustments

Tables 6, 7, 8 and 9 show the exhaustiveness adjustments for GDP according to the output, expenditure and income approach.

Table 6. Output approach, adjustment to GVA

| NACE compo-nent | Public & private non-financial corporations | | | | Households (unincorporated units) | | | | Total sectors | | | |
| | T4 | T5 | Total | % of GDP* | T4 | T5 | Total | % of GDP* | T4 | T5 | Total | % of GDP* |
	(billion Lei)				(billion Lei)				(billion Lei)			
D	44 691	52 341	97 031	6.4	13 759		13 759	0.9	58 450	52 341	110 791	7.3
F	7 764	2 585	10 349	0.7	3 947	5 593	9 540	0.6	11 711	8 178	19 889	1.3
G-H	19 299	3 271	22 570	1.5	23 057	11 914	34 971	2.3	42 356	15 185	57 541	3.8
I	26 747	9 864	36 611	2.4	5 924	549	6 473	0.4	32 671	10 413	43 084	2.8
J-O	13 582	6 017	19 599	1.3	11 983	4 748	16 731	1.1	25 565	10 765	36 330	2.4
Total	**112 083**	**74 078**	**186 160**		**58 670**	**22 804**	**81 474**		**170 753**	**96 882**	**267 635**	

* Total GDP = 1514750.9 billion lei

Table 7. Output approach, adjustment to GVA for VAT fraud and underground economy

| | T4 | T5 | Absolute | % of GDP |
	(billion Lei)			
VAT fraud	74 077.6		74 077.6	
Total underground economy	244 830.6	22 803.5	**267 634.1**	**17.7**

Table 8. Expenditure approach

| Expenditure component | Type of NOE coverage (billion Lei) | | Total | Share in GDP (per cent) |
	T4	T5		
Household final consumption expenditure				
Industry	87 121.1		87 121.1	5.8
Construction	3 452.0	3 355.7	6 807.7	0.4
Trade, hotels, restaurants	5 648.4	10 007.8	15 656.2	1.0
Transport	12 810.6		12 810.6	0.8
Services	9 875.4	4035.7	13 911.1	0.9
Total final consumption	**118 907.5**	**17 399.2**	**136 306.7**	**9.0**
Gross fixed capital formation				
Construction	10 211.6		10 211.6	0.7
Total GFCF	**10 211.6**		**10 211.6**	**0.7**
Changes in inventories				
Industry	1 468.0		1 468.0	**0.1**

Table 9. Income approach

NACE component	Absolute (billion Lei)		Per cent of GDP	
	Compensation of employees	Gross operating surplus	Compensation of employees	Gross operating surplus
Non-financial corporations				
D		97 031.4		6.4
F		10 349.1		0.7
G-H		22 569.5		1.5
I		36 610.3		2.4
J-O		19 599.2		1.3
Households (unincorporated units)				
D	1 767.2	11 991.9	0.1	0.8
F	730.7	8 809.4	0	0.6
G-H	2 131.7	32 839.8	0.1	2.2
I	674.1	5 798.9	0	0.4
J-O	691.9	16 039	0	1.1
Total	**5 995.6**	**251 289.5**	**0.4**	**16.6**
Total underground economy (income approach)	**257 285.1**		**17.0**	
Total underground economy (output approach)	**267 634.1**		**17.7**	

RUSSIAN FEDERATION

1. Introduction

When compiling macroeconomic indicators, the Federal Service for State Statistics of Russia (RosStat) takes underground and informal production into account. These types of producing activities are legal, but are not fully recorded in economic statistics, either because of concealment or understatement by the producers, or because of the informal nature of production. At present, illegal economic activities are not accounted for. Adjustments for the non-observed economy have been in the range of 22% to 25% of the GDP of Russia.

Adjustments for non-observed economic activities are made for each of the three approaches to measuring GDP: the production approach, income approach and expenditure approach, including capital formation, exports and imports. The adjustments are generally made using the balancing method.

2. Sources and estimation methods

2.1 General overview

For almost all branches of the economy, the estimates of output are based on sample surveys using the register of enterprises. In addition, industry output measured by the surveys is increased to take account of the output produced by individual unincorporated businesses and for hidden output.

The Russian Classification of Economic Activities was introduced on 1 January 2005. It is harmonized with NACE at the four-digit level. The two previous years comprised a transition period and certain statistical data were produced in accordance with the two classifications using conversion keys.

During 2004 and the first half of 2005, RosStat switched to a database constructed on the basis of the Russian Classification of Economic Activities for the compilation of the production and income accounts. These were compiled for the period from 2002 to Q1 2005. In June 2005, the results were published on the RosStat website (www.gks.ru) and in the publications on social and economic situation in Russia.

The new methodology was accompanied by changes in data sources for the non-financial corporations sector and was supported by developing structural surveys.

2.2 Enterprises (non-financial corporations)

The programme for structural surveys of enterprises has been unified for all enterprises irrespective of the kind of activity and type of property. Structural surveys have been developed in stages. Industrial enterprises were surveyed in 1998-1999. In 2000-2001, the survey was extended to enterprises in construction, trade, and catering. The report for 2002 covered organizations in all branches of the economy, with the exclusion of small businesses, government and financial institutions.

The annual structural survey programme describes a system of variables which characterize the structure and the evolution of enterprises, their use of the factors of production, and the results of their productive activity. The conceptual design of the structural survey is close to that of the enterprise census.

The programme is based on the international standards stipulated in official documents, in particular in EU Council Regulation No 58/97[31] regarding structural business statistics. All large and medium-sized enterprises are to report annually to the state statistical bodies on turnover, production volume, value added, personnel costs, total purchases of goods and services, purchases of goods and services for resale, gross investment in tangible goods, and number of persons employed. This list is obligatory for all enterprises. For other activities it includes some other indicators.

The basic reporting unit of the annual structural survey is the legal entity. All the data are reported for the enterprise as a whole, and the most important indicators are reported for those comprising statistical observation units.

The elaboration of the annual structural survey and the production of results on the basis of the Russian Classification of Economic Activities allowed data to be more systematically presented on the main and secondary activities of large and medium-sized non-financial corporations. Harmonization of this information with other statistical data on production of goods and services resulted in more reliable estimates of the production and income accounts. Estimates of the shadow and informal activities were obtained with the help of transition keys from the Russian Classification of Branches of the Economy to the Russian Classification of Economic Activities. For other sectors of the economy, production and income accounts were compiled using similar transition keys. This work allowed estimating the size of the non-observed economy in Russia (Table 1).

2.3 Informal Sector

The high share of the informal sector in the Russian economy explains RosStat's efforts to improve the statistical estimates in this sphere. In recent years, attention has been paid to measuring informal employment.

To ensure consistency, the definition of the boundaries of the informal sector is in line with the principle of determining the household sector in the System of National Accounts.

---

[31] Official Journal of the European Communities No L14, 17.1.1997

Table 1. Value added of non-observed economy by economic activities, 2003

	Non-observed economy as % of total VA for the sector	of which:		VA of non-observed economy	
		Shadow transactions of legal entities as % of total VA for the sector	Household sector as % of total VA for the sector	Shadow transactions of legal entities as % of total non-observed VA	Household sector as % of total non-observed VA
Agriculture, hunting, and forestry	66.5	3.9	62.6	1.6	33.3
Fishing, fisheries	75.2	65.7	9.4	2.2	0.4
Mining and quarrying	5.0	4.8	0.2	2.0	0.1
Manufacturing	13.3	11.2	2.2	11.9	3.2
Electricity, gas and water supply	0.5	0.5	0.0	0.1	0.0
Construction	24.0	16.2	7.8	6.3	4.1
Wholesale and retail trade, repair of motor vehicles, motorcycles and personal and household goods	59.8	37.6	22.2	52.7	42.0
Hotels and restaurants	43.1	30.7	12.3	1.6	0.9
Transport and communication	12.2	7.8	4.4	5.3	4.1
Financial intermediation	0.0	0.0	0.0	0.0	0.0
Real estate, renting and servicing	31.6	21.2	10.4	14.4	9.6
Public administration and defence, compulsory social security	0.0	0.0	0.0	0.0	0.0
Education	3.8	1.1	2.7	0.2	0.6
Health and social work	9.0	4.5	4.4	0.9	1.2
Other community, social and personal services	9.8	5.9	3.9	0.7	0.6
TOTAL				100	100
Total as % of GDP	24.3	13.9	10.3		

The units of the informal sector are defined according to only one criterion: "lacking the state registration as a legal entity". Therefore, the informal sector comprises household enterprises, or unincorporated enterprises owned by households which produce goods and services to be sold on the market who do not have a status of a legal entity. The informal sector comprises:

- individuals doing business, irrespective of whether they are registered as entrepreneurs;
- farm owners registered as individual entrepreneurs;
- individuals providing professional and/or technical services (such as doctors, notaries, auditors), irrespective of whether they are registered as entrepreneurs;
- persons providing paid services to households (maids, guards, drivers, tutors, nannies, cooks, secretaries), irrespective of whether they are regarded as employees or self-employed;
- persons working as employees of individual entrepreneurs;

- simple partnerships established under an agreement between individual entrepreneurs;
- persons producing, within households, agricultural, forestry, hunting, and fishing products for sale in the market.

The informal sector does <u>not</u> include:

- financial and industrial groups, investment funds, agents, affiliated and other separate units of legal entities, despite the fact that these organizations are not considered legal entities;
- farmers' households registered as legal entities;
- domestic and personal services provided on a voluntary basis and also production of agricultural, forestry, hunting and fishing products for own final consumption.

The total population employed in the informal sector includes all persons who during the period under survey, were employed in at least one of the production units of the informal sector, irrespective of whether this was the principal or secondary job.

In order to make estimates of total labour expenditure for producing goods and services within the SNA production boundaries, the households producing agricultural, forestry, hunting and fishing products for own final consumption are singled out as a separate category.

According to the guidelines of the 17th International Conference of Labour Statisticians, *informal employment* or employment in the informal sector includes:

- persons employed in the informal sector (as defined above);
- hired workers engaged in informal jobs in formal sector enterprises;
- contributing family members working in formal sector enterprises.

Employment in the informal sector is estimated on the basis of the integration of the labour market survey data and enterprise statistics.

In addition to estimating employment in the informal sector, estimates are obtained of the number of informal work places and the amount of time worked in formal sector enterprises.

"Informal work places in enterprises belonging to the formal sector" are those where people work on the basis of an oral agreement without a formal contract, and those where people work on the basis of contracts and other legal agreements, which, though written, lack clauses dealing with social protection of employees.

2.3.1 Analysis of the data on informal employment on the basis of the Labour Force Survey

Statistical observation of persons employed in the informal sector has been organized since 2001 through quarterly Labour Force Surveys. The survey is conducted in all regions of Russia (except the Chechen Republic). It covers about 67 000 persons per quarter (0.06 per cent of the total population of the age surveyed) and about 270 000 persons per year (0.25 per cent).

The survey includes indicators necessary to identify the population engaged in the informal sector and in informal jobs of the formal sector. The classification is done based on the question about the work place. The results of the Labour Force Surveys show a steady growth in informal employment in recent years. In 2004, 12.7 million (18 per cent) of jobs in the economy were classified as informal, of which 11.9 million (94 per cent) were attributed to the informal sector and 0.8 million to informal work places in the formal sector.

Over the period 2001-2004 the number of instances of informal employment increased by 2.7 million (27 per cent), thus increasing the number of jobs in Russia by 758 thousand, or alternatively a 1.3 per cent decrease in the number of formal jobs (Figure 1).

Figure 1. Work places of informal employment by type in 2001-2004

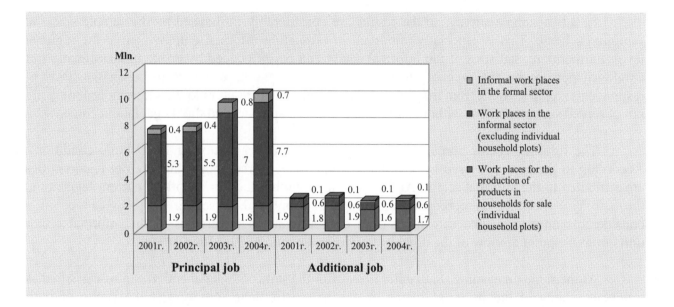

In the total number of informal work places, 10.3 million (81 per cent) were attributed to the main job and 2.4 million (19 per cent) to a secondary job. Growth of informal employment over the period 2001-2004 was mainly due to the increase of the number of principal jobs (Table 2). In 2004, 15 per cent of the total number of principal jobs were informal, as were 87 per cent of additional jobs.

Table 2. Number of persons employed in the informal sector of economy by type of employment in 2004

	Total	of which		Persons employed in the informal sector as % of total employed population
		at principal (single) job	at additional job	
	1 000 persons			Per cent
Total	11 500	9 594	1 906	17
Urban population	6 696	6 208	488	13
Rural population	4 804	3 386	1 418	31
Men	5 961	4 976	985	17
Women	5 539	4 618	921	17

2.3.2 Problems and limitations in using Labour Force Surveys to measure employment in the informal economy

Utilization of the results of the Labour Force Survey for estimating employment in the informal economy reveals representative categories of employed persons, determines the fields where informal employment is concentrated, and shows its distribution. However, limitations exist in utilizing labour force surveys to characterize numbers and conditions of employment in the informal sector because of the nature of the source of information.

LFS is a sample survey, so the results are considerably influenced by the sample size and sampling scheme. This is especially important in estimating informal employment at the regional level. Furthermore, statistics of the informal sector can be influenced by errors in classification of employed persons by the type of enterprise where they work, which is made on the basis of respondents' replies. Apart from that, some other marginal contributors to the informal economy are not observed such as persons without a definite place of residence, and the illegal labour force.

The informal sector borders can change along with legislation and economic conditions. According to the approach used by RosStat, all individual entrepreneurs that are not legal entities are attributed to the informal sector. At the same time, within the framework of current legislation, the activity by certain entrepreneurs and usage of employed personnel by them can be of a considerable dimension, and can differ from conventional characteristics of the informal sector units from the point of view of the organization of production and labour relations.

At the same time, some small enterprises with the status of a legal entity, can be classified as production units of the informal sector by the nature of their activity and the status of their employees.

Thus, in order to obtain more complete information and specify more precisely the approaches to determine the borders of the informal activities, it is necessary to have additional sources of information, such as special surveys of the informal sector units, additional questions in LFS, and computations based on data from different sources.

2.3.3 Computations of the number of persons employed in the informal economy based on data from different sources

To meet the requirements of SNA93, RosStat and its regional bodies have been making computations of gross labour expenditure since 2004 by combining methods based on integration of labour force and enterprise survey data and other sources of information (including administrative). Estimates of the number of persons employed in the informal economy are made in the framework of these computations.

Integrated data on labour expenditure for the economy as a whole (including the informal work places) are formed for the following indicators: number of principal and additional jobs, number of man-hours worked at all jobs and total full-time equivalents worked.

In computations of gross labour expenditure the population employment survey provides data on the number of work places and average hours worked per week. The second source of information is a survey of legal entities.

Data are used from special surveys of individual entrepreneurs in different branches of the economy, conducted by state statistical bodies. In particular: owners of lorries; individual entrepreneurs in retail trade and industry; and provision of domestic services.

One of the sources of information on the official number of individual entrepreneurs is a register of enterprises and organizations maintained by the state statistical bodies. The following data from tax authorities are also used:

- number of entrepreneurs (not registered as legal persons including heads of farmers' households);
- number of notaries in private practice;
- number of individual entrepreneurs paying social tax;
- number of workers hired by individual entrepreneurs and
- individuals on whose remuneration the single social tax was paid.

In addition, data of licensing authorities are used, for example on transport.

The procedure of integrating all these data consists of several stages, which include:

- making the data on employment and working time comparable, taking into account the methodology of calculation of indicators received from various sources;
- choosing a basic source of information; comparing data obtained from different sources; assessing the quality of information; analysing the causes of deviations; determining the scale of corrections;
- assessing integrated indicators of employment and time worked by selected types of work;
- assessing the summary indicators of labour expenditure on the production of goods and services at all types of work.

Data obtained from the enterprise surveys are taken as the basic source of information on the number of work places in legal entities by comparable categories. The data obtained from the enterprise surveys are compared with those obtained from the population employment surveys with respect to the main jobs of persons employed by labour contracts. The aim is to determine: possible underestimation of the number of work places in enterprises; the scale of utilization of unrecorded labour force; the scale of adjustments due to inaccurate classification of enterprises where they worked; and the level of interregional labour migration.

In the process of data integration, the size of any possible adjustment is taken in the framework of the system of integrated computations of data obtained from both enterprise surveys and Labour Force Surveys. Integration of the data obtained from different sources made it possible to adjust the estimates of work places both in the formal sector, and in the informal sector.

Elaboration of the procedures for estimating employment in the informal sector and informal work places in the formal sector provides the estimates of the production and generation of income accounts for the households sector.

3. Illegal activities

Attempts to measure some illegal activities are at the stage of theoretical models. For example, the Bank of Russia developed a model for estimating the illegal turnover of narcotics in cooperation with the Ministry of Interior.

This model allows making the following estimates:
- the quantity of narcotics on the market and their market price;
- the quantity and value of narcotics produced in Russia;
- the quantity and value of imported narcotics;
- the value of imported narcotics using average prices in the producing country.

The Interior Ministry made estimates for 1998-2001 of the overall narcotics turnover, in kind and in cash, using regional data. The estimates of turnover in each region were made in two ways: based on the seized (confiscated) drugs and on the consumption of drugs.

The Bank of Russia focused on an experimental measurement of the exports and imports to be included in the balance of payments using the two ways mentioned above.

The starting point for the calculations was the turnover by type of narcotics. The turnover estimates for 1998-1999 were made and the results were similar. For 2000-2005 it was decided to use the lower estimate of turnover that was based on seized quantities.

The origin of narcotics coming to Russia from other countries is now recorded. Until 2000, a large part of imported drugs in the opium group was supposed to come from the "golden triangle" countries. At present, countries such as Afghanistan, Tajikistan and Kyrgyzstan are considered as the main suppliers. Therefore, average drug prices determined at the time of purchase in the exporting country were revised. For example, FOB import prices of opium decreased by almost 3 times, of heroin by 2.7 times, and of hashish by 8 times.

Estimates of the imported quantities are made for 12 extended groups of natural and synthetic drugs. The Interior Ministry provides information on the market sources. The volume of drugs imported for domestic consumption, the volume of drugs in transit and the volume of export of drugs produced in Russia are measured. However, these data cannot be considered reliable.

Determining reliable prices is not expected to become possible in near future because of the lack of regular and reliable data sources. As a rule, the necessary figures are derived from publications issued in foreign countries and from data provided to the Interior Ministry by its colleagues abroad. Such information usually comes with a long delay. The calculations can be considerably distorted when retrospective prices are used for present estimates, as the supply prices for some types of narcotics are subject to strong fluctuations. The fact that Russia is not a large-scale exporter to the world market is taken into consideration for defining narcotics prices. However, transit of drugs is taking place on its territory. The price of drugs leaving Russia is estimated to be only 1.5 times the FOB import price.

As a result of this work, the annual value of the illegal narcotics imported for 1998-2003 in FOB prices was estimated to be about 200 million dollars, and the value of the exported drugs less than 25 million dollars. However, the estimation was done on an experimental basis and it is not included in the GDP estimates.

SERBIA

1. Introduction

In 2004 and 2005, the Statistical Office of the Republic of Serbia took part in the OECD regional project on non-observed economy for the Western Balkan countries. The main objectives of the project were to improve the exhaustiveness of the national accounts, to define the various types of non-exhaustiveness and to identify the main shortcomings of available data sources. The project also attempted to measure the impact of the non-observed economic activities on the GDP estimations according to the production approach. The Eurostat's Tabular Approach was used to define the types of non-observed economy.

The starting point for identifying the non-exhaustiveness elements were the available statistical and administrative data sources. However, there were several aspects that limited the statistical office's capacity to identify all non-exhaustiveness types and to select adequate adjustment methods as recommended in the Eurostat Tabular Approach. For example, there is still no statistical business register in Serbia and full cooperation with the Tax Authority is not yet established. The reference year for the NOE Project was 2003 but the Value Added Tax was introduced only in 2005 and the application of international accountancy standards in financial reports started in 2004. Complete data of Labour Force Survey (LFS) according to the ILO classification are still not available. The calculation of GDP by expenditure approach is not yet developed and supply-and-use tables are not used.

The non-financial corporate sector and the households sector together produce over 80% of GDP. Therefore, the assessment of NOE elements mostly covered these two institutional sectors. Due to the intensive process of privatization, the Serbian economy is characterized by a large number of small productive units (small and medium-sized enterprises, individual entrepreneurs) that are often unrecorded and use irregular employment. For example, out of the total 70 178 enterprises in the non-financial sector, 61 349 are privately owned, of which 60 619 are classified as small-size enterprises. A significant share of private ownership and small-size enterprises can be seen in manufacturing, construction, wholesale and retail trade, repair of motor vehicles, hotels and restaurants, transport, storage and communications, real estate, renting and business activities. Therefore the estimation of NOE elements was focused mostly on these branches, privately owned small enterprises and entrepreneurs.

Table 1 shows the total adjustments made by the Statistical Office of the Republic of Serbia (SORS) for reference year 2003, covering different non-exhaustiveness types (N1 to N7) by economic activities and institutional sectors. In total, exhaustiveness adjustments equal to 14.56% of GDP for the year 2003.

The relative share of the non-exhaustiveness types can be seen as a percentage in Table 1. Misreporting (N6) by producers stands for the largest exhaustiveness adjustment - 44.1%. The branches with the largest exhaustiveness adjustments were NACE sections G, O, F, D and K.

Table 1. Summary of exhaustiveness adjustments to GVA, 2003
(million Din.)

Sectors/NACE sections	Type of non-exhaustiveness adjustment							Total	
	N1	N2	N3	N4	N5	N6	N7	Absolute	% of GDP
Non-financial corporations	33 745.0			25 226.0		49 270.7	256.9	108 498.6	9.90
Government sector							436.4	436.4	0.04
Households	13 153.0	10 561.1			1 794.3	21 131.6	3 945.2	50 585.2	4.62
NACE Sections:									
A				5 206.9	181.5	386.8		5 775.2	0.53
B				19.3		9.7		29.0	0.00
C				621.4	13.3	19.4		654.1	0.06
D				4 550.7	1 163.2	11 382.5		17 096.4	1.56
E				0.0				0.0	0.00
F	12 275.0			1 007.8		11 084.3	30.0	24 397.1	2.23
G	13 989.0	3 258.7		3 294.2	333.8	28 235.3	95.7	49 206.8	4.49
H	1 675.0			427.1		925.5	360.7	3 388.3	0.31
I				2 760.9		1 532.2	6.4	4 299.5	0.39
J	4 856.0			1 006.5	102.4	35.0		5 999.9	0.55
K				2 646.4		11 695.0		14 341.4	1.31
L				2 661.9				2 661.9	0.24
M	242.0			195.9		116.4	3 506.6	4 060.9	0.37
N				44.2			480.5	524.7	0.05
O	13 861.0	7 302.4		782.8		4 980.2	152.3	27 078.7	2.47
P				0.0			6.3	6.3	0.00
Total:	**46 898.0**	**10 561.1**		**25 226.0**	**1 794.3**	**70 402.3**	**4 638.5**	**159 520.3**	
Share in total NOE adjustment	**29.4**	**6.6**		**15.8**	**1.1**	**44.1**	**2.9**	**100.0**	
Adjustment as % of GDP	**4.28**	**0.96**		**2.30**	**0.16**	**6.43**	**0.42**		**14.56**

Exhaustiveness adjustments are most significant in non-financial corporations and households sectors (Table 2).

Table 2. Breakdown of total exhaustiveness adjustments by institutional sector

Share (%) in GVA adjustment for the institutional sectors

Breakdown by institutional sector	Non-financial corporations	Financial corporations	General government	Households	Non-profit institutions	Total
%	68.0	-	0.3	31.7	-	100.0

It should be stressed that some figures may still be revised as a result of further findings and inclusion of new data sources.

2. Sources and estimation methods

2.1 Type N1 – producers not registering

2.1.1 Labour Input Method

The exhaustiveness adjustment for N1 in 2003 was based on the estimation of the number of unregistered employment within the private sector (Table 3). At that time, the Labour Force Survey data was not yet available. The analysis of the relationship of intermediate consumption, output and gross value added per employee showed that the share of intermediate consumption in output was larger and the GVA per employee was smaller in private enterprises when compared to the mixed and public sector. The analysis did not include the government sector since it comprises large companies with monopolistic status, especially in mining and quarrying, electricity, gas and water supply, transport, storage and communications (railway transport, air transport, postal services and telecommunications). The estimated new GVA per employee within the private sector according to the weighed average in the mixed and public sectors was used to calculate the new number of employees. The difference between the calculated and the existing number of employees was multiplied by the corrected GVA per employee. The total amount equals to 29 477 million din., that is 2.7% of GDP.

Concerning entrepreneurs (the households sector) (Table 3), the GVA per employee was found to be higher than in the small enterprises. The number of employees was increased and the respective GVA was recalculated relative to small enterprises. The correction was made in the sectors E – Electricity, gas and water supply, F – Construction, H – Hotels and restaurants and N – Health and social work. The correction for households amounts to 0.6% of GDP, and for both sectors together to 3.3%. It does not include adjustments for practicing certain activities as a secondary job, such as non-registered taxi drivers, priests, housemaids, artists, craftsmen, magicians, astrologists, masseurs and private teachers, or similar activities, which would make the adjusted GVA even higher.

Table 3. Non-exhaustiveness adjustment - type N1[1]

NACE section	Private enterprises				Entrepreneurs				Total adjustment to GDP (%)
	Estimates of employed persons	Correction of employed	GVA adjustment (million din.)	% of GDP	Estimates of employed persons	Correction of employed	GVA adjustment (million din.)	% of GDP	
A	11 804	4 092	1 241.1	0.11					0.11
D	150 782	25 426	11 923.5	1.09					1.09
E					14	4	1.1	0.00	0.00
F	31 087	7 730	3 385.3	0.31	32 536	12 249	3 760.4	0.34	0.65
G	132 657	20 143	12 165.6	1.11					1.11
H					59 085	20 676	2 770.5	0.25	0.25
K	17 096	1 187	761.6	0.07					0.07
N					6 249	1 429	261.5	0.02	0.02
Total:	343 426	58 578	29 477.0	2.69	97 884	34 358	6 793.5	0.62	3.31

[1] Sources: Financial statements and survey on entrepreneurs.

2.1.2 Preliminary results of the LFS

When the results of the Labour Force Survey according to the ILO standards became available, new calculations were made. The results were very similar to the method described above. However, the LFS results are still preliminary, they relate to 2004 and the sample quality has not yet been assessed.

The full time equivalent employment (FTE) was assessed on the basis of working hours in the LFS. The difference between the number of employees presented in financial reports and statistical surveys on entrepreneurs was multiplied by the GVA per employee of the existing calculations. The resulting correction amounts to 4.3% of the GDP (full time jobs). According to the ratio of employment taken from financial statements to employment taken from the survey on entrepreneurs, 1.2% of the GDP for the corrected GVA comes from the households sector and 3.1% from non-financial sector (Table 4).

Table 4. Non-exhaustiveness adjustment - type N1

NACE section	Employed		Coefficient (LFS/FS)	VA adjustment (mill. din.)	Per cent of GDP
	LFS full-time equivalent	Private enterprises and entrepreneurs FS [1]			
F	136 680	105 527	1.30	12 275	1.12
G	398 541	344 141	1.16	13 989	1.28
H	73 386	63 943	1.15	1 675	0.15
J	43 455	40 065	1.08	4 856	0.44
M	132 044	131 197	1.01	242	0.02
O	103 096	65 879	1.56	13 861	1.27
Total:	**887 202**	**750 752**		**46 898**	**4.28**

[1] Sources: Financial statements and Survey on entrepreneurs.

Full time equivalent employment (FTE) data are still preliminary, as they show significant discrepancies compared to full-time employment data. Therefore, the total non-exhaustiveness adjustment of 7.5% of the GDP (Table 5) is not included in Table 1.

Table 5. Non-exhaustiveness adjustment - type N1

NACE section	Employed		Coefficient full-time equivalent	GVA adjustment (mill. din.)	Per cent of GDP
	LFS full-time equivalent	Private enterprises and entrepreneurs [1]			
F	164 686	105 527	1.56	23 311	2.13
G	470 249	344 141	1.37	32 428	2.96
H	86 529	63 943	1.35	4 006	0.37
I	172 073	156 672	1.10	7 918	0.72
J	45 751	40 065	1.14	8 146	0.74
K	84 512	79 787	1.06	5 927	0.54
M	132 805	131 197	1.01	459	0.04
Total:	**1 156 606**	**921 332**		**82 194**	**7.50**

[1] Sources: Financial statements and survey on entrepreneurs.

2.2 Type N2 – illegal activities

The most important types of illegal economic activities in Serbia were distribution of drugs, prostitution, smuggling of people, fencing (reselling) of stolen goods, especially stolen vehicles, and unauthorized copies of software programs. An estimation of the first two types of illegal activities (drugs and prostitution) was made for 2003.

The following sources were used: information from the police, health authorities, expert estimates and assumptions, experience from other countries, international surveys (UNODC – World Drug Report 2005), Internet, press, TV, etc.

2.2.1 Drugs

Research and statistical data indicate increase in the number of drug addicted persons, number of arrests that are connected with drugs, seizures of drugs, number of people under drug addiction treatment, number of drug addicted people in prison, etc. Drug users most commonly sought treatment because of heroin use (77%). That is estimated to be only 10-20% of the total number of drug users. The second most often used drug was cannabis, followed by cocaine. There was a strong increase in consumption of synthetic drugs, such as ecstasy. The geographical position of Serbia plays an important role, as it is part of the "Central Balkan route" where illegal drugs are being trafficked from South East towards Western Europe. Drugs that are consumed in Serbia are mainly imported, although there is also some local production (cannabis and ecstasy).

Cooperation is established with the Ministry of Interior and the Institute of Addictive Disorders (IAD). Information on quantities and rate of drug seizures, imports and production, domestic use and transit, street and wholesale prices, purity of drugs, number of people under drug addiction treatment, kinds of drugs in use and doses was available from these sources and also from research journalists and other sources mentioned above.

Estimations of drug consumption for 2003 were made from the supply side and from the demand side. Although the information was considered reliable, estimations are still experimental and have not been incorporated into 2003 national accounts because of the sensitivity of the subject (Table 6).

From the supply side, estimation of final consumption was based on the following data: quantity and rate of drug seizures, quantity of drugs for domestic use and transit, purity of imported drugs and drugs sold on the street, and prices of drugs sold on the street. Regarding transit of drugs, it is assumed that organizers are mainly foreign citizens. Serbian citizens are usually taking part in transportation. They keep small amounts of drugs and sell them in the street.

Table 6. Estimate of final consumption of drugs from the supply side, 2003

Drug	Seized amount (gr. or pcs.)	Rate of seizure	Domestic use (%)	Purity of imported drugs (%)	Purity of drugs sold on streets (%)	Price of drugs sold on streets (Euro per gr./pcs.)	Final consumption (thousand EUR)	Final consumption (million din.)
Heroin	262 995	10%	10	85	15	30	4 023.8	2 623.5
Cocaine	5 337	10%	10	85	50	50	408.3	26.6
Cannabis	774 285	30%	90	65	20	2	105 698.0	689.1
Amphetamines – pcs. (0.5 gr.)	406 067	30%	90	100	100	11	9 357.0	610.1
Ecstasy – pcs.	76 194	20%	100	100	100	3	914.3	59.6
Total:							**61 486.9**	**4 008.9**

From the demand side, estimation was based on the number of drug users, price of drugs sold on the street and average daily and annual consumption by kinds of drugs (Table 7).

Table 7. Estimate of final consumption of drugs from the demand side, 2003

Drug	Number of drugs users	Price of drugs sold in street (EUR per gr./pcs.)	Average annual consumption (gr. or pcs.)	Final consumption (thousand EUR)	Final consumption (million din.)
Heroin	7 350	30	182.5	40 241.3	2 623.7
Cocaine	270	50	30	405.0	26.4
Cannabis	62 170	2	85	10 568.9	689.1
Amphetamines – pcs. (0.5 gr.)	5 670	11	150	9 355.5	610.0
Ecstasy - tablet	3 050	3	100	915.0	59.7
Total:	78 510			**61 485.7**	**4 008.9**

Estimations of drug consumption from both sides gave us the opportunity to check the reliability of the results and of basic data such as number of drug users and daily doses.

The value added was calculated by deducting quantities for domestic use from final consumption, multiplied by import (wholesale) prices.

The total exhaustiveness adjustment in 2003 – type N2 (drugs) would be 3259 million din. or 0.3% of the GDP (Table 8).

Table 8. Non-exhaustiveness adjustment - type N2 (drugs)

Drug	VA (thousand EUR)	VA (million din.)
Heroin	35 504.3	2 314.9
Cocaine	264.2	17.2
Cannabis	9 349.5	609.6
Amphetamines – pcs. (0.5 gr.)	4 253.2	277.3
Ecstasy - tablet	609.6	39.7
Total:	**49 980.8**	**3 258.7**

Consumption of drugs as % of GDP	**0.37**
VA in production of drugs as % of GDP	**0.30**

2.2.2 Prostitution

The growth of prostitution can be seen as marked growth in the number of massage parlours, night bars and demand for certain vocational profiles (dancers, masseuses, hostesses, strippers etc.). The most widespread forms of prostitution are: street prostitution, hotel and bar prostitution, escort services, elite prostitution and prostitution by advertising in newspapers and on the Internet.

The Ministry of Interior estimated that there were 800 registered prostitutes in Belgrade in 2003. The estimation of prostitution is based on data of research journalists. According to their estimation, there are around 7000 prostitutes in Serbia. Available data from research journalists and Ministry of Interior were: prices per services, total number of prostitutes and monthly earnings of prostitutes. The production costs, such as the purchases of clothes, cosmetics, taxi etc. are estimated to be about 20% of the output and are reported as intermediate consumption.

The exhaustiveness adjustment in 2003 – type N2 (prostitution) would be 7302 million din. or 0.67% of the GDP (Table 9).

Table 9. Non-exhaustiveness adjustment - type N2 (prostitution), 2003

	Million EUR	Million din.
Output	140	9 128
Intermediate consumption	28	1 826
Value added	**112**	**7 302**
% of GDP	**0.67**	**0.67**

The total exhaustiveness adjustment for type N2 (both drugs and prostitution) in 2003 would be 10561 million din. or 0.97% of the GDP.

2.3 Type N3 – producers not required to register

Non-exhaustiveness type N3 covers production for own final consumption – crops and livestock products, processing of agricultural products and construction of dwellings. Estimates of value added in crop and vegetable production as well as production of livestock are based on reliable data in special annual reports by municipalities, and also price and trade statistics. The value of total agricultural production is included in the gross output. Valuation is made using the quantity – price method. There is no need for specific adjustments of non-coverage. Regarding construction of dwellings, the procedure for obtaining building permits has been simplified and penalties in case of illegal construction are now stipulated by law. In recent years the own account construction has become negligible.

2.4 Type N4 – enterprises registered but not surveyed

Up to 2005, the Statistical Office of the Republic of Serbia was maintaining the administrative register of legal persons. It included the identification number of the unit and the code of kind of activity at the time of registration. Both legal persons and their business units were registered. The changes in the code of kind of activity were made based on a request by the legal person. Deletion from the Register was done based on information from the Commercial Court. Although the Register is of excessive volume and not updated as required, it is still used as a frame for statistical surveys. The information provided through surveys on kind of activity, address, status of activity, etc. has not been used as feedback to update the Register or the survey frames. SORS has commenced the project of establishing the statistical business register by using databases from several administrative sources: financial statements register, tax payers register, VAT payers register. From 2005, the Serbian Agency for Business Registers is in charge of the administrative register of business entities.

Within the system of national accounts, the main sources for the GDP calculation are the financial statements that are compiled by the National Bank of Serbia – The Solvency Centre. This is the primary source providing good coverage for defining the active status of enterprises. In 2003, 10% of the enterprises failed to submit financial statements. These are the enterprises where non-exhaustiveness of type N4 can occur. Part of the enterprises that were closed in 2003 were also included as they had been active for a certain period of the year. Comparing the status on 31/12/2003 as presented in the administrative register and that according to the Tax Identification Number (TIN) from the Tax Authority, the enterprises with active status in 2003 were identified. For those failing to submit financial statements, the GVA was determined according to the average of the sector to which they belong. The GVA was then corrected by the ratio of the number of VAT payers and the total number of tax payers, based on the assumption that those who paid turnover tax in fact had a turnover and, therefore, should be included in the calculation. The frame for the GDP calculation was defined by adding the legal persons who terminated their activities during the year. It is necessary to determine for all legal persons with TIN who failed to submit financial statements the precise period of activity and whether they realized a turnover and paid taxes and contributions. For this purpose monthly data on closing dates is needed from the tax authority. This issue should be stipulated by the Protocol on cooperation between the Tax Authority and the SORS. Table 10 shows the results of the calculation and the exhaustiveness adjustment for N4 (2.3% of the GDP).

Table 10. Non-exhaustiveness adjustment - type N4

	Legal persons of 31.12.03.	Submitted financial statements	Difference	VA adjust. mill.din.	VA adjust. mill.din.[1]	Cessation 2003 with TIN	Adjustment for cessation mill.din.[2]	Total adjustment mill.din.	% of GDP
	1	2	3=(1-2)	4	5	6	7	8=(5+7)	9
A	4 291	3 782	509	17 587.3	4 942	23	264.9	5 206.9	0.48
B	75	64	11	61.9	17	1	1.9	19.3	0.00
C	204	183	21	1986.9	558	2	63.1	621.4	0.06
D	17 463	16 078	1 385	14 516.1	4 079	135	471.6	4 550.7	0.42
E	243	249	0	0	0	0	0.0	0.0	0.00
F	4 273	3 961	312	3 275.2	920	25	87.5	1 007.8	0.09
G	39 519	35 333	4 186	10 484.2	2 946	417	348.1	3 294.2	0.30
H	1 053	939	114	1 376.8	387	10	40.3	427.1	0.04
I	4 703	4 234	469	8 922.7	2 507	40	253.7	2 760.9	0.25
J	723	685	38	3 184.3	895	4	111.7	1 006.5	0.09
K	7 745	7 184	561	7 814.9	2 196	97	450.4	2 646.4	0.24
L	4 828	4 149	679	8 956.6	2 517	33	145.1	2 661.9	0.24
M	3 508	3 452	56	607.2	171	7	25.3	195.9	0.02
N	1 168	1 188	-20		0	3	44.2	44.2	0.00
O	18 550	16 683	1 867	2 745.8	772	23	11.3	782.8	0.07
P	0	0	0	0	0	0	0.0	0.0	0.00
Q	0	0	0	0	0	0	0.0	0.0	0.00
Total:	108 346	98 164	10 188	81 519.9	22 907	820	2 319.0	25 226.1	**2.30**

[1] Estimated according to the ratio of VAT-payers and taxpayers in 2005 (28%).

[2] Assuming that they were active for four months on average.

2.5 Type N5 – registered entrepreneurs not surveyed

The SORS is maintaining the Unique Register of Shops based on data received from the local government (municipalities) who maintain their registers of private entrepreneurs. Although the local government is legally bound to inform the statistical office on all changes within three days, actually they do so once per month or a few times per year. Certain municipalities have failed to provide data for several years. The crucial problem for the Register is the time lag of data from municipalities that causes certain discrepancies with some other sources. Another problem is the determination of the principal activity, which is defined by municipalities according to declaration given by the entrepreneur. In the contract issued by the municipality, several activities may be entered. However, only one is recorded in the Register, specified by the municipality. It is uncertain whether the activity is correctly indicated and whether the municipality provides us with timely information on the change of principal activity. Entrepreneurship is rather dynamic and SORS cannot update the database without notices from municipalities since the Unique Register of Shops presents a compilation of municipal registers. No discrepancies are allowed. The activity code and the activity status given in the Register of the Tax Authority and in the Unique Register of Shops do not fully correspond.

After the establishing procedure has been completed, the entrepreneur is granted a TIN and registered with the Tax Authority. However, the statistical office may include the records only after receiving the notice from the local government (municipality). In 2005, the difference was about 4000 entrepreneurs.

In determining the non-exhaustiveness type N5, all the aspects mentioned above were taken into account. On the other hand, there was available data from the statistical survey of entrepreneurs, provided by the municipal tax administration. The survey provided aggregated data at the activity level on the number of employers and employees, wages, taxes and other contributions paid. These data are used to calculate output, intermediary consumption and value added for the household sector. The coverage of the survey is very good when comparing the Unique Register of shops to the Tax Authority register. The GVA adjustment was carried out for the following sectors: A – Agriculture, hunting and forestry, C – Mining and quarrying, D – Manufacturing, G – Wholesale and retail trade, motor vehicles repair and J – Financial mediation. Where the coverage of the statistical survey was lower compared to the registry of enterprises featuring TIN, as well as for the enterprises closed in 2003, the adjustment was made based on the estimated number of employment and the average GVA per employee in small enterprises of the private sector. The exhaustiveness adjustment for N5 was 1794 million din., or 0.16% of GDP (see Table 11).

Table 11. Non-exhaustiveness adjustment - type N5

NACE section	Number of entrepreneurs 31/12/03 with TIN	Cessation 2003 with TIN	Total frame	Number of entrepreneurs from survey	Difference of entrepreneurs	Estimates of employed	VA adjustment (million din.)	% of GDP
	1	2	3=(1+2)	4	5=(3-4)	6	7	8
A	933	106	1 039	756	283	436	181.5	0.02
C	103	2	105	90	15	24	13.3	0.00
D	29 149	2 675	31 824	30 129	1 695	2 693	1 163.2	0.11
G	73 379	10 690	84 069	83 721	348	615	333.8	0.03
J	491	39	530	372	158	296	102.4	0.01
Total:	**104 055**	**13 512**	**117 567**	**115 068**	**2 499**	**4 064**	**1 794.3**	**0.16**

2.6 Type N6 – misreporting

The largest part of the NOE is recorded as a consequence of underreporting by businesses in order to reduce tax payments and social security contributions. The individual data on the turnover and the taxes and contributions paid in 2003 are not available in the tax authority. Therefore, the results of the statistical survey on entrepreneurs and the financial statements of enterprises were used to assess the non-exhaustiveness type N6. The estimation was based on the assumption that small-size enterprises have been mainly privatized and have a small number of employees. In order to be competitive on the market, these enterprises have to be more productive than the large ones. Also, the individual entrepreneurs have to act as small-size enterprises.

Double correction was made: to correct both for the overestimation of intermediate consumption and underestimation of VA and output per employee. The total exhaustiveness adjustment in 2003 – type N6 was 70402 mill.din. or 6.43% of the GDP (Table 12).

Table 12. Non-exhaustiveness adjustment - type N6
(million din.)

NACE section	VA	Intermediate consumption	VA corrected	Intermediate consumption corrected	VA adjustment in enterprises	% of GDP	VA adjustment entrepreneurs	% of GDP	Share in GDP %
A	5 013.4		5 302.3		288.9	0.03	97.9	0.01	0.04
B							9.7	0.00	0.00
C							19.4	0.00	0.00
D	28 504.9		37 952.6		9 447.7	0.86	1 934.7	0.18	1.04
F	11 045.6	36 487.9	22 129.9	30 330.5	11 084.3	1.01			1.01
G	27 969.1	45 699.7	45 328.6	38 706.1	17 359.5	1.58	10 875.8	0.99	2.58
H	1 254.7		2 180.2		925.5	0.08			0.08
I							1 532.2	0.14	0.14
J							35.0	0.00	0.00
K	13 116.2	27 586.0	19 259.0	23 193.7	6 142.8	0.56	5 552.2	0.51	1.07
M							116.4	0.01	0.01
O	2 653.1	3 936.650	6 675.0	2 402.006	4 021.9	0.37	958.3	0.09	0.45
Total:	**89 557.0**	**113 710.2**	**138 827.7**	**94 632.3**	**49 270.8**	**4.50**	**21 131.6**	**1.93**	**6.43**

2.7 Type N7 – other statistical deficiencies

Resulting from the ad hoc statistical survey carried out within the NOE project, non-exhaustiveness type N7 for the Republic of Serbia equals to 0.42% of GDP. Data from the survey were used to summarize certain elements of NOE and to estimate and calculate the GVA adjustments. The corrections were based on the household final consumption expenditure for health services in private sector, for education (private tuition) and on the information on tips of various kinds: in restaurants, bars and cafes, hairdressers and beauty shops, for taxi, craftsmen and other services. For various services, the value of the tips ranges from 6% to 10% of the value of the services. For health care, the correction was done concerning direct payments by the households. These were considered as wages and salaries in kind (Table 13).

Table 13. Non-exhaustiveness type N7

NACE section	VA adjustment (million din.)	Per cent of GDP
F	30.0	0.00
G	95.7	0.01
H	360.7	0.03
I	6.4	0.00
M	3 506.6	0.32
N	480.5	0.04
O	152.3	0.01
P	6.3	0.00
Total:	**4 638.5**	**0.42**

SPAIN

1. Concepts and definitions

The current annual data estimation process and the revision policy of the Spanish National Accounts takes into consideration the exhaustiveness requirements set by the European Community. Special attention is paid to the base year estimates. The results from the newly revised series, with 2000 as a base year, were published in May 2005.

Major changes and revisions in national accounts are implemented in benchmark years. For instance, when the base year was last changed, national accounts were revised so as to include data from alternative sources such as the new Labour Force Survey (LFS). The LFS featured both a new methodology and an increase in the total population emanating from the 2001 Population Census. Furthermore, new surveys developed by the National Statistical Institute (INE), specifically in the services sector, have been included among the basic sources. Both the quality and quantity improvements of the sources allow for more exhaustive estimations of GDP.

The Spanish approach is based on the OECD *Handbook on Measuring the Non-observed Economy*, as well as the tabular approach to exhaustiveness used in the Eurostat exhaustiveness projects and in the UNECE survey on the Non-Observed Economy 2003.

The analysis of the different types of non-exhaustiveness are as follows (based on the Eurostat tabular framework):

1.1 Statistical underground (T1, T2, T3)

The incidence of these three types in Spain is very small. Firstly, since 1992, economic statistics have been based on the Central Business Register (DIRCE), which has a total coverage for the NACE93 Rev.1 set of activities. DIRCE compiles data from tax registers, social security and statistical sources. It is updated on a regular basis: the data of the register are published for external users, with reference date 1st of January of each year.

Secondly, all INE statistics include a treatment of survey non-response following internationally recommended procedures. The non-response is treated in industrial surveys (energy and manufacturing industries), in services surveys, in the construction survey, in the household budget survey and the LFS.

Of the three components, the most explicit adjustments are made for T3. For example, although companies with no salaried employees are included in the DIRCE, INE industrial surveys do not include them, so they are specially accounted for as described in 2.1.

1.2 Economic underground (T4, T5)

The problem areas encountered under this heading are measured and analysed in the Spanish national accounts. In practice, it is not easy to separately evaluate the two types (T4 and T5), although the reasons for lack of coverage are different. Therefore, T4 and T5 are considered together.

1.3 Informal sector (T6)

This type of economy is no longer significant in Spain.

1.4 Illegal production (T7)

A part of illegal activities is being reflected in statistical sources and in national accounts under different (legal) activity codes. For example, part of prostitution is included as activity of health or massage clubs, and illegal gambling as activity of nightclubs. Spain makes no adjustment with respect to other illegal activities that are not included implicitly in the national accounts.

1.5 Other types of under-coverage (T8)

The other types of under-coverage do have an incidence in Spain. For example, in the case of tips and payment in kind, there exists specific legislation pertaining to their measurement in order to ensure the exhaustiveness of Gross National Income (GNI). Nonetheless, the differentiation between the types T8 and T4 is not clear. For example, if tips are not declared by the person receiving them, output and income are being undervalued.

Figure 1. Exhaustiveness estimation

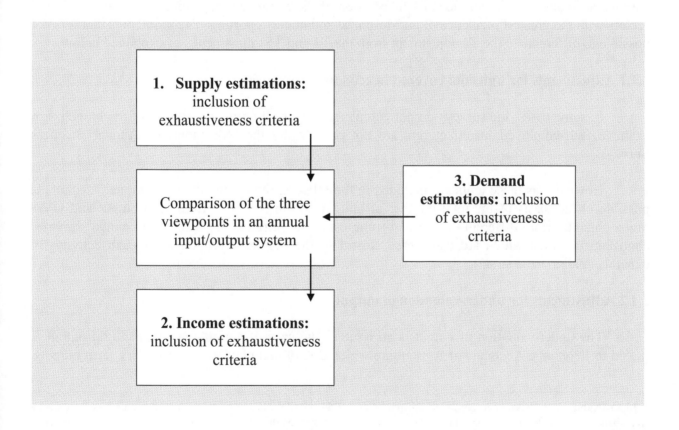

2. Sources and estimation methods

The national accounts calculation in Spain uses all three approaches- production, expenditure and income approach. Balancing the annual supply-and-use tables[32] is considered as the optimal method for improving the exhaustiveness of national accounts. Disaggregated balances are made by products and industries.

All estimations of the Spanish NA series are linked with estimations by employment, using as primary sources the LFS, data from registries (DIRCE and Social Security) and employment data from structural surveys.

2.1. Output estimations

The output estimates are based on structural business surveys, which are conducted by INE or by other agencies in coordination with INE. The survey frame for these structural surveys is based on DIRCE, which complies with a series of quality and coverage requirements. For example, all active units are registered and there are no duplicates. The register is updated regularly based on fiscal sources, other registers and statistics. No T2 type adjustments are therefore made.

All INE surveys incorporate a statistical non-response treatment according to the international standards. Therefore, the T1 adjustment is not considered explicitly in the national accounts. This does not imply that T1 adjustments are not considered implicitly.

However, as explained below, the balancing of input-output tables and other checks in national accounts occasionally lead to the revision of the results corresponding to the activities and sectors with the greatest incidence of non-response and under-reporting. The problem is that it is not possible to differentiate the T1 adjustment from the T4 and T5 adjustments, as explained below.

2.1.1 Adjustments for units not covered in economic statistics

In some cases, the surveys do not completely cover all units or activities of the branch. For example, self-employed manufacturers are not covered by the INE Industrial Annual Business Survey.

However, as these units are included in the DIRCE, their estimation in national accounts is possible on the basis of the total number of units according to the DIRCE and output and GVA ratios obtained from different sources. In some cases, these ratios are taken from annual surveys, choosing the strata which are considered closest to the non-surveyed units for each activity (in general, smaller-sized strata).

2.1.2 Adjustments for under-valuation of output

The under-valuation of output is an issue in the case of agriculture. Agricultural output is linked to Economic Accounts of Agriculture which do not include data on secondary farm outputs.

---

[32] Input-Output tables have been compiled in Spain since 1954. Until 1985 their interval was more or less once every five years and thereafter every year. The current system, which applies the ESA95 methodology, comprises annually: a source table, destination table at purchase prices, a destination table at basic prices (broken down into internal flows and imported flows) and ancillary matrices of taxes, subsidies and distribution margins (trade and transport). A symmetric Input-Output table is compiled every five years.

Therefore, the secondary output has to be estimated separately in collaboration with the Ministry of Agriculture. Such secondary output is often generated by hunting, organising bullfights and horse breeding.

Some industries are mainly composed of self-employed entrepreneurs and small-sized companies, which are subject to less auditing and fiscal control. Underestimation of output arises either due to under-reporting of production or over-valuing of the costs. In this particular case, a supply and demand comparison in national accounts, with annual supply-and-use tables, enables the detection of some of these under-valuations.

In other cases, under-valuation can be also detected through an analysis of the discrepancy between per employee remuneration and surplus per productive unit and/or per self-employed. The adjustment procedure is similar to that of the industrial branches and relies on ratios obtained from the small-sized strata of surveys and other sources of information. The industries mostly affected are: market services and commercial activities such as catering, shop-keeping, transport and business and personal services.

Construction stands out as a special case. Sub-contracting in this industry has been the object of ongoing large-scale studies. These studies have unravelled that there exists an inconsistency between the initially assigned output value by the subcontracts and the actual output of subcontractors. The productivity ratios obtained from the smallest-sized company stratum in the structural survey are applied and this difference is added to the mixed income of the self-employed subcontractors.

In distribution services (trade and transport), there is sufficient additional information available to calculate the margins for some products. This information can then be compared with the estimations done in structural surveys.

Education is another case where coverage may lack, as the structural surveys only reflect public education. This problem has been tackled through special surveys of units excluded from regular structural surveys.

Housekeeping services in Spain constitute a significant niche of a statistically non-observed economy. Conventional sources such as the Household Budget Survey or the Labour Force Survey do not cover this activity. In order to estimate employment in housekeeping services, the INE has used specific surveys carried out by the Ministry of Labour on the immigrant population, which is the main supplier of labour for this particular activity. Lastly, the employee compensation is estimated from ratios obtained with the Household Budget Survey, although the estimates may suffer from coverage problems.

2.2 Income estimations

Income estimates are considered separately from output estimates, although the distinction between output and income adjustments is often blurred. A good proportion of the estimates made in order to ensure exhaustiveness of output directly affect income estimates and vice versa. For example, when using employment from the LFS as a source of comparison, adjustments take the form of remuneration and/or mixed income.

Both for output and for income, adjustments are made to cover tips (T8), especially for those activities where they are used as a form of additional income such as in hotels, bars and restaurants, transport (taxi), public entertainment, gambling and personal services. Various surveys and specific studies are used in order to determine their amounts. Two kinds of tips can be distinguished: relatively fixed amounts and those that vary with the price paid for the service. This calls for two types of treatment where the amounts depend on either quantitative indicators or on the value of the output.

Wages and salaries in kind are also subject to some adjustments. The estimation of these variables is facilitated due to the fact that Spanish tax laws and the General Accounts Plan force companies to record payments in kind as earned income. These payments are therefore theoretically included in the data of the structural surveys that serve as the basis for national accounts.[33]

Furthermore, adjustments are made in specific cases such as in bar and restaurant services. In Spain, bars and restaurants are often small-sized companies maintained by households where income in kind (and tips) complements the low monetary wages and unpaid family workers. The estimations of these aspects in the national accounts are based on specific information and studies of the sector.

2.3 Expenditure estimations

2.3.1 Household final consumption expenditure

To estimate household final consumption expenditure, INE tries to achieve the maximum possible coverage using the Household Budget Survey (HBS) as a basic source. The data provided by this survey are compared with other types of information, especially with the supply data, in order to ensure the exhaustiveness of the estimations.

If GDP estimates were based solely on the HBS, problems inherent to this source would arise. HBS undervalues household expenditure on a series of items such as alcoholic beverages, tobacco, gambling services, etc. In Spain, the possible under-valuation of these sectors is mitigated by the tight control exerted by the public authorities on some of these products, for example, tobacco and gambling. Tobacco has been a public distribution monopoly for many decades and is currently an oligopoly with a marked presence of quasi-public companies. Gambling is entirely regulated and supervised by the Government. Therefore, consistent estimations of expenditure on those items can be made. These estimations may not be considered strictly as adjustments for exhaustiveness, but rather as special cases where the basic data source is replaced by alternative sources with better quality and coverage.

The HBS poses a statistical problem for T3 of NOE: the expenditures made collectively by households are not covered. It is therefore necessary to introduce expenditure estimation adjustments for this population group who are not covered by the survey (specifically, censuses and municipal registers) to ensure full population coverage.

2.2.2 Gross fixed capital formation

The methodology followed to estimate gross fixed capital formation (GFCF) is based on a commodity-flow type procedure. First, the supply of domestic and imported capital goods available in the economy is analysed. An initial estimate of the GFCF is obtained from production and

---

[33] The statistics on labour costs (an exhaustive bi-annual survey) is used as a source. Furthermore, the INE structural business surveys always include questions on labour costs, encompassing payment in kind.

foreign trade statistics. This is then revised through the balancing of supply-and-use tables. In the case of imported goods, foreign trade statistics provide an approximation of the types of products used.

Supply is then compared with demand estimates based on the Structural Business Surveys, and by means of elaborating a GFCF matrix defined by products and by industry.[34]

With regard to own-account gross capital formation, a large part of the statistical sources available (industrial surveys) provide information on own-account output. For some activities, however, it is necessary to include additional estimates. For example, in agriculture a specific estimation is carried out in national accounts on the basis of a study made by the Ministry of Agriculture.

3. Implications and effects on national accounts and GDP estimates

The data presented in the Table 1 have some overlap due to the identification of some of the problem types defined in the NOE. This is the case for T4 and T5, but also partially for T1[35]. T3 includes all cases where the main source of information cannot be replaced by an exhaustive one. Data for T7 are not provided, since illegal economy is not estimated[36].

Table 1. Adjustments in national accounts for different types
of the non-observed economy, 2000
(per cent of GDP)

Industries (A6)	T3	T4/ T5	T8[37]
Agriculture, hunting, forestry and fishing	0.03	0.02	
Industry, including energy	0.25	1.22	
Construction[38]		1.31	
Wholesale and retail trade, hotels and restaurants, transport and communication		4.20	0.65
Financial, real estate, renting and business activities			
Other service activities	2.67	0.80	0.04
TOTAL	**2.95**	**7.55**	**0.69**

---

[34] These matrices are published yearly in the Spanish NA.

[35] Concerning T1: the non-response adjustments are directly made in the basic statistics themselves, that is, they are carried out prior to compiling the national accounts. T2 is not applicable as the main register of the Spanish statistical system (Enterprises Central Register) is updated on a continuous basis through different sources, such as tax registers, social security data, specific surveys, census, business registers, etc.

[36] Part of illegal activities are already recorded in other elements of the estimates (for example, the revenues from prostitution are eventually recorded as part of the output of the accommodation or recreational services).

[37] The cases mentioned in the manual might be allocated either to T8 or within category T4. For instance, non-declared tips or wages and salaries in kind are an under-declaration of the output and income.

[38] T3 is included within the assessment of procedures T4 and T5. T6 and T7 are not explicitly estimated.

SWEDEN

1. Introduction

In the Swedish national accounts two independent estimates of GDP are compiled using the production and expenditure approaches.

Independent industry-by-industry calculations of GDP from the income side were undertaken partly as an experiment for the period 1980-1993. Since the changeover to SNA93, however, complete income calculations have not been carried out although it is the intention to resume them.

The main approach in the calculations is geared to the use side. The statistical basis is well developed, with possibilities for comparison between different independent sources. The annual calculations are balanced in a system of supply-and-use tables. The system also includes employment calculations, with average numbers of employees and hours worked.

For the time being, no explicit estimate is included for illegal production. However, experimental calculations have been made in spring 2005 for prostitution, drugs, and smuggling of alcohol and tobacco, and an estimate will be included in the near future. The estimate for illegal activities would affect GDP by 0.15 percentage points.

2. Definitions and concepts

The non-observed economy refers to all productive units that may not be captured in the basic data sources used for the compilation of the national accounts. The three main types are underground production, informal activities and illegal activities.

3. Sources and estimation methods

Methods used for measuring informal/black economy could be grouped into direct and indirect methods. Direct methods include measurements based on statistical surveys, interviews, tax evasion, etc. Indirect methods include analysis based on discrepancies between for instance national accounts data and model-based calculations, by drawing comparisons between income and outlay for various groups; between working hours and income for employees and sole proprietors; analysis of secondary income for some trade groups; comparisons between employment measured in Labour Force Surveys and in business reports.

The following methods are used:
- comparing information from different data sources for the same activity;
- comparing the results from Labour Force Survey with estimates obtained from Business Statistics and from Labour Statistics based on administrative sources;
- the commodity flow method;
- balancing of national accounts data within the supply-and-use tables;
- comparison of ratios of input to output per industry and over time;
- comparison of earnings per industry over time;

- imputation methods for non-response;
- focus on special industries, e.g. cash trades providing a high degree of personal services; and
- tax evasion.

In order to achieve exhaustiveness, specific adjustments for each industry are made for wages in kind, tips and the black economy.

4. Implications and effects on national accounts and estimates of the size of non-observed economy in the GDP estimates

4.1 The production approach

GDP calculated from the production side is based on an exhaustive register of production units. Conceptual differences between business reporting and SNA definitions are accounted for in detail. A consistent estimate of GDP according to the production and expenditure approaches is obtained within the reconciliation of the supply-and-use tables.

Business statistics are the main source for the output calculations. From 2000, the entire population of non-financial corporations is included. However, the national accounts still obtain information from other sources for NACE 01-05. The calculations of agricultural output are almost entirely based on the EAA-Manual (Economic Accounts for Agriculture). The Swedish Board of Agriculture is in charge of compilations and calculations and provides national accounts with the relevant data.

The value of forestry output is defined on the basis of the activities and products involved and produced in close cooperation with the National Board of Forestry. The industry is functionally defined and consists of institutional units or parts of institutional units, with responsibility for and access to stocks of forestry raw materials and which are able to control the difference between additions to and withdrawals from these stocks. Output comprises both market output and output for own use. As regards fishing, NACE 05, estimates from the business statistics can now be used for national accounts calculations. Also for NACE 65-67, financial corporations, full annual censuses are carried out. Enterprises in NACE 65-66 are subject to supervision by the Financial Supervisory Authority, and statistics from all enterprises are collected and reported in the publication *Finansiella företag* (Financial corporations). NACE 67 is covered by the business statistics and is also subjected to a full census. Apart from these sources, special inquiries are used to collect more detailed information on output and intermediate consumption in some industries, e.g. manufacturing industries and energy companies.

Explicit supplements for the output value of unrecorded activity are applied for a number of industries. The industries affected by this adjustment are agriculture, manufacturing, construction, distribution including motor repairs, restaurants, taxis, haulage firms, other business services (cleaning), gaming and personal services (hairdressers etc.).

An inquiry carried out by the National Audit Office in 1997 shows that hidden activity occurs in the industries listed above. However, it is difficult to quantify hidden output value or value added from this inquiry. Therefore, the scale of the supplements applied is based also on analysis of the supply-and-use tables.

The supplement for the hairdressing industry is explicitly calculated as the difference between the values of the 1995 Household Budget Survey (HBS) and the business statistics.

In construction, output is measured with the aid of investment and repair expenditure, so that problems of hidden data in the construction industry are substantially reduced. The explicit supplement for construction activity covers work on owner-occupied dwellings.

4.1.1 Income in kind (benefits) and gratuities

Table 1 describes the contribution of hidden and informal activities to value added and to GDP in Sweden in 2000.

The most significant income in kind in Sweden concerns concessionary cars, which an employer provides for his employees. Car benefits are added to the employer's output value and to households' consumption. The other benefits in kind are meal benefits and concessionary housing. Meal benefits arise almost exclusively through the sale by an employer of restaurant vouchers to his employees at a reduced price. This benefit is included in the supplement applied to households' consumption expenditure in relation to the results of the household budget surveys. Concessionary housing is captured by the application of the calculation model. A rental value is calculated for all dwellings in the country and is assigned to final use. Gratuities are relatively uncommon in Sweden. The tips are given mainly in the restaurant and taxi trades, and possibly hairdressing.

**Table 1. Explicit adjustments for hidden and informal activities
and the relation to value added in these industries and to GDP, 2000**
(million SEK)

	Activity	Value added		
		Hidden	Open+ hidden	Share of hidden activities (%)
22	Publishing, printing and reproduction of recorded media	587	28 598	2.1
28	Manufacture of fabricated metal products, except machinery and equipment	342	36 764	0.9
29	Manufacture of machinery, equipment n.e.c.	165	53 091	0.3
33	Manufacture of medical, precision and optical instruments, watches and clocks	168	12 449	1.3
45	Construction	6 145	78 955	7.8
50-52	Distribution	2 230	208 265	1.1
55	Restaurants	4 591	30 537	15.0
6022	Taxis	1 346	7 073	19.0
6024	Haulage	4 846	31 070	15.6
74	Cleaning, etc	4 809	125 731	3.8
92	Gaming, etc	1 496	23 650	6.3
93	Hairdressing, etc	2 460	7 277	33.8
	Total for these industries	29 185	643 460	4.5
	GDP	29 185	2 194 967	1.3

Earlier a special exhaustiveness addition for agriculture was added to the figures obtained from the Swedish Board of Agriculture. The Board has now included such figures in their accounts and Statistics Sweden does not have to make exhaustiveness adjustments to the figures.

4.2 The income approach

The income approach for the economy as a whole is determined by the level of GDP from the use side. That portion of income which consists of wage and salary totals includes income in kind in accordance with the rules laid down by the tax authorities. In addition, an adjustment is made covering car benefits from the year 1997 onwards, in which the utility value is deemed to exceed the limit laid down. Gratuities are taxable income and must be declared as pay and reported as the amounts actually received. Adjustment for cases in which these amounts have not been reported is covered by a supplement for "black" wages and mixed income.

In order to obtain the GDP level calculated from the use side, substantial adjustments must be made for wages and salaries and mixed income compared to the values obtained from the tax authorities.

The adjustment for "black" wages in 2000 amounted to SEK 14 billion, which represents 1.6 per cent of the total payroll excluding "black" wages. For mixed income the adjustment amounts to SEK 99 billion, which represents 73 per cent of the mixed income recorded in the national accounts.

4.2.1 Income in kind and employer declarations

The employer declarations contain information on income in kind, which is treated as income by the taxation authority and added to wages and salaries in the national accounts. Income in kind is valued at market prices by the taxation authority. The information covers all types of income in kind as free meals, rentals, cars, fuel, interest, etc.

A special arrangement has been made in Sweden for personal computers in order to improve the use of computers. The employee can rent a PC from his employer and pay the rent by reducing the wages. This rent is regarded as income in kind in the national accounts and added to wages and salaries and household consumption. Output of PC rentals is also added to the output figures for different industries.

4.2.2 Tips

Tips are not very common in Sweden and exist in some restaurants and for taxis. Tips are included in the Household Budget Survey (HBS) so the information used to estimate the level of household consumption by resident households includes tips. The value of tips is, however, not explicitly shown in the survey. The HBS information does not include consumption by non-resident households in Sweden so they are added to the figures in order to cover all consumption. The source for estimating consumption by non-resident households is the currency exchange. This source also includes tips since all money used by non-residents in Sweden is registered.

4.3 The expenditure approach

4.3.1 Household consumption expenditure

Data on household consumption consistent with the national accounts definitions are not available in any one statistical inquiry. A large number of different sources are therefore used in order to calculate the various consumption items. The calculations are based on both expenditure amounts measured annually and on the updating of benchmarks for a certain year with the aid of value and volume indicators, which are obtained from statistical inquiries and administrative material. In certain cases extensive balancing operations are carried out. For example, in 1995, comparisons were undertaken between all conceivable sources, which could be brought together. Thus there is a sound benchmark for 1995. For subsequent years, updating methods and annual calculation methods are used on different parts of the material. Annual calculations are carried out for about 34 per cent of the consumption value.

Household budget statistics (HBS)

The household budget statistics are the only consistent inquiry which measures household consumption expenditure as such. In these intermittent inquiries Statistics Sweden has endeavoured to measure the expenditure of households with definitions that are as close as possible to those of the national accounts. HBS material is available for 1995, '96, '99, 2000, 2001 and 2003. But since the HBS is a relatively small sample survey, the material produced is scrutinised. In cases where the HBS estimate is not consistent with data from other sources and there is reason to place greater confidence in other sources, the HBS estimate is discarded. Special attention is devoted to those items which tend to be underestimated in HBS inquiries, and expenditure which is poorly covered because of the composition of the sample, for example households of persons aged over a certain age.

Turnover statistics, VAT records, business statistics

In order to estimate the trend from an initial year onwards, in many cases quarterly turnover statistics for the retail trade and service industries are used. The trend in turnover statistics is continuously compared with the turnover trend obtained when the data on VAT payments are processed statistically. The trend figures from the turnover statistics are also compared on an annual basis with the results obtained when the annual business statistics are processed. Comparisons of trend figures in the first instance, but also turnover, are undertaken for industries of interest in this context.

Industry-goods matrix

The turnover statistics measure total turnover in each sub-industry. By combining industry turnover figures with the goods and services sold by each industry, an industry-goods matrix is obtained. Inquiries on sales per product of goods and services are made on a five-year basis. The matrix consists of 70 industries, whose turnover is allocated to 103 different goods and services groups.

Further balancing procedures

In the calculations, use is also made of a variety of other detailed information that can be collected for various goods and services. Examples of such material are records of departments and agencies of government, trade associations and membership organisations, or supervisory bodies that exercise surveillance, collect charges or pay grants in relation to the scale of an activity. Register material for vehicles, real estate and other matters and intermittent industry inquiries as well as reports and studies on different activities are also used.

The Swedish national accounts are based on a supply-and-use system in the context of which all production and use of goods and services is arranged in a system of 400 product balances. This provides an opportunity to check calculated consumption of goods and services for household consumption and other use against the supply of the corresponding goods and services.

If there are differences between supply and use, a residual item arises. Special analysis is then devoted to the good or service in question and necessary measures are taken to balance supply and use.

The product balancing technique means that benchmarks in household consumption can be affected. For example, in the benchmarking for 1995, an important criterion in the evaluation of household budget data were the results obtained from the product balance reconciliations. The calculations for households' petroleum consumption are made in the national accounts special energy balances. Statistics from a number of sources for petroleum products are coordinated in five different product balances where the allocation to different user groups is specified.

Analysis, balancing and adjustments thus arise for all the 230 product groups, which are the smallest building blocks of household consumption allocated to purposes.

4.3.2 General government consumption expenditure

The material provides complete coverage since data are collected for all activities. Separate inquiries are conducted for both central and local government consumption. These are geared to the needs of the national accounts and cover all components of government final consumption. Statistics Sweden always carries out a plausibility check of the information when it is received. Comparisons in the form of time-series are also made in order to detect any major divergences between years. As regards the local government statistics, the result of the inquiry is also returned to the data providers, inter alia in the form of key figures, which facilitate comparisons between different municipalities. The respondents then have an opportunity to correct their data if they consider that any error has arisen.

Adjustment for definitional differences between ESA and the statistical sources is carried out.

4.3.3 Gross fixed capital formation

A number of sources are used in the calculation of gross fixed capital formation. Business statistics provides investment data in accordance with Swedish accounting rules for all enterprises in Sweden (with the exception of NACE 65-66). Additional information is used when there are differences between the accounting rules and the national accounts definitions. This applies, for example to a 1-2 year investment and to software purchased and produced on own account and investment through financial leasing.

In order to overcome the problem that short-term investment (1-2 year investment) is not included as investment in Swedish accounting practice, the national accounts have conducted a special survey in cooperation with those responsible for the investment surveys. The results are used to determine the proportions of investment in the accounts of business statistics representing consumption inventories and short-term inventories.

Purchased software is calculated with the aid of inquiries about the production of standard and customer-specific software by computer consultancies. For software produced on own-account, model-based data are produced.

For construction investment, special calculations are carried out in industries where purchases and sales play a major role, since in business statistics the net recording of buildings purchased minus buildings sold does not always give data with satisfactory quality at industry level. Data on investment in new buildings are used instead.

The value of new construction, extensions and reconstruction of buildings is obtained from a number of sources in addition to the business statistics, first and foremost from investment surveys.

For industries where both business statistics for enterprises and investment surveys lack coverage or provide poor coverage, alternative sources are drawn upon. This applies in particular to agriculture, forestry and fishing, and to real estate management.

4.3.4 Changes in inventories

Changes in inventories are calculated for agriculture, forestry, quarrying, manufacturing, energy, construction, distributive trades, other service industries and for central government military inventories. Information is collected from quarterly surveys, business statistics and also from the Swedish Board of Agriculture, the National Board of Forestry and from energy statistics.

4.3.5 Trade in goods and services

Estimates for trade in goods and services are derived from three main sources. Data on trade in goods with countries outside the EU is collected via customs import and export declarations. Data on trade with countries within the EU is based on a monthly survey. Trade in services is collected in a quarterly survey. The estimates are continuously checked against VAT information.

4.4 Employment method

4.4.1 Comparison between Labour Force Survey and business statistics

In order to ensure completeness in the national accounts the Labour Force Survey (LFS) is compared with business statistics, which provide consistent information on employment and output.

Total hours worked

Sources and methods

Three methods are used to calculate the volume of hours worked in the Swedish economy:
- direct method: the total hours actually worked are estimated according to LFS and business statistics (BS);
- accounts method: data on the number of employed persons are combined with actual working time in LFS;

- hours worked in the hidden economy are based on estimates of wages and hourly earnings paid in the hidden economy.

The direct method is used for total hours worked where the LFS, with a few supplements, are used, as well as for market producers by industry where the BS is used. Table 2 shows the link between total hours worked according to NA and LFS.

Table 2. Total hours worked (x10 000) according to LFS and NA

Domestic concept	2000	2001	2002
Total hours worked, LFS	676 801	680 328	671 224
Adjusted to ESA 95 definition			
Hours worked by persons aged 65 and older	8 085	8 077	8 708
Hours worded by persons aged 15 and younger	2 161	2 140	2 048
Illicit work	3 239	3 280	3 263
Conscripts	2 527	2 535	2 048
Total hours worked by employees, NA (annual average)	**692 813**	**696 360**	**687489**

The accounts method is used for estimates of hours worked in central and local government and also for non-profit institutions serving households (NPISH). The number of employees in the government sector and NPISH are based on administrative sources. To estimate the volume of hours worked, annual working time according to LFS is used (Volume of hours worked = Number of employees x annual working time).

The Swedish National Audit Office prepared a report on illicit work in Sweden during 1997. The study covered the extent of hours worked, compensation and the structure of illicit work in Sweden. The report is the basis for calculations of the total amount of hours worked as well as hours worked by industry. The amount of hours is based on compensation of employees and estimates of hourly earnings (compensation by industry/hourly earnings = number of hours worked).

Verifying the validity of total hours worked

The validity of total hours worked is verified by a direct and indirect method. The direct method compares estimates across different sources for employment. The number of employed persons and hours worked are measured both by LFS and BS. To compare the sources, adjustments for conceptual and coverage differences are done. An exhaustive comparison of the LFS and BS is presented in Table 3.

The indirect method is used to compare estimates in national accounts with the results of other enterprise surveys conducted by Statistics Sweden. This can be done by calculating wages per hour according to estimates in national accounts and comparing these results with survey estimates of wages, salaries and labour costs.

Table 3. Comparison between LFS and the business statistics (BS), 1998
(Hundred persons)

SNI	Labour Force Survey						Reduction for NPISH	Business surveys		Difference LFS and BS	
	Hours	Hours self employed	Hours x 53 weeks	Average annual working hours	Number of full time employees	Addition over-and under-aged		Adjusted number of full time employees	Number of full time employees	Absolute	%
C,D	2 283	95	100 000	1 800	7 002	50		7 052	7 311	-259	-3.7
E	95	0	5 035	1 800	280	2		282	264	18	6.3
F	471	81	29 256	1 800	1 625	8		1 633	1 697	-64	-3.9
G	1 277	189	77 698	1 800	4 317	117		4 434	4 180	254	5.7
H	245	35	14 840	1 800	824	45		869	713	156	18
I	692	67	40 227	1 800	2 235	11		2 246	2 485	-239	-10.6
K	947	147	57 982	1 800	3 221	171		3 392	3 131	261	7.7
M	74	7	4 293	1 800	239	14		253	133	-120	47.3
N	166	19	9 805	1 800	545	17		562	570	-8	-1.5
O	301	25	17 278	1 800	960	21		981	514	467	47.6
Total					**21 247**	**456**	**-846**	**20 857**	**20 998**	**-141**	**-0.7**

Note: In the comparison between the Labour Force Survey and business statistics some adjustments must be made. The business statistics measure full time equivalents and the Labour Force Survey number of employed persons on average throughout the year. In the comparison, full time equivalents are calculated in the LFS as hours worked per person through average hours worked per person per year.

Confronting estimates

This section describes how separate estimates for employment, compensation of employees and production are confronted and adjusted to reach the final estimates. The adjustments in this step of the process are done within the limits of first estimates of totals for employment, compensation and production. Adjustments are mainly done for detailed economic activities where some discrepancies between the sources may appear. If, however, major differences occur, this will lead to further investigation on potential errors in primary statistics. The process is described in Figure 1.

The first estimates are compared on a detailed level of economic activity to evaluate if results are reliable. Does combining of data on compensation of employees, hours worked and production give reasonable results? If not, experts responsible for different industries go back to primary statistics to find out what is causing the problem. Adjustments are done in either production, compensation of employees or hours worked.

Estimates are combined for analytical purposes. The main analytical variables are:
- comparing earnings per person and per hour in national accounts with data on earnings and labour cost;
- comparing hours worked and production on a very detailed industry level (133 activities).

Figure 1. Confronting separate estimates

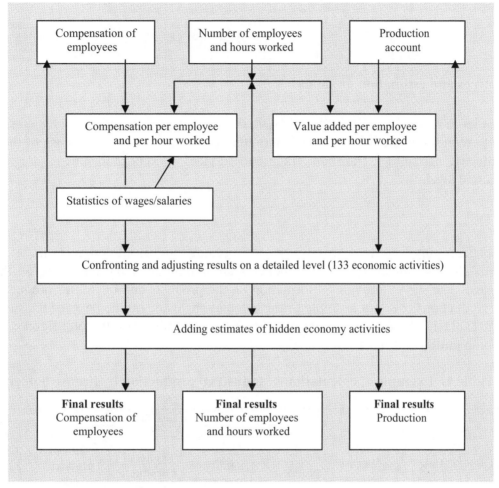

The analytical variables are reviewed with the help of other statistical sources. For example, hourly earnings are compared with statistics of wages and salaries according to statistics produced by the Department of Labour and Education Statistics.

When data sets have been compared and the balancing procedure is finished the final step is to add estimates of hidden economy. The adjustments for illicit work in Sweden are calculated by using national accounts estimates together with information according to a study by the Swedish National Audit Office. The basis for adjustment of hidden compensation of employees is the residual between GDP by income and GDP by production. Compiling GDP by the income approach does not sum up to total value added which indicates occurrence of unregistered income. The report from the Swedish National Audit Office presents results of a study carried out in 1997 with information on structures, levels of wages and which economic activities that are involved. The study shows that persons employed in regular work carry out illicit work. For this reason no additional employed persons are added in national accounts estimates but only additional hours worked. The amount of hours worked is based on total incomes combined with hourly earnings.

TAJIKISTAN

1. Data sources and estimation methods

In order to ensure exhaustiveness of GDP, the estimates of the different elements of the non-government sector are made by the State Committee for Statistics for all branches of the economy, such as industry, agriculture, transport, trade and services. Certain adjustments are made at the macroeconomic level.

1.1 Industry

Statistical surveys are carried out to measure industrial production by individual entrepreneurs (license holders). Lists of producers are compiled by the tax office on the basis of licenses issued. The survey provides information on the products and quantities produced, average prices and production costs. An example of the calculations made on the basis of the survey results is shown in Table 1. The estimated volume of production is added to the total figures by industry for each month until the next survey.

Table 1. Example of calculation of industrial production by license holders

| Product | Unit | Number of license holders | Surveyed license holders | | | | Estimated volume of production by all registered license holders, somoni |
			Number	Quantity of products	Value of product, somoni	Average value of products per producer, somoni	
1	2	3	4	5	6	7 (6:4)	8 (7x3)
Food products							
Vegetable oil	liters	100	10	200	380	38	3800
Light industrial products							
Trousers	Pieces	50	5	15	150	30	1500
Wooden articles							
Doors	Pieces	30	3	12	960	320	9600
Total		180	18	x	x	x	14900

Note: 1 somoni equals approximately 0.30 US dollars

1.2 Transport

The statistical office also conducts sample surveys of commercial cargo transportation by entrepreneurs-owners of cargo transport vehicles, and of passenger transportation by entrepreneurs-owners of passenger vehicles. The survey is carried out once per quarter over seven days. From all license holders, 10 per cent of the owners of cargo vehicles and 20 per cent of the owners of passenger vehicles are surveyed.

The following information is collected in the survey:
- the model of the transport vehicle and its carrying capacity;
- the distance of transportation and volume of carried cargo in tons or number of passengers transported during the survey period;
- the freight turnover during the survey period;
- number of trips per day;
- number of workdays per week;
- income received;
- fuel consumed.

In processing the results of the survey, the average value of indicators collected from the sample are grossed up to the total number of entrepreneurs active in the area.

1.3 Services

Sample surveys of payments made to private individuals for personal services are also conducted. They provide the following information: how often and what kind of services of private individuals are used and how much is paid (per month) for these services. The services covered are: sewing clothes; repair of footwear; repair of domestic equipment; repair and maintenance of motor vehicles (including technical inspection, car washing, paid parking); repair and construction of dwellings; services of hairdressers; etc.

1.4 Other

Special surveys are conducted in trade, construction, medical care (services of private doctors and other medical personnel), education (tuition, additional studies, preparation of course and diploma papers), and agricultural production by individuals.

2. Implications and effects on GDP estimates

The statistical office bases its estimates of the non-observed economy on data from surveys of the private sector. Adjustments are made for gross output, intermediate consumption and value added for inclusion in GDP calculations. At present, these adjustments constitute more than 25 per cent of GDP.

The quality of the surveys is not always good but they are as accurate as possible given that no special surveys are currently conducted.

3. Future plans

The Statistical Office is working on improving the methodology of national accounts compilation according to SNA93. Following receipt of grant assistance, methods of calculation for all branches of the economy were analysed. Special attention was paid to the examination of the available data sources. Recommendations were given on their use for the assessment of estimates.

It is planned to enhance the scope of national accounts and improve the estimates of NOE, and to ensure further implementation of SNA93 by reviewing current methodology, concepts, definitions and sources.

THE FORMER YUGOSLAV REPUBLIC OF MACEDONIA

1. Introduction

The statistical office regularly produces annual GDP by production, income and expenditure approach at current prices, as well as quarterly GDP by production approach according to SNA93 and ESA 95. The main methodological improvements have been achieved through:
- the Eurostat Pilot Project on Exhaustiveness (PPE) ;
- participation in the European Comparison Programme in 1996 when GDP by expenditure approach was improved;
- major data revision in 2000 to improve the data sources, estimations of non-observed economy as well as applying the NACE Rev.1 classification in GDP calculations.

In 2004, a Eurostat-OECD NOE Project for Western Balkan Countries (WBC) was started. Its objective was to enable these countries to tackle the NOE in a sustained and systematic manner and to bring about fundamental long-term improvements in the data collection systems underlying their economic statistics. This objective is to be achieved by applying the Eurostat Tabular Approach and by following the guidelines of the OECD Handbook. The first phase of the project was carried out from September 2004 until January 2006. Continuation of the project would depend on the progress made during this fifteen month period and on the availability of funds.

2. Definitions and concepts

The definitions of activities that are not directly observed through the standard statistical surveys are based on the standard terminology used within the Eurostat Pilot Project on Exhaustiveness. Eight types of NOE (T1-T8) were considered.

3. Sources and estimation methods

In line with the Trade Company Law, all legal entities and sole traders, except small unincorporated units with low level of turnover (less than 400 Euros) and with less than two employees are obliged to submit annual financial reports to the Central Register. This information provides the bulk of data for GDP output estimates of value-added in the market sector.

Depending on their activity-code and on how they are financed, legal units are grouped as:
- non-financial enterprises;
- central and local government;
- government sector (health, education, etc.);
- non-profit institutions;
- banks;
- insurance companies;
- individual entrepreneurs (with or without paid employees).

The units are obliged to present financial reports, including data from balance sheets and income statements that permit estimation of the gross and net value added for each legal unit.

These estimates are systematically checked against other data sources within a national accounts data warehouse set up by the statistical office. The warehouse stores data from the various sources of business statistics, namely the Central Register Office, Ministry of Finance, Pension Fund, Tax Office, Health Insurance Fund, Employment Bureau, and the National Bank. Moreover, indicators of activity at the NACE Rev.1 activity level are also checked to ensure that growth rates are plausible.

Data on the unincorporated units that are not required to provide annual reports to the Central Register are obtained from a number of sources. Data on small-scale unincorporated entrepreneurs, for example, is provided by the Public Revenue Office whose data comes from local authorities where the entrepreneurs are registered. In addition, data on crafts activities is provided by the Register of Craftsmen, managed by the Chamber of Craftsmen.

Based on the analyses and consultations made with tax and accounting experts, the National Accounts Department concluded the following:
- Income statements and balance sheets of financial corporations, government units and NPISH's give true picture of their activities and major exhaustiveness adjustments are not needed. National Accounts staff makes just an adjustment of the consumption of fixed capital of government units and an adjustment of the cash to accrual data.
- Income statements of the non-financial corporations contain underestimated sales, wages and salaries and number of employees and overestimated costs.
- There are a significant number of un-registered unincorporated units.

It can be concluded that the basic data sources do not provide total coverage of activities in the non-financial corporations sector and households sector.

Estimations for achieving the exhaustiveness of GDP are done for business units belonging to the non-financial corporations sector and for the household sector.

3.1 Misreporting

Underreporting is one of the main types of non-exhaustiveness in the country. The main reasons for underreporting are to avoid payments of turnover tax, import duties, personal taxes and employers' social contributions.

Underreporting is thought to be significant in the non-financial enterprises sector, as well as in the household sector, so adjustments for underreporting are made for non-financial enterprises and unincorporated enterprises.

Adjustments for underreporting were made on a very detailed level of activities. They were made in following steps:
- assessment of underreported wages;
- assessment of over-reported intermediate consumption;
- assessment of non-registered employment;
- assessment of non-registered sales in trade.

For **assessment of underreported wages** data for net wages from the annual financial reports are compared with the data from the Labour Department. Wages obtained from the Labour Department are usually higher than those reported in the Income Statement. The value of adjustment is calculated as a difference between both data sources, multiplied by the number of registered employees. This adjusted value is added to the value of gross output and compensation of employees.

For a producer who works in specific activities in the household sector and whose income is below the minimum income (according to expert assessment), an adjustment is made in order to reach that limit. Additional adjustments are made for those producers whose average income is lower than the average net wages obtained from the Labour Department.

An **adjustment of intermediate consumption** is also made on the basis of the data comparison between the previous and current year and intermediate consumption of related branches.

Assessment of non-registered employees is made by comparing data for the registered number of employees from annual financial reports and the number of employees from the LFS.

Analyses are made at a very detailed level of activities for all kinds of units. The nature and characteristics of particular branches are taken into account when comparing the data. Generally, the data on the total number of LFS employees is taken as an indicator of the actual number of employees. In specific activities performed by public enterprises or by big enterprises, the data from the Central Register is usually considered as more reliable, so adjustment for non-registered employees was not made.

The number of employees from the LFS is considered more reliable for activities performed by small enterprises (newly created private enterprises). The adjustment of non-registered employees relate only to small enterprises. The share of the small enterprises in the total number of enterprises is 98%, the share of the number of employees in small enterprises in the total number of employees is 56% and the share of value added of small enterprises in total value added is 47%. Total adjusted number of employees is close to the number of employees taken from the LFS. Adjustment of the number of employees was multiplied with the value of output per employee in order to make adjustments to the gross output.

Assessment of non-registered sales in trade. In order to avoid value added tax, trade enterprises do not register the sales in their book-keeping. Therefore, total registered sales in financial reports tend to be underreported. Adjustments of the sales of merchandisers are based on total supply and demand of goods, which pass through trade channels. An appropriate trade margin is applied to the total value of these undeclared sales so as to correctly record their output. The difference between the derived gross output and declared gross output for trade activity is the value of adjustment.

3.2 Assessment of author's fees

Payment of author's fees, according to the accounting standards, is a cost paid by enterprises for using certain services. It is treated as part of intermediate consumption. In order to balance the supply and use of goods and services according to the System of National Accounts, it is necessary to record their contribution in the output of activities where they are produced.

Paid author's fees are treated as separate units classified in related activity (K-real estate, renting and business activities). The value of these services is estimated on the basis of the available data for paid personal taxes obtained from the Ministry of Finance. 20% of the value of paid author's fees are estimated as intermediate consumption, and 10% as consumption of fixed assets.

3.3 Accommodation of tourists in rooms under individual ownership

The value added from accommodating tourists in privately owned rooms is estimated on the basis of information available in the Department of Catering Trade and Services. The total number of nights spent is multiplied with the average price per night to calculate the gross output. Intermediate consumption and depreciation are estimated on the basis of regular statistical surveys for value added of corporations and unincorporated enterprises. The average price per night spent is estimated based on information from the Tourist Bureau or Tax Department. Gross value of production minus intermediate consumption and depreciation is attributed to the category of mixed income. Information on the number of tourists and nights spent in private rooms is also available from the Tourist Bureau.

3.4 Unincorporated household enterprises that have very small-scale market output

Data for very small-scale market output produced by unincorporated household enterprises are obtained from the Tax Office. The producers with very small-scale output are obliged to pay annually a fixed amount of tax. They are not obliged to submit financial reports because their income is below a prescribed threshold. Data obtained from the Tax Office, such as net income, income tax, contributions for pension and health insurance, and other taxes represent a mixed income. To calculate intermediate consumption and depreciation from mixed income, some coefficients based on expert estimates are used.

These coefficients are different for different activities. Using the data from LFS, some adjustments are made for individuals who provide services for their friends or neighbours during weekends or after working hours, and take remuneration in cash or in kind. They are not declared as private craftsmen or traders. This group includes some other services performed by individuals, such as cleaning, babysitting, private tuition etc. The individuals providing the services do not fill in tax declarations with respect to these activities. They are also not covered by statistical surveys, therefore indirect methods of estimation are used. The estimated number of non-registered employees is multiplied by net income per employee.

3.5 Illegal activities

An estimate of the annual value of consumption of drugs is made using available data on registered drug-users and an estimate of the number of non-registered users, the average price of drugs on the illegal market and average consumption per day. No drugs are produced in the country, all drugs are imported. Therefore, it is assumed that quantities consumed are also quantities imported.

The statistical office has also estimated output of smuggling of people (human trafficking) through the country. Due to lack of available data, the revenue from smuggling of people was assumed to be equal to value added. However, these estimates are considered not to be accurate because of lack of data, and need further analysis. The current estimates are only experimental and are not included in official estimates of GDP.

4. Implication and effects on national accounts and GDP estimates

The adjustments made for the period of 2000-2003 are presented in Table 1.

Table 1. Adjustments of value added by selected economic activities, 2000-2003
(per cent)

| | Adjustments for economic underground (T4) | | | | | | | | Adjustments for informal sector (T6) | | | | Total | | | |
| | Non financial sector | | | | Households sector | | | | | | | | | | | |
	2000	2001	2002	2003	2000	2001	2002	2003	2000	2001	2002	2003	2000	2001	2002	2003
Value added at basic prices- total	**8.5**	**8.9**	**8.6**	**10.3**	**1.1**	**1.3**	**1.1**	**1.0**	**3.2**	**4.6**	**4.7**	**5.0**	**12.9**	**14.9**	**14.4**	**16.3**
of which:																
Manufacturing	2.2	2.2	2.0	4.1	0.1	0.1	0.1	0.1	0.4	0.6	1.2	1.2	2.7	3.0	3.3	5.4
Construction	0.4	0.4	0.4	0.3	0.0	0.0	0.0	0.0	1.0	1.2	1.3	2.1	1.4	1.6	1.6	2.4
Wholesale and retail trade; repair of motor vehicles motorcycles and personal and household goods	4.1	4.6	4.6	4.3	0.4	0.5	0.4	0.4	0.2	0.3	0.3	0.2	4.7	5.3	5.3	4.9
Hotels and restaurants	0.4	0.4	0.4	0.7	0.1	0.1	0.1	0.1	0.3	0.4	0.5	0.4	0.8	0.9	0.9	1.1
Transport, storage and communication	0.6	0.6	0.5	0.2	0.2	0.1	0.1	0.1	0.4	0.7	0.4	0.4	1.1	1.5	1.1	0.6
Real estate, renting, and business activities	0.5	0.5	0.5	0.5	0.1	0.3	0.3	0.3	0.7	0.9	0.8	0.6	1.3	1.6	1.5	1.4

TURKEY

1. Introduction

The national accounts figures in Turkey are compiled according to the SNA 68. The breakdown into the productive sectors is based on ISIC rev.2. The Turkish Statistical Institute (TURKSTAT) is making a big effort to introduce the SNA 93 and ESA 95 in the accounts by adapting the sources in order to comprise the new concepts and methodologies. GDP is estimated by the production, expenditure and income approaches.

National Accounts Department of TURKSTAT is in the process of revising Turkey's national accounts figures according to 1998 supply-and-use tables. The base year of national accounts, which depends mainly on estimation of GDP by production and expenditure approaches, will be changed from 1987 to 1998.

Quarterly estimates are made since 1990 on a regular basis and annual estimates are mainly derived as the sum of the four quarters. When input-output tables are compiled, annual sources and their exhaustiveness are taken into account more systematically. The most recent table is for 1998. In the quarterly and annual compilation of the Turkish national accounts, explicit exhaustiveness adjustments are only made in some specific cases. In the 1998 input-output table, a special effort has been made to adjust certain activities. For example, the adjustment for manufacturing is based on a comparison between the LFS and enterprise-based data on employment. It takes into account the discrepancy in the number of workers. Adjustments for misreporting (under-reporting of gross output and over-reporting of intermediate consumption) are not systematically made for any economic activity.

In a recent revision of national accounts, some adjustments were made and some indirect methods were developed to cover the unregistered activities in the GDP estimates. Illegal production is not included in the GDP estimates for Turkey.

2. Sources and estimation methods

2.1 Registers and basic data sources

The last Industrial Census for 2002 was conducted in 2003. Setup of the statistical business register that is fully compliant to the EU requirements will be completed by the end of 2006.

Quarterly and annual surveys exist for most branches. Data sources on employment are abundant. Therefore employment data (especially the LFS) are an important source for NA estimation in areas where other information is not available. They are also a potentially important source for making exhaustiveness adjustments for a wider range of activities than currently covered.

TURKSTAT engages in a systematic approach to achieve exhaustiveness in the NA, with a full examination of all individual NOE components. However, a complete, detailed and systematic estimation of all components of the NOE does not yet exist.

A project on exhaustiveness of national accounts is carried out in the context of upgrading the statistical system of Turkey. The main objective of the project is to determine the elements missing from national accounts, including all components of non-observed economy.

An important source for under-coverage (informal and hidden units) is the LFS.

2.2 Evaluation methods

2.2.1 Agriculture

Value added of production of dairy products, such as butter, cheese etc. and processing of agricultural products, such as production of flour by milling, tanning of skins etc. were calculated by using the Household Budget Survey results and added to the agriculture sector.

2.2.2 Industry

The regular quarterly Household Labour Force Survey (HLFS) contains questions on the volume of the informal sector. Therefore, TURKSTAT uses the regular HLFS as the main data source for information on informal sector employment. In light of the experiences with the regular HLFS, this was considered to be the most fruitful approach for obtaining NA adjustments for informal sector employment.

There is a difference between employment information recorded in the LFS and enterprise-based sources because of non-coverage in the business register or the sampling list, and incomplete or incorrect responses in surveys.

The labour statistics were used as a basic indicator to determine the value added of manufacturing industry. The results of Manufacturing Industry Census and Household Labour Force Survey were compared and analyzed and a discrepancy observed. The reported number of persons employed in manufacturing was lower than that of the HLFS. It was assumed that some of the manufacturing establishments conceal part of their production activities. Therefore, the difference in the number of workers was multiplied by the average value added per capita obtained from annual industry survey and the result was added to the original estimate of value added of manufacturing industry.

The HLFS also indicated that a number of households were engaged in household manufacturing. Average hours worked per week were calculated from the HLFS and converted to a full-time equivalent. The average value added per capita in small-scale manufacturing was applied to the resulting number of employees to obtain estimates of the total value added (Table 1).

2.2.3 Trade and transport

The value added of trade and transportation sectors is estimated by using trade and transport margins on produced and imported goods. This approach allows to cover some part of non-observed activities. The margins were updated from the last supply-and-use tables (1998).

Table 1. Share of non-registered activities and household production in total manufacturing industry and GDP
(per cent)

Year	2000		2001		2002		2003		2004		2005	
	% of industry	% of GDP	% of industry	% of GDP	% of industry	% of GDP	% of industry	% of GDP	% of industry	% of GDP	% of industry	% of GDP
Small-scale industry (non-registered)	5.86	1.12	5.62	1.16	5.64	1.13	5.69	1.14	5.85	1.19	5.86	1.22
Household manufacturing	2.42	0.46	2.56	0.53	2.52	0.51	2.48	0.49	2.30	0.47	2.20	0.46
TOTAL	**8.28**	**1.59**	**8.18**	**1.68**	**8.16**	**1.64**	**8.16**	**1.63**	**8.15**	**1.66**	**8.15**	**1.67**

2.3 Informal sector survey

TURKSTAT conducted an independent Informal Sector Survey in 2000 to estimate the basic characteristics of informal sector employment. With technical assistance from the ILO, investigations were carried out into the development of: a definition of the informal sector that is in line with the particular conditions in Turkey; a survey methodology to measure employment in this sector; the survey sample and questionnaire forms; and a pilot test of the survey.

For the purpose of the survey, the informal sector is defined as all unincorporated non-agricultural economic units (establishments whose legal status is individual ownership or simple partnership), which pay either a lump sum tax or no tax at all, and have fewer than 10 employees. The survey covers persons aged 16 years and over, working as self-employed or as an employer. The sample covers all settlements in urban areas with a population of 20 000 or more.

The survey includes both households and establishments. The questionnaire is composed of two main parts:
- Household questionnaire: collects information on the demographic characteristics of household members, their employment status in the last 12 months, source of household income and average net monthly household income.
- Establishment questionnaire: collects information on the demographic characteristics of the operators, working hours, total number of persons employed, taxation method, type of legal organization/ownership, number of hours worked, operating surplus, input-output, etc.

Two reference periods were used: the "last 12 months" and the "last month that economic activity was carried out". The survey was conducted in February, May, August and November of 2000.

In addition to the independent Informal Sector Survey that was conducted in 2000, the Turkish Statistical Institute has added some questions to a revised HLFS that started in 2000, aimed at estimating informal sector employment more precisely.

TURKMENISTAN

1. Introduction

Turkmenistan is systematically developing methodological approaches for assessing the volume of non-observed activities that are not covered by regular statistical surveys. Special attention is paid to updating the register of enterprises and organizations, register of physical persons and improvement of survey methods.

The National Institute of Statistics and Forecasting of Turkmenistan has developed methodological recommendations for measuring the NOE based on SNA 93 and the OECD Handbook. The assessment is done according to the three approaches: production, expenditure and income approach, where the production approach is the main method. Corrections are done for most of the branches of economy: industry, trade, transport, communication, construction, agriculture, fishing, health, education, services, etc.

According to the expenditure approach, estimation is made of the share of NOE in household final consumption expenditure and fixed capital formation. According to the income approach, only the compensation of employees is evaluated.

Among the different methods to measure NOE, the main methods are special surveys, balancing supply and use of resources, indirect and mixed methods based on branch statistics and data from governmental agencies.

Until 2002, the National Institute of Statistics and Forecasting of Turkmenistan included under the NOE the informal and illegal activities, following the recommendations of SNA 93. At present, the NOE is classified into 5 types according to the OECD Handbook: underground, illegal, informal activities, households production for own final use and statistical deficiencies. In addition, the Eurostat tabular framework is followed since 2003.

2. Sources and estimation methods

2.1 Producers deliberately not registering (underground) - N1

This type of NOE comes from the household sector and makes up 7% of GDP. To this type belong transport services by unregistered entrepreneurs (owners of private vehicles), sewing clothes, renting, and other services provided to physical persons without registration (without a licence). This sector covers most branches of the economy. The share of these activities is most significant in trade, transport, services, construction and culture. Data sources for activities of type N1 are: statistics on households, transport, trade and investment; social and demographic statistics; special surveys of private entrepreneurs transporting passengers and cargo; surveys of households who use the services of the informal sector, and individual entrepreneurs providing the services; employment surveys; market surveys, etc.

2.2 Producers not registering - illegal activities - N2

Under this type, Turkmenistan includes the economic activities carried out by legal, physical persons without licence. This includes:
- illegal production of alcohol;
- illegal fishing;
- private tuition;
- lawyers;
- medical services (surgery and childbirth).

This type of non-observed activities makes up 0.8% of GDP.

Illegal fishing, alcohol production and legal services are estimated by a balancing method, as the difference between total consumption (according to the budget statistics) and output from official statistics.

Medical services are estimated based on the number of operations and informal payments identified through anonymous interviews with citizens. Private tuition is estimated based on the number of pupils on middle, special and high schools, share of pupils having private teachers (from the budget surveys on expenditure on private tuition) and prices of these services.

Other types of illegal activities, like gambling, sales of stolen goods, production and sales of counterfeit goods and unauthorised copies of artistic originals are traditionally not widespread in Turkmenistan. Output of prostitution, production and sales of drugs and arms smuggling are not included in GDP because of ethical reasons. In addition, such activities in Turkmenistan do not take place on a large scale.

2.3 Producers not required to register - N3

In Turkmenistan, this type covers household production for own final consumption and for selling, e.g. production of national costumes, carpets, everyday items, home-baked bread etc. This type provides over 8% of GDP. The estimation of production of households is based on data from the budget surveys and social and demographic statistics, statistics on prices and agriculture. The list of products produced by households for own final consumption is constantly updated.

2.4 Legal persons not surveyed - N4

This type does not exist in Turkmenistan as all registered legal persons are covered by statistical surveys.

2.5 Registered entrepreneurs not surveyed - N5

Until 2001, the National Institute of Statistics and Forecasting of Turkmenistan did not have a register of entrepreneurs, and the estimation was done based on the number of units not surveyed. In 2002, the statistical office has set up a register of physical persons together with the Tax Office. Type N5 does not exist in Turkmenistan as all registered entrepreneurs declare their income to the Tax Office.

2.6 Producers deliberately misreporting - N6

This type of activities is estimated based on tax audits. The additional tax payments and value added are used to estimate the hidden production in different branches. The results are grossed up for all enterprises in the register. Type N6 activities make up 2% of GDP. This type of NOE can be found in trade, construction, industry and services.

2.7 Other statistical deficiencies - N7

To this type belong exhaustiveness adjustments to the data on surveyed enterprises, especially concerning small enterprises. The non-responding (potentially active) enterprises are identified from the statistical register (the difference between registered and reporting enterprises). These data are corrected using a coefficient of active enterprises (ratio of active enterprises to all enterprises). The resulting number of "potentially active" enterprises makes up the estimation to active enterprises. It is used to correct all data collected from small enterprises, including output, intermediate consumption, wages and salaries, changes in inventories, etc. The basic indicator is output.

Type N7 makes up 0.3 % of GDP of Turkmenistan.

3. Summary of exhaustiveness adjustments

The NOE is estimated for two sectors of the economy: non-financial enterprises and households. In the non-financial enterprises sector, two types of NOE are estimated: N6 and N7. The share of this sector was 2.6 % of GDP in 2005 (4.3% in 2002). Reduction of NOE is mainly due to the decrease of production that is hidden from the tax office.

For the household sector, 3 types of non-observed activities are estimated: N1, N2, N3. The share of this sector in GDP was 17% in 2005 (5 percentage points more than in 2002). The increase is due to the growth of non-observed activities in transport, construction and services.

In total, the NOE made up 18.1% of GDP in 2005. According to the different types of NOE, the biggest share belongs to the type N3 (over 40%), N1 (over 38%), and N6 (11%). Type N2 forms 3.9 and N7 1.4% of NOE.

UKRAINE

1. Introduction

Since the early 1990s, the State Statistics Committee of Ukraine (Goskomstat) has increasingly focused on the problem of estimating the underground economy. Efforts were aimed at estimation of household production, misreporting and non-response by enterprises.

The estimation methods of non-observed activities have been constantly improved throughout this period. In particular, international standards were introduced for structural enterprise statistics, household surveys and employment statistics. Special statistical surveys were carried out on taxis, markets and individual housing construction. The compilation of input-output tables made it possible to use the commodity flow method. In 2004, a survey of experts was established, to provide advice on the levels of non-observed economic activities in agriculture, industry, construction, trade and transport.

Currently work continues to improve estimation of the volume of NOE in line with SNA93 and ESA95.

2. Definitions and concepts

Goskomstat uses the Eurostat T1-T8 types of non-exhaustiveness, while definitions and concepts correspond to the recommendations of the OECD *Handbook on Measuring the Non-Observed Economy* (2002) and the 1993 International Conference of Labour Statisticians' definition of informal sector.

3. Sources and estimation methods

The main sources of data for estimating non-observed activities are:
- structural statistics of enterprises in the non-financial corporations sector (volumes of products sold, composition of expenditure and number of employees, with detailed breakdown by types of economic activity and size of enterprise, and with information on the reasons for non-response);
- household surveys (expenditure on goods and services with detailed breakdown by place of purchase);
- labour statistics (wages and number of employees);
- sample surveys of population (households) on economic activity (number of persons employed and time worked by types of economic activity and categories of employment);
- sample surveys of markets and taxis;
- statistics of agriculture (volume of output and gross value added of the households sector, output of products for own final consumption);
- administrative data (registers of legal entities and individual entrepreneurs, licenses for construction issued to individuals, balance of payments).

4. Estimation of volume of output

The calculation methods used for the types of non-observed economy are developed on the basis of Eurostat recommendations.

4.1 Statistical underground (types T1-T3)

Calculations are based on the analysis of reasons for non-response to Structural Surveys of Enterprises in the non-financial sector. Data on the enterprises that have not submitted reports are estimated on the basis of the number of non-responding enterprises, reasons for non-response, and the output and expenditure of enterprises of similar size and kind of activity.

4.1.1 Non-response to surveys (T1)

The volume of output per small enterprises by type of economic activity is determined using the reported data on the number and output of small enterprises contained in the annual Structural Survey of Enterprises (SSE).

On the basis of the data from SSE, the number of non-responding enterprises by type of economic activity is established. The reason for non-response is also indicated, such as refusal to report, absence of management, absence of documents, untimely submission of reports, etc.

Since it is mainly small enterprises that refuse to report, the volume of activities is determined by multiplying the number of non-responding enterprises by average volume of output per reporting small enterprise.

4.1.2 Out-of-date registers (T2)

From the SSE, the number of enterprises that were not found at the given address is determined, by type of economic activity. Assuming that small enterprises are more likely to change addresses or give a wrong address, the volume of hidden activities is calculated by multiplying the number of enterprises not found at the given address by average output per small enterprises from the SSE.

4.1.3. Unregistered units (T3)

From the SSE is determined the number of enterprises that have not submitted their reports because of the following reasons:
- shut down in the reporting year;
- declared bankrupt;
- refused to report because of suspension of activities in the reporting year.

Taking into account that small enterprises are more frequently shut down and created, the volume of hidden activities is calculated by multiplying the number of these enterprises by the average output of reporting small enterprises from the SSE.

The resulting figure is divided by two, based on the assumption that the liquidated enterprises were active on average for half a year.

4.2 Economic underground (T4-T5)

Misreporting is identified by comparing the level of production per employed person and levels of intermediate consumption per unit of produced products for enterprises engaged in the same kind of activity.

The volume of output per worker is determined based on SSE data by type of economic activity and by size of enterprise. The indicators of the volume of output per worker are compared for large- and medium-sized and for small enterprises. Adjustments for small enterprises are made when the output per worker in large and medium-sized enterprises exceeds corresponding indicators for small enterprises.

When analysing structural indicators, units with output significantly below average and intermediate consumption significantly above average are determined by type of activity and number of employees. Adjustments for under-reporting of output for such enterprises are made on the basis of average output per worker and average number of workers. The criteria for determining such enterprises are based on expert opinions for each type of economic activity. Analysis and comparison of the shares of value added elements (wages, profit) are also made.

In case of deliberate non-registration, economic activity data from population surveys are used. The output of employers or employees who are not registered taxpayers is calculated based on data on small enterprises.

4.3 Informal economy and production of households for own final consumption (T6 and T8)

To determine output, data from household surveys (volumes of purchases at markets and from individuals), surveys of market turnover, household surveys of economic activity (number of self-employed, non-paid family workers employed in individual household plots), as well as information on licenses issued for construction of individual houses and household buildings, and on agricultural production of households is used. Similar sources of data are used for the estimation of other kinds of non-observed activities, including production for own final consumption, tips, and payment in kind.

The number of persons hired by households and employers is estimated on the basis of sample surveys of population (households). The volume of production is calculated by multiplying the number of persons hired by households and employers by the volume of output per worker in small enterprises, based on the SSE data.

By comparing the resulting volume of output with the data of the State Tax Administration (STA) on the volume of production by individual entrepreneurs, the volume of hidden activities due to intentional non-registration of employees is determined. If the Tax Administration data on production by individual entrepreneurs exceed the volume of production calculated on the basis of the number of employees, the difference can be attributed to type T6.

Output of households in the informal sector is estimated on the basis of household survey data. Goods which are not produced in the informal sector, but which are purchased at markets and from citizens, are considered to be resold.

Statistics on market turnover are used to estimate the output of trade (trade margin). Certain volumes of output of goods and services are grouped by type of economic activity.

The volume of individual housing construction is calculated on the basis of data on construction and capital repairs of cottages, garages, and individual houses and on the basis of statistics on investments and construction.

Agricultural production by citizens for own consumption is estimated on the basis of agricultural statistics.

Tips and production of products for own use (T8) is included in T6 because of the difficulty of distinguishing it from informal activities.

4.4 Illegal activities (T7)

A partial accounting of illegal economic activities is made. The National Bank is making adjustments for exports and imports within the balance of payments framework. Some estimates are made of the production of selected products (e.g. tobacco products and alcohol). However, a lack of sufficient administrative data prohibits an accurate estimation of this activity.

5. Estimation of intermediate consumption and gross value added

Adjustments of value added and intermediate consumption for the non-financial corporations sector (T1-T3) are made using data from the Structural Survey on Enterprises. The adjustement are based on the volume of hidden output of products and structural proportions between output and intermediate consumption and value added in small enterprises carrying out corresponding types of economic activities. For type T4, misreporting, adjustments are made for overstatement of intermediate consumption and understatement of wages on the basis of the same data for large and medium enterprises or for small enterprises.

The volume of intermediate consumption and gross value added for the household sector is determined by expert estimates taking into account the structural proportions of small enterprises for corresponding types of economic activity.

6. Implications and effects on national accounts and GDP estimates

Tables 1 and 2 contain estimates of the non-observed economy in Ukraine based on the production approach.

About half of the contribution to NOE in Ukraine is made by agriculture, where nearly two thirds of total output is produced in the informal sector, although in recent years its share has been decreasing. Within the different NOE types, a high level is recorded for economic underground in industry and trade. Most of the adjustments are made in agriculture, trade, construction and industry.

The adjustments for NOE in GDP calculations by categories of final use are given in Table 3.

Table 1. Share of NOE in GDP
(per cent)

NACE activity	2001	2002	2003	2004
Agriculture, hunting, forestry and fishing	9.2	9.3	8.0	7.2
Mining and quarrying, manufacturing, production and distribution of electricity, gas and water	2.6	3.3	3.0	3.7
Construction	0.7	0.6	0.6	1.1
Wholesale and retail trade, hotels and restaurants	2.3	2.8	3.5	3.5
Transport and communication	0.3	0.6	0.6	1.4
Other activities	1.0	1.1	1.5	2.0
Total	**16.3**	**17.7**	**17.2**	**18.9**

Table 2. Share of NOE in GDP by non-exhaustiveness type, 2002-2003
(per cent)

NACE activity	Statistical under- ground T1-T3		Economic under- ground T4-T5		Informal and other T6-T8	
	2002	2003	2002	2003	2002	2003
Agriculture, hunting, forestry and fishing	0.0	0.0	0.7	0.7	8.6	7.3
Mining and quarrying, manufacturing, production and distribution of electricity, gas and water	0.5	0.3	1.8	2.5	1.0	0.2
Construction	0.1	0.1	0.5	0.5	0.0	0.0
Wholesale and retail trade, hotels and restaurants	0.4	0.6	2.4	2.6	0.0	0.3
Transport and communication	0.1	0.1	0.5	0.4	0.0	0.1
Other kinds of economic activity	0.1	0.2	0.4	0.6	0.6	0.7
Total	**1.2**	**1.3**	**6.3**	**7.3**	**10.2**	**8.6**

Table 3. Share of NOE in GDP
(per cent)

	Share of adjustments			Share of GDP		
	2002	2003	2004	2002	2003	2004
Final consumption expenditure of households	25.8	23.5	19.0	14.2	12.9	10.0
Gross fixed capital formation	5.9	4.7	5.1	1.1	1.0	1.2
Total adjustments				**15.4**	**13.8**	**11.1**

UNITED KINGDOM

1. General overview

The UK makes significant efforts to ensure its national accounts are of the highest quality. This starts by making decisions about whether to use administrative or survey sources for the components of each of the three measures of GDP and culminates in balancing these measures through supply-and-use tables (SUTs). One acknowledged weakness of the UK accounts is that at present no explicit estimate is made for illegal production. However, certain illegal production can feed into the overall measure of GDP through the balancing process because it will generally be picked up in one of the measures of GDP. For example, income from selling stolen goods may be spent legally and therefore picked up in the expenditure measure of GDP.

2. Sources and estimation methods

Exhaustiveness is ensured in three main ways: ensuring data quality, surveys and confronting data at a macro level.

2.1 Ensuring data quality

The three measures of GDP are all based on different administrative or survey sources. These sources can be affected by hidden activity to varying degrees. When administrative data are used, data may be 'hidden' from the collecting authority (e.g. tax evasion can affect Inland Revenue data). Surveys are more likely to suffer from non-response or poor quality data.

This makes the choice of data sources quite difficult and consequently decisions have to be made on a case-by-case basis. For example, in the production approach, published company accounts can be used for industries dominated by a few large enterprises (e.g. telecommunications) but industries populated by a large number of small firms are better covered by sample surveys because small firms are more likely to try to avoid taxation.

2.2 Surveys

The Office for National Statistics (ONS) has invested in high quality business and household surveys, which have been specifically designed to produce results for the national accounts. The business surveys, such as the Annual Business Inquiry (ABI) are supported by a comprehensive Inter Departmental Business Register (IDBR), which ensures these surveys remain representative of the whole economy. Sound survey methodology is used to make appropriate allowances for non-response through imputation, and use of the business register ensures accurate grossing.

The household surveys, such as the Family Expenditure Survey (FES) are run continuously throughout the year and based on a sample of the population derived from post office records.

These surveys are often cross-referenced against relevant business sources (e.g. household final consumption is estimated from both household and business surveys) to ensure quality.

Adjustments are made when it is known that these surveys under-record, for example, in the case of expenditure on tobacco.

Use of surveys must be balanced against effective use of administrative data wherever it can be used as an alternative source of information (e.g. tax records in the income approach). Administrative data may also be used as a check against survey data (e.g. using published accounts at industry level in the production approach or VAT data for the expenditure approach). Effective use of administrative sources can both increase quality and reduce the burden on survey respondents (businesses or individual householders).

2.3 Confronting data at a macro level

2.3.1 Balancing the accounts

In the UK much of the exhaustiveness work is focussed on the production approach, which is considered the best measure of GDP and consequently drives the SUTs balancing process. However, since this balancing process takes place at the relatively detailed 123 Input-Output group level this allows ONS to make use of the most accurate measure of GDP on a case by case basis, with the other measures constrained to the best total.

2.3.2 Use of employment data to cross-check output data

A global examination of the comparability between data derived from the production inquiries underlying the national accounts and the Labour Force Survey has been carried out. There is no evidence that there is significant hidden employment producing output that is not measured in the existing national accounts.

2.3.3 The supply approach to measuring fixed investment

Increasing use is being made of the supply approach to the measurement of fixed capital formation as a check on the results from the expenditure-based estimates. The two approaches give similar results, but adjustments have been made to the expenditure-based estimates for industries where there are most likely to be weaknesses in the coverage of the inquiries.

3. Production approach

The production approach to measuring GDP is based largely on the National Statistics Annual Business Inquiry (ABI), which draws a sample from the Inter Departmental Business Register (IDBR). Inquiry based estimates are further supplemented by estimates of earned income in kind and a number of other adjustments where necessary. Adjustments to the production measure are made on an industry-by-industry basis.

3.1 Data quality

3.1.1 Inter Departmental Business Register (IDBR)

The IDBR is the sample frame used for all of the main business surveys; it is a comprehensive register of UK businesses. It holds information on nearly 2 million enterprises, covering approximately 98 per cent of UK economic activity, but excluding private households.

It is regularly updated from both VAT and Pay-As-You-Earn (PAYE) sources. The IDBR provides a single, reliable set of employment estimates, improving the consistency of the national accounts and the quality of the productivity and unit wage cost estimates.

HM Customs and Excise (C&E), the government department which ensures compliance with the law governing payment of VAT, regularly feeds back information to the IDBR (for example any new VAT registrations are notified to ONS on a weekly basis). These quality checks mean that some firms who might otherwise have evaded the fiscal authorities (and therefore statistical records) will be included in the register and it is more likely that they will be included in the correct size band. These effects on the IDBR can be regarded as implicit adjustments for non-registration because of VAT evasion in the production approach to measuring GDP.

3.1.2 The Annual Business Inquiry (ABI)

The main source of data for the production approach is the ABI. The introduction of the ABI, which covers retail, wholesale, manufacturing and a host of other industries, has led to large improvements in the coverage of UK businesses and standardisation of inquiry procedures. The ABI covers Northern Ireland and includes small businesses in its sample selection and grossing procedures – these were sometimes weaknesses of the former separate inquiries used in the UK.

3.2 Adjustments made to ensure exhaustiveness

3.2.1 General adjustments

In most industries within the SUTs framework, the ABI provides sufficient information to calculate gross value added. This is supported by, for example, Prodcom in the manufacturing industries and Department of Trade and Industry (DTI) data in the oil/gas extraction industry. The basic data sources (mainly ABI) are subjected to the following general adjustments in all industries:
- ONS compile an industry-by-industry measure of GDP in terms of production and income. These two methods are balanced in the SUTs process to provide the best possible measure of GDP by the production approach;
- An estimate of "income in kind" (based on Inland Revenue data supplied at I-O group level) is added for every I-O level industry;
- Generally good methodology and data validation techniques are employed in the ABI. However, as an additional check, odd movements in large companies (from ABI data) are often checked against companies' annual reports and accounts. More use is made of this approach in industries dominated by large businesses, for example, telecommunications;
- Estimates of VAT based turnover and VAT paid (supplied by Inland Revenue at I-O group level) are used to validate the production-based estimates of turnover and gross value added (GVA);
- The income-based estimate of GVA is used in industries where source data for the production approach is considered to be poor or is absent altogether.

3.2.2 Specific adjustments

In addition to the general exhaustiveness adjustments mentioned above, the following industry specific adjustments are also used:

Agriculture

The Ministry of Agriculture, Fisheries and Food (MAFF) provides estimates of the gross output, intermediate purchases, value added (and the product composition of purchases less sales) of the national farm, and of intra-farm transactions. This is used as an alternative, more comprehensive source of data in the production approach. These estimates do not cover all of the activity of non-farm based agricultural enterprises and therefore an adjustment is made to cover this type of activity.

Construction industry

Construction output is based mainly on Department of the Environment Transport and the Regions (DETR) data, although this is crosschecked against ABI data. Additionally, ONS make a hidden economy adjustment for self-employed builders based on DETR data, which is also applied consistently in the expenditure approach.

Wholesale and retail industry; Hotels and restaurants

Additional quality checks are applied to the base ABI data. Particularly, extra analysis of returns from large businesses including: year-on-year analysis; time series comparisons with quarterly data sources; and checks against annual reports and accounts. Additionally, there is an adjustment to ABI data for under-coverage of small outlets – based on special analyses undertaken in collaboration with the Department of Trade and Industry (calculation based on reported self-employment income in the industry and an estimate of under-coverage by the IDBR).

Transport

Data are checked against annual reports and accounts (particularly in communications industry, which is dominated by large businesses).

Under-coverage of taxis is dealt with by an adjustment based on number of registered cabs and expert opinion on taxi driver earnings (this adjustment is less important than it was, due to improvements to IDBR coverage). Additionally, Civil Aviation Authority data are used to check ABI data for the airlines.

4. Income approach

In the UK, the income approach is heavily reliant on information derived by the Inland Revenue (the UK government's tax collecting body) as a by-product of the tax system. Although this provides an independent approach for measuring GDP, it does have a number of weaknesses, which are overcome through a series of exhaustiveness adjustments in each of the income components. These adjustments aim to:
- capture hidden activity (e.g. below the tax threshold);
- adjust for coverage (e.g. include pension fund data);
- utilise alternative data sources that are regarded as better quality or more timely (e.g. MAFF data).

4.1 Data quality

In the UK, income tax is charged under a series of "schedules" and "cases", each representing a different type of income (e.g. Schedule D, Case 1 represents corporations/quasi-corporations tax on profits and Schedule E represents income from employment and pensions).

This system of recording income for tax purposes provides an ideal base for estimation of most of the components of the income approach. The main drawback is timeliness, since there is some delay in providing this information. However, this is not an issue when the accounts are finalised for GNP purposes.

The tax data utilised in the UK national accounts is provided by three main sources within the Inland Revenue: Pay-As-You-Earn data, Survey of Personal Income and Corporations Tax Returns.

4.1.1 Pay-As-You-Earn (PAYE) data

For the vast majority of employees who receive income under Schedule E (income from employment) the tax due on that income is calculated by the employer and the appropriate amount deducted before the employee is paid. This system, known as Pay-As-You-Earn (PAYE), ensures that these individuals do not usually need to complete an annual tax return or make any direct payment to the Inland Revenue.

About 90 per cent of all UK individuals liable to income tax are chargeable under schedule E and almost all of income tax chargeable under schedule E is collected under the PAYE system. This system therefore provides an excellent base for the calculation of compensation of employees.

After the end of each tax year, employers send details of pay and tax contributions for each employee to the Inland Revenue. Estimates of wages and salaries for those within the PAYE system are derived from a 1 per cent sample of tax deduction documents. The Inland Revenue under statutory authority sends these documents to the Department of Social Security (DSS), which notes the details of social security. A separate computer file based on 1 per cent of these records is compiled for statistical analysis including details of pay and tax. The total number of tax deduction documents exceeds 30 million each year and 300 000 records are sufficient to estimate total wages and salaries with a standard error of about ¼ per cent.

The estimate of pay obtained for the whole PAYE population is obtained by multiplying the 1 per cent sample estimates by appropriate grossing factors. These are obtained by comparing the employees' National Insurance contributions (NICs) totals obtained from the 1 per cent sample with the total employees NICs recorded.

Employers are allowed to submit computerised returns to the Inland Revenue derived from their payroll systems and, in practice, include some employees falling below the tax/NIC threshold.

However an exhaustiveness adjustment is required (outlined below) to fully cover individuals who fall below the threshold.

4.1.2 The Survey of Personal Incomes

The Survey of Personal Incomes is an annual survey that covers individuals in receipt of income from self-employment (partnerships and sole traders) for whom income tax records are held by the Inland Revenue. The survey is based on a stratified sample of tax records.

The data from the survey is used in the calculation of mixed income (sole traders) and quasi-corporations (partnerships) gross operating surplus. This includes doctors and dentists practising under the National Health Service but excludes the salaries of members of the professions chargeable to tax under Schedule E (i.e. doctors who are full-time hospital employees, nearly all teachers and HM Forces pay), which are all included in PAYE data.

The Survey of Personal Incomes also includes details of rental income, which is used in the calculation of household operating surplus when earned by individuals classified to the household sector.

4.1.3 Corporation tax returns

The Inland Revenue data used by the ONS in the calculation of non-financial corporations gross operating surplus cover the taxable trading profits/losses of all industrial and commercial companies operating in the UK. The data are obtained from the Inland Revenue inquiry on trading profits of industrial and commercial companies assessed to UK corporation tax. The Inland Revenue data does not include quasi-corporations, which are supplied as part of the Survey of Personal Incomes (see above).

All companies must complete regular corporation tax returns regardless of their size or whether they are in profit or loss, so coverage of the sector is 100 per cent. Consistency is assured since the national accounts figures are taken from these standard tax returns.

Schedule D Case 1 profits is net of capital allowances but the national accounts definition of gross trading profits requires that these allowances not be deducted. Information for each company sampled includes the capital allowances given by the tax inspector, so that these can be added back to the Schedule D Case 1 profits. The resulting estimates (known as Schedule D Gross Case 1 profits, or losses) are used in the calculation of gross operating surplus of non-financial corporations.

The Schedule D Case 1 profits definition is different from the national accounts definition of gross trading profits in several other respects (e.g. the treatment of finance lease rental payments) so ONS make adjustments to align the overall estimate to a national accounts (ESA95) basis.

4.2 Adjustments made to ensure exhaustiveness

4.2.1 Compensation of employees

A number of specific adjustments are made to cover hidden activity:
- estimates of incomes not covered because employees are below the threshold at which the PAYE system becomes operative are based on the numbers concerned and their average annual earnings (from the Family Expenditure Survey (FES));
- estimates for informal activity, e.g. tips, are based on information from the Inland Revenue;

- a specific estimate based on the FES is made for the earnings of those outside the National Insurance scheme, principally the earnings of those under 16 years of age.
- many of the workers in domestic service and agriculture are paid at rates below the PAYE system thresholds. A specific adjustment is therefore made for these workers, based on information from the FES and from MAFF.

A number of other adjustments are required in order to ensure complete coverage in compensation of employees. "Profit related pay" and "shares appropriated under profit-sharing schemes" are taken from Inland Revenue sources as "expenses, payments and benefits in kind assessed as taxable income". Employees' contributions to superannuation funds are taken from government administrative sources (for public sector employees) and National Statistics inquiries (for private sector employees). A number of estimates of non-taxable income in kind are based on expenditure estimates (e.g. imputed rental value of housing provided free by employers and value of food provided in canteens etc. including meal vouchers) are also added.

Additionally, it is recognised that PAYE data do not adequately cover "compensation" of HM Forces, which includes a large proportion of income in kind (accommodation etc.). For this reason a substitute estimate is obtained from government administrative sources.

4.2.2 Mixed income

The main exhaustiveness adjustment within the UK measure of mixed income in hidden activity is an allowance for income tax evasion, which is significant in this sector.

The following additional adjustments are made to ensure exhaustiveness in the coverage of mixed income:
- employers' contributions to the NHS pension fund (from the Government Expenditure Monitoring System);
- Lloyds Names income (from Bank of England data).

4.2.3 Gross operating surplus of non-financial corporations

The only exhaustiveness adjustment for hidden activity applied is a small (historically based) evasion adjustment based on 0.3 per cent of the gross trading profits of non-financial corporations.

4.2.4 Gross operating surplus of households

Although no specific exhaustiveness adjustments are required, the following coverage adjustments are required to fully cover gross operating surplus:
- households' tax-free rental income (ONS estimate based on Inland Revenue information);
- imputed rental income of owner - occupiers (ONS estimate).

5. Expenditure approach

5.1 Data quality

5.1.1 Household final consumption expenditure

Estimates of consumers' expenditure are built up commodity-by-commodity from a variety of independent sources. For each commodity or service the source used is the one which is judged to provide the most reliable estimate of the level and changes in expenditure for that commodity or service. In many cases a combination of sources is employed so as to make the best use of available information.

The primary sources of information fall into three main categories: sample surveys of consumers' expenditure; statistics of retail and other traders' turnover; and statistics of supply and sales.

Sample surveys of consumers' expenditure

The principal surveys used in the UK estimates are the National Food Survey (NFS) and the Family Expenditure Survey (FES).

The Ministry of Agriculture, Fisheries and Food (MAFF) conduct the NFS, which covers households in Great Britain. It covers all household expenditure on food other than meals and snacks and other items bought and consumed outside the home. Each household participating in the survey records, for one week, the quantity and value of food bought. The survey includes an "eating out extension", to cover those meals and snacks eaten outside the home.

The FES, which like the NFS is taken continuously throughout the year, covers expenditure on all goods and services by all household members of aged 16 or over, whether the goods and services are consumed inside or outside the home. Members of each household participating in the survey record for two weeks the value of their expenditure and give particulars of their income. The household is also asked to provide details of those payments which may recur regularly but less frequently, such as electricity and gas bills, rent, and travel season ticket purchases.

Statistics of retail and other traders' turnover

The second approach used in measuring consumers' expenditure is to collect statistics of turnover by retailers and other businesses selling goods and services direct to consumers. A sample of businesses can cover a far higher proportion of the population's spending than can be covered by a consumer survey of practicable size. This approach requires retailers and other businesses to provide a commodity analysis of their sales, which they are asked to do in the NS Annual Retail Inquiry.

Statistics of supply and sales

A third approach is to make use of statistics of supplies or sales to consumers of particular goods and services. This approach is used for measuring expenditure on energy products, rail and bus travel, post and telecommunications, alcoholic drink and, to a certain extent, cars and motorcycles. For items such as gas and electricity, these direct estimates are highly reliable. But for other categories there are problems in assessing the proportion of the supplies used for business purposes (e.g. vehicles, rail travel and petrol).

5.1.2 Gross fixed capital formation

The overall calculation of GFCF is complex but estimates rest heavily on the capital expenditure and inventories inquiries conducted by ONS on a quarterly basis. These inquiries are the benchmark against ABI data.

Fixed investment in new dwellings by the private sector is derived from statistics of construction output from DETR sources. In the public sector, estimates for the larger public corporations are based on their annual accounts supplemented by returns they make to ONS about the sources and uses of their funds.

Figures for central government are based on the Appropriation Accounts presented to Parliament; local government data are based on their returns to DETR etc.

Estimates of GFCF by unincorporated businesses (other than dwellings) are compiled using the IDBR as the population frame, in the same way as estimates for incorporated businesses. Thus the estimates of GFCF will cover all unincorporated businesses which are registered for VAT either directly through statistical returns received or on the basis of their turnover declared to the tax authorities.

5.1.3 Trade in goods and services

Estimates for trade in goods are derived mainly from C&E, which is regarded as a high quality source. For services, estimates are derived from a wide variety of data sources but mainly the International Trade in Services (ITIS) and International Passenger Survey (IPS).

5.2 Adjustments made to ensure exhaustiveness

5.2.1 Household final consumption expenditure

Table 1 lists some of the main exhaustiveness adjustments for coverage made to household final consumption.

5.2.2 Gross fixed capital formation (GFCF)

New dwellings

For GFCF in new dwellings, construction output estimates which are derived from the IDBR are supplemented by estimates for construction operatives with low turnover. This will allow for at least some part of activity in the hidden economy. The supplement uses as its basis the difference between the numbers of self-employed construction workers captured by the Labour Force Survey and the number on the IDBR.

Table 1. Adjustments for coverage made to household final consumption

Category	Main data source	Adjustment
• Food and non-alcoholic beverages	• NFS	• Adjustments from trade sources: • Expenditure on soft drinks • Casual purchases (chocolate, ice cream etc.) • Food items consumed outside the home
• Alcoholic beverages, tobacco and narcotics	• HM Customs and Excise (HMCE)	• Deduction to remove business expenditure on alcoholic beverages • Smuggling adjustment from 2001 Blue Book
• Clothing and footwear	• Retail Sales Inquiry	• Adjustment for cleaning and repair (from FES)
• Imputed rental	• ONS estimate	• Movement in number of owner-occupiers (from DETR) and change in average rents (from FES and LA data)
• Goods and services for routine domestic maintenance	• FES	• Upward adjustment to allow for income in kind
• Purchase of vehicles	• ABI (motor trades)	• Deductions for sales to businesses • Upward adjustment to allow for income in kind from company cars (income approach)
• Motor vehicle repairs	• FES	• Upwards adjustment for payments by insurers (Association of British Insurers)
• Rail travel	• DETR	• Deduction for business expenditure
• Buses and coaches	• DETR	• Deduction for business expenditure and general government expenditure
• Air travel	• IPS/CAA	• Deduction for business expenditure
• Audio/visual equipment	• ABI (retail)	• Upwards adjustment film/tapes/repairs (FES)
• Other recreational items	• ABI (retail)	• Upwards adjustment to expenditure on garden supplies/ veterinary services (FES)
• Recreational and cultural services	• FES	• Upwards adjustment for juvenile expenditure in cinemas • Upwards adjustment for television/video hire
• Games of chance	• HMCE /OFLOT	• Upwards adjustment for on course bookmakers
• Newspapers / magazines	• FES	• Upwards adjustment for under recording in FES
• Restaurants and hotels	• FES	• Deduction for foreign tourists expenditure (IPS) • Upwards adjustment for income (food) in kind • Upwards adjustment HM forces income in kind (MOD) • Upwards adjustment medical staff income in kind (NHS)
• Personal care	• FES	• Upwards adjustment for expenditure on toiletries etc. (ABI retail)
• Personal effects	• ABI (retail)	• Deduction for capital formation
• Social protection	• FES	• Adjustment for residential nursing homes (ONS benchmark survey)
• Insurance	• FES	• Deduction for service charges (association of British insurers)
• Financial services	• BOE/ Inland Revenue	• Various adjustments for service charges

Improvements to dwellings

The hidden economy is thought to be particularly active in the house improvement market. Therefore, in addition to the reported construction output, the estimates of total GFCF on housing improvement work include an additional adjustment, worth approximately 25 per cent of the reported income of the self-employed in the construction industry. This is intended to allow for hidden economy home improvement work by this industry.

Gross output of construction

The hidden economy allowance is based on the use of expenditure estimates, such as the periodic English House Conditions Survey, to estimate the under-recording of output in a 'benchmark' year. The DETR can provide employment in construction estimates consistent with their gross output figures. The Department for Employment and Education (DEE) also collects information on the labour force in employment (it is the higher of the two). The hidden economy allowance from a benchmark year is then taken forward in line with movements in the difference in the DETR and DEE estimates.

5.2.3 Trade in goods and services

Goods

Estimates for trade in goods are derived mainly from C&E records. Regular quarterly samples drawn from the recorded transactions are checked and analysed to allow any necessary under-coverage adjustments to the statistics on trade in goods to be calculated.

Separate exercises are carried out periodically on both imports and exports to check for actual errors in the recording of various data in the Customs system, including the value of goods. These results have led to an adjustment being incorporated for over-valuation of exports.

Services

In recent years, efforts to improve exhaustiveness have been focused on improving the coverage and quality of the basic data sources (i.e. to ensure comprehensive coverage of and accurate reporting by registered and economically active units).

6. Illegal activities in the UK accounts

Work published in the July 1998 edition of UK Economic Trends suggests that the activities considered could generate value added to the UK economy within the range shown in Table 2. However, these are only broad estimates.

The potential effects on the accounts from the introduction of illegal activities are:
- income from illegal activities (value added) would be included under income from self- employment;
- consumers' expenditure on illegal activities would be included under household final consumption expenditure;
- imports of illegal drugs would be included under imports of goods.

Table 2. Illegal activities generating value added, 1996

	Value added (per cent of GDP)	Consumers expenditure (per cent)
Drugs	0.5 – 1.1	0.9 –2.1
Prostitution	0.2	0.2
Selling stolen goods	0.1	0.1
Illegal gambling	0.1	0.2
Total	**0.9 –1.5**	**1.4 –2.6**

The vast majority of illegal activities are consumed by, and generate income for, the household sector and are recorded in neither the income, expenditure or output sides of the accounts. Illegal activities are thus unlikely to explain any discrepancies within the accounts.

Although the UK accounts are in other respects consistent with ESA95, in common with most other national statistical institutes, the ONS has not yet been able to make specific adjustments to include illegal activities (e.g. selling heroin) due to the difficulty in finding suitable and accurate data sources.

However, several types of transactions which are illegal but not hidden are already recorded in the national accounts. In the UK these will include sales of alcohol and tobacco to children under the age of 18, and selling tickets to 18 certificate films to children under 18. No attempt is made to remove these kinds of illegal transactions from the accounts.

One notable development is that the accounts published in September 2001 included, for the first time, estimates from 1995 of household expenditure on alcoholic drink and tobacco products (cigarettes etc.), which are smuggled into the UK. These estimates are based on HM Customs and Excise intelligence on the level of smuggling taking place, together with assumptions about the prices at which the smuggled goods are sold to consumers through different types of outlets.

The data sources examined in the 1998 report produce estimates that would need substantial refining before they could be included in the national accounts. There is also a major problem in obtaining a time series for these sources. Additionally, links between the illegal economy and the legal economy need to be better understood (whether the income from illegal production is channelled through legitimate businesses) in order to correctly classify activities, and check against existing data.

Based on the results of the 1998 study, the UK currently has no plans to include specific adjustments for illegal activity within the accounts. The exception to this is the inclusion of the smuggling estimates mentioned above.

7. Concealed income (evasion) adjustment

The Office for National Statistics re-evaluated its methodology for estimating concealed income, which was implemented in the 1998 Blue Book. Revisions to GDP (income measure) from implementing this methodology were incorporated from 1989 and described in the 1998 GNP Questionnaire. The work that was undertaken is presented in Box 1.

Box 1. Concealed income (evasion) adjustment

Eurostat document CPNB/152 reported on the exhaustiveness of the UK's GNP estimates and recommended that adjustments made for tax evasion in the income measure of GDP should be improved. This resulted in a re-evaluation of the methodology for estimating concealed income, which was implemented in the 1998 Blue Book. Revisions to GDP (income measure) from implementing this methodology were incorporated from 1989 and described in the 1998 GNP Questionnaire. Subsequently, the exhaustiveness reservation on the UK accounts was lifted.

The original work undertaken comprised two main components: use of a much improved Inter Departmental Business Register (IDBR) to improve the production measure of GDP; and use of a new model to estimate hidden activities based on this improved production measure.

First, for the 1998 Blue Book, various revisions were processed (re-balancing the years 1989-96 through the input-output framework) including the transition onto the new register. This had been developed using VAT and PAYE information providing a much more exhaustive register and thereby improving estimates from ONS business inquiries. In particular, the coverage of small businesses was improved since the old register relied mainly on VAT data and excluded many businesses under the VAT threshold.

Most of the register changes had little direct effect on the components of income-based GDP since they rely mainly on administrative data from UK tax systems rather than inquiries based on the register.

Second, the ONS compiled an enhanced model based on detailed industry information on production and incomes (from the Inland Revenue) to estimate adjustments to allow for the hidden economy. This replaced the former method for estimating the evasion adjustment, which operated only at the whole economy level.

The production approach sources information from the IDBR in compiling an 'exhaustive' estimate of gross value added. In this process, adjustments are made for known under-coverage, such as construction, taxis, agriculture, retail and catering - with detailed comparisons of the production and income estimates. For industries other than construction or agriculture, the new model describes a path for concealed income from 1988 onwards. It covers income concealment by the self-employed (mixed income) and by employees (compensation of employees). Essentially the same model framework is used in both cases -there are differences but the basic outlines are the same.

The models assume that:

a)   Annual estimates of concealed income are based upon the estimated level of concealed income in the UK in 1994 (according to the discrepancy between GDP production) and GDP (income);

b)   The level of income concealment in any following year depends on:

- the level of income concealment in the previous year;
- the growth in a factor which is the best indicator available of the change in demand (either mixed income or compensation of employees);
- from 1995, the methodology has a further improvement reflecting information on turnover by industry for sole proprietors and partnerships as an input to the model (from the IDBR); and
- the change in taxes affecting self-employed and employees.

Therefore:

Level$_{n-1}$ = Level$_1$ * Change in income (or turnover) * Change in tax

In the UK, income is assumed to be mainly concealed by the self-employed and, to a much lesser extent, by employees. Therefore, the income concealment adjustment only affects the series for mixed income and compensation of employees. In 1994 (benchmark year) the concealed income adjustment for compensation of employees amounted to 0.25 per cent of total compensation of employees whereas the adjustment for mixed income amounted to 23.3 per cent of total mixed income.

Incorporated businesses will have some incentive to conceal operating surplus, but the practice is thought to be on a relatively minor scale and the comprehensiveness of the PAYE and VAT register makes evasion by companies difficult. It is more likely that incorporated businesses exploit legal means of minimising their tax payments by hiring tax consultants rather than evading taxes and breaking the law. However a small adjustment is made to corporation tax data to allow for evasion.

Benchmark

1994 was used as the benchmark year for this "evasion" methodology. Once all the information from all sources was available and had been scrutinised as part of the validation and balancing process it was evident that there was a shortfall in the early estimates of the income measure compared to the production and expenditure measures. Various judgements and adjustments are made to components of all measures of GDP as part of this process. The production measure was the highest of the three GDP measures. In order to achieve the optimum balance for GDP at current prices, the difference between the production and income measures was deemed to be due to missing hidden economy activity. This difference supplemented the provisional estimate of hidden economy activity (i.e. pay under tax threshold etc.) and formed the benchmark for the model. This was then allocated across industries and worked back to 1989. The model using this benchmark has been used to make estimates for the hidden economy for later years.

The last step analysed the whole time series to check that there was no discontinuity between the 1988 and 1989 estimates on account of the new methodology.

UNITED STATES

1. Introduction

The text that follows provides the latest available information on how hidden and informal economic activities are reflected in the U.S. national income and product accounts (NIPAs).

The Bureau of Economic Analysis (BEA) published a series of three articles in the May, June, and July 1984 issues of the *Survey of Current Business* (a list of references is shown in box 1) that describe the current framework for the treatment of hidden and informal economic activity in the NIPAs.[39] BEA published a fourth article on the topic in the April 1985 *Survey* that discussed a technique for measuring the underground economy.[40] The scope of these articles is sufficient to inform readers of BEA's treatment of the underground economy within the NIPAs.

Some illegal economic activity is captured in the NIPAs, although the recording of the associated receipts and expenses may be misclassified or mistimed. To the extent that illegal income is "laundered" through legal business operations, and the resulting income is used to purchase goods and services in legal markets, this illegal economic activity would be captured in national economic statistics. Because the U.S. market is so large, it is likely that a substantial amount of illegal economic activity carried out in the United States is captured in the NIPAs in this way.

While the impact of the unmeasured and misallocated components of illegal activity is not insignificant – in contrast to other countries where its significance is larger – improving the estimates of illegal activities is not one of the United States' major statistical priorities. BEA, like other national accounting agencies, is ill equipped to make analytical headway in using the few existing estimates of U.S. illegal economic activity or in developing new estimates. Thus, it is not cost-effective for BEA to devote resources to measure illegal economic activities. Instead, BEA's account-improvement initiatives are aimed at better measuring new types of <u>legal</u> economic activity such as non-reporting or misreporting of legal activities in income tax statistics, in employee compensation, in costs of production, and in market prices.

The text below presents a summary of the key articles mentioned above, addresses definitional issues and estimation methodologies, and provides information on the impact of such estimates on the NIPAs. It draws from and builds upon the *Survey* articles, but it does not attempt to replicate them.

2. BEA and the underground economy

Carol Carson authored the first of the companion articles in the May 1984 issue of the *Survey* entitled "The Underground Economy: An Introduction." The May article defines the underground economy from BEA's perspective and discusses the incentives for agents to engage in such activity, provides a synopsis of numerous methods that have been used to measure

---

[39] For full citations, see Carol S. Carson (A and B) and Robert P. Parker in the references.

[40] See De Leeuw in the reference.

underground economic activity in the United States and elsewhere around the world, and highlights the effects of underground economic activity on U.S. economic statistics.

The second companion article, which appeared in the June 1984 *Survey,* was authored by Robert P. Parker and is entitled "Improved Adjustments for Misreporting of Tax Return Information Used to Estimate the National Income and Product Accounts, 1977." The Parker article presents and discusses newly developed estimates of unreported and misreported economic activity that were incorporated into the NIPAs, and it highlights the methodologies used to prepare the old and improved misreporting adjustments. The improved misreporting adjustments are primarily based on analyses of Federal income tax return data from businesses and individuals.

Carson's second article in the July 1984 *Survey* elaborates further on the coverage of the underground economy within the NIPAs. It differentiates between the types of economic activities that are included in the NIPAs and those that are excluded. It discusses appropriate interpretations of NIPA estimates with respect to their coverage of the underground economy. Finally, it explains the effects of the underground economy on NIPA estimates by presenting an analysis of how the underground economy affects major source data underlying the NIPAs.

Frank de Leeuw prepared a related article in the April 1985 issue of the *Survey* entitled "An Indirect Technique for Measuring the Underground Economy." This article reveals an econometric technique for analyzing 56 "suspect," "well-measured," and "intermediate" industries (based on the extent to which underground economic activity was present), in order to estimate the amount of underground economic activity during the period 1949-1982. De Leeuw finds, "subject to considerable uncertainty, that the underground economy causes the growth of national income in private domestic industries to be understated by an average of one-quarter of 1 per cent" over the period.

These articles are the best available explanation of how BEA defines and treats the hidden and informal economy in the NIPAs.

3. Definitions

The *System of National Accounts, 1993* SNA defines the production boundary to include:

" ... a physical process, carried out under the responsibility, control and management of an institutional unit, in which labour and assets are used to transform inputs of goods and services into outputs of other goods and services. All goods and services produced as outputs must be such that they can be sold in markets or at least be capable of being provided by one unit to another, with or without charge." (Paragraph 1.20)

The following additional restriction is applied; i.e., economic activity must be:

" ... carried out under the instigation, control and responsibility of some institutional unit that exercises ownership rights over whatever is produced." (Paragraph 1.23)

Further, paragraph 6.30 states:

"Despite the obvious practical difficulties in obtaining data on illegal production, it is included within the production boundary of the system."

Although BEA estimates of gross domestic product generally follow the guidelines in *1993 SNA* paragraphs 1.20 and 1.23, the NIPAs do not reflect illegal economic activity. In fact, it has been a NIPA convention to exclude, to the extent possible, illegal activities.[41] At least two reasons underpin this convention. First, by definition, illegal activities are "antisocial" or "bads" rather than "goods" sufficiently so that they are outlawed.[42] Second, illegal activities are difficult to measure. "To a large extent, they must be deliberately concealed if they are to take place at all."[43]

Carson (1984, B) notes that there are three important clarifying points to the statement that the NIPAs do not reflect illegal economic activity: (1) The NIPAs exclude those "illegal" activities that would otherwise be considered production; e.g., growing, manufacturing, and the distribution of goods and services; (2) the NIPAs exclude only the value of goods and services produced despite prohibitions – i.e., there are no carry backs or forwards; (3) NIPA exclusions are not dependent on the status of producers.

The foregoing statements outline BEA's intent; however, practice may differ somewhat from intent. This outcome results because some source data that are used to prepare the NIPAs include some production and income associated with illegal goods and services that are reported as legal. Also, goods and services produced legally may not be reported in source data used to prepare the NIPAs because the goods and services are removed from legal markets through illegal activities.

Generally, BEA includes "legal source" underground economic activity in the NIPAs, where possible, by adjusting source data to include the value of "legal" economic activity that is **not** reported or that is misreported (underreported). BEA's adjustments do not distinguish between those that are required to correct for errors due to misinterpretation of reporting requirements and intentional misreporting or evasive reporting tactics. These adjustments are primarily to source data that are based on business or individual income tax returns. A brief description of the sources and methods used to develop the adjustments is presented in the next section.

4. Misreporting adjustments: estimation methodologies

Efforts to capture and reflect the underground economy in NIPA estimates is restricted by the extent to which adjustments can be made to data sources that are used to prepare the estimates. Federal Tax return data constitute a major source of information for the NIPAs. Given that it is feasible to adjust Federal Tax return data to account for misreporting, BEA uses this approach to capture "legal source" underground economic activity. The administrative and logistical costs of developing misreporting adjustments for all other source data that underlie NIPA estimates are high.

Table 1 shows the components of gross domestic product (GDP), gross domestic income (GDI), and personal income (PI) that are based on Federal Tax return information and the sources of that tax return information (entries for components of GDI that are also components of PI are only shown once). Table 2 shows 1997 aggregate and component estimates of GDP, GDI, and PI.[44] For each series, the table shows the published value, along with the proportionate value of the series that is derived from Federal tax return information. The two tables show that: (1) about 4 per cent of the value of GDP is derived from tax return information, (2) about 51 per cent of the total value of

---

[41] See U.S. Department of Commerce (1954).

[42] See U.S. Department of Commerce (1936) and Denison (1982), respectively.

[43] See Carson (1984, B), page 106.

[44] Estimates are not shown for a more recent period because 1997 is the last year for which BEA has published Input-Output table estimates where misreporting adjustments are separately identifiable.

GDI is based on tax return information, and (3) about 56 per cent of PI is based on tax return information.

The U.S. Department of the Treasury, Internal Revenue Service (IRS), developed misreporting adjustments for tax return data under the Taxpayer Compliance Measurement Program (TCMP) and the Information Return Program (IRP). To prepare misreporting adjustments, the IRS conducted intensive audits of tax returns under the TCMP and compared tax returns with information returns under the IRP. BEA combined this information with the results of an Exact Match Study (EMS) program that was conducted by the Census Bureau. For the EMS program, the Census Bureau compared tax returns with income information reported by taxpayers in an independent government survey (the Current Population Survey (CPS)) under tight confidentiality conditions. Combined, the TCMP, IRP, and EMS programs produced tax compliance information that was used to adjust legal source income of individuals and businesses that file and those that do not file income tax returns.[45] BEA uses this information to develop misreporting adjustments that are added to the tax data that underlie the NIPA estimates. Details on BEA's methodologies for preparing misreporting adjustments using TCMP, IRP, and EMS program information are provided in Parker, pp. 22-4.

5. Impact of misreporting adjustments

Table 3 shows aggregate and component estimates of GDP, GDI, and PI for 1997, associated misreporting adjustment values, and misreporting adjustments as a per cent of the corresponding estimates. The table shows that misreporting adjustments accounted for 0.8 per cent of GDP. Within GDP, the largest misreporting adjustments are to personal consumption expenditures. Misreporting adjustments accounted for 5.0 per cent of GDI; non-farm proprietors' income, profits before tax, and private wages and salaries had the largest adjustments. Misreporting adjustments accounted for 4.4 per cent of PI.

6. Summary

Carson (1984 A, p. 25) reports that, for the period 1974-81, estimates of legal source underground economic activity – the type intended to be captured in the NIPAs – ranged from 4 to 8 per cent of GDP. Although Table 3 indicates that BEA's misreporting adjustments accounted for only 0.8 per cent of GDP for 1997, such adjustments accounted for 5.0 per cent of GDI. In 1997, GDP and GDI differed by $70.7 billion (the statistical discrepancy). Therefore, the combination of adjustments to GDP and GDI to capture "legal source" underground economic activity places BEA's adjustments at the lower range of those cited by Carson.

In the summer of 2007, BEA plans to publish the final 2002 benchmark input-output accounts. Misreporting adjustments for 2002 will be available at that time. BEA will then prepare an updated version of this report that reflects the 2002 input-output benchmark estimates some time in 2008.

---

[45] The TCMP and IRP reflect adjustments for selected years beginning in 1963, while the EMS program reflects adjustments for selected years beginning in 1973. The last TCMP adjustments were prepared for 1988; BEA continues to prepare misreporting adjustments based on the TCMP by extrapolation. For a more detailed discussion of the TCMP, IRP, and EMS Programs, see Carson (1984 A, p. 26).

Box 1. List of References

Carson, Carol S. (1984 A). "The Underground Economy: An Introduction." *Survey of Current Business*. May, pp. 21-37.

Carson, Carol S. (1984 B). "The Underground Economy: An Introduction." *Survey of Current Business*. July, pp. 106-17.

Commission of the European Communities, International Monetary Fund, Organisation for Economic Cooperation and Development , United Nations, and World Bank (1993).   *System of National Accounts, 1993*. New York, New York.

De Leeuw, Frank (1985). "An Indirect Technique for Measuring the Underground Economy." *Survey of Current Business*. April, pp. 64-72.

Denison, Edward F. (1982). "Is U.S. Growth Understated Because of the Underground Economy? Employment Ratios Suggest Not." *The Review of Income and Wealth*, Ser. 28.2, March, pp. 1-16.

Parker, Robert P. (1984). "Improved Adjustments for Misreporting of Tax Return Information Used to Estimate the National Income and Product Accounts, 1977." *Survey of Current Business*. June, pp. 21-37.

U.S. Department of Commerce (1997). Bureau of Economic Analysis. "The Statistical Discrepancy." *Survey of Current Business*. August, p. 19.

U.S. Department of Commerce (1936). Bureau of Foreign and Domestic Commerce. *National Income in the United States, 1929-35*. Washington, DC: Government Printing Office.

U.S. Department of Commerce (1954). Office of Business Economics. *National Income* (A Supplement to the *Survey of Current Business*). Washington, DC: Government Printing Office.

Table 1. Sources of tax return information used to prepare estimates of the National Income and Product Accounts, 1997

Component	NIPA estimates	Source of tax-based information*
GROSS DOMESTIC PRODUCT		
Personal consumption expenditures		
• Durable goods	All durable goods (small establishments)	A
• Nondurable goods	All nondurable goods (small establishments) except gasoline and oil; fuel oil and coal; prescription drugs; food furnished employees; food produced on farms; and net foreign remittances	A
• Services	Small establishments of services covered in economic census (primarily hotels and motels; automobile services; personal) services; miscellaneous repair services; health services; professional services; recreational services; educational services; and welfare services)	A
	Financial services furnished without payment by investment companies	B
Gross private domestic investment		
• Fixed investment		
• Non-residential	All private equipment and software (small establishments)	A
• Residential	Residential equipment and manufactured homes (small establishments)	A
• Change in private inventories	Change in book value for construction, manufacturing, mining, and trade	B,C
GROSS DOMESTIC INCOME		
Wages and salaries	All private industries, except farms, railroads, private households, non-profit institutions not included in the Census of Wages and Employment; and tips	D
Supplements to wages and salaries	Employer contributions for private employee pensions and supplemental unemployment	E
Net interest	Domestic net monetary interest of corporations, sole proprietorships, and partnerships; imputed interest paid by investment companies	B,C
Business current transfer payments to persons	Corporate donations	B
Non-farm proprietors' income	All industries	C
Rental income of persons	Royalties	F
	Non-farm non-residential properties	B,C
Corporate profits before tax	All domestic industries except Federal Reserve banks, other federally sponsored credit agencies, and mutual depository institutions; state and local corporate profit tax accruals; and the cost of trading or issuing corporate securities	B
Capital consumption allowances with capital		
• Consumption adjustment	Capital consumption allowances for corporations and non-farm sole proprietors and partnerships	C
PERSONAL INCOME		
Personal dividend income	All domestic industries except Federal Reserve banks, other federally sponsored credit agencies, and credit unions	B

* Sources:

A. Various reports from the 1997 economic census. In the census, tax return information is used to define the universe to be covered and to provide employment, payroll, and receipts data for small firms that are not sent a Census report form.

B. Statistics of Income – 1997, Corporation Income Tax Returns – tabulations of IRS form 1120 series.

C. Statistics of Income – 1997, Sole Proprietorship Returns – tabulations of IRS form 1040 schedule C and Statistics of Income – 1997, Partnership Returns – tabulations of IRS form 1065.

D. Employment and Wages – 1997 – tabulations of the Census of Wages and Employment.

E. Private Pension Plan Bulletin – Abstract of IRS form 5500 annual reports.

F. Statistics of Income – 1997, Individual Income Tax Returns – tabulations of IRS form 1040.

Table 2. National Income and Product Accounts: estimates and amounts derived from tax return information, 1997

	NIPA estimates	Amount derived from tax return information[1]
	(billion dollars)	
GROSS DOMESTIC PRODUCT	**8 304.3**	**329.8**
Personal consumption expenditures	**5 547.4**	**296.8**
• Durable goods	692.7	26.5
• Nondurable goods	1 619.0	91.8
• Services	3 235.8	178.4
Gross private domestic investment	**1 389.8**	**33.0**
• Fixed investment	1 317.8	31.9
• Non-residential	968.7	0.0
• Structures	250.3	0.0
• Equipment and software	718.3	0.0
• Residential	349.1	0.0
• Change in private inventories	72.0	1.2
Net exports of goods and services	**-101.6**	**0.0**
• Exports	955.3	0.0
• Goods	687.7	0.0
• Services	267.6	0.0
• Imports	1 056.9	0.0
• Goods	885.3	0.0
• Services	171.5	0.0
Government consumption expenditures and gross investment	**1 468.7**	**0.0**
• Federal	530.9	0.0
• National defence	349.6	0.0
• Non-defence	181.3	0.0
• State and local	937.8	0.0
GROSS DOMESTIC INCOME	**8 233.7**	**4 168.8**
Compensation of employees, paid	**4 666.1**	**3 179.5**
• Wage and salary accruals	3 879.1	3 088.8
• Government	668.1	0.0
• Private	3 211.0	3 088.8
• Supplements to wages and salaries	787.0	90.7
• Employer contributions for employee pension and insurance funds	497.5	90.7
• Employer contributions for government social insurance	289.5	0.0
Taxes on production and imports	**612.0**	**0.0**
Less: Subsidies	**32.9**	**0.0**
Net operating surplus	**2 014.1**	**989.3**
• Private enterprises	2 001.5	989.3
• Net interest and miscellaneous payments	489.2	-168.7
• Business current transfer payments (net)	49.9	8.4
• To persons (net)	19.4	8.4
• To government and the rest of the world (net)	30.5	0.0
• Proprietors' income with inventory valuation and capital consumption	576.0	540.9
• Farm	34.2	0.0
• Proprietors' income with inventory valuation adjustment	40.1	0.0
• Capital consumption adjustment	-5.9	0.0
• Non-farm	541.8	540.9

	NIPA estimates	Amount derived from tax return information[1]
• Proprietors' income	500.7	500.7
• Inventory valuation adjustment	1.0	0.0
• Capital consumption adjustment	40.2	40.2
• Rental income of persons with capital consumption adjustment	128.8	12.5
• Rental income of persons	137.9	12.5
• Capital consumption adjustment	-9.1	0.0
• Corporate profits with inventory valuation and capital consumption adjustments	757.5	596.2
• Profits before tax	687.2	540.0
• Inventory valuation adjustment	14.1	0.0
• Capital consumption adjustment	56.2	56.2
• Current surplus of government enterprises	12.6	0.0
Consumption of fixed capital (CFC)	**974.4**	**0.0[2]**
• Private	800.3	617.1
• Domestic business	675.2	617.1
• Capital consumption allowances (CCA)	756.5	714.0
• Less: Capital consumption adjustment	81.3	96.9
• Households and institutions	125.1	0.0
• Government	174.1	0.0
Addendum:		
• Statistical discrepancy	70.7	0.0
PERSONAL INCOME	**6 915.1**	**3 858.4**
Compensation of employees, received	**4 664.6**	**3 179.5**
• Wage and salary disbursements	3 877.6	3 088.8
• Private industries	3 211.0	3 088.8
• Government	668.1	0.0
• Supplements to wages and salaries	787.0	90.7
• Employer contributions for employee pension and insurance funds	497.5	90.7
• Employer contributions for government social insurance	289.5	0.0
Proprietors' income with inventory valuation and capital consumption adjustments	**576.0**	**540.9**
Rental income of persons with capital consumption adjustment	**128.8**	**12.5**
Personal income receipts on assets	**1 181.7**	**117.1**
• Personal interest income	848.7	-168.7
• Personal dividend income	333.0	285.8
Personal current transfer receipts	**951.2**	**8.4**
• Government social benefits to persons	931.8	0.0
• Other current transfer receipts, from business (net)	19.4	8.4
Less: Contributions for government social insurance	**587.2**	**0.0**
Statistical discrepancy	70.7	0.0

1. Government receipts that are derived from tax return information are not included as such in this table. They are not included because the focus is on NIPA estimates for which adjustments for taxpayer misreporting are needed to raise NIPA estimates to actual levels. Government receipts and their counter entries are already at their actual levels.

2. As indicated the $0.0 entry, tax return information is not used to prepare the estimate for consumption of fixed capital (CFC), although tax return information is used to estimate portions of the components of private CFC. For private capital consumption allowances (CCA), $714.0 billion is derived from tax return information. The private capital consumption adjustment is the difference between private CCA and private CFC. The $96.9 billion entry in the private capital consumption adjustment that was derived from tax return information is the part of that difference associated with the portion of private CCA derived from tax return information. Government CFC is not derived from tax return information.

Table 3. BEA adjustments for misreporting of tax return information in the National Income and Product Accounts, 1997

	NIPA Estimates	Misreporting Adjustment	Misreporting adjustment as a per cent of estimate
	(billion dollars)		
GROSS DOMESTIC PRODUCT	**8 304.3**	**67.0**	**0.8**
Personal consumption expenditures	**5 547.4**	**63.8**	**1.1**
• Durable goods	692.7	5.0	0.7
• Nondurable goods	1 619.0	14.1	0.9
• Services	3 235.8	44.6	1.4
Gross private domestic investment	**1 389.8**	**3.2**	**0.2**
• Fixed investment	1 317.8	3.2	0.2
• Change in private inventories	72.0	0.1	0.1
Net exports of goods and services	**-101.6**	**n.a.**	**n.a.**
Government consumption expenditures and gross investment	**1 468.7**	**n.a.**	**n.a.**
GROSS DOMESTIC INCOME	**8 233.7**	**413.7**	**5.0**
Compensation of employees, paid	**4 666.1**	**78.5**	**1.7**
• Wage and salary accruals	3 879.1	78.5	2.0
• Government	668.1	n.a	n.a
• Private	3 211.0	78.5	2.4
• Supplements to wages and salaries	787.0	0.0	0.0
• Employer contributions for employee pension and insurance funds	497.5	0.0	0.0
• Employer contributions for government social insurance	289.5	n.a	n.a
Taxes on production and imports	**612.0**	**n.a.**	**n.a.**
Less: Subsidies	**32.9**	**n.a.**	**n.a.**
Net operating surplus	**2 014.1**	**335.2**	**16.6**
• Private enterprises	2 001.5	335.2	16.7
• Net interest and miscellaneous payments	489.2	-11.3	-2.3
• Business current transfer payments (net)	49.9	0.0	0.0
• To persons (net)	19.4	0.0	0.0
• To government and the rest of the world (net)	30.5	n.a	n.a
• Proprietors' income with inventory valuation and capital consumption adjustments	576.0	237.3	41.2
• Farm	34.2	n.a	n.a
• Proprietors' income with inventory valuation adjustment	40.1	n.a	n.a
• Capital consumption adjustment	-5.9	n.a	n.a
• Non-farm	541.8	237.3	43.8
• Proprietors' income	500.7	227.0	45.3
• Inventory valuation adjustment	1.0	n.a	n.a
• Capital consumption adjustment	40.2	10.3	25.6
• Rental income of persons with capital consumption adjustment	128.8	1.5	1.2
• Rental income of persons	137.9	1.5	1.1
• Capital consumption adjustment	-9.1	n.a	n.a
• Corporate profits with inventory valuation and capital consumption adjustments	757.5	107.7	14.2

	NIPA Estimates	Misreporting Adjustment	Misreporting adjustment as a per cent of estimate
• Profits before tax	687.2	107.7	15.7
• Inventory valuation adjustment	14.1	n.a	n.a
• Capital consumption adjustment	56.2	0.0	0.0
• Current surplus of government enterprises	12.6	n.a	n.a
Consumption of fixed capital (CFC)	**974.4**	**n.a**	**n.a**
• Private	800.3	n.a	n.a
• Domestic business	675.2	n.a	n.a
• Capital consumption allowances (CCA)	756.5	10.3	1.4
• Less: Capital consumption adjustment	81.3	-10.3	-12.7
• Households and institutions	125.1	n.a	n.a
• Government	174.1	n.a	n.a
Addendum:			
• Statistical discrepancy	70.7	n.a	n.a
PERSONAL INCOME	**6 915.1**	**306.0**	**4.4**
Compensation of employees, received	**4 664.6**	**78.5**	**1.7**
• Wage and salary disbursements	3 877.6	78.5	2.0
• Private industries	668.1	0.0	0.0
• Government	3 211.0	n.a.	n.a.
• Supplements to wages and salaries	787.0	0.0	0.0
• Employer contributions for employee pension and insurance funds	497.5	0.0	0.0
• Employer contributions for government social insurance	289.5	n.a.	n.a.
Proprietors' income with inventory valuation and capital consumption adjustments	**576.0**	**237.3**	**41.2**
Rental income of persons with capital consumption adjustment	**128.8**	**1.5**	**1.2**
Personal income receipts on assets	**1 181.7**	**-11.3**	**-1.0**
• Personal interest income	848.7	-11.3	-1.3
• Personal dividend income	333.0	0.0	0.0
Personal current transfer receipts	**951.2**	**0.0**	**0.0**
• Government social benefits to persons	931.8	n.a.	n.a.
• Other current transfer receipts, from business (net)	19.4	0.0	0.0
Less: Contributions for government social insurance	**587.2**	**n.a.**	**n.a.**

n.a. – not applicable

UZBEKISTAN

1. Introduction

The State Committee of the Republic of Uzbekistan on Statistics (Goskomstat) has been estimating the volume of the non-observed economy since 1995.

In accordance with the definitions and concepts of non-observed economy specified in the System of National Accounts (SNA93) and the OECD manual *Measuring Non-observed Economy* (2003), Goskomstat estimates informal economic activities for which information is not available through the regular statistical reporting.

The informal sector includes the activities of households and individual entrepreneurs working with or without licenses on producing:
- industrial goods and services for own final consumption and for sale;
- transport services (cargo and passengers);
- construction and repairs of dwellings and other household buildings, including for own final use;
- personal, educational, health, cultural and other services;
- owner occupied housing;
- renting out private dwellings.

2. Data sources

Special sample surveys are conducted by the subject-matter divisions of the statistical office. For the time being, these surveys are the main source of information for estimating the non-observed economy. However, they do not provide all necessary information for national accounts, e.g. it is not possible to estimate intermediate consumption.

In addition, all other possible sources of information are used, such as household budget surveys, administrative sources (mainly the State Tax Committee), and analysis of the input-output ratio between different groups of enterprises, as well as indirect and expert estimates.

3. Estimation methods

The first experimental estimates of production in the informal sector were made in industry, construction, agriculture, retail and services to the public. The first adjustments for GDP on the production side were made on the basis of these estimates.

Drawing on the experience acquired, Goskomstat has prepared *Methodological recommendations on statistical accounting, economic estimates and adjustments for the non-public sector of the economy in total volume of production, goods and services*.

In accordance with these recommendations, the branch units in Goskomstat make regular estimates of the volume of production by non-public sector, which include both legal entities and individuals. Such estimates are made both at the national and regional levels.

3.1 Labour input method

In order to create a system for quantitative assessment of economic activities and employment in the informal sector, a TACIS project was conducted jointly with the Italian Institute of Statistics (ISTAT). The aim of the project was to determine the possibility of using the labour input method by adapting it to the conditions of the national economy of Uzbekistan. If the project is successful, it will be a basis for a methodology of estimating the non-observed economy.

A special pilot household budget survey was conducted. Household budget surveys are carried out in Uzbekistan on a regular basis. Since 2001, a new scheme of the survey is used with the support of the World Bank. 10 000 families per year participate in the survey with a monthly rotation of 833 families.

To collect information on informal employment, new questionnaires were developed with ISTAT which included additional questions on second and third jobs, and the number of hours worked at additional places of work. Also, questions concerning the types of second jobs became more concrete, and the types of unregistered services used by households were defined.

In addition to the sample surveys, studies of employed persons, based on the data of labour statistics and other official sources were conducted.

Comparison of the number of employed persons from the household budget survey and from labour statistics and administrative sources has shown that the data cannot be fully reconciled and there is a need to conduct additional studies.

Analysis of employment in different branches of the economy from different sources, such as the data on demand and supply and the contribution of labour by branches, has proved that the number of employed persons in the economy is significantly higher than shown by the household budget survey. It is logical that already the household budget survey shows higher numbers of employed persons than official labour statistics, because it is assumed that the respondents do not need to conceal their employment from state statistical bodies.

However, the numbers of employed persons according to the special pilot household survey exceeded the numbers obtained by the regular survey by more than 8 per cent.

On the basis of the data on employment and number of hours worked from the sample survey, the calculation of the volume of production of informal activities by industries was made.

By comparing the volume of production, determined by traditional methods and the estimated data based on the sample survey, additional volume of production was calculated that is not accounted for by regular statistical observations. With the use of this method, the share of hidden production activities can be 5 to 6 per cent higher than the official estimates at present.

As a result of the survey, the questions in the household budget surveys on the production of agricultural products on household plots, farms and family enterprises were expanded. Questions on the number of hours worked overtime both during the surveyed week and during a month, as well as on payment actually received for the second or third jobs, were added to the questionnaire.

At present, estimates of additional volume of production are made using the newly received information.

4. Impact on GDP

Estimates of the informal sector of the economy are made in the final annual calculations of macroeconomic indicators, and in the compilation of national accounts. They are carried out by the specialists of the National Accounts Division, who take final responsibility for the calculations.

The total estimated share of informal activities in the produced GDP of the Republic of Uzbekistan amounts to approximately 29-30 per cent. The informal output of industrial products makes up 1.3 per cent, agricultural production 16.5 per cent, construction 1.3 per cent, trade and catering 2.9 per cent, transport services 2.1 per cent, and services to the public 5.4 per cent.

Annex: THE T1-T8 FRAMEWORK

The T1-T8 framework broadly categorises the NOE problem areas as statistical under-coverage, economic underground, illegal production, informal sector that is not illegal or underground, and other types of deficiencies. The eight categories under this broader framework are of the following types[46]:

Statistical undercoverage

T1-Non-response

Undercoverage arises due to non-response to statistical questionnaires or non coverage of active units in administrative files. This may be attributable to the time required to complete questionnaires, belief that information will be used for other than statistical reasons and poorly designed questionnaires.

T2-Out of date registers

Undercoverage occurs due to units missing from statistical registers or out of date registers that may contain incorrect information.

T3-Units not registered or not surveyed

Undercoverage results from non-coverage because of established thresholds for registration, non-coverage of certain activities, exclusion of newly created units and due to the disappearance of units in the course of the year.

Economic underground

T4-Under-reporting of turnover/income

Enterprise owners may intentionally under-report gross output or over report intermediate consumption to evade income tax, value added tax or other such taxes or to avoid meeting social security obligations.

T5-Units intentionally not registered

Units may not be covered because they are intentionally not registered to avoid tax payments or social security obligations. This could apply to both the entire enterprise or parts of it.

Informal sector

T6-Unregistered units

Units may not be required to register due to their small-scale in production (typically household units) such as agricultural production for own use in non-agricultural households, non-agricultural production in households for own use, own account construction, occasional and temporary activities and work on service contracts.

Illegal production

T7-Unregistered units

Production units do not report or register their illegal activities

Other

T8-Other types of GDP undercoverage

Undercoverage in this residual category can arise due to several reasons but frequently stem from production for own final use, tips, and wages and salaries paid in kind.

---

[46] OECD, 2002, *Measuring the Non-observed Economy: A Handbook*, Paris.

DA